LANGUAGE AND LITERACY
LEARNING IN SCHOOLS

CHALLENGES IN LANGUAGE AND LITERACY

Kenn Apel, Barbara J. Ehren, Elaine R. Silliman,
and C. Addison Stone, Series Editors

Language and Literacy Learning in Schools

Edited by

ELAINE R. SILLIMAN
LOUISE C. WILKINSON

Series Editor's Note by C. Addison Stone

THE GUILFORD PRESS
New York   London

© 2004 The Guilford Press
A Division of Guilford Publications, Inc.
72 Spring Street, New York, NY 10012
www.guilford.com

Printed in the United States of America

This book is printed on acid-free paper.

Last digit is print number: 9 8 7 6 5 4 3 2 1

Library of Congress Cataloging-in-Publication Data

Language and literacy learning in schools / edited by Elaine R. Silliman,
    Louise C. Wilkinson.
        p. cm.—(Challenges in language and literacy)
    Includes bibliographical references and index.
    ISBN 1-59385-065-4 (hardcover : alk. paper)
    1. Language arts.   2. Literacy.   3. Interdisciplinary approach in
education.   I. Silliman, Elaine R.   II. Wilkinson, Louise Cherry.   III. Series.
LB1576.L2932 2004
372.6—dc22   2004014031

About the Editors

Elaine R. Silliman, PhD, CCC-SLP, is Professor of Communication Sciences and Disorders and Cognitive and Neural Sciences at the University of South Florida in Tampa, Florida. She is a Fellow of the American Speech–Language–Hearing Association (ASHA) and the International Academy for Research on Learning Disabilities, and received the Honors of the New York State Speech–Language–Hearing Association and the Distinguished Alumni Achievement Award from the Graduate Center of the City University of New York. Dr. Silliman also served as Coordinator of the ASHA Special Interest Division, Language Learning and Education; Editor of the ASHA journal, *Language, Speech, and Hearing Services in Schools*; and on the first Specialty Board on Child Language. Her research and publications focus on language learning disabilities and the language basis of literacy. Her current research interests include oral language–literacy connections in monolingual English-speaking children with social dialect variations, bilingual (Spanish–English) children, and children who are struggling with reading, writing, and spelling. Her previous books include *Communicating for Learning: Classroom Observation and Collaboration* (coauthored with Louise C. Wilkinson), *Speaking, Reading and Writing in Children with Language Learning Disabilities: New Paradigms in Research and Practice* (coedited with Katharine G. Butler), and *Handbook of Language and Literacy: Development and Disorders* (coedited with C. Addison Stone, Barbara J. Ehren, and Kenn Apel). Dr. Silliman has taught at Tel Aviv University and Hunter College of the City University of New York and has served on review panels for the U.S. Department of Education.

Louise C. Wilkinson EdD, is Dean of the Syracuse University School of Education and Distinguished Professor of Education, Psychology, and Communication Sciences. Her extensive research on children's language and literacy learning has been published in 125 articles, chapters, and volumes. She coauthored *Communicating for Learning: Classroom Observation and Collaboration* (with Elaine R. Silliman) and coedited *Communicating in the Classroom*, *The Social Context of Instruction*, *Gender Influences in Classroom Interaction*, and *The Integrated Language Arts*. She has served on the boards of major journals on literacy, language, and education, the National Advisory Board of the National Reading Research Center, and on the governing boards of the National Association of Universities and the Land-Grant Colleges' Commission for Human Resources and Social Change. Elected Fellow of the American Psychological Association, the American Psychological Society, and the American Association of Applied and Preventative Psychology, Dr. Wilkinson has chaired national review panels for the U.S. Department of Education and the National Science Foundation. She also served as U.S. Delegate to the Organization for Economic Cooperation and Development and the Asia–Pacific Economic Cooperation organization, Vice President and National Program Chair of the American Educational Research Association, and on the Council of Academic Policy Advisors to the New Jersey Legislature. She chairs the Urban Deans' Network of the International Reading Association and was appointed Honored Guest Professor of Education at Beijing Normal University (2001–2005). Dr. Wilkinson has taught at Harvard, Massachusetts Institute of Technology, Boston University, University of Wisconsin–Madison, the City University of New York Graduate Center, and Rutgers University.

Contributors

Kenn Apel, PhD, CCC-SLP, Department of Communicative Disorders and Sciences, Wichita State University, Wichita, Kansas

Anthony S. Bashir, PhD, CCC-SLP, Department of Communication Sciences and Disorders, Emerson College, Boston, Massachusetts

Robin L. Danzak, MA, Department of Communication Sciences and Disorders PhD Program, University of South Florida, Tampa, Florida

Mavis L. Donahue, EdD, College of Education, University of Illinois–Chicago, Chicago, Illinois

Kailonnie Dunsmore, PhD, School of Education, University at Albany, State University of New York, Albany, New York

Barbara J. Ehren, EdD, CCC-SLP, Center for Research on Learning, University of Kansas, Lawrence, Kansas

Carol Sue Englert, PhD, College of Education, Michigan State University, East Lansing, Michigan

Sharon K. Foster, MS, CCC-SLP, Consolidated High School District 230, Orland Park, Illinois

Linda B. Gambrell, PhD, School of Education, Clemson University, Clemson, South Carolina

Ronald B. Gillam, PhD, CCC-SLP, Department of Communication Sciences and Disorders, University of Texas at Austin, Austin, Texas

Brenda K. Gorman, MA, Department of Communication Sciences and Disorders, University of Texas at Austin, Austin, Texas

Pam Hart, PhD, CCC-SLP, Department of Communication Disorders, Central Missouri State University, Warrensburg, Missouri

Katherine Hilden, BA, Department of Counseling, Educational Psychology, and Special Education, Michigan State University, East Lansing, Michigan

Julie J. Masterson, PhD, CCC-SLP, Department of Communication Sciences and Disorders, Southwest Missouri State University, Springfield, Missouri

Lesley Mandel Morrow, PhD, Graduate School of Education, Rutgers University, New Brunswick, New Jersey

Michael Pressley, PhD, Department of Teacher Education, Michigan State University, East Lansing, Michigan

Elaine R. Silliman, PhD, CCC-SLP, Department of Communication Sciences and Disorders, University of South Florida, Tampa, Florida

Bonnie D. Singer, PhD, CCC-SLP, Innovative Learning Partners, Boston, Massachusetts

Shane Templeton, PhD, Center for Learning and Literacy, College of Education, University of Nevada, Reno, Reno, Nevada

Gary A. Troia, PhD, CCC-SLP, College of Education, University of Washington, Seattle, Washington

Geraldine P. Wallach, PhD, CCC-SLP, Department of Communicative Disorders, California State University, Long Beach, Long Beach, California

Christina Pennington Whitaker, PhD, School of Education, Clemson University, Clemson, South Carolina

Louise C. Wilkinson, EdD, School of Education, Syracuse University, Syracuse, New York

Series Editor's Note

I am pleased to present the fourth volume in the Challenges in Language and Literacy series. In their original prospectus for this volume, Elaine Silliman and Louise Wilkinson characterized their goal as the production of a book that provided "practitioners and those preparing to enter the profession with the conceptual frameworks and empirical bases for the collaborative incorporation of effective language and literacy practices into the everyday life of the general education classroom." In the ensuing book, the editors have fulfilled this purpose admirably. The book is notable for its combination of solid scholarship and rich examples of practice, its integrative treatment of the linguistic basis of literacy learning, and its reasoned call for cross-disciplinary scholarship and practice.

One prominent theme in this book is collaboration. Although a good deal has been written about the importance of collaboration in meeting the educational needs of children who are at risk for literacy learning, this book provides a fresh perspective. In addition to a focus on the integration of general education and special education, a central theme of the book relates to the importance of collaboration between speech–language specialists, general educators, and special educators. The book's important premise is that effective literacy instruction is grounded in a focus on the interplay of language and literacy skills.

An additional asset of the book is its emphasis on the importance of shared *knowledge* as well as shared responsibility. Frequently, discussions of collaboration focus primarily on the issues of responsibility and collegiality. Clearly, these are important issues in effective collaboration, and they are not neglected in this book. However, collaboration without shared knowledge runs the distinct danger of becoming "parallel play." True collaboration requires not just shared responsibility but a shared perspective on the task at hand and a genuine appreciation of where and how one's role dovetails with the roles of fellow professionals. Such a shared perspective requires not only common goals but also overlapping knowledge.

Collectively, the chapters in this volume address the knowledge base concerning the interplay of language and literacy that must be shared by all professionals who work in literacy instruction. Speech–language specialists will know more about language than do general or special educators; general and special educators will know more about reading and writing than do speech–language specialists. This book provides that knowledge base in a way that speaks equally effectively to scholars and practitioners from the various disciplines represented.

One important factor in the success of the volume is the editors' wise choice of authors. Each topic in the book is covered in two or more chapters written by respected scholars who represent multiple disciplines. In addition, each chapter, regardless of the primary discipline represented by the author, addresses the central issue of the relation between language and literacy skills, as well as the potential for collaboration among professionals.

An additional asset of the volume is its combination of solid scholarship and rich examples. Each author provides a set of principles and recommended practices that are grounded in research—both that of the authors, who are themselves productive researchers, and that of others. In addition, the authors draw on their experiences as researchers and as practitioners to illustrate key points with detailed examples. Some of these examples focus on children with language and literacy challenges; others focus on effective instructional environments. In both instances, the reader gains sensitivity about how the principles delineated by the authors play out in practice.

One final asset is the volume's breadth of coverage regarding both language and literacy practices. There is solid treatment of now standard topics in the field, including word recognition, spelling, and phonological processes. In addition, however, there is deep coverage of issues related to higher-level language processes, reading comprehension, and written composition. The reader will learn a good deal about how syntactic processing and linguistic inference relate to reading comprehension, how morphological processing relates to spelling and vocabulary, how phonological processing relates to word recognition and spelling, as well as how higher-level language processing influences lower-level reading/spelling processes. In all of these areas, considerable attention is devoted to instructional goals and activities that foster the interplay of language and literacy learning, as well as to current and future research agendas.

This book embodies many of the themes in other volumes in the Challenges in Language and Literacy series, which aim to integrate interdisciplinary perspectives on language and literacy with empirically based programs and practices for promoting effective learning outcomes in diverse students. The series is based on the premise that oral and written language skills are functionally intertwined in individual development. Understanding the complexity of this relationship requires the collaborative contributions of scholars and practitioners from multiple disciplines. The series focuses on typical and atypical language and literacy development from the preschool years to young adulthood. The goal is to provide informative, timely resources for a broad audience, including practitioners, academics, and students in the fields of language science and disorders, educational psychology, general education, special education, and learning disabilities.

I am confident that this book will do what we had in mind for the entire series, that is, to stimulate the thinking and the practice of professionals devoted to the integration of work on language and literacy in myriad settings devoted to research and practice. The book is an important step forward in the integration of disciplinary perspectives on the acquisition of literacy.

C. Addison Stone

Acknowledgments

We gratefully acknowledge the many people who worked on this volume, which is part of the Challenges in Language and Literacy series. The idea for this book originated with a major symposium: "Maximizing Students' Language and Literacy Learning," cosponsored by the Rutgers Graduate School of Education and the Seton Hall School of Medical Education on April 19, 2002, in New Brunswick, New Jersey. Special recognition is given to Dr. Brian Shulman, Seton Hall University, for his outstanding contributions as codirector of the conference. The purpose of the conference was to provide general and special education teachers, speech–language pathologists, and those preparing to enter these professions with knowledge about how to collaborate effectively in schools in order to optimize students' language and literacy learning. Through Seton Hall University, the American Speech–Language–Hearing Association approved the conference for professional continuing education; in addition, the conference qualified as continuing professional development for educators through Rutgers University, an approved provider of programs for educators in New Jersey.

We thank all those who participated in the conference. These participants included the presenters, who also wrote chapters in this volume, the attendees from whom we learned, and the staff of the Rutgers Graduate School of Education Office of Continuing Education and Global Outreach, including the Director, Dr. Darren Clarke. Our appreciation is also extended to Jane Sherwood of the Rutgers Graduate School of Education Dean's Office for her assistance in all phases of this work and to Jeanne Federico and Belinda Fusté of the University of South Florida, Department of Communication Sciences and Disorders, who assisted in the multiple phases of manuscript preparation. We also want to acknowledge Acquisitions Editor, Rochelle Serwator, and Editor-in-Chief, Seymour Weingarten, of The

Guilford Press for their continual support of this project from its inception to its completion. Their conviction that professional books can transcend disciplinary and professional boundaries warrants recognition. Lastly, to all of our supporters and colleagues, and to our respective spouses, Paul and Alex, we are very appreciative of their patience, assistance, and continued belief in our work.

ELAINE R. SILLIMAN

LOUISE C. WILKINSON

Contents

LANGUAGE AND LITERACY
LEARNING IN SCHOOLS

❧

PART I

Challenges and Choices in the New Educational Landscape

1

❧

Collaboration for Language and Literacy Learning

Three Challenges

ELAINE R. SILLIMAN
LOUISE C. WILKINSON

The purpose of this book is conveyed well by a general education teacher who has a student with disabilities in her classroom for part of the day:

> Are there any benefits to teaching students with disabilities in my general education class? . . . The advantage of having additional adults working alongside . . . very often a special education teacher and/or a specialist, such as a speech–language pathologist . . . is that those additional staff members are available to work with other students with special needs, not just with the special education student(s). General education teachers can then offer individualized help to other students in need of a little extra attention. General education teachers are also able to receive specialized professional development to learn strategies and techniques that work well with both special education and general education students. ("A Teacher's Perspective on the Reauthorization of IDEA," 2003)

As this teacher implies, key stakeholders in the education of children, regardless of their areas of expertise or roles as practitioner or researcher, must communicate and collaborate more effectively across disciplinary and professional boundaries to achieve a common goal. The goal to attain involves doing what's right for all students by narrowing the literacy achievement gap for those whose diversity and socioeconomic status and/ or language learning difficulties put them at increased risk for chronic academic failure.

This book provides a strong foundation for both teachers and speech–language pathologists who work with children learning to become literate in English as a first or second language. It includes the perspectives of researchers with well-established bodies of original research on the development of effective practices in literacy education and language intervention. It is unfortunate that while both perspectives—the educational and the clinical—are integral to a comprehensive approach to language and literacy learning, they have not informed each other in systematic ways. This volume brings together both perspectives to focus on the core contents of literacy: Word recognition, oral and reading comprehension, writing, and spelling.

The gulf between researcher viewpoints also appears at the professional level. From a practical perspective, classroom teachers, who are versed in the teaching of literacy, and speech–language pathologists, who are professionally prepared in the components of spoken language, have remained separated from one another in the educational setting. For example, in spite of the fact that the 1997 reauthorization of the Individuals with Disabilities Education Act (IDEA) specified that services were to be provided in the least restrictive environment possible, federal data show that, nationally, speech–language pathologists were "providing 82.8% of their services in special education settings, such as resource rooms for students with speech–language impairments" (U.S. Department of Education, Office of Special Education Programs, 2002a, p. III-7). Most services are provided for students with language and/or articulation impairments.

One reason for this continued separation is the broad variation among states in their policy changes and disability criteria for such categories as specific learning disabilities and speech–language impairment (U.S. Department of Education, Office of Special Education Programs, 2002b). These variations often promote fragmentation of services and rigid professional boundaries (Silliman, Butler, & Wallach, 2002). In other words, regular and special education are considered to be two different systems without common bonds. A second reason for the divide stems in large part from federal and state education laws and regulations, including Title I, that differentiate elementary and secondary education from special education and related services. However, the current federal and state commitments to standards-based educational reform impacts both classroom teachers and speech–language pathologists. As a result, rich opportunities are available to bridge the divide in innovative ways through collaboration with the goal of narrowing the achievement gap for all students.

In the first part of the 21st century, the catchphrase for educational reform is the implementation of scientifically based practices, or evidence-based practices, as these practices have emerged from the considerable research on learning to read and the prevention of reading failure in children at risk (Snow, Burns, & Griffin, 1998; National Reading Panel, 2000). For the first time, the inclusion of scientifically based practices in the elementary education reading curriculum is now federal educational policy as reflected in the No Child Left Behind Act (NCLB; 2002). Educational policy results from the social translation of scientific knowledge into politically approved practices that then shape how federal monies and technical assistance are allocated (Lo Bianco, 2001). President George W. Bush articulated the policy vision of NCLB when he signed this far-reaching legislation into law in January 2002:

> Too many children in America are segregated by low expectation, illiteracy, and self-doubt. In a constantly changing world that is demanding increasingly complex skills from its workforce, children are literally being left behind. It doesn't have to be this way. . . . In America, no child should be left behind. (Bush, 2002)

There can be little argument with a vision of educational equity that seeks to "make educational excellence the rule" (Haycock & Wiener, 2003, p. 5), including educational excellence for students covered under the current provisions of IDEA (President's Commission on Excellence in Special Education, 2002). However, few topics provoke as much controversy as do the subjects of educational reform and the stress on results as found in the concept of accountability in NCLB. It is also likely that the NCLB notion of accountability will transform the identification procedures and instructional practices of a reauthorized IDEA, still in progress as of this writing.[1] Based on Senate bill S. 1248 (U.S. Senate Health, Education, Labor, and Pensions Committee, 2003; hereafter referred to as the U.S. Senate HELP Committee), the most significant changes will align IDEA with the NCLB accountability system in order for a united accountability structure to exist. In addition, three themes from the President's Commission on Excellence in Special Education (2002) are incorporated into the amended IDEA bill: (1) a focus on results, not on process; (2) shifting from a model of "wait to fail" to a model of prevention; and (3) considering children with disabilities as general education children first. A prevention model emphasizing early identification might not require the demonstration of a severe discrepancy between IQ and achievement to determine eligibility. Instead, identification could take place in the classroom through a process of children's responses to scientific, research-based intervention (for a fuller discussion of the response-to-instruction model, see Silliman, Wilkinson, and Brea-Spahn, 2004). The aim is to reduce unnecessary referrals to special education for learning disabilities for children whose struggles to read may be the product of inadequate experiences with emerging literacy experiences combined with inadequate educational opportunities.

It seems that, over the past three decades, U.S. education has been in a perpetual cycle of reform, with one set of "best practices" quickly replaced by another set of "best practices." It is no wonder that many practitioners, whether classroom teachers in regular or special education or speech–language pathologists, feel confused, if not dismayed, by the constant change in the meaning of and evidence for "best practices" (Gersten, 2001). In this chapter we address three challenges to the adoption of best practices: (1) the lack of clarity in the meaning and scope of NCLB for all students, including those with disabilities, and the educators responsible for them; (2) the proper role of accommodations for students with special needs in the high-stakes assessment required for aligning IDEA with NCLB; and (3) the establishment of workable criteria for highly qualified general education and special education teachers.

Following this discussion of challenges to cross-disciplinary collaboration, we then present an overview of the book's chapters, relating them to possible avenues for collaboration between teachers and speech–language pathologists in implementing best practices in literacy. It should be noted that the linguistic distinction between "teacher" and "speech–language pathologist" reflects to some extent the discord between the educational frames of teachers and the clinical frames of speech–language pathologists (Duchan, 2004), who frequently do not view themselves as teachers. We make clear here that this conflict in frames is not one we support, since the educational versus clinical distinction in the school setting is often an arbitrary, rather than a substantive, division.

THREE CHALLENGES TO COLLABORATION

Challenge 1: Learning to Live with NCLB

The Basis of Reform: The NCLB Act and Title I

NCLB, or Public Law 107-110, is a significant reform of the federal Elementary and Secondary Education Act (ESEA), initially passed in 1965. The nucleus of this far-reaching law requires states to assure that all grade-3 students, *including students with disabilities*, will read proficiently no later than the 2013–2014 school year (NCLB, 2002). By 2005–2006, states must start annual testing of students in grades 3–8 in reading (or language arts) and mathematics, and these tests must be aligned with state standards. Grade-3 science assessments are to begin by the 2007–2008 school year. Moreover, representative samples of students in grades 4 and 8 across states must now participate in biennial reading and mathematics assessments of the National Assessment of Educational Progress (NAEP) if states are to continue receiving Title I funds (NCLB, 2002).[2] The NAEP serves as a national benchmark of state standards, assessments, and student achievement outcomes (for a more complete discussion of NCLB–NAEP issues, see Silliman et al., 2004).

Currently, Title I funds affect approximately 12.5 million students enrolled in public (and private) schools, primarily those in grades 1–6 (U.S. Department of Education, Office of Elementary and Secondary Education, 2002). Funds may be allocated for the improvement of instructional programs in two situations: (1) for schoolwide programs that serve all children when at least 40% of the enrolled students are from poor families, and (2) as targeted assistance in schools whose poverty rate is below 40% or when schools select not to operate a schoolwide program (U.S. Department of Education, Office of Elementary and Secondary Education, 2002). Therefore, the financial risks are high for states and local education agencies if they do not show adequate evidence of progress toward meeting literacy goals since schools can lose federal funding provided under the Title I section of the ESEA.

Under NCLB, Title I funds are intended to help children who are failing, or who are most at risk for failing, to meet high academic standards for literacy. Those eligible for services include children who are economically disadvantaged who have disabilities, who are English language learners (ELLs), or whose families are migrants or homeless, among others. Children from low-income groups or who are ELLs are more susceptible to multiple risk factors that are associated with literacy learning difficulties. These risk factors include mother's education being less than high school, living in a single-parent household, living in a family receiving welfare benefits, or having parents whose primary language is other than English (U.S. Department of Education, National Center for Education Statistics, 2001). Moreover, the proportion of first-time kindergartners with two or more risk indicators is three times greater for Hispanic children and four times greater for African American children than for their Caucasian peers (U.S. Department of Education, National Center for Education Statistics, 2003a, 2003b). These two groups of children also tend to be referred to special education in proportions greater than their representation in the school-age population,[3] especially for a specific learning disability, emotional/behavioral disturbance, or mental retardation (President's Commission on Excellence in Special Education, 2002; U.S. Department of Education, Office of Special Education Programs, 2002a). Of note, Title I funds may be used to *coordinate* or *supplement* other services required by law for these same groups of children, including children already covered under IDEA, who meet eligibility requirements for Title I funds (see NCLB, 2002, Section 1115 b[3]). Title I also incorporates two other new federally supported reading programs: Early Reading First, which is designed to increase the quality of preschool education, and Reading First, which is dedicated to improving reading achievement in kindergarten through grade 3.

The Cornerstones of NCLB

As summarized in Table 1.1, NCLB is built on four cornerstones: (1) increasing accountability for student outcomes, (2) expanding parental choices when Title I schools consistently fail in their efforts to improve, (3) emphasizing learning to read by improving teacher quality and relying on scientifically based research for reading programs, and (4) allowing more flexibility to states and local school districts in how federal grants are spent to meet the NCLB goals. Bloomfield and Cooper (2003) describe these keystones as the *federalization* of education whereby the federal government, not individual states, is now setting educational standards; the *standardization* of curriculum, assessment, and accountability; and *privatization*. National standardization results from a comparison of student performance on the required NAEP with state test results "to see whether the states are 'dumbing down' their test results [to attain high proficiency percentages] to look better on national comparisons" (Bloomfield & Cooper, 2003, p. 8). "Privatization" refers to the opening of public education to the private sector. Included under this domain would be private providers who offer supplementary educational services; charter schools, which are publicly funded but managed on a for-profit or a nonprofit business model; and the use of vouchers as tuition aid for low-income children to attend religious or secular private schools.

TABLE 1.1 The Four Cornerstones of the No Child Left Behind Act

Cornerstone	How operationalized
Increased accountability	Assess outcomes via adequate yearly progress (AYP)—results matter.
Increased choices for parents and students in Title I schools	Identify schools "in need of improvement"—unsuccessful corrective actions after 2 years lead to options for supplemental services and school choice.
Putting reading first	Employ only highly qualified teachers; offer reading programs based on proven scientific research—quality of instruction and evidence-based practices are essential.
Expanded flexibility at the state and local school levels	Manage Reading First grants in ways that will meet goals—financial/technical resources matter.

As might be expected, after 2 years of implementation, NCLB is experiencing a backlash from many in the educational community. At best, some members of the public press give a mixed grade to NCLB (e.g., Allen, 2004). The education press reports that, in implementing the grant funds from the Reading First Initiative, the commercial reading programs that states have selected tend to be the same ones, which raise the danger of a single instructional approach (Manzo, 2004). In general, criticisms of NCLB focus on the interpretation of "adequate yearly progress" (AYP) and the meaning of schools in need of improvement, accommodations for students with disabilities in this era of high-stakes assessment, and the highly qualified teachers provision of the Reading First Initiative.

Adequate Yearly Progress and Identification of Schools in Need of Improvement

AYP means that specific goals must be set for student learning, assessments must be conducted to measure whether students enrolled in the school for *one academic year* are attaining these goals, and, as a consequence, educators are held responsible for raising student achievement in reading and math for all students (Haycock & Wiener, 2003). Included under the term "all" are the four subgroups of students cited earlier: the economically disadvantaged, those from the major racial and ethnic groups, those who have disabilities, and those who are ELL. To assure that schools are not masking the performance of the four subgroups through relying on average school performance, NCLB requires that not only must school scores be reported as a whole, but also that the scores for the four subgroups must be disaggregated, or separated, for reporting purposes.

Adequate Yearly Progress and High-Stakes Assessment. Figure 1.1 outlines the AYP process, which obliges states to set goals—for example, in reading—and to measure whether individual schools and students in these schools are meeting those goals. AYP is premised on high-stakes testing for schools and students. For example, a requirement is that 95% of students in a school must take the assessments. In 2003 six states (Delaware, Florida, Louisiana, New Jersey, North Carolina, and Texas) were using high-stakes tests to determine *both* grade promotion and graduation from high school with a diploma (Thompson & Thurlow, 2003; Wasburn-Moses, 2003). By 2008, 28 states will mandate a high-school exit examination for a diploma (Goertz & Duffy, 2003). Cochran-Smith (2000) describes high-stakes tests as analogous to gambling in a poker game:

> The term is used to indicate the potential for both great losses and great wins when one makes the choice to play at the big-money table . . . [but]

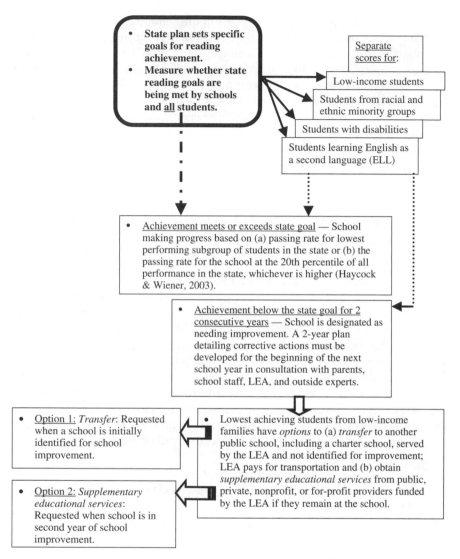

FIGURE 1.1. Process for determining adequate yearly progress for Title I schools under the No Child Left Behind Act (2002). (LEA, Local Education Agency).

test takers caught in the high-stakes national testing movement have had no choice about whether they will play in the big-money game, a game that is rigged from the start in favor of teachers and students from suburban and other highly resourced communities. (p. 269)

Similarly, Thurlow and Johnson (2000) criticize high-stakes tests for students with disabilities The concern is that, since the reauthorization of IDEA in 1997, students with disabilities must participate in assessments that, generally, are not designed for those receiving a variety of special education services and do not necessarily reflect what these students know and can do. On the other hand, nonparticipation in state- and district-mandated assessments could lead to other unintended consequences for these students, such as being granted an alternate diploma rather than a standard high-school diploma that then limits their postsecondary choices.

Supplementary Educational Services. When a school does not meet AYP criteria for 2 consecutive years, then the school is designated as "needing improvement." At this point, while the school develops a plan to raise achievement, one option becomes available to all low-income students and parents: transfer to another public school within the district that is making AYP, with transportation paid by the Local Education Agency (LEA). A second option becomes operative for students from low-income families when schools are at the end of their second year of school improvement: to obtain supplementary educational services from a state-approved list of public or private providers, with the services also paid for by the LEA, again, up to a certain limit (U.S. Department of Education, Office of Innovation and Improvement, 2003). Public providers can include public schools (including charter schools), LEAs, and educational service agencies. Private providers, consistent with the privatization principle ((Bloomfield & Cooper, 2003), may include faith-based organizations and private businesses, such as private tutoring services or, in the case of speech–language services, private practitioners who meet a state's criteria for approval as a provider (U.S. Department of Education, Office of Innovation and Improvement, 2003).

Supplementary educational services can consist of such academic assistance as "tutoring, remediation, and other educational interventions" (U.S. Department of Education, Office of Innovation and Improvement, 2003, p. 39) that are consistent with the LEA's content and instruction, are aligned with the state's academic standards, are research-based, and are provided outside the regular school day. For students with disabilities, the NCLB regulations, finalized in December 2002, specified that parents must be supplied with names of *some* approved providers (whether public or private) who can offer necessary accommodations for the child, but neither the State Education

Agency (SEA) nor the LEA were obligated to offer assistance with accommodations for the provision of supplementary educational services. In contrast, according to the regulations, ELL students receiving supplementary educational services must also have language assistance linked with the supplementary services; otherwise the LEA must offer language assistance. Of interest for school specialists, such as speech–language pathologists and learning disability specialists, public schools may provide supplemental educational services to students at risk of failing the state's academic achievement standards but who are not low income; however, there are restrictions on how Title I funds may be used in this situation. In other cases that involve students with disabilities or ELL students, the LEA can be a provider if parents request direct services from the LEA. The qualification is that "LEAs are not permitted merely to assign those students whose parents request assistance to a district- or school-administered program" (U.S. Department of Education, Office of Innovation and Improvement, 2003, p. 26).

Adequate Yearly Progress Myths. A final comment on AYP pertains to two myths surrounding the concept (Haycock & Wiener, 2003). First, contrary to the interpretation of the public and the press, NCLB does not require that states identify schools as "failing." It requires that schools be identified for improvement in certain areas where there have been chronic problems in achievement for certain groups of students, such as persistent reading failure. Despite this fine point in the law, most likely, the public perception, as well as the perceptions of educational staff and their students, is that the "needing improvement" designation does mean failure. Second, the perception exists that AYP means that schools must improve test scores every year to avoid being labeled as needing improvement. Haycock and Wiener (2003) point out that AYP refers to *"adequate* yearly progress" and not *"annual* yearly progress." However, what AYP means actually depends on individual state definitions. The result is wide disparities among states in the meaning of reading proficiency. For example, one state improvement plan requires that 50% of students must be proficient readers in 2004. In 2003, the school improved significantly, raising the percentage of proficient students from 40% to 55%, but in 2004 the proficiency percent declined slightly to 52%. In this example, according to Haycock and Wiener (2003), the school will not be designated as needing improvement because the 2004 score remained above the state's 50% target. However, if the school does not meet the 50% target for 2 consecutive years, then it would be identified as needing improvement.[4]

Summary: The Accountability Challenge Is Here to Stay. Concerns about the AYP requirement focus on two aspects (Keegan, Orr, & Jones, 2002). One set of criticisms focuses on the absence of consensus about the meaning of "adequate," much less "proficient," a controversy that is linked to high-stakes assessments and "mismatches between what is taught and what is tested" (Committee on Assessment in Support of Instruction and Learning of the National Research Council, 2003, p. 17). The outcome of high-stakes assessments then becomes one where teachers concentrate less on students' meaningful learning and more on strategies for "learning the test." For example, in preparing for the 10th-grade state test in writing, a Florida high school student who enjoys creative writing nevertheless indicated that she would use the mechanical writing formula she had been taught to pass the essay test—that is, five paragraphs that make three points with the use of the transitional connectives *first*, *next*, and *in conclusion* (Catalanello, 2004). A second form of disapproval pertains to the questionable use of assessment for the dual purposes of accountability at the district and state levels and determining instructional outcomes at the classroom level (Committee on Assessment in Support of Instruction and Learning of the National Research Council, 2003; Keegan et al., 2002).

Regardless of the trepidations expressed and the multiple policy clarifications still needed, districts and states are now being held accountable for the achievement of all students, and there are serious consequences if state-mandated standards are not met over a 5-year period of improvement. These consequences can include the withholding of Title I funds or the restructuring of the school, which may include changing the school's governance or appointing a trustee to administer LEA affairs instead of a superintendent and school board (NCLB, 2002). The bottom line and the challenge for all professional stakeholders serving children is that AYP means "Process is not enough; it's results that count" (Keegan et al., 2002, p. 2). However, over the long term, students' perspectives on this new accountability challenge might be captured best in this tale from Delpit (2003):

> The 100 year old man lies on his deathbed, contemplating his long life. . . . He has lived a good life—there have been good times and bad times but he has accomplished much that he is proud of. . . . One of his favorite grandsons looks into his eyes and asks, "Grandpa, is there anything you regret in your life?" The old man closes his eyes. Just when his family thinks he has drifted off to sleep, he opens them again and says with an expression of deep, wistful longing, "Son, I just really wish with all my heart that I would have scored higher on the state-mandated achievement tests." (p. 14)

Challenge 2: Learning to Reconcile IDEA with NCLB: Accommodations and High-Stakes Assessment

Since the 1997 IDEA reauthorization, students with disabilities must be included in the assessment programs of states and districts, with the results of their performance reported separately from general education students. NCLB (2002) added the new stipulation that states were now accountable for the AYP of students receiving special education services who had individualized education plans (IEPs). For example, the requirement that 95% of students in a school must participate in the testing programs for reading also applies to students with IEPs, as well as to students who are ELL and have attended school in the United States for 3 consecutive years. In other words, 95% of these two student groups must participate (see note 4). The bar has been set high. NCLB requires that, by 2013–2014, 100% of students in a state, including students with disabilities, are to meet state proficiency standards in reading and math (Ralabate & Foley, 2003). Moreover, the amended IDEA bill (U.S. Senate HELP Committee, 2003) makes clear that a critical aspect of reauthorization is holding states, districts, and schools accountable for the AYP of students with significant disabilities.

According to an analysis of state data by *Education Week* (2004) for the 2002–2003 school year, the participation rates for students with IEPs in grade-4 reading tests ranged from a low of 48% in California (which reported only 2001–2002 data) to a high of 100% in five states (Delaware, Kansas, Maryland, Massachusetts, and Nebraska). However, two major issues impacting on the validity of participation rates are that not all states administer assessments to students in grades 4, 8, and 12, and states differ in how they determine participation rates when students require accommodations. Topics often not well understood concern distinctions between "standard accommodations" and "modifications" and the relationship of alternate assessments to the AYP accountability standard.

What Are Allowable Testing Accommodations under IDEA for Accountability?

There are three ways in which students with disabilities can participate in state assessments (Lehr & Thurlow, 2003). First, they can participate *without accommodations*. In 2002–2003, according to the *Education Week* (2004) analysis, only 10 states reported that students participated without accommodations. Second, they can participate *with accommodations*, a situation that occurred in all 50 states and the District of Columbia in 2002–2003. Third, they can participate in *alternate assessments* when accommodations are not sufficient to allow participation in general assessments. Alternate assessments were administered in 48 states and the District of Columbia in 2002–2003 (*Education Week*, 2004). Thus, the vast majority of students with IEPs require accommodations to participate in high-stakes testing or the substitute alternate assessments. It should be noted that NCLB (2002) regulations, as well as the amended IDEA bill (U.S. Senate HELP Committee,

2003), specify that, at the state, district, and school levels, alternate assessments must be an integral part of state standards and assessment programs, must be constructed so that scores are generated in reading and math, and must meet the AYP requirements.

Testing accommodations are defined as minor changes made to the test setting, the timing of the test, its presentation format, or the response mode (Minnesota Department of Education, 2003) to "help students show what they know on assessments without being impeded by their disability" (Elliott, McKevitt, & Kettler, 2002, p. 154). Standard accommodations are not supposed to alter the nature of the content being assessed and therefore compromise the reliability, validity, or security of the test (Minnesota Department of Education, 2003). Instead, accommodations are intended to provide access to the content in order to equalize the opportunities for students to display what they know. While marked disparities are evident among state policies in permissible, or standard, accommodations, the most frequently used accommodations involve the presentation format. These include extended time or additional breaks, reading aloud the directions or questions to a student, student dictation of answers to a scribe, and small-group or individual testing (Lehr & Thurlow, 2003; Wasburn-Moses, 2003). It is the responsibility of IEP teams to select the appropriate accommodations for students and to familiarize students with these accommodations during actual instruction *before testing* (Ralabate & Foley, 2003; Thurlow & Johnson, 2000). Furthermore, accommodations must be selected in accord with state or district guidelines and, under the assessment provisions of IDEA, detailed in the student's IEP (Elliot et al., 2002). Nonetheless, there appear to be broad variations across a state's school districts in the extent to which IEPs contain detailed documentation on curriculum and instructional accommodations, much less the degree to which these accommodations are then explicitly linked to testing accommodations at the appropriate time (Shriner & Destefano, 2003). In 2002–2003, all states and the District of Columbia reported that in their large-scale assessments they included students who participated without accommodations or with standard accommodations (*Education Week*, 2004). However, as noted earlier, not all states report their data by grade (4, 8, and 12).

What Are Testing Modifications versus Accommodations?

In contrast to the minor adjustments that characterize accommodations, *modifications* involve changes to the content of a test that then alter what the test assesses (Elliott et al., 2002). For example, modification may occur when the IEP team establishes a lower passing score for an individual student on the state accountability measure (Minnesota Department of Education, 2003), which then may invalidate the test. In 2002–2003, 26 states and the District of Columbia reported that students took their state assessments with modifications (*Education Week*, 2004). However, across states, the boundary between an accommodation and a modification is often controversial because acceptable modifications in one state may not be suitable as a standard accommodation in another state (Lehr & Thurlow, 2003).

Another controversy concerns specific testing accommodations that may influence the validity of test scores for students with disabilities. For example, there is little research to provide guidance on whether the test scores of students with disabilities in the standard conditions (no accommodations) differ in their magnitude from the scores of students who have test directions and questions read aloud to them as an accommodation (Elliot et al., 2002). Thus, the absence of this information makes it difficult to interpret state reading proficiency rates for students with disabilities. To illustrate this point, an analysis of state reading proficiency rates for 2002–2003 (*Education Week*, 2004) indicated a major achievement gap in reading proficiency of at least 30 percentage points between students with and without disabilities in grades 4, 8, and 12. However, these data are not further separated by students who participated in testing without accommodations contrasted with those who required accommodations (and what type of accommodation), or even separated by disability category. Moreover, the proportion of low-income ELL or African American students with disabilities who read below proficiency levels was also unreported.

Prior to the 1997 IDEA, students with disabilities who required accommodations were often excluded from state or district assessments because their inclusion lowered overall school performance. As Thurlow and Johnson (2000) comment, exclusion was frequently translated into lower expectations and reduced access to the general education curriculum. There can be little debate that, regardless of the language and literacy problems that children have, all should be challenged in academic, social, and linguistic discourse domains with the expectation that they can learn. But, at this point in time, the consequences of high-stakes assessments for students with disabilities under a realigned IDEA remain speculative relative to such critical issues as further limiting or enlarging their access to educational opportunities, the use of test scores for either retention or promotion, and the awarding or denial of a high-school diploma (Thurlow & Johnson, 2000).

How Will Alternate Assessments Become Part of an Integrated IDEA–NCLB Accountability System?

The answer to the alignment issue is that it will not come easily. Alternate assessments were initially instituted under the 1997 IDEA with implementation required by 2000; therefore, in advance of the passage of NCLB, most states had alternate assessments in place, although there remain wide disparities in the extent to which states have validated their alternate assessment standards or even implemented a standards-based approach. These new standards cannot be geared to functional skills, with some exceptions, but must be aligned with state academic content standards in reading and math (Lehr & Thurlow, 2003).

Forms and Functions of Alternate Assessments. Approximately 20% of students with disabilities, or about 2% of the total student population, are not able to participate in high-stakes assessments (Thurlow & Johnson, 2000). Typically, these are students with the most severe cognitive disabilities.[5] However, under a new NCLB regulation, for Title I, this term refers to students whose intellectual functioning and adaptive behavior are –3 standard deviations or more below the mean. In other circumstances, states can individually define the meaning of "students with the most significant cognitive disabilities," a potentially confusing situation since a severe cognitive disability is not one of the 13 disability categories in IDEA. Thus, state definitions can encompass any of the existing 13 disability categories, including speech or language disability (American Speech–Language–Hearing Association, ASHA; 2004). A major concern is that states and LEAs will interpret this regulation as referring to mental retardation only, with the result that "low-performing" students will be misclassified as severely cognitively disabled and placed in educational programs well below their potential (Olson, 2003). Regardless, the scores of students who take alternate assessments must be reported separately from the scores of students who participate in the large-scale assessments with or without accommodations (Ralabate & Foley, 2003).

The most common form of alternate assessment across states is the portfolio, or body-of-evidence, approach (Thompson & Thurlow, 2003). Less commonly used are rating scales or checklists and an analysis of progress on the IEP goals and objectives that usually requires a body of evidence on student performance. The latter type of assessment meets the twin goals of documenting IEP progress and the purpose for assessment, such as whether the student has met graduation requirements (Lehr & Thurlow, 2003; Thurlow & Johnson, 2000). Thompson and Thurlow (2003) report that, based on state special education outcomes, alternate assessments are most often independently scored by trained teachers from outside the student's district or by the test developer contractor.

Out-of-Level Assessments. Related to alternate assessments is the issue of out-of-level testing for those students with disabilities who are not participating in grade-level curriculum. This form of assessment entails administrating a test at a grade level typically below the student's grade level

(Minnema & Thurlow, 2003). Instead, measures are designed for students' instructional level. State reporting practices tend not to provide the specific standards for determining AYP under this type of assessment (Olson, 2003). As a consequence, clear results from out-of-level assessments are not available and it remains questionable at the current time whether these students are included in accountability data (Minnema & Thurlow, 2003).

Summary: Meeting the Accommodations and Alternate Assessment Challenge. Accommodations are an everyday event in the regular education classroom as a way to provide temporary assistance to individual children, such as giving a child more time to finish reading assignments (Carlisle & Rice, 2002). In contrast, students with disabilities often require a variety of accommodations that are not short term.

The challenge confronting many is how to align the diverse individual needs of students with disabilities, some of whom may not even be able to participate in alternate assessments, with the NCLB accountability standards. As a starting point for resolving this concern, Thurlow and Johnson (2000) suggest that better collaboration among regular and special educators in policy decisions, such as joint decision making about the long-term social consequences of different diploma options, might result in only 1–2% of students with disabilities requiring alternate assessments at any grade level, in contrast with the current 20% who need alternate assessments. Collaborative involvement in policy decisions about the educational improvement of all students also has two added advantages that Roach, Salisbury, and McGregor (2002) articulate. One is that practitioners are assisted to understand the motivations and impact of policy on practice from the classroom to the district level. The second benefit of collaboration among all key stakeholders is the meshing of multiple perspectives that can result in the shared frame of reference critical to achieve if standards-based practices are to enhance the quality of learning outcomes for all students.

Challenge 3: Learning to Implement Evidence-Based Practices Well—The Highly Qualified Teacher Dilemma

Reading Instruction and the Quality Problem

A major cornerstone of NCLB (see Table 1.1) is that improved instruction in reading is premised on highly qualified teachers who are skilled in implementing evidence-based education. According to Whitehurst (2002), evidence-based education results when decisions about the delivery of reading instruction are the product of well-developed professional judgment integrated with the best available scientific evidence for effective practices.

NCLB requires that, by 2005–2006, states must have highly qualified teachers in every classroom who can deliver evidence-based education, a mandate that also applies to teachers in charter schools. This provision of the law stems from the long-standing concern that low-income students in Title I elementary, middle, and high schools are more likely to be taught by general education teachers who are less experienced and do not have certification in the core academic subjects that they are teaching (U.S. Department of Education, 2003b). (The 12 core academic subjects are listed in Table 1.2.) The Title I section of NCLB largely leaves to states the task of developing their own definitions of "highly qualified" as long as these definitions include (1) at least a bachelor's degree, (2) full state certification or licensure (which can be obtained through alternate routes), and (3) a rigorous method for assessing an individual's subject knowledge and teaching skills in the content area. The methods for demonstrating content knowledge in the case of experienced teachers may include a combination of experience, college course work, professional development, or other measures that a state determines (Education Trust, 2003).[6] Each state submitted plans to the U.S. Department of Education on September 1, 2003, specifying how they would meet the "highly qualified" provision.

The option for experienced teachers to demonstrate content knowledge in forms other than a college/university specialty or the passing of a test is known as the "High Objective Uniform State Standard of Evaluation" (the HOUSSE provision) (Education Trust, 2003—the Education Trust is an independent, nonprofit organization whose mission is to work for the high academic achievement of all students). The concern expressed in the Education Trust analysis is that states have interpreted this provision for objective assessment as meaning almost any kind of demonstration resulting in a "HOUSSE of cards" (p. 7). For example, some states permit teachers to self-assess their content knowledge as an acceptable process for demonstrating content knowledge, while others allow veteran teachers to meet the content knowledge standard through obtaining a satisfactory score on their annual performance evaluations.

TABLE 1.2. The 12 Core Content Areas in the No Child Left Behind Act

• Reading	• Civics
• Language arts	• Government
• English	• Economics
• Mathematics	• Arts
• Science	• History
• Foreign languages	• Geography

What Do Teachers Need to Know to Teach Reading Well? In addition to the state plan for meeting the highly qualified requirement, each state also had to provide a statewide baseline on the percentage of classrooms currently taught by highly qualified teachers and separately detail the same information for high-poverty (Title I) schools. In an analysis of these state data by the Education Trust (2003), the information submitted was found to be less than reliable. For example, a number of states had not yet defined "highly qualified," and only two states (Colorado and Tennessee) incorporated measures of student progress in their procedures for evaluating whether current teachers were highly qualified. One state even designated the dubious categories of "fully highly qualified" and "interim highly qualified."

The contentious part of the highly qualified requirement is neither the degree nor the certification requirements, but the elusive definition of teaching quality (Cochran-Smith, 2003; Education Trust, 2003). One source of difficulty in defining "quality" in literacy instruction is attributed to teacher education curricula. For example, Berninger and Richards (2002) describe teacher education as atheoretical because its primary focus is "different instructional options from which to select" (p. 304), not the conceptual frameworks consistent with the factors known to facilitate positive literacy outcomes for individual children. Others (e.g., McCutchen & Berninger, 1999; Moats & Lyon, 1996) express concern that, while mastery of content, or domain, knowledge is expected for the teaching of high-school mathematics and English, research is missing on the specialized content knowledge elementary teachers actually need for attaining expertise in classroom reading instruction (Moats & Foorman, 2003).

The absence of research on the disciplinary knowledge base that supports best practices in reading instruction is not a trivial oversight (McCutchen et al., 2002). The expectation is that, nationwide, teachers will implement evidence-based instruction in their teaching of reading. To illustrate this expectation, the findings of the National Reading Panel (2000) have been repackaged for and distributed to many elementary teachers as a framework for implementing evidence-based instruction in phonemic awareness, phonics, fluency, vocabulary, and text comprehension (Armbruster, Lehr, & Osborn, 2003). However, Moats and Foorman (2003) challenge whether this framework can be translated into and sustained as effective practices crafted to meet the needs of all children unless teachers possess explicit metalinguistic knowledge of the conceptual relationships between language and reading. In other words, are credentials, experience, and professional development activities as measures of highly qualified teachers equivalent to having strong content knowledge in the subject domain to be taught (Education Trust, 2003)?

The Scope of the "Highly Qualified" Problem. Moats and Foorman (2003) designed and refined a teacher knowledge survey instrument intended to access teachers' awareness of domains and concepts crucial for understanding reading development in kindergarten to grade 3. Results showed that too many kindergarten- to grade-4 teachers who worked in high-poverty urban schools did not know that diagraphs (letter combinations) in English orthography often represented a single phoneme as found in a word like *chip*. Only 16% were able to select from four choices that *tacked* was only one syllable (vs. the foils *peaches, able, quiet,* and *higher*), and only 7% could select *anxiety* as a word without a prefix, root, or suffix from four other choices (*prevalidate, subtraction, returnable,* and *unhistorical*). Overall, only one-third of teachers showed the high level of metalinguistic content knowledge about basic concepts and relationships in phonology, morphology, syntax, and orthography necessary for the effective teaching of reading, writing, and spelling.

These significant knowledge gaps indicate that for evidence-based instruction to achieve positive outcomes at least four systemic changes must co-occur:

- Extensive restructuring of elementary teacher education in reading (Berninger & Richards, 2002).
- Intensive, ongoing professional development experiences that include the analysis of children's work, such as the analysis of error patterns in oral reading and spelling (McCutchen et al., 2002).
- At the school level, "informed instructional leaders who can press a well-articulated [reading] initiative for several years" (Foorman & Moats, 2004, p. 58).
- Ongoing consultative assistance for teachers and other educational staff to support their transfer of new knowledge into informed practices that are sustained (Case, Speece, & Malloy, 2003).

Without these systems in place, too many teachers will continue to be less than qualified to diagnose children's decoding and comprehension needs appropriately and, further, unprepared to assist a diverse array of children with the differentiated instruction that might help them succeed.

The Special Educator and the Speech–Language Pathologist: Are They Highly Qualified?

The NCLB–IDEA Dilemma. A challenge for both special educators and speech–language pathologists is how their status will be defined in an alignment of IDEA's general definition of qualified personnel with the NCLB standards for the highly qualified. Under NCLB (2002) and its regulations, special education (and related services) are not explicitly identified as a core subject academic area; however, as the National Education Association points out (Ralabate & Foley, 2003), almost "all special education teachers either teach or support instruction in one or more core academic areas" (p. IV-3). Because of the wide variability among states in their standards for teacher certification, it remains blurry whether or not special educators or related service staff, such as speech–language pathologists, who work in Title I schools meet the highly qualified provision of NCLB even if they meet state requirements for teacher certification or professional licensing (see also note 6).

However, at least two predicaments are unique to school-based speech–language pathologists. First, IDEA 1997 contains a "highly qualified" provision wherein states are obliged to recognize the highest standards in the state that apply to a specific profession or discipline. In the case of speech–language pathologists, the entry-level degree for the profession, as regulated by the national ASHA standards, is the master's degree combined with 1-year of supervised professional experience and the passing of a national examination. This higher standard is recognized by many states for employment in the public schools. Whether this long-standing provision will be retained, modified, or eliminated in the 2004 reauthorization of IDEA is unknown at this time (Snyder, 2003).

The second quandary pertains to variances among states in their education regulations. Although IDEA considers speech–language pathology services a related service, in a number of states speech–language services are defined as a special education service. In those states, a speech–language pathologist may function as a classroom teacher of children with language impairment, team-teach with another special educator in a classroom, or provide auxiliary support in a related service role. Because of this flexibility in role assignments, a few states have attempted to reconcile the IDEA–NCLB dilemma in their HOUSSE process for "not new" teachers. One illustration comes from the Florida Department of Education (2002). Speech–language pathologists will have to meet the highly qualified requirement if they are the "teacher of record" for a core academic subject (see Table 1.2). The designation as "highly qualified" in this situation is through credentialing. This may include a state-issued professional license in speech–language pathology or a state Educator Certificate in Speech–Language Impaired in combination with the other NCLB requirements for highly qualified. In contrast, the HOUSSE processes of other states do not mention either speech–language pathologists or special education teachers.

Because of this marked disparity among states in their regulations for the delivery of speech–language services, it can be expected that the reconciliation of NCLB provisions with IDEA provisions about "highly qualified" will be a rocky road. To redress the gap between the two laws, the U.S. Senate HELP Committee's (2003) version of a reauthorized IDEA mandates that, by the end of the 2006–2007 school year, all special education teachers teaching in elementary, middle, and high schools must be highly qualified. This same bill also weakens somewhat the highest qualified standard for related service personnel, as just discussed, but retains its basic elements (Snyder, 2003).

The Federal Government's Road to Developing Quality Indicators for Special Education and Speech–Language Services. On the second anniversary of NCLB, a *New York Times* editorial ("Leaving Some Children Behind," 2004) sounded a clarion call for teachers who know how to teach children, particularly those with learning- or language-related disabilities. So a key question is the quality of those educators who are responsible for students with disabilities.

To begin the long process of answering this question, as well as illuminating issues related to retention and attrition, the U.S. Department of Education commissioned an exploratory study, *The Study of Personnel Needs in Special Education* (SPeNSE; Carlson, Brauen, Klein, Schroll, & Westat, 2002).[7] Five quality indicators were identified and built into an interview process that involved 8,061 service providers, including 510 speech–language pathologists who provided direct service to students with disabilities. These indicators of individuals' quality were (1) teaching experience; (2) credentials, especially level of certification; (3) self-efficacy; (4) professionalism (e.g., the number of journals read, professional association memberships, etc.); and (5) selected classroom practices that exemplified best practices in teaching reading. In addition, demographic characteristics were included as a quality indicator for the "workforce as a whole . . . because of pervasive differences in the demographics of students and their teachers" (Carlson, Lee, Schroll, Klein, & Westat, 2002, p. 3).

The limitations of an interview process dependent on self-reports are well known. Moreover, the SPeNSE design, in delving into the meaning of quality, did not include the critical outcome variable of student achievement. However, the next step is testing the validity of the teacher quality model relative to how characteristics of language arts teachers are associated with the academic achievement of students with disabilities (U.S. Department of Education, Office of Special Education Programs, 2002a). A concern is that the SPeNSE factors are global indicators only in contrast with the teacher knowledge focus of Moats and Foorman (2003), which attempted to pinpoint specific linguistic content essential for implementing effective reading instruction. Moreover, as the SPeNSE report (Carlson, Brauen, et al., 2002) acknowledges, unraveling discussions of teacher quality from discussions of teacher quantity become highly complex, particularly for special education teachers, due to the serious nationwide shortage of qualified individuals, estimated at over 12,000 vacant positions. These shortages then result in less-qualified individuals being hired. Contrary to expectations, there appears to be a minimal shortage of school-based speech–language pathologists on a nationwide basis (U.S. Department of Education, Office of Special Education Programs, 2002a). Given these caveats, the quality indicator profiles, summarized in Table 1.3, provide two kinds of snapshots. One is the characteristics of a nationally drawn representative sample of special educators and speech–language pathologists; the other suggests how these data may be used ultimately to formulate new educational policies for students with disabilities.

- First, both groups were demographically similar—that is, primarily white, suburban, middle class, and female (Carlson, Lee, et al., 2002)—a profile that differed considerably from the diverse student population served. As a group, speech–language pathologists were more demographically homogeneous than the special education group.
- Second, both groups were also similar in terms of their years of teaching experience. But school-based speech–language pathologists are an aging group with the largest cohort in this sample aged 45 or older (U.S. Department of Education, Office of Special Education Programs, 2002a). The SPeNSE data show that, while there is a mild shortage of qualified speech–language pathologists nationwide, retirements in the next 15 years will provoke major shortages. The rate of younger individuals entering the profession is insufficient to meet future needs (U.S. Department of Education, Office of Special Education Programs, 2002a).
- Third, approximately 59% of special educators have a master's degree, contrasted with 87% of speech-language pathologists. From an educational and credentialing perspective, the U.S. Department of Education describes speech–language pathologists as being "highly qualified for their positions" (U.S. Department of Education, Office of Special Education Programs, 2002a, p. III-13), an evaluation due in part to the fact that ASHA certification or a state professional license depends on the passing of a national examination. In contrast, not all states require testing for certification as a special education teacher. The problem with less-qualified teachers is particularly acute for the teaching of students with emotional disabilities.
- Fourth, the special educators and speech–language pathologists in this sample were similar in their sense of self-efficacy. Both groups saw themselves as competent relative to managing their job responsibilities and in their understanding of factors that contributed to a positive school climate. Both articulated similar gaps in their knowledge. For speech–language pathologists, knowledge gaps were broader for those with 6 or more years of experience. Those with less than 6 years of experience were more likely to believe that their academic and clinical preparation prepared

them to plan accommodations for students with cultural and linguistic diversity, translate research into useable practices, and use technology for intervention purposes (U.S. Department of Education, Office of Special Education Programs, 2002a).

• Finally, a common theme for the attrition of special educators was a sense of powerlessness in not being able to meet the complicated needs of children with multiple disabilities. For speech–language pathologists, caseload size combined with the complexity of serving students in many different disability categories fueled their desire to leave. The average median caseload of speech–language pathologists is 53 students (ASHA, 2000), which exceeds the recommended ASHA *maximum* caseload of 40 students. Moreover, some state educational policies (e.g., Arizona, Colorado, Florida, Ohio, and Texas, among others) allow 100 or more students on a caseload (ASHA, 2000). To retain qualified speech–language pathologists and to reduce their attrition, the U.S. Department of Education suggests that caseloads be limited to 46 or fewer students (U.S. Department of Education, Office of Special Education Programs, 2002a), consistent with the ASHA (2000) recommendation.

The Three Challenges: Some Conclusions

Three challenges to collaboration in the new world of standards-based education for all students have been dissected. One challenge is learning how to deal with the "high-stakes" accountability provisions of NCLB for students covered by Title I. Becoming informed about educational policies at federal and state levels and how policies are actually implemented at the local level is essential to meet this challenge. At the same time, it is equally vital to deal more responsively with the second challenge: meeting the accountability requirements of a revised IDEA for students with language and literacy learning problems who require accommodations or alternate assessments. The third challenge is equally as complex as the first two. Practitioners, including speech–language pathologists, must focus on developing a rich conceptual knowledge base about the central relationships between language and literacy learning if evidence-based practices are to be implemented in a manner that will explicitly connect students' learning with the quality of that learning.

Without question, the roles, responsibilities, and practices of speech–language pathologists have expanded into the literacy domain (ASHA, 2001). However, just as it is apparent that too many elementary education teachers (and, perhaps, special education teachers) do not have sufficient metalinguistic knowledge about the linguistic and discourse systems that support reading, writing, and spelling, at the same time it cannot be presumed that the depth of this same body of knowledge is sufficiently rich

TABLE 1.3. Quality Indicator Profiles of Special Educators and School-Based Speech–Language Pathologists

Profile	Special educators	Speech–language pathologists
Demographic characteristics	• 85% female • 86% white • Mean age: 43 years	• 96% female • 94% white • Mean age: 43 years
Average teaching experience	• 14.3 years	• 14 years
Highest-level degree held	• Master's degree—59%	• Master's degree—87%[a]
Credentials	• 92% fully certified for main teaching assignment • Certification test required—58% • 10% serving students with emotional disturbances held an emergency certificate, twice the rate of any other group	• 92% held the state professional license • 86% held a teaching certificate • 71% held the ASHA Certificate of Clinical Competence[b] • 3% were working under an emergency certificate
Self-efficacy • Perceptions of competence	• Planning effective lessons, monitoring progress, and modifying instruction accordingly	• Interpreting results of standardized measures, planning effective services, using appropriate clinical skills, monitoring student progress, and modifying instruction accordingly

- Perceptions of needs

- Perceptions of school climate and support from colleagues and administrators

- Most cited reason for wanting to leave profession as soon as possible

- Accommodating learning needs of culturally and linguistically diverse students, applying research findings to address instructional problems, and using technologically based instruction

- Associated with attitudes toward manageability of the assigned workload and intent to remain in teaching

- Attrition related to teaching of students with four or more different primary disabilities

- Accommodating language learning needs of culturally and linguistically diverse students, applying research findings to address problems in service delivery, using technologically based instruction, and supervising paraprofessionals

- Positive attitudes associated with manageability of workload and intent to stay in the profession

- Attrition related to caseload size, including caseloads with six or more different disabilities represented

Note. Based on Carlson, Brauen, Klein, Schroll, and Westat (2002) and U.S. Department of Education, Office of Special Education Programs (2002a).

[a]A total of 36 states require at least a master's degree for employment; seven states allow employment with a bachelor's degree without a requirement that a master's degree must be obtained within a specified period of time (Alabama, Arizona, Nevada, New York, Pennsylvania, South Carolina, and Tennessee) (U.S. Department of Education, Office of Special Education Programs, 2002a .

[b]The greater the years of experience, the less likely it is that a speech–language pathologist holds the ASHA Certificate of Clinical Competence (U.S. Department of Education, Office of Special Education Programs, 2002a).

across all speech–language pathologists in order for them to take on new collaborative roles in literacy education under both Title I of NCLB and IDEA. To maximize the quality of the knowledge base and its realization in evidence-based instruction that alters students' performance in positive directions, at least three changes merit consideration.

1. We need to refocus graduate education content in language learning and impairment. Traditionally, the curriculum in this domain focuses on the components and dimensions of spoken language development alone. It becomes essential for an enriched knowledge base that the spoken domain be interconnected *with* emerging literacy and the subsequent development of reading, writing, and spelling abilities. Also, it is unknown how many graduate programs in communication sciences and disorders provide students with an in-depth understanding of applied linguistics and its applications to the analysis of children's strengths and needs in learning the language of schooling.

2. Shift the emphasis of continuing professional development activities from the passive " 'sit and get' stand-alone workshops" (Klingner, Ahwee, Pionieta, & Menedez, 2003, p. 411) to active learning embedded in policy-related goals. The aim is to create collaborative opportunities for teachers, speech–language pathologists, and researchers to forge a community of problem solvers who can craft strategies for translating research into sustainable literacy-related practices that will eventually result in large-scale classroom change for at-risk students and those with disabilities. This process of translation, infusion, and maintenance as made evident in improved student performance is referred to as "scaling up," or sustainability, and currently is a major focal point of research in literacy education and learning disabilities (e.g., Cutter, Palincsar, & Magnusson, 2002; Denton, Vaughn, & Fletcher, 2003; Foorman & Moats, 2004; Gersten & Dimino, 2001; Klingner et al., 2003). The sustainability of research-based practices has yet to be addressed systematically in language impairment.

3. Finally, encourage changes in attitudes at state and local levels about the new roles and responsibilities of speech–language pathologists that will enhance their identity as valued members of the school community who are visibly supported by administrators and the full teaching staff (U.S. Department of Education, Office of Special Education Programs, 2002a). Retention of the most highly qualified speech–language specialists is dependent not only on reduced caseloads but also on increased flexibility in the design of service delivery models that can meet the individualized language and literacy needs of students who are most at risk for being left behind.

CHAPTER ORGANIZATION

The contributors to this volume are literacy educators, special educators, and speech–language pathologists who are well known for their research and publications in language and literacy learning. The volume's aim is to provide access to the differing disciplinary perspectives on the evidence-based practices that should guide preprofessional and professional education, as well as professional collaboration in educational environments.

All of the chapters blend the theoretical and the applied. Each chapter includes a statement and definition of the topic within the general domain of language and literacy learning, an overview of the existing research literature pertinent to the work presented, a summary of an original piece of research that includes illustrations from real case materials, and, finally, some practical recommendations regarding the assessment and instruction of individual students who are struggling to master English reading, writing, and spelling.

Challenges and Choices in the New Educational Landscape

Continuing Part I, Geraldine P. Wallach and Barbara J. Ehren in Chapter 2 address classroom collaboration. They present a decision-making framework for speech–language pathologists to create collaborative modes of instruction and intervention through designing curriculum relevant therapy. This decision-making process is accompanied by practical examples for producing positive outcomes.

Word Recognition and Reading Comprehension: Perspectives on Instructional and Intervention Practices

Next, Part II focuses on the complex interactions between word recognition and reading comprehension. In Chapter 3, Ronald B. Gillam and Brenda K. Gorman take a language-based view of information processing in their dynamic systems perspective of word recognition and text interpretation. Their premise is that reading is a complex dynamic system in which a variety of linguistic and discourse knowledge reciprocally interacts with processing units and the reader's language and real-world experiences. The dynamic systems model is then related to collaborative assessment and intervention.

In Chapter 4, Gary A. Troia, also taking a language-based view, concentrates on the ways in which empirically validated instructional practices for word recognition can build high-quality reading programs. The contributions of the speech–language pathologist's knowledge base to building collaborative reading programs are highlighted throughout the chapter. Also described in depth are instructional guidelines for the teaching of phonological awareness, grapheme–phoneme correspondences, and decoding skills.

The next three chapters shift the focus to reading comprehension. In Chapter 5, Christina Pennington Whitaker, Linda B. Gambrell, and Lesley Mandel Morrow introduce the literacy perspective that text comprehension entails continuous interactions among the reader, the text to be understood, and the social context of the reading activity. They then present a brief history of comprehension assessment and instruction that, in the past several years, culminated in national reports identifying the key features of exemplary comprehension instruction. Rich examples are then offered concerning how exemplary teachers in grades 1 and 4 foster reading comprehension and vocabulary learning.

In Chapter 6, Michael Pressley and Katherine Hilden extend the literacy viewpoint through a description of the stakeholders and the instructional components that must be blended into a common frame in order for comprehension strategy instruction to become an integral part of a reading curriculum at every grade level. This description serves as a backdrop for a detailed review of the research on comprehension strategies instruction. The case made is that transactional strategies instruction, combined with decoding and vocabulary instruction and the promotion of worthwhile world knowledge, yield the best outcomes.

Next, in Chapter 7, Mavis L. Donahue and Sharon K. Foster take readers into new territory in reading comprehension. Using a fictional story whose understanding depends on the detection of incongruities, they built the argument that individual differences in narrative reading comprehension are not a simple result of whether mastery of decoding, fluency, vocabulary, or even sentence types has been attained. Instead, narrative text comprehension is approached as social decision making, requiring the ability to infer and integrate multiple social perspectives. Donahue and Foster draw on examples of individual differences among middle- and high-school students with language learning difficulties who read the same fictional story but arrived at differing conclusions depending on whether they relied on text-based information or their personal storehouse of social scripts. Guidelines are then suggested for collaboration on interpreting patterns of student responses and for analyzing the social information-processing demands of written texts.

Writing and Spelling: Perspectives
on Instructional and Intervention Practices

Part III focuses on writing and spelling. In Chapter 8, Carol Sue Englert and Kailonnie Dunsmore ground their argument on the writing process from a Vygotskian perspective and the role of the instructional dialogue in marshalling the potential of the inclusion classroom as a learning environment for children with language and learning disabilities. Their grade-1 inclusion classroom, cotaught by a regular education teacher and a special education teacher, is part of the LEAP (Literacy Environments for Accelerated Progress) project. Four principles guide instruction: (1) situated language activity (the acquisition of the language of schooling in the authentic context of the academic curriculum), (2) apprenticeship in learning, (3) teacher scaffolding of the child's zone of proximal development, and (4) developing instructional talk as a mediational tool to support the process of writing. The telling case of Joseph, a child with a language learning disability, is highlighted over the course of several months as he is supported to discover the functions of writing tools and approach writing as a problem solving activity.

Bonnie D. Singer and Anthony S. Bashir, in Chapter 9, shift readers in the next chapter to a clinical perspective in their description of the EmPOWER™ approach to expository writing in middle-school students with language learning disabilities. In their research review on the writing abilities of these students, the authors point out that their chronic problems with planning, organizing, producing, and revising written text cannot be separated from their difficulties with language production. The EmPOWER approach is intended to foster the explicit dialogue that students need to have with themselves in order to manage, regulate, and write expository text in a consistent way. The approach, described in detail, is also designed for collaboration between teachers and speech–language pathologists.

The final two chapters concentrate on spelling, a major reason why many children chronically struggle with writing. While some may view the orthography of English spelling as chaotic and irregular and its function as primarily mechanical, Shane Templeton, in Chapter 10, encases spelling in a broader literacy frame. The analysis of students' spellings is a window into their lexicon and offers rich opportunities to examine the foundations of literacy knowledge. In other words, a student's pattern of spelling errors provides information on his or her lexical access of phonological, orthographic, and morphological structures and indexes the student's knowledge of word structure. Following a description of the layers of information that spellings represent and the associated phases of spelling development, two cases are presented as the prelude to effective word study instruction. Principles of word study are outlined as a guide for the active engagement of any student in instruction.

Taking a perspective that complements Shane Templeton, in Chapter 11 Kenn Apel, Julie J. Masterson, and Pam Hart approach spelling from a language-based standpoint and describe the multiple linguistic factors that influence spelling development. In this framework, children employ multiple strategies and different kinds of linguistic knowledge at varying points in their development to expand their spelling knowledge. Following a review of spelling instruction approaches, the multiple-linguistic-factor model is outlined as the focus of classroom-based spelling instruction. The authors conclude with future instructional and research challenges for an integrated approach with students, the integration of spelling into the curriculum, and the integration of professional expertise, including the linguistic expertise of the speech–language pathologist, into evidence-based spelling practices.

Part IV brings the book to a close concentrating on the integration of educational and clinical practices. In Chapter 12, Elaine R. Silliman, Louise C. Wilkinson, and Robin L. Danzak frame the book's themes through the story of Betsy, a student with a language learning disability. Likening her voyage through school from the preschool years through high school graduation to the Humpty Dumpty tale, the aim is to bring to life the voice of a youngster with a fractured language-processing system whose multiple strengths in language and literacy were never adequately understood by the many school-based professionals with whom she interacted. Her story crystallizes the major point of this vollume. There are significant long-lasting effects for students with language learning difficulties when the integration of educational and clinical practices is undervalued and a shared perspective does not exist on what really "counts" as meaningful language and literacy learning.

NOTES

1. Congressional action on IDEA, initially scheduled for reauthorization in 2002, is not expected until the fall of 2004 at the earliest.

2. Under the Title I provisions of NCLB, Congress authorized that eligible local education agencies receive approximately $13 billion in fiscal year 2002, $16 billion in fiscal year 2003, and an estimated $18.5 billion for fiscal year 2004 (NCLB, 2002). However, the funds actually appropriated were approximately $6 billion short of the amount Congress authorized when NCLB was passed ("School Reform Left Behind," 2004).

3. According to data from the U.S. Department of Education, National Center on Education Statistics (2003a, 2003b), in 2000 African American students and Hispanic students each comprised 17% of the school-age population; how-

ever, the rate of growth for the two groups differed considerably from 1972 to 2000. The African American school-age population increased by 2%, while the Hispanic school-age population increased by 11%. In the 10-year period from 1990 to 2000, the numbers of ELL students rose from 2.1 million to more than 3.7 million (U.S. Department of Education, 2003a).

4. In response to criticism from school boards on the NCLB policy for determining participation rates in testing, Rod Paige, Secretary of the U.S. Department of Education, modified this policy on March 29, 2004. States can now average participation rates over 3 years as the basis for meeting the AYP standard. A 2- or 3-year average must still meet or exceed the requirement that at least 95 percent of all students in a school participated in assessment.

5. Effective January 8, 2004, the Office of Elementary and Secondary Education of the U.S. Department of Education issued new final regulations for students with the most severe cognitive disabilities. According to an analysis by the American Speech–Language–Hearing Association (ASHA; 2004), the new regulation sets a 1% cap on the number of students in a school district having the most severe cognitive disabilities who, on alternate assessments, can score as proficient or advanced based on the development of alternate assessment standards. In other words, the 1% cap pertains to alternate assessment standards, not grade-level standards, that can be included in the determination of AYP. Proficient and advanced scores obtained on alternate assessments that are grounded to grade-level standards can be counted in the AYP calculations.

6. On March 15, 2004, Secretary Paige announced new flexibility provisions for teachers in small, rural, and isolated areas who often teach multiple subjects. Also special educators who do not teach core subjects or who only provide consultation, such as for curricula adaptations, will not be required to demonstrate subject matter competency in those subjects. For further information, see: http:// www.ed.gov/news/pressreleases/2004/03/03152004.html

7. The SPeNSE report (Carlson, Brauen, et al., 2002) also comprises a portion of the *Twenty-Fourth Annual Report to Congress on the Implementation of the Individuals with Disabilities Act* (U.S. Department of Education, Office of Special Education Programs, 2002a), which was not released until September 2003.

REFERENCES

Allen, M. (2004, January 9). Bush's education plan gets mixed grades on anniversary. *Washington Post*, p. A9. Retrieved January 15, 2004, from http://www. washingtonpost.com.

American Speech–Language–Hearing Association. (2000). *2000 Schools Survey*. Rockville, MD: Author.

American Speech–Language–Hearing Association. (2001). Roles and responsibilities of speech–language pathologists with respect to reading and writing in children and adolescents (Position statement, Executive Summary of Guidelines, Technical Report). In *ASHA Supplement 21* (pp. 17–27). Rockville, MD: Author.

American Speech–Language–Hearing Association. (2004, January 12). Analysis of ED's 1% rule for students with the most significant cognitive disabilities.

Retrieved February 5, 2004, from http://www.asha.org/about/legislation-advocacy/federal/nclb/.

Armbuster, B. B., Lehr, F., & Osborn, J. (2003). *Put reading first: The research building blocks for teaching children to read* (2nd ed.). Washington, DC: Partnership for Reading. Retrieved February 2, 2004, from http://www.nifl.gov/nifl/publications.html.

Berninger, V. W., & Richards, T. L. (2002). *Brain literacy for educators and psychologists*. San Diego, CA: Academic Press.

Bloomfield, D. C., & Cooper, B. S. (2003). NCLB: A new role for the federal government: An overview of the most sweeping federal education law since 1965. *T. H. E. Journal, 30*(Suppl. 10), 6–32.

Bush, G. W. (2002, January 8). *No Child Left Behind framework*. Retrieved August 12, 2003, from http://www.ed.gov/nclb.

Carlisle, J. F., & Rice, M. S. (2002). *Improving reading comprehension: Research-based principles and practices*. Baltimore: York Press.

Carlson, E., Brauen, M., Klein, S., Schroll, K., & Westat, S. W. (2002, July). *Study of personnel needs in special education: Key findings*. Washington, DC: U. S. Department of Education, Office of Special Education Programs. Retrieved May 2, 2003, from http://www.ed.gov/about/offices/list/osers/osep/index.html.

Carlson, E., Lee, H., Schroll, K., Klein, S., & Westat, S. W. (2002, August). *SPeNSE final report: Methods*. Washington, DC: U. S. Department of Education, Office of Special Education Programs. Retrieved May 2, 2003, from http://www.ed.gov/about/offices/list/osers/osep/index.html.

Case, L. P., Speece, D. L., & Molloy, D. E. (2003). The validity of a response-to-instruction paradigm to identify reading disabilities: A longitudinal analysis of individual differences and contextual factors. *School Psychology Review, 32*, 557–582.

Catalanello, R. (2004, February 1). Kicking "FCAT essay" habit. *St. Petersburg* (FL) *Times*, pp. 1A, 14A.

Cochran-Smith, M. (2000). Gambling on the future. *Journal of Teacher Education, 51*, 259–261.

Cochran-Smith, M. (2003). Teaching quality matters. *Journal of Teacher Education, 54*, 95–98.

Committee on Assessment in Support of Instruction and Learning of the National Research Council. (2003). *Assessment in support of instruction and learning: Bridging the gap between large-scale and classroom assessment*. Washington, DC: National Academies Press.

Cutter, J., Palincsar, A. S., & Magnusson, S. J. (2002). Supporting inclusion through case-based vignette conversations. *Learning Disabilities Research and Practice, 17*, 186–200.

Delpit, L. (2003). Educators as "seed people" growing a new future. *Educational Researcher, 7*(32), 14–21.

Denton, C. A., Vaughn, S., & Fletcher, J. M. (2003). Bringing research-based practice in reading intervention to scale. *Learning Disabilities Research and Practice, 18*, 201–211.

Duchan, J. F. (2004). *Frame work in language and literacy: How theory informs practice.* New York: Guilford Press.

Education Trust. (2003, December). *Telling the whole truth (or not) about highly qualified teachers: New state data.* Retrieved January 10, 2004, from http://www2.edtrust.org.

Education Week. (2004, January 8). Quality counts 2004. *Education Week, 23*(17). Retrieved January 15, 2004, from http://www.edweek.org/sreports/qc04/article.cfm?slug=17test.h23.

Elliott, S. N., McKevitt, B. C., & Kettler, R. J. (2002). Testing accommodations research and decision making: The case of "good" scores being highly valued but difficult to achieve for all students. *Measurement and Evaluation in Counseling and Development, 35,* 153–166.

Florida Department of Education. (2002, October 4). *No child left behind—Highly qualified teacher requirements.* Retrieved February 6, 2004, from http://info.fldoe.org/dscgi/ds.py/Get/File-718/NCLB-HQ Option Chart-Rev2.pdf.

Foorman, B. R., & Moats, L. C. (2004). Conditions for sustaining research-based practices in early reading instruction. *Remedial and Special Education, 25,* 51–60.

Gersten, R. (2001). Sorting out the roles of research in the improvement of practice. *Learning Disabilities Research and Practice, 16,* 45–50.

Gersten, R., & Dimino, J. (2001). The realities of translating research into classroom practice. *Learning Disabilities Research and Practice, 16,* 120–130.

Goertz, M., & Duffy, M. (2003). Mapping the landscape of high-stakes testing and accountability programs. *Theory into Practice, 42*(1), 4–11.

Haycock, K. & Wiener, R. (2003, April 4). *Adequate yearly progress under NCLD.* Paper presented at the National Center on Education and the Economy Policy Forum: Implementing the No Child Left Behind Act. Retrieved January 10, 2004, from http://www2.edtrust.org.

Keegan, L. G., Orr, B. J., & Jones, B. J. (2002, February 13). *Adequate yearly progress: Results, not process.* Paper presented at the 2002 conference Will No Child Truly Be Left Behind?: The Challenges of Making the Law Work, sponsored by the Thomas B. Fordham Foundation. Retrieved May 9, 2003, from http://www.edexcellence.net/NCLBconference/NCLBconferenceindex.html.

Klingner, J. K., Ahwee, S., Pionieta, P., & Menedez, R. (2003). Barriers and facilitators in scaling up research-based practices. *Exceptional Children, 69,* 411–429.

Leaving Some Children Behind. (2004, January 27). *New York Times,* p. A26.

Lehr, C., & Thurlow, M. (2003, October). *Putting it all together: Including students with disabilities in assessment and accountability systems* (Policy Directions No. 16). Minneapolis: University of Minnesota, National Center on Educational Outcomes. Retrieved January 29, 2004, from http://education.umn.edu/nceo/.

Lo Bianco, J. (2001). Policy literacy. *Language and Education, 15*(2–3), 212–227.

Manzo, K. K. (2004, February 4). Reading programs bear similarities across the states. *Education Week, 23*(21). Retrieved February 4, 2003, from http://www.edweek.org.

McCutchen, D., & Berninger, V. W. (1999). Those who *know*, teach well: Helping teachers master literacy-related subject-matter knowledge. *Learning Disabilities Research and Practice, 14*, 215–226.

McCutchen, D., Harry, D. R., Cunningham, A. E., Cox, S., Sidman, S., & Covill, A. E. (2002). Reading teachers' knowledge of children's literature and English phononogy. *Annals of Dyslexia, 52*, 207–228.

Minnema, J., & Thurlow, M. (2003). *Reporting out-of-level test scores: Are these students included in accountability programs?* (Out-of-Level Testing Report 10). Minneapolis: University of Minnesota, National Center on Educational Outcomes. Retreived February 6, 2004, from http://education.umn.edu/nceo.

Minnesota Department of Education. (2003, December 2). *Accommodations and modifications for students with special needs on Minnesota statewide assessments.* Retrieved January 29, 2004, from http://education.state.mn.us/stellent/groups/public/documents/translated content/pub_041416.pdf.

Moats, L. C., & Foorman, B. R. (2003). Measuring teachers' content knowledge of language and reading. *Annals of Dyslexia, 53*, 23–45.

Moats, L. C., & Lyon, G. R. (1996). Wanted: Teachers with knowledge of language. *Topics in Language Disorders, 16*(2), 73–86.

National Reading Panel. (2000). *Teaching children to read*. Bethesda, MD: Department of Health and Human Services, NICHD Clearinghouse.

No Child Left Behind Act of 2001. (2002, January 8). *Bill summary and status for the 107th Congress.* Retrieved January 15, 2004, from http://thomas.loc.gov.

No Child Left Behind Act: Title I: Improving the Academic Achievement of the Disadvantaged. (2002, November 26). *Summary of final regulations.* Retrieved January 17, 2004, from http://www.ed.gov/programs/titleiparta/index.html#reg.

Olson, L. (2003, November 19). Delay on special education rules prompt concern. *Education Week*, pp. 23, 25. Retrieved February 12, 2004, from http://www.edweek.org.

President's Commission on Excellence in Special Education. (2002, July). *A new era: Revitalizing special education for children and their families.* Retrieved July 12, 2002, from http://www.ed.gov/inits/commissionsboards/whspecialeducation/index.html.

Ralabate, P., & Foley, B. (2003, May). *IDEA and ESEA: Intersection of access and outcomes.* Retrieved February 5, 2004, from the National Education Association website: http://www.nea.org/specialed/ideaeseaintersection.html.

Roach, V., Salisbury, C., & McGregor, G. (2002). Applications of a policy framework to evaluate and promote large-scale change. *Exceptional Children, 68*, 451–464.

School Reform Left Behind. (2004, January 10). *New York Times*, p. A30.

Shriner, J. G., & Destefano, L. (2003). Participation and accommodations in state assessments: The role of individualized educational programs. *Exceptional Children, 69*, 147–161.

Silliman, E. R., Butler, K. G., & Wallach, G. P. (2002). The time has come to talk of many things. In K. G. Butler & E. R. Silliman (Eds.), *Speaking, reading, and writing in children with language and learning disabilities: New paradigms in research and practice* (pp. 3–25). Mahwah, NJ: Erlbaum.

Silliman, E. R., Wilkinson, L. C., & Brea-Spahn, M. R. (2004). Policy and practice imperatives for language and literacy learning. In C. A. Stone, E. R. Silliman, B. J. Ehren, & K. Apel (Eds.), *Handbook on language and literacy: Development and disorders* (pp. 97–129). New York: Guilford Press.

Snow, C. E., Burns, M. S., & Griffin, P. (Eds.). (1998). *Preventing reading difficulties in young children.* Washington, DC: National Academies Press.

Snyder, N. (2003, June 19). *Side-by-side comparison of personnel standards language in current IDEA law, H. R. 1350, and S. 1248.* Retrieved February 12, 2004, from http://www.asha.org/about/legislation-advocacy/federal/IDEA.

A Teacher's Perspective on the Reauthorization of IDEA. (2003, December 30). Message posted to http://pub60.ezboard.com/fourchildrenleftbehindfrm2.

Thompson, S., & Thurlow, M. (2003, December). *2003 state special education outcomes: Marching on.* Minneapolis: University of Minnesota, National Center on Educational Outcomes. Retrieved January 19, 2004, from http://education.umn.edu/nceo.

Thurlow, M. L., & Johnson, D. R. (2000). High-stakes testing of students with disabilities. *Journal of Teacher Education, 51,* 305–314.

U.S. Department of Education. (2003a). *NCLB desktop reference.* Retrieved February 6, 2004, from http://www.ed.gov/admins/lead/account/nclbreference/page_pg17.html?exp=0.

U.S. Department of Education. (2003b, October 8). High school leadership summit. Retrieved February 6, 2004, from http://www.ed.gov/searchResults.jhtml#SeeAlso.

U.S. Department of Education, National Center for Education Statistics. (2001). *Entering kindergarten: A portrait of American children when they begin school* (NCES 2001-035). Retrieved February 1, 2001, from http://nces.ed.gov.

U.S. Department of Education, National Center for Education Statistics. (2003a). *Status and trends in the education of Hispanics* (NCES 2003-008). Retrieved April 15, 2003, from http://nces.ed.gov.

U.S. Department of Education, National Center for Education Statistics. (2003b). *Status and trends in the education of blacks* (NCES 2003-034). Retrieved October 14, 2003, from http://nces.ed.gov.

U.S. Department of Education, Office of Elementary and Secondary Education. (2002, November 26). Title I, Part A Program, Purpose. Retrieved January 17, 2004, from http://www.ed.gov/programs/titleiparta/index.html.

U.S. Department of Education, Office of Innovation and Improvement. (2003, August 22). *No Child Left Behind: Supplemental education services—Nonregulatory guidance.* Retrieved January 19, 2004, from http://www.ed.gov/policy/elsec/guid/suppsvcsguid.doc.

U.S. Department of Education, Office of Special Education Programs. (2002a). Twenty-fourth annual report to Congress on the implementation of the Individuals with Disabilities Act. Retrieved September 25, 2003, from http://www.ed.gov/about/reports/annual/osep/2002/index.html.

U.S. Department of Education, Office of Special Education Programs. (2002b,

October). *IDEA Part B data fact sheet: Child count*. Retrieved May 15, 2003, from http://www.ed.gov/OSERS.

U.S. Senate Health, Education, Labor, and Pensions Committee. (2003, November). *Title I—Amendments to the Individuals with Disabilities Education Act* (Senate Reports 108-185). Retrieved January 30, 2004, from http://thomas.loc.gov/.

Wasburn-Moses, L. (2003). What every special educator should know about high-stakes testing. *Teaching Exception Children, 35*(4), 12–15.

Whitehurst, G. J. (2002, October). *Evidence-based education (EBE)*. Presentation at the Conference on Student Achievement and School Accountability sponsored by the U.S. Department of Education, Office of Elementary and Secondary Education. Retrieved February 6, 2004, from http://www.ed.gov/admins/lead/account/sasaconference02.html.

2

❧

Collaborative Models of
Instruction and Intervention

Choices, Decisions, and Implementation

GERALDINE P. WALLACH
BARBARA J. EHREN

Professionals working in school settings with increasingly diverse and challenged populations of students have much to think about as they try to find ways to help the children and adolescents in their care succeed academically and socially. The challenges facing regular and special education teachers, speech–language pathologists, reading and learning disability specialists, and other practitioners who work both within and outside of postmillennium classrooms come from many sources. The issues facing educators and specialists in this inclusive milieu include keeping up with the demands of a fast-moving curriculum, meeting the special needs of students who cannot move as quickly or who move differently through the curriculum, and understanding who does what to whom with a curriculum, particularly when several professionals provide complementary, and in some cases, overlapping services for the same students. Indeed, members of different disciplines, all with well-meaning instructional and intervention goals, are challenged to develop and implement collaboratively created programs that will maximize students' language and literacy learning—as the title of this text suggests. Creaghead (2002), talking about speech–language pathologists but making points that other specialists may relate to, noted recently:

> The major concern of our members in school settings is caseload size,
> with paperwork a close second. If we are to be successful in reducing
> caseloads or the paperwork burden, we will need to collaborate with
> special educators, regular educators, administrators, and parents. (p. 35)

The chapter covers three major subtopics as part of a general discussion of collaborative models of instruction and intervention. It focuses on some of the specific opportunities speech–language pathologists, classroom teachers, reading specialists, and other frontline professionals have to work together. The first section of the discussion briefly addresses the culture of schools: the interaction of teacher knowledge, values, and style; student knowledge, values, and styles; and materials and instructional styles. Assumptions about what is learned, how it is learned, and "what to do next" when students fail to "fit the mold" are outlined. The central theme of this section is the primacy of language in literacy learning and learning in general. Examples of the linguistic abilities assumed for various tasks are presented to highlight some of the challenges facing students with language learning disabilities. The importance of collaboration is introduced along with the reality underlying Creaghead's (2002) words: too many students with too many problems, and professionals with too little time. The first section sets the tone for some of the "shared knowledge" that forms a piece of the collaborative puzzle and recognizes the unique challenges and choices facing all educational practitioners who are involved in collaboration with "struggling communicators."

The second section of the chapter covers the nuts and bolts of the collaborative challenge. Selective collaborative models are outlined. Some of the choices facing professionals are discussed. Aspects of both decision-making and implementation processes are reviewed. The section has two intersecting topics: understanding the student with special needs and understanding the professionals who serve those students. Using the language arts content area of the curriculum as a template, a service delivery model is outlined. The language teaching continuum discussed includes highlights of several components adapted from Ehren (2000): (1) the *what* (the subject area), (2) the *how* (how the subject is delivered), (3) the *by whom* (classroom teacher, speech–language pathologist), and (4) the *for whom* (the student with a language learning disability versus the student with a language difference). Differences between "instruction" and "intervention" are highlighted as part of the discussion. The dynamic and ever evolving roles and responsibilities of different professionals are considered from a shared responsibility perspective that recognizes professionals' unique training and abilities.

The final section of the chapter summarizes some of the key points relating to maximizing the language and literacy successes of children and adolescents with language learning disabilities in schools. It covers where we have been and suggests where we might be going as frontline professionals continue to explore ways to help students with special needs survive and thrive in inclusive settings. Many of the concepts introduced in this chapter, specifically those that relate to curricular content, are covered in greater depth in the chapters that follow.

THE CULTURAL AND LINGUISTIC DEMANDS OF SCHOOL: STRANGERS IN A STRANGE LAND

Knowing Where We're Coming From: A First Step

In the quest to help students survive and ideally thrive in school, two pieces of shared knowledge among the regular educators, special educators, and other professionals may prove helpful especially when attempting to find some common ground: (1) understanding the culture of schools; and (2) understanding the primacy of language in learning. Clearly, as noted by Apel (1999) in his discussion of theory-to-practice gaps, professionals' "definitions" or "perceptions" of what things "are" or "are not" influence what they do on a daily basis. For example, if a reading specialist views reading as a visual process, his remediation/intervention might go in that direction (Apel, 1999). Similarly, if a speech–language pathologist believes that there is some relevance to the terms "one-step command," "two-step command," and "three-step command," he might create listening comprehension activities that mirror that belief. If a special education teacher thinks that there is validity to the concepts of an "auditory learner" or a "visual learner," her classroom groups might reflect this notion. Along these same lines, if a kindergarten teacher believes that literacy relates only to the acquisition of reading and writing, her focus might ignore some critical oral language foundations.

The four examples presented in the previous paragraph remind readers that professionals from diverse backgrounds and training bring their preconceived notions about language, literacy, and learning with them to their classrooms, clinical rooms, and resource rooms. Fey and Johnson (1998), and Meline and Paradiso (2003) also talking about the theory-to-practice gap, add that bringing researchers and practitioners together starts with recognizing the differences between the two groups—that is, practitioners and researchers should acknowledge and attempt to understand their differences and value what each has to offer. Perhaps collaborators from different disciplines including readers of this text might consider taking the advice of Fey and Johnson. Indeed, *creating opportunities to explore each other's unique contributions might represent a small first step toward developing truly collaborative language-based literacy programs.*

Knowing more about each other's points of view may represent a beginning. But collaborative frames of mind, formed with a willingness to learn and a level of shared knowledge, should begin at the preservice level. Professionals from diverse backgrounds are expected to collaborate with one another when they, in reality, have had limited preparation for doing so. Most professionals play "catch-up" on the road to creating and implementing collaborative programs for instruction and intervention. Speech–language pathologists, reading specialists, and special and regular educators typically experience few interdisciplinary moments in their undergraduate or graduate programs. They may share similar ideals and goals—for example, to help children and adolescents succeed academically—but those ideals and goals may be expressed in different lexicons, reflect different philosophical slants, and be based on different bodies of research, among other things. Formal and informal opportunities for education majors, speech–language pathology, and reading/literacy majors should be built into the curriculum.

For example, future reading specialists and speech–language pathologists might have as an assignment the completion of a series of interviews with each other (those in training) and with professionals from outside of their field of study. Specific questions about one's definition of literacy, the role of oral language in writing, and the grouping of children as "auditory" or "visual" learners are among the areas that might be explored, with discussions of the findings to follow. Likewise, mock case presentations formed with interdisciplinary teams could also provide preprofessional experiences, among many others, including experiences that foster an understanding of school as both a cultural and a linguistic experience.

School as a Cultural Experience

Children are immigrants in a foreign land when they enter a school building for the first time (Donahue, 2002). They not only have to adapt to a new culture but they also have to adapt to a new language. In their classic article "Talking to Learn: Social and Academic Requirements of Classroom Participation," Weade and Green (1985) remind professionals that the classroom is a complex maze of teacher, student, materials, and group interaction. This maze, represented by four overlapping circles, highlights the key components of school culture. According to Weade and Green (1985), both students and teachers bring with them to the classroom knowledge, abilities, experiences, beliefs, and preferences that influence how they perform academically. A clash of cultures can occur if a student's home culture is markedly different from a teacher's culture. For example, the preschool experiences students bring with them when they start their academic careers, such as having been read to and practicing with sound–letter correspondences, may influence the teacher's view of them as students. Van Kleeck (1998) and Dodd and Carr (2003), among others, talk about the importance of the preliteracy/preschool period on academic success, a point that is reinforced by Weade and Green (1985). Teachers also bring with them curricular and pedagogical knowledge, skills, experiences, and expectations; students bring with them strategies for "studenting" and curricular expectations. Classroom materials have their own structure and format, presenting subject matter and topics in language. And classroom groups take on lives of their own. The class may function as a whole group, there may be small-group activities, specified instructional groups (e.g., reading or math groups), and peer-group activities. This complex system of interconnected factors, about which volumes have been written, reminds us that "problems are not just within children—and neither are solutions" (Nelson, 1998, p. 12). As the Nelson quote suggests, collaborative programs are created by considering what students bring with them to the academic table as well as teacher expectations, the nature of the materials used, and the overall functioning (i.e., the culture) of the classroom.

A number of questions might be raised that cut across disciplines. For example, what are the personal frames of reference students bring to a lesson (or a therapy or resource room session) that might influence their participation? What will be the social and academic expectations for participating? Do students "read" both the social and the academic requirements for participating? Have they read all the expectations? Or only part of them? How will groups be organized and how will expectations for participating vary within and across groups? How will turn-taking procedures be organized? What frames of reference for "doing" the lesson will be shared by the teacher and the student? What is the structure of the text being used? When a student responds to a question inappropriately, what happens? Whereas these are only a few of the questions one could pose, the opportunities appear golden for professionals who work both within and outside of classrooms to create a dialogue around these types of questions. As noted earlier and in the preservice discussion, creating a discourse among one another, which may take the form of an in-service workshop, a consultation, an informal discussion, or the like may be a starting point for creating and implementing programs that maximize students' language and literacy learning.

The concept that children use "talking to learn," for example, reminds practitioners that language and academic success have an intimate relationship (Bashir, Conte, & Heerde, 1998; Cirrin, 1999; Fey, Catts, & Larivee, 1995; Wallach & Butler, 1994; Wallach, in press). Further, Weade and Green's (1985) inclusion of "social," in the *social* and *academic* requirements of classroom participation, reinforces the notion that a critical core of the learning process resides within the communicative interactions that occur between students, their peers, and the professionals who serve them (see Donahue & Foster, Chapter 7, this volume; Hay, Payne, & Chadwick, 2004; Mastergeorge, 2001; Vygotsky, 1987). The dynamic interplay of social, communicative, and linguistic factors come together to define what is learned, when it is learned, and how it is learned. While mastery of a school curriculum presents new challenges for many students, it presents a particular challenge for students with spoken and written language learning problems who have to master simultaneously the curriculum's content and the social-communicative rules that regulate access to the curriculum. While seemingly overwhelming in some ways, there is hope for these students, as several intervention studies suggest (Hadley, Simmerman, Long, & Luna, 2000; Hyter, Rogers-Adkinson, Self, Simmons, & Jantz, 2001; Mastergeorge, 2001). For example, Hyter et al. (2001) demonstrated that some children diagnosed with emotional/behavioral disorders (E/BD) improved in their classroom performance after a collaborative in-class language program stressing expressive and pragmatic aspects of communication was implemented. The results of the program demonstrated that many students with E/BD exhibited undiagnosed language disorders. At the same time, findings showed the strength of speech–language pathologists and special education teachers working together to develop and achieve consistent language/academic goals.

School as a Linguistic Experience

Nelson (1998) expands the discussion of instructional discourse, taking the communicative component further and moving beyond the overall view of schools as a cultural adaptation for students. Aspects of instructional language Nelson covers include: (1) meeting classroom management expectations, (2) understanding peer interaction rules, and (3) processing and comprehending instructional language.

Meeting classroom management expectations includes abilities like responding to teacher's signals of task reorienting, knowing when to try for the teacher's attention, and knowing how to pass a turn or guess appropriately. Peer interaction rules include actions such as whether one can solicit help in acceptable ways and times, give appropriate help to classmates, and participate in group decision making through appropriate conversational rules of turn taking. Processing and comprehending instructional language includes being metalinguistic (i.e., can talk about language, can reflect upon language, and can analyze language), successfully accessing textbook language, and applying strategies for correcting misunderstood content information.

Furthermore, Blank (2002) points out that classroom discourse is filled with verbal concepts. Examples include new topic knowledge to be acquired and implicit meaning—for example, figuring out what the teacher really wants. Blank notes a twofold challenge for mastering school content. She indicates that (1) the language of school is informationally loaded, and (2) school discourse presumes a good deal of "already-known" information, as well as inferential and integrative processing ability. Indeed, "within instructional exchanges, including discussing, questioning, responding, and summarizing, teachers and students construct and make explicit the content of the curriculum" (Bashir et al., 1998, p. 10).

Given what is known about school culture and school language and given what practitioners have to do to help students, what roles might different team members share to guide students through the culturally different, discourse-dense, and informationally loaded world of school? These are among the questions collaborators should be asking one another. Answers to these questions and others may provide professionals with a foundation for understanding the connections between the demands of the classroom and the abilities students bring with them to succeed (Bashir et al., 1998).

A Key Question for All Collaborators: What Language Abilities Are Assumed?

Regardless of the disciplines represented by the readers of this text and frontline teams in schools, all professionals who are interesting in literacy learning and learning in general are engaged in the study and "practice" of language, albeit in different ways and with overlapping and different populations (Dickinson & Tabors, 2001a; Ehren, 2000; Silliman, Butler, & Wallach, 2002). A key question that must be raised is: What language abilities are necessary to become literate? As suggested by Weade and Green (1985), many students with language learning disabilities learn to talk but are not proficient at talking to learn (Bashir et al., 1998). Asking about language abilities might be considered an obvious arena for speech–language pathologists, but the question "What does it take?," relative to language skills, should concern curricular committees, administrators, and all professionals who work with children and adolescents with language, reading, academic, and behavioral problems.

The three examples that follow remind professionals of the broad spectrum of language abilities needed to be successful across a variety of curriculum activities. The examples also represent different levels of literacy and offer opportunities for how team members can work together to explore and understand the language abilities that are "assumed" or "needed" to complete various literacy and academic tasks.

1. What does it take to understand and use (a) and (b) to facilitate comprehension?

a.   Baq to Baq: Lakers Do It Again!
b.   Christopher Columbus: How History Was Invented

A headline or title can facilitate comprehension and prepare students for what might be coming up in the text *if* both language knowledge and background knowledge are available and applied to the task (see also Whitaker, Gambrell, & Morrow, Chapter 5, and Pressley & Hilden, Chapter 6, this volume). Consider the first headline: "Baq to Baq: Lakers Do It Again!" The headline provides the reader with some information about the topic. It notes one of the main "characters" (players) in the text as well as using the play-on-words from his name to mean "back to back." It tells readers (or listeners) that the "Lakers" have done it again; they've repeated something that appears to be a good thing. But the headline, while providing information, assumes a great deal of background and linguistic knowledge. Does the reader understand that the headline refers to the Los Angeles Lakers? Does the reader know anything about sports and this particular sport, basketball? Further, can the reader unravel the figurative language, the creative play-on-words, to comprehend the headline? More specifically, the spelling of *baq* is a play on the spelling of the name of Lakers' star *Sha*quille O'Neal. The headline refers to the Lakers' second consecutive National Basketball Association championship, a headline that is now obsolete given the Lakers' "three peat"—another play-on-words that will be comprehensible to most residents of Southern California and basketball fans everywhere.

Regarding the second example, does the middle-school student comprehend the true meaning of the phrase "How history was invented?" in the second "headline"/title. The phrase changes the intent of the Christopher Columbus passage (Hennings, 1993). (The text makes the point that Columbus may not have been the "hero" we have known and read about.) Consequently, while headlines and titles may be used by practitioners (and textbook authors) as a tactic to facilitate text processing and comprehension, they must be aware of the kinds of background and linguistic knowledge assumed accessible to make them useful.

2.   What does it take to construct a writing piece like the one that follows? (The piece is retyped from the original, which was handwritten with "illustrations." Spelling attempts are noted by slashes. The typed version also maintains word boundaries as written and punctuation or the lack thereof.)

Today at about 7:00 I woke my dad up and then I saw a dear he was looking for grass and he was come/coming cloeser then my dad got the camer and took picc/picshers/pichers of it then it came aroud to the front of the house and he was oney about a feet away and then he went back in the woods then when we were going to get some food we saw

a frog and my dad said to get out and take it and said pick it up then I
said no you pick it up and then he hoped away.

This personal narrative, written by a second grader without language
or learning problems, provides some insights into this child's advancing
language and literacy proficiency. While one might be tempted to focus
on the spelling, grammar, and punctuation in the piece, it might be more
important at this age level to observe what the piece says about this young
writer's language knowledge (see Englert & Dunsmore, Chapter 8, and
Singer & Bashir, Chapter 9, this volume). Again, one should ask: What language abilities are assumed to be intact in order to produce a piece like the
one presented?

Justin, the author of the piece, understands something about recount-
ing events (Westby, 1994). He also knows that stories, in this case, a personal narrative, consist of a series of sentences. He knows about internal
mental states and uses quoted dialogue in stories, even though he fails
to mark these character dialogues with quotes. Justin also knows about
expressing events in a logical sequence. His use of linguistic forms (temporal connectives), such as "and then," "then," and "when," while somewhat oral in style, help readers of the narrative to understand the order
of events.

While Justin has much more to learn about composing written stories,
including learning more about spelling patterns and print conventions, his
oral and written language experiences have helped him evolve to this point
as a writer. For example, he has had practice telling spoken narratives. His
parents, caretakers, and teachers have read to him. He has played language
awareness games at home and in school, including rhyming games, segmenting games, and sound identification games, and he has practiced with
print. (See Troia, Chapter 4, this volume, for additional information on
facilitating the integration of decoding and spelling activities with beginning readers and writers.)

3. What does it take to unravel the information from this social studies text?

Melanesia[1]

Each tribe exchanged goods with other tribes such as food, animals, clay,
and wooden bowls, woven mats, weapons, and even canoes. Religious
ceremonies were often used to protect crops from harm or to increase
their yields. Melanesia is a relatively unknown country. Some of the
islands of Melanesia are large single islands (New Britain and New Ire-
land), and some are made up of island groupings (The Solomon Islands
and New Hebrides). Often villagers used magic to protect themselves
from enemies or against villagers who failed to pay a debt or who broke
a rule.

This last example, the Melanesia excerpt, from a classic study by Ohlhausen and Roller (1988), reminds practitioners about the complexity of materials in many sixth-grade textbooks. The Melanesia passage contains unfamiliar content expressed in complex structures. In additional to the new and unfamiliar content students have to master (including learning about the location, customs, foods, etc. of Melanesia), they must also deal with the way the information is transmitted, that is, through compound and complex sentences, organized in an expository text format. The metaphorical double-edged sword of content and structure challenges students in middle school with and without language problems as they try to absorb the information across subject areas from school textbooks.

Ohlhausen and Roller (1988) hypothesized that improving the way passages like this one about Melanesia are written could help middle-school children absorb its content. For example, the Melanesia passage could be reorganized to begin as a series of sentences like: "Melanesia is a relatively unknown country. It consists of a series of islands. . . . We are going to study the following topics about Melanesia." As predicted, reordering the sentences and reorganizing the sequence of information facilitated the retention and memory of the sixth-grade students for the Melanesia unit. The research, presented as an example, reminds professionals to pay close attention to how a text is organized as well as to what it has to say.

Summary: What the Language Examples Say

The three examples remind collaborators that there is much they can do together. Common ground can be established by asking the question: "What language abilities underlie literacy and learning?" Addressing this question forms a foundation for the development and implementation of literacy programs that are truly collaborative and language-based. The Melanesia excerpt and the other two examples presented in this section remind readers that there are many questions to ask about what language is required or assumed to underlie many of the academic tasks facing their students on a daily basis.

The next step in learning how to collaborate involves the delivery of services that complement, not replicate, one another. Indeed, the who-does-what-to-whom question looms large in school settings. But, hopefully, one can take some logical steps toward the process of creating complementary services from heeding the three examples in the previous section. For example, the regular or special education classroom teacher might be responsible for teaching the content of the Melanesia unit whereas the speech–languagepathologist might help the students with language learning disabilities in her class to develop strategies for using clues in the text and understanding the structure of expository text. Likewise, the speech–language pathologist and reading specialist might assume consultative roles with kindergarten and Grade 1 teachers to create programmatic sequences that take into account the oral language, narrative, and print prerequisites, among others, required to complete a writing piece like Justin's. Speech–language pathologists and other specialists working with the same students might agree to use the content of the curriculum (e.g., the Columbus unit) as a context or backdrop for the more specific interventions necessary for individual students (Ehren, 2000; see also Figure 2.1 on p. 53). Ehren (2000) uses the term "curriculum relevant therapy" to describe the ways in which specific interventions, including speech–language therapy, interface with the curriculum.

Regardless of the diversity of disciplines represented on most school teams serving students with language learning disabilities, one of the toughest challenges facing practitioners is to avoid becoming lost in labels and materials at the expense of focusing on the development of a shared understanding of language-based literacy instruction and intervention and the implementation of innovative programs. The collaborate choices and challenges facing professionals are considered in greater detail next.

COLLABORATIVE CHALLENGES, CHOICES, AND IMPLEMENTATION: KNOWLEDGE COMES FIRST

An Overview

As Cook and Friend (1991) put it, collaboration involves at least two *co-equal partners* who are involved in a *voluntary*, problem-solving process for the purpose of achieving a *common goal* (cited in Lue, 2001, p. 244). While one may recognize the positive ideas reflected in this definition and understand that no one discipline has all the information needed to meet the diverse needs of children and adolescents with language learning disabilities, professionals are also well aware of the challenges facing them. There is much to consider when making decisions about how to implement collaborative programs for instruction and intervention in various settings within an inclusive world. For example, professionals' perceptions about how to operationalize programs that are *truly* collaborative may differ (Peña & Quinn, 2003).

Providing integrated language/literacy services for students with difficulties in the classroom "requires teachers and speech–language pathologists . . . [reading and other specialists] . . . to rethink teaching approaches and commit to a collaborative course of action" (Bashir et al.,

1998, p. 4). Collaboration can take many forms and occur within many service delivery models. Indeed, as with any complex issue, there is good news and bad news. Table 2.1 outlines some of the benefits and challenges involved in collaboration. Working professionals will, no doubt, be familiar with the sampling of ideas represented in Table 2.1 and will add their own items to the list.

As Lue (2001) and other school-based professionals point out, the benefits of collaboration are tremendous for teachers, for specialists, and for students. The necessityof sharing responsibilities in language and literacy is reflected in many of the concepts discussed in this chapter and throughout this text. Knowing that one is not alone in helping students navigate their way through the sometimes turbulent waters of schools (their culture, their language, their content) should provide encouragement to frontline teams. The ever-present challenges can be overcome as professionals gain knowledge of the language–literacy relationship, one another, and the collaborative choices available to them.

Collaborative Models of Service Delivery: Some Broad Choices

Professionals across disciplines will also recognize the various models of service delivery presented here and will weave the collaborative process into each of these models in different ways (DeKemel, 2003). Silliman (2004;

TABLE 2.1. The Benefits and Challenges of Collaboration

Benefits

- Individuals involved develop mutual goals that are specific enough so that their expertise complements, not replicates, services.
- An atmosphere of equally valued professional contributions develops over time.
- Professionals share resources, decision-making authority, etc.
- Programs (individualized education program goals) become more integrated (in the truest sense).

Challenges

- Administrative support and structure fails to be in place.
- Time for consultation and collaboration is insufficient or nonexistent.
- Conflicts arise between what educators would like to do and what they are able to do.
- A lack of shared knowledge base, training, and confusion regarding roles and responsibilities exists.

Note. From Lue (2001). Published by Allyn and Bacon. Boston, MA. Copyright 2001 by Pearson Education. Reprinted by permission of the publisher. See also DiMeo, Merritt, and Culatta (1998).

see also Silliman & Wilkinson, Chapter 1, and Silliman, Wilkinson, & Danzak, Chapter 12, this volume) discusses four models that recognize students' needs at different points in time: (1) the *direct service model*, (2) the *classroom-based service delivery model*, (3) the *consultative model of service delivery*, and (4) the *community-based service delivery model*. The direct service model, as used here, refers to the more traditional "pull-out" model. Students are taken out of their classrooms for speech–language therapy, resource room, or other services that operate on a one-on-one or small-group basis outside of the classroom.

The classroom-based service delivery model, popular among speech–language pathologists today, involves interacting within the context of the classroom and may take the form of working with small groups, the whole class, or individual students (see Ehren, 2000; Hadley et al., 2000; Hyter et al., 2001; Silliman, Bahr, Beasman, & Wilkinson, 2000). While direct service and classroom delivery models are mentioned separately here, most school-based people would classify classroom-based intervention under the direct service model as long as the intervention involves the professional's caseload. Thus, pull-out and classroom-based service can both be aspects of direct services.

The consultative model of service, sometimes known as "indirect service," involves team members working on various aspects of instruction and intervention from planning to modifying the curriculum, among other activities. In the consultative model, for example, a speech–language pathologist might make suggestions to a teacher about how to modify lessons, tests, and assignments based upon the language demands inherent in the tasks and materials and the particular student's language abilities (Ehren, 2000). The speech–language pathologist, in the consultative role, would not be working directly with the student or students. Similarly, a special education teacher might provide the speech–language pathologist or reading specialist with a tutorial about what her social studies unit might look like for the next 6 weeks to facilitate an understanding of classroom expectations. Finally, community-based services, like home-based literacy programs, provide services to clients where they "live."

Lue (2001), summarizing the work of Borsch and Oaks (1993) also outlines four service delivery models that complement the models Silliman (2004) describes. The four "teaching" models, on a continuum from "outside" to "inside" classrooms are (1) *resource management*, (2) *supportive teaching*, (3) *complementary teaching*, and (4) *team teaching* (DiMeo, Merritt, & Culatta, 1998, p. 79; Lue, 2001, p. 249). All models involve classroom activity but with varying degrees of involvement by team specialists (e.g., speech–language pathologists, reading specialists). All involve teachers and specialists working together to plan, monitor, and make decisions about the goals and materials for their students with language learning disabilities (Lue,

2001). In resource management, the speech–language pathologist, reading specialist, or learning disability specialist would observe in the classroom periodically to ensure that mutual goals are being met and to work with teachers when curricular adaptations are necessary. In supportive teaching, a specialist might conduct a demonstration lesson targeting specific language and literacy goals. For example, a speech–language pathologist might conduct a demonstration lesson for Grade 1 teachers on phonemic segmentation (see Troia, Chapter 4, this volume). A reading specialist might present a demonstration lesson on reading comprehension strategies (see Pressley & Hilden, Chapter 6, and Donahue & Foster, Chapter 7, this volume). Complementary teaching, somewhat like supportive teaching, involves the teacher teaching the core of a lesson and the specialist teaching portions of the lesson that relate to his or her area of expertise. For example, a teacher might read a story to the children and ask general questions about the story while the speech–language pathologist might organize more specific activities that help students appreciate story grammars and attend to the mental states of characters that serve as motivations for characters' actions (Westby, 1999). Team teaching involves the teacher and specialist in the classroom for an entire subject or day. Both teach skills as well as curricular content. Finally, beyond the models and options discussed, several program developers also note the important role that parents can and should play in the collaborative process (Dickinson & Tabor, 2001b; Giangreco, 2000).

A Closer Look at Collaborative Choices: Becoming Aware of the "Too Many Cooks" Syndrome

Studying the various collaborative choices available can be a useful endeavor. Most professionals have experience with all or some of the service delivery models presented earlier. No doubt, practitioners have tried many collaborative strategies including written communication, conversation, demonstrations, in-services, and conferences (DiMeo et al., 1998). Many have also used a "cut and paste" approach to make things work based on the needs of the children and adolescents in their care and the realities of their particular settings. Certainly, readers of this text may be well aware of the reality that many recommendations look better on paper than they do in the real world.

For example, there are often hidden glitches to the collaborative choices made. These glitches are varied and include such questions as the following (see Ehren, 2000; Norris, 1997):

1. Is the team-teaching option an appropriate one for specialists?
2. Should speech–language pathologists teach both the skills and the *content* of the curriculum along with the classroom teacher?

3. Do highly trained specialists fall into the "tutor trap" by helping students complete homework assignments and other class work?
4. Can classroom lessons target the students who need the most help?

Choices must be continuously evaluated from many perspectives including assessing the roles and responsibilities that collaborators accept. It is important to question new trends as well as to evaluate the research base that supports those trends and popular practices (Apel, 1999; Fey & Johnson, 1998). Finally, it is most important to recognize that none of us can be all things to all students.

An Example: The Decision-Making Process

As shown in Figure 2.1, Ehren (2000) describes a "language teaching continuum" to help professionals engage in decision making related to four aspects of collaboration. These aspects are (1) delineating their roles to match their expertise and to maximize what they can do, especially when different professionals are working with the same student; (2) articulating the differences between "instruction" and "intervention" (or therapy) and developing language/literacy/learning goals accordingly; (3) recognizing the differences between teaching the content of the curriculum versus teaching its language underpinnings; and (4) understanding the populations for whom each professional is responsible.

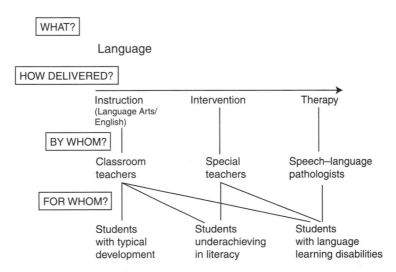

FIGURE 2.1. The language teaching continuum of service delivery. From Ehren (2000). Copyright 2000 by B. J. Ehren. Reprinted by permission.

Regardless of the discipline one represents, the questions that Ehren (2000) poses—the what, how delivered, by whom, and for whom—offer a template for consideration. The model also helps professionals appreciate their uniqueness.Clearly, adaptations to the model are always possible. The varied ways in which professionals can collaborate, as noted throughout the chapter, remain fluid, dynamic, and continuously changing. The model for the language teaching continuum represents a way to begin to think about the primary role of teachers and specialists, and at the same time allows for creative ways to cross the lines in a metaphorical sense.

What?

Language arts is the content area discussed by Ehren (2000). It is a major component of the school curriculum that has more formal predominance in the elementary grades. Other content areas like science, math, or social studies could be substituted in the "What" section. As discussed throughout this chapter, language cuts across all content areas and underlies many academic tasks. All students must learn to listen, speak, read, and write to survive and thrive in classrooms. All educational collaborators are involved in the business of language. Facilitating language and literacy is our shared responsibility. However, shared responsibility does not imply that every professional functions in the same way. Shared responsibility involves recognizing the different ways professionals might "deliver" language to their students. The "What" aspect in the model provides an example of how "language"—a continuum from language arts to language therapy—may be described.

How Delivered?

After the "what" is determined, the question of "how" the language arts curriculum is delivered to students is considered. The type of teaching that occurs in the normal course of events in a school curriculum is referred to as *instruction*. Children without language, learning, and literacy difficulties benefit from regular "language arts" instruction. When typical instruction is insufficient to produce the mastery required in the curriculum, schools respond by offering a variety of *intervention* services (e.g., Reading Recovery, English as a Second Language programs, speech–language therapy). In this continuum, *therapy* is considered a very specific, more intense type of intervention. As noted in the model, students with language learning disabilities may require specific, intense therapy. The typical language arts' curriculum is insufficient for them. Rather, "curriculum-relevant therapy" is required (Ehren, 2000, 2002). Curriculum-relevant therapy includes helping students master the language foundations or underpinnings that will enable them to access the curricular content (Ehren, 2000, 2002; see also page 49, this chapter). For example, therapy might include learning how to process and use expository text structure for handling social studies pieces like the Melanesia example presented earlier.

By Whom and for Whom?

In the inclusive world of schools, the roles played by teachers and specialists are continuously evolving. The model suggests a way in which professionals can begin to consider a "core role." How does each professional "deliver language content" to his or her students? What is his or her *primary* responsibility? For which population is he or she *primarily* responsible? As outlined in the model, regular classroom teachers "deliver language" to students with typical development. Clearly, the inclusive milieu of schools today changes the equation for classroom teachers, and makes collaboration a critical component in the education process. Speech–language pathologists, on the other hand, are involved primarily with students with language learning disabilities in the intervention/therapeutic arena. Speech–language pathologists may be involved in numerous collaborative options to reach that population (some of whom may be in regular classes at least part of the time). The perspective underlying the model is that the speech–language pathologist, the reading specialist, and other specialists are not primarily responsible for typical learners as Figure 2.1 might suggest. Similarly, students who are underachieving in literacy may be involved in the intervention arena serviced by special education teachers and other specialists who are generally not speech–language pathologists. Does the model convey that professionals never cross disciplinary lines? Indeed not. For example, specialists who are not classroom teachers may "cross the line" when they shift from a "failure" model to a "prevention" model. From the prevention perspective, speech–language pathologists may have a consultative role to play in strengthening the quality of instruction to prevent or minimize failures in literacy learning (see also page 49, this chapter).

The Model and Collaboration: Final Thoughts

The concept of the language teaching continuum demonstrates how professionals can begin to talk about complementary roles and responsibilities, and perhaps make some reasonable choices about who does what to whom. By weaving together aspects of the collaborative models discussed earlier, including in-class service and consultation, professionals can achieve their goal of creating and implementing *complementary* services. Reminiscent of the points made at the beginning of this chapter, it is important for professionals to understand "where" their choices originate from—choices that relate to the what, the how, the by whom, and the for whom. For example, speech–language pathologists, reading specialists, and other specialists are not responsible for teaching how a bill becomes a law. However, a speech–language pathologist should facilitate the spoken/written expression of a sequence of ideas, including helping the student to use appropriate clauses and transition words. The speech–language pathologist could use the "bill becomes a law" unit as a context for her curriculum-relevant therapy (Ehren, 2000, 2002). Likewise, speech–language pathologists, reading specialists, or learning disability specialists (who are not classroom teachers) would not be teaching the names of the 13 original colonies to students with memory problems. It might be more effective for them to teach their students with language learning disabilities mnemonic techniques to help them learn the names of the colonies for a test. Similarly, it is not the responsibility of speech–language pathologists to preteach the science vocabulary; that is the domain of the science teacher (and one could not keep up with the fast-moving curriculum in any case). However, the speech–language pathologist might teach words and phrases like *was caused by*, *the result of*, and so on—the specific linguistic glue—that holds the science lesson or textbook together. Highly trained specialists should not be helping their students with language learning disabilities finish the problems on a math sheet. Again, it might be more effective for the appropriate specialist to work on those "tricky" math words like *above*, *after*, *as many as*, *before*, *below*, *between*, and the like (see Cirrin, 1999; Ehren, 2000, 2002).

THE LONG ROAD TO A REASONABLE END: THREE FINAL POINTS

Where might professionals go from here with so much to consider? Three final points are made for future consideration. First, some of the preliminary research on the effectiveness of collaborative and inclusive programs is positive (e.g., Ogletree, 1999; Hadley et al., 2000; Hyter et al., 2001; Throneburg, Calvert, Sturum, Paramboukas, & Paul, 2000). Second, professionals have specialized training and expertise, which should be recognized. Teachers need not become speech–language pathologists and speech–language pathologists need not become teachers, among other combinations one could name. Team members have unique, important, and complementary roles to play on the educational stage.

Third, professionals should recognize that there are small steps they can take to launch collaborative programs (Norris, 1997). J. Ysseldyke (personal communication, 1990) reminds school-based professionals to give themselves time. They are asked to think about the answer to this metaphorical question: How do you move a graveyard? One body at a time.

Sometimes collaborative change comes slowly. Collaboration that meets rigorous efficacy standards will be a gradual process that includes exploration, evaluation, and change. Small steps may lead the way. It may be that working with one teacher or one specialist will suffice initially to create a joint language/literacy program. It may be that starting with one demonstration lesson in one class may create interest in one's school. It may be that a checklist going back and forth from teacher to specialist is a way to begin a broader and longer term collaboration. Collaboration comes from the Latin word *collaboratus*, which means "to labor together" (Lue, 2001, p. 244). And laboring together means that professionals have partners with whom they can make the world a little bit better for students who reside both within and outside their classrooms.

NOTE

1. From Ohlhausen and Roller (1988, p. 75). Copyright 1988 by the International Reading Association. Reprinted by permission of the International Reading Association. All rights reserved.

REFERENCES

Apel, K. (1999). Checks and balances: Keeping science in our profession. *Language, Speech, and Hearing Services in Schools, 30*, 98–107.

Bashir, A. S., Conte, B. M., & Heerde, S. M. (1998). Language and school success: Collaboration, change, and choices. In D. D. Merritt & B. Culatta (Eds.), *Language intervention in the classroom* (pp. 1–36). San Diego, CA: Singular.

Blank, M. (2002). Classroom discourse: A key to literacy. In K. G. Butler & E. R. Silliman (Eds.), *Speaking, reading, and writing in children with language learning disabilities: New paradigms in research and practice* (pp. 151–173). Mahwah, NJ: Erlbaum.

Borsch, J., & Oaks, R. (1993). *The collaboration companion: Strategies and activities in and out of the classroom*. East Moline, IL: LinguiSystems.

Cirrin, F. (1999). Assessing language in the classroom and the curriculum. In J. B. Tomblin, H. L. Morris, & D. C. Spriestersbach (Eds.), *Diagnosis in speech–language pathology* (2nd ed., pp. 283–314). San Diego, CA: Singular.

Cook, L., & Friend, M. (1991). Collaboration in special education. *Preventing School Failure, 35*(2), 4–24.

Creaghead, N. A. (2002). Health care and schools services—More coalitions and collaborations. *ASHA, 7*(4), 35.

DeKemel, K. (2003). Alternative service delivery models: The move toward collaborative and consultation and classroom-based intervention. In K. DeKemel.

Intervention in language arts: A practical guide for speech–language pathologists (pp. 109–126). Philadelphia, PA: Butterworth-Heinemann.

Dickinson, D. K., & Tabors, P. O. (Eds.). (2001a). *Beginning literacy with language.* Baltimore: Brookes.

Dickinson, D. K., & Tabors, P. O. (2001b). Bringing homes and schools together. In D. K. Dickinson & P. O. Tabors (Eds.), *Beginning literacy with language* (pp. 289–312). Baltimore: Brookes.

DiMeo, J. H., Merritt, D. D., & Culatta, B. (1998). Collaborative partnerships and decision making. In D. D. Merritt & B. Culatta (Eds.), *Language intervention in the classroom* (pp. 37–97). San Diego, CA: Singular.

Dodd, B., & Carr, A. (2003). Young children's letter–sound knowledge. *Language, Speech, and Hearing Services in Schools, 34*(2), 128–137.

Donahue, M. L. (2002). "Hanging with friends": Making sense of research on peer discourse in children with language and learning disabilities. In K. G. Butler & E. R. Silliman (Eds.), *Speaking reading, and writing in children with language learning disbilities: New paradigms in research and practice* (pp. 239–271). Mahwah, NJ: Erlbaum.

Ehren, B. J. (2000). Maintaining a therapeutic focus and shared responsibility for student success: Keys to in-classroom speech–language services. *Language, Speech, and Hearing Services in Schools, 31*, 219–229.

Ehren, B. J. (2002). Speech–language pathologists contributing significantly to the academic success of high school students: A vision for professional growth. *Topics in Language Disorders, 22*(2), 60–80.

Fey, M. E., Catts, H. W., & Larivee, L. S. (1995). Preparing preschoolers for the academic and social challenges of school. In M. E. Fey, J. Windsor, & S. F. Warren (Eds.), *Language intervention: Preschool to elementary years* (pp. 3–37). Baltimore: Brookes.

Fey, M. E., & Johnson, B. W. (1998). Research to practice (and back again) in speech–language intervention. *Topics in Language Disorders, 18*(2), 23–34.

Giangreco, M. F. (2000). Related services research for students with low-incidence disabilities: Implications for speech–language pathologists in inclusive classrooms. *Language, Speech, and Hearing Services in Schools, 31*, 230–239.

Hadley, P. A., Simmerman, A., Long, M., & Luna, M. (2000). Facilitating language development for inner-city children: Experimental evaluation of a collaborative classroom-based intervention. *Language, Speech, and Hearing Services in Schools, 31*, 280–295.

Hay, D. F., Payne, A., & Chadwick, A. (2004). Peer relations in childhood. *Journal of Child Psychology and Psychiatry, 45*, 84–108.

Hennings, D. G. (1993). On knowing and reading history. *Journal of Reading, 36*(5), 362–370.

Hyter, Y. D., Rogers-Adkinson, D. L., Self, T. L., Simmons, B. F., & Jantz, J. (2001). Pragmatic language intervention for children with language and emotional/behavioral disorders. *Communication Disorders Quarterly, 23*(1), 4–16.

Lue, M. S. (2001). *A survey of communication disorders for the classroom teacher.* Needham Heights, MA: Allyn & Bacon.

Mastergeorge, A. M. (2001). Guided participation in sociocultural learning: Intervention and apprenticeship. *Topics in Language Disorders, 22*(1), 74–92.

Meline, T., & Paradiso, T. (2003). Evidence-based practice in schools: Evaluating research and reducing barriers. *Language, Speech, and Hearing Services in Schools, 34*(4), 273–283.

Nelson, N. (1998). *Childhood language disorders in context: Infancy through adolescence.* Needham Heights, MA: Allyn & Bacon.

Norris, J. A. (1997). Functional language intervention in the classroom: Avoiding the tutor trap. *Topics in Language Disorders, 17*(2), 49–68.

Ogletree, B. (1999). Practical solutions to the challenges of changing professional roles: Introduction to the special issue. *Intervention in School and Clinic, 34,* 131.

Ohlhausen, M., & Roller, C. (1988). The operation of text structure and content schemata in isolation and interaction. *Reading Research Quarterly, 23,* 70–88.

Peña, E. D., & Quinn, R. (2003). Developing effective collaboration teams in speech–language pathology. *Communication Disorders Quarterly, 24*(2), 53–63.

Silliman, E. R. (2004). Inclusion models for children with developmental disabilities. In R. D. Kent (Ed.), *MIT encyclopedia of communication disorders* (pp. 307–311). Cambridge, MA: The MIT Press.

Silliman, E. R., Bahr, R., Beasman, J., & Wilkinson, L. C. (2000). Scaffolding for learning to read in an inclusive classroom. *Language, Speech, and Hearing Services in Schools, 31,* 265–279.

Silliman, E. R., Butler, K. G., & Wallach, G. P. (2002). The time has come to talk of many things. In K. G. Butler & E. R. Silliman (Eds.), *Speaking, reading, and writing in children with language learning disabilities: New paradigms in research and practice* (pp. 3–25). Mahwah, NJ: Erlbaum.

Throneburg, R. N., Calvert, L. K., Sturum, J. J., Paramboukas, A. A., & Paul, P. J. (2000). A comparison of service delivery models: Effects on curricular vocabulary skills in the school setting. *American Journal of Speech–Language Pathology, 9*(1), 10–20.

van Kleeck, A. (1998). Preliteracy domains and stages: Laying the foundation for beginning reading instruction. *Journal of Childhood Communication Development, 20*(1), 33–51.

Vygotsky, L. S. (1987). *The collected works of L. S. Vygotsky* (Vol. 1). New York: Plenum Press.

Wallach, G. P. (in press). Over the brink of the millennium: Have we said all we can say about language learning disabilities? *Communication Disorders Quarterly.*

Wallach, G. P., & Butler, K. G. (Eds.). (1994). *Language learning disabilities in school-age children and adolescents: Some principles and applications.* Needham Heights, MA: Allyn & Bacon.

Weade, R., & Green, J. L. (1985). Talking to learn: Social and academic requirements of classroom participation. *Peabody Journal of Education, 62*(3), 6–19.

Westby, C. E. (1994). The effects of culture on genre, structure, and style of oral and written texts. In G. P. Wallach & K. G. Butler (Eds.), *Language learning disabilities in school-age children and adolescents: Some principles and applications* (pp. 180–218). Needham Heights, MA: Allyn & Bacon.

Westby, C. E. (1999). Assessing and facilitating text comprehension problems. In H. W. Catts & A. G. Kamhi (Eds.), *Language and reading disabilities* (pp. 154–219). Needham Heights, MA: Allyn & Bacon.

PART II

❧

Word Recognition and Reading Comprehension
Perspectives on Instructional and Intervention Practices

3

❧

Language and Discourse Contributions to Word Recognition and Text Interpretation

Implications of a Dynamic Systems Perspective

RONALD B. GILLAM
BRENDA K. GORMAN

This chapter concerns the language and discourse processes that play a role in *word recognition*, which we view as the ability to construct meaning while attending to printed words. Our view of word recognition is predicated on the belief that reading is a complex dynamic system in which various kinds of language and discourse knowledge impact on one another in a reciprocal fashion. Our assumptions about the reading process are consistent with connectionist theories of text comprehension (Evans, 2002; Gernsbacher, 1995; Goldman & Rakestraw, 2000; Graesser, Gernsbacher, & Goldman, 1997; Kintsch, 1994b; Rawson & Kintsch, 2002) and reading (Berninger & Abbott, 2002; Berninger, Abbott, & Alsdorf, 1997; Plaut, McClelland, Seidenberg, & Patterson, 1996; van Kleeck, 2003; Whitehurst & Fischel, 2000). Specifically, we believe that the reader's interpretation of a printed text emerges out of simultaneous mental connections among different processing units. These include orthographic (letter) processing units, phonological (sound) processing units, lexical (word) processing units, semantic (propositional meaning) processing units, morphosyntactic (grammatical) processing units, and contextual (discourse circumstances) processing units. The extent of the contribution that a particular processing unit makes to word recognition varies as a function of the relationships between the reader's prior knowledge about the topic, the reader's language and situational knowledge, and the difficulty level of the words and sentences in the text. Some children may have difficulty with word recognition because they have weakly organized knowledge about a topic. They may not be familiar with the vocabulary and the basic concepts in the text. Other children may have difficulty with word recognition because they have reduced neural connections between parts of the brain that are critical for literacy development. They may not be able to access networks that enable them to easily and rapidly connect letters, sounds, and words as they read.

Because multiple levels of language knowledge and language processing contribute to reading, it should not be surprising that children with reading disabilities often present concomitant problems with oral language comprehension or use. It should not be surprising that children with language impairments are at high risk for reading disabilities (Catts & Kamhi, 1999). In fact, Catts and his colleagues (Catts, Fey, Zhang, & Tomblin, 1999) found that over 70% of the poor readers in their study of 604 children in Iowa had a history of language deficits in kindergarten.

A dynamic view of reading has a number of implications for assessment and teaching. In performing assessment, classroom teachers, special educators, and speech–language pathologists should use a combination of task-specific and authentic measures to determine children's strengths and weaknesses and to determine what to do to help children read better. *Task-specific measures* (e.g., standardized tests) provide information about children's knowledge and ability within specific domains. *Authentic measures* (e.g., reading miscue inventories, classroom observations, and language samples) that examine how children use their knowledge of language as they engage in functional listening, speaking, reading, and writing contexts provide information about children's ability to integrate their knowledge to support literacy. In teaching, classroom teachers, special educators, and speech–language pathologists should work together to decide what specific instruction to provide to help children read better and to make sure students receive the necessary support they need to transfer the skills and strategies learned in supportive contexts to typical classroom contexts. This approach involves augmenting authentic reading in classroom contexts with small-group mini-lessons that focus the reader's energies on the specific skills they need to read successfully, providing readers with practice in using those skills, teaching strategies for applying their new skills, and then supporting readers as they use new skills and strategies in regular classrooms.

KNOWLEDGE REPRESENTATIONS
IN A DYNAMIC SYSTEM

There is no question that prior linguistic and discourse knowledge play important roles in the reading process. In connectionist and dynamic systems models of cognition, knowledge is characterized as networks of connections between neurological idea units that are referred to as "nodes." Knowledge networks that are well established, like the networks that are activated as you drive your car, have three characteristics: (1) they are efficient (i.e., a minimal number of nodes are activated); (2) they are robust (i.e., strong connections between nodes are activated automatically); and (3) they are stable (i.e., the same sets of connections are activated each time). These principles support consistent and expert performance.

On the other hand, emerging knowledge networks are thought to contain an abundance of weakly interconnected nodes. When learners approach a new task or a new experience, as happens when teenagers are learning to drive, they may not have the requisite prior knowledge and skills that are needed to support maximum performance in a wide variety of contexts. When novice learners are faced with unfamiliar information, like navigating through a busy parking lot to get to the drive-up window at a fast-food restaurant, they may tentatively activate many connections between nodes. This results in inconsistent performance that is highly susceptible to interference. For example, the novice driver in our example may stop unexpectedly because he or she is not sure who has the right-of-way in a parking lot, may not enter the drive-up lane correctly, or may not pull up close enough to the window to easily exchange money for food (for more information on knowledge networks, see Elman, 1993, 1995; Jenkins, Merzenich, Ochs, Allard, & Guic-Robles, 1990; Merzenich, 1990; Rumelhart, 1994; Xerri, Merzenich, Jenkins, & Santucci, 1999).

According to dynamic systems theory, the neural networks in a complex process like reading are "softly assembled" in novices. The term *softly assembled* means that there are weak connections between nodes (Evans, 2001). As readers become more fluent, the complex system of networks involved in reading begins to self-organize, and connections between nodes strengthen. This self-organization is driven by interactions between the knowledge networks that comprise the system, the reading material, and the nature of instruction that each child receives. This self-organization appears to mirror the statistical and probabilistic properties of interactions among the system, the reading material, and the nature of instruction. High-frequency and low-frequency patterns of words and sentences are reflected in the way the connections in mental networks are organized. This means that knowledge networks organize themselves (i.e., "learn") to encode frequently encountered words that play consistent syntactic and semantic roles in short, easy sentences (see Elman, 1993, for an example of this principle).

Over time, the learning system gradually organizes itself to narrow the range of performance (Thelen & Smith, 1994). Less-adept readers may have reading systems that are slow to self-organize. Children with reading difficulties may have systems that are organized in unusual ways, resulting in a greater range of reading behaviors. They may look much like typically achieving children in some reading contexts (as when they read a familiar or well-rehearsed story), but they can look like very poor readers in other reading contexts (such as when they read a new story that contains words and concepts that they have not encountered before).

A DYNAMIC MODEL
OF WORD RECOGNITION

Reading, from a dynamic systems account, is viewed as a spontaneous, continuous, self-organizing process that evolves with practice. We do not conceive of reading as a step-by-step, bottom-up process in which readers see a word, sound it out, recognize it, access meaning, and then move on to repeat the same process with the next word in the sentence. Our view of the reading process, depicted in Figure 3.1, follows ideas that have been proposed by Walter Kintsch (1994a, 1994b, 1998, 2000), who has studied discourse comprehension, reading, and writing for many years. Imagine a student who is reading a short story. She attends to the perceptual inputs (letters) and activates knowledge networks that contain potential words that are consistent with the perceptual input she is receiving. A small number of lexical nodes are selected, and each one activates connections with some of its strongest semantic neighbors in the knowledge network. While the reader is busy interpreting the words she has just read, she integrates the meanings of those words with the meanings of the words that preceded them. The meanings she creates are known as "propositions," and they consist of the main idea, called the "predicate," and its associated ideas, called "arguments."

At the same time our imaginary reader is busy accessing her mental lexicon for words that match the sequences of letters and sounds to which she is attending, she is also creating propositional networks for the words, activating what she knows about the likely grammatical roles the words are playing. She also activates discourse knowledge and world knowledge that are held in long-term memory and uses that knowledge to build an interpretation of the text as a whole.

As she builds an interpretation of the entire text, her working memory system must hold numerous propositions in a state of readiness so that she

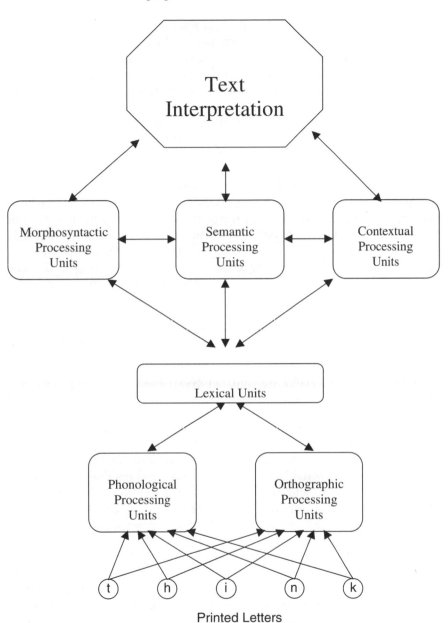

FIGURE 3.1. A dynamic model of word recognition.

can relate the meaning of what she has read already to what she is currently reading and what she expects to read next. As more information about the semantic, syntactic, and discourse context become available, the meaning of the story evolves. Kintsch refers to this as "sense elaboration," which involves the exploration and elaboration of multiple meanings at the word, sentence, and text levels.

But let's not forget that while all this is going on, our reader is busy attending to the next words on the page. She uses her evolving interpretation of the text to delimit the number of lexical choices that match the sequence of letters she is attending to at any given moment. Her working memory system organizes the lexical nodes that have been activated with the associative and semantic neighbors of those nodes. Her long-term memory organizes networks of propositions that clarify the meaning of the sentence and discourse contexts in which the newly encountered words participate. Inferences and elaborations on the overall meaning of the text arise as a system of interrelated knowledge networks emerges. The key concept is that all of these processes occur in parallel (concurrently) as the reader continues through the text.

Orthographic Processing Units

In the simplified dynamic model of reading depicted in Figure 3.1, the reader attends to the word *think* on a page. Orthographic and phonological processing units are simultaneously activated when the reader focuses attention on the word. The orthographic processing units are a complex network of neurons that encode letters (orthography) and their order. Research suggests that skilled readers "see" letters and words in their mind's eye, even though their eye-movement patterns indicate that they do not fixate on each individual letter at a time. The mind resolves a number of letters on both the left and the right side of each fixation point while relating the information to previous text and programming the next eye movement (Inhoff, Starr, & Shindler, 2000; Reichle, Rayner, & Pollatsek, 1999).

Readers who apply an orthographic strategy use the word's visual information to directly access mental representations of pronunciations in memory (Buchanan, Hildebrandt, & MacKinnon, 1999). With experience, spelling patterns (i.e., orders of letters) become associated as "expected" sets of letters, so readers can actually fill in the blanks of missed letters as their fixation points move across the text. This skill appears to begin with the ability to identify letters. For example, Badian (1998) tested 234 children 6 months before kindergarten, at the end of first grade, and into second grade. At the preschool level, the most reliable predictor of first-grade reading skills was children's ability to name letters and memorize sentences. In addition, a visual–orthographic task was the only measure before kindergarten that predicted good versus poor reading skills in first and second grade. Badian proposed that children with good letter knowledge learned to decode words more quickly and accurately. That is likely to have happened because mental effort that would have been devoted to figuring out what the letters in a word were could be reallocated to other mental processes that play a role in decoding.

Phonological Processing Units

The phonological processing units are networks of neurons that enable readers to encode letters as sequences of sounds, known as "phonological encoding," and to consciously reflect on and manipulate the sounds in words, known as "phonological awareness." Some readers use a phonological strategy in which they convert letters to mental representations of sound sequences, and activate words in the *lexicon* (the dictionary of known words that comprises part of long-term memory) that share the same sound sequences. This is what happens when readers sound out words they do not recognize automatically. Early in the literacy development process, some readers have the ability to rapidly blend letters into visual word forms and use these forms to access words in the lexicon, but this skill seems to be limited to words they have read frequently. For unfamiliar words, readers tend to resort to the slower phonological decoding strategy.

Many researchers and teachers have stressed the critical role of phonological awareness in learning to read. A number of studies, like the one by Lundberg, Frost, and Petersen (1988), have shown that children who received phonological awareness training before receiving reading instruction learned to read faster than children who did not receive such training. However, the critical importance of phonological awareness training alone (apart from instruction in decoding) might be overstated. Bus and van IJzendoorn (1999) reviewed the educational outcomes of over 36 studies of phonological awareness and 34 studies on reading. Their meta-analysis indicated that phonological awareness accounted for approximately 12% of the variance in reading skills. Bus and van IJzendoorn remind us that while readers appear to be successful on posttests of decoding skills, not all studies of phonological awareness show increases in actual word identification skills. Moreover, the long-term effects of phonological awareness training are inconclusive. Of the studies included in their meta-analysis, seven showed moderate long-term effects, but eight others (including Lundberg et al., 1988) did not demonstrate significant long-term effects for phonological awareness training. The authors suggest that phonological awareness may have a limited, short-term effect, and that other skills such as word-specific print-to-meaning connections may play an increasing role during later stages of reading.

Other authors have drawn similar conclusions about the limited importance of phonological awareness. In his review of three meta-analysis studies of the cognitive, linguistic, and processing abilities that predict reading skill, Hammill (2004) pointed out that orthographic knowledge (knowledge of letters and writing conventions) predicts reading better than phonological awareness ability, intelligence, spoken language, and rapid naming. Similarly, Scarborough (1998) wrote that print-specific abilities like letter identification and rapid naming are the most useful predictors of which children are at risk for reading problems.

A more limited view of the necessity of phonological awareness is easily assimilated into a dynamic systems model of reading. Some children's systems will self-organize toward phonological strategies for accessing the lexicon during reading. Other children's systems will tend to organize toward orthographic strategies of word recognition. Most children, however, use a combination of both approaches depending on the level of difficulty and the amount of pictorial support in the book.

Lexical Units

Activation of orthographic and phonological processing units spreads to lexical units (i.e., words in the lexicon) that share the letter and/or sound patterns that the reader attends to (see Figure 3.1). The activation of words in the mental lexicon spreads naturally to the activation of associated meaning networks as readers build *propositions* (meaningful associations between actors, actions, and things acted upon) across sentences.

During reading development children transition from word-specific coding, in which they access the lexicon by "sounding out" the letters in the printed word, to abstract orthographic coding, in which they access the lexicon by recognizing the sequence of letters. Movement from word-specific coding to orthographic coding may occur because the ability to generalize to "orthographically regular" words grows with the number of specific words that have been learned. As the number of "learned" words increases, the "orthographic neighborhoods" become very dense and gradually allow identification of both familiar and new words (Aarnoutse, Leeuwe, Voeten, & Oud, 2001; Cunningham, Perry, Stanovich, & Share, 2002; Nation & Hulme, 1996). Another possibility is that the visual word form evolves from word-specific processing to more general orthographic processing due to increased fluency in phonemic decoding. With increased fluency in letter-to-sound decoding, the top-down processing demands placed on the visual word form system may change, progressing to more demand to activate smaller networks of orthographic units (Manis, Doi, & Bhadha, 2000; Torgesen et al., 1999; Torgesen et al., 2001).

Once a candidate network of words is activated through analysis of the orthographic and phonological features of the letters that are being attended to, readers begin what Kitsch and his colleagues (Ericsson & Kintsch, 1995; Kintsch, 1994a, 2000) have referred to as "sense elaboration." In our simplified model, the lexical nodes activate knowledge networks related to morphosyntactic (grammatical) knowledge, semantic knowledge, and contextual (situational) knowledge (see Figure 3.1). Knowledge from these networks supports some meaning networks and suppresses others. During reading, some tentative word choices are retained as others are discarded, just as some tentative interpretations of the text are retained while others are not. That is why there are arrows leading toward and away from each of the processing units in the second level of our model.

Morphosyntactic Processing Units

As mentioned previously, access to visual orthographic images appears to promote recognition of unfamiliar words that are orthographically similar to words that the reader is familiar with. Lexical access also involves activation of *morphosyntactic processing units* that are related to the grammar of sentences. A *morpheme* is the smallest unit of meaning. "Morphological awareness" refers to knowledge of base words, inflections, and derivations. *Base words*, also known as "root words," can exist alone or with other morphemes. *Compound words* contain two base words (e.g., *butterfly, ladybug*). *Inflections* are morphemes that are added to base words to play a grammatical role by denoting number (*dogs*), case (*boy's*), verb tense (*runs, jumped, swinging*), comparatives (*faster*), and superlatives (*slowest*). *Derivational morphemes* play a semantic role by adding specific meaning to the root word. Derivational morphemes include prefixes (*preheat, tricycle, unable*) and suffixes (*quickly, happiness, connection*).

Morphological awareness involves knowing which words can take on particular morphemes, how morphemes affect words' meanings, and how the addition of morphemes may change words' part of speech. For example, prefixes alter the meaning of base words but do not change their part of speech. *Able* is an adjective, and remains an adjective when it becomes *unable*. In contrast, suffixes alter the word's meaning and its part of speech. *Happy* is an adjective, but *happiness* is a noun.

Numerous studies have compared the effects of phonological awareness and morphological awareness on reading ability. Carlisle and Nomanbhoy (1993) administered one phonological awareness task and two morphological awareness tasks to children in first grade. The phonological awareness task was phoneme deletion. For the morphological awareness tasks, children had to produce base words within morphologically complex words and identify whether or not pairs of words in sentences were morphologically related.

Results indicated that all three tasks together accounted for 37% of the variance in word reading. For reading comprehension, these tasks also accounted for an increasing portion of the variance of reading comprehension of second graders (34%), third graders (43%), and fifth graders (55%; Carlisle, 1995, 2000).

Another aspect of morphological awareness that has been studied is the ability to read both transparent and opaque derivatives. A word is considered a *transparent derivative* if the addition of a morpheme to a base word does not change the base word's pronunciation (e.g., *happy→happiness*). In contrast, when an added morpheme changes the pronunciation, such as the vowel sound and/or stress pattern, the word is considered an *opaque derivative* (e.g., *total→totality*; *clean→cleanliness*). Fowler and Liberman (1995) found that poor readers identified the semantic relationship between base words and suffixes in transparent derivatives as well as good readers, but performed significantly poorer on opaque derivatives. Results of this study indicated that performance on opaque derivatives accounted for 10% of the variance in children's word identification.

In a similar study, Windsor (2000) tested children between the ages of 10 and 12 to assess their morphological knowledge of whether or not there was a relationship between base words and derivatives in the midst of recognizing visual orthographic similarity. She found that the ability to identify the morphological structure of derivatives contributed significantly to both word identification and comprehension. Like Fowler and Liberman (1995), Windsor also found that identification of opaque derivatives predicted reading achievement better than identification of transparent derivatives. Windsor proposed that the ability to analyze the phonological changes that occur when derivations are added to words may help explain the relationship between morphological awareness and reading achievement.

As shown in Figure 3.1, morphological awareness appears to draw on orthographic, phonological, and semantic processing units. Windsor (2000) found that poor readers performed better on transparent derivatives than on opaque derivations. For example, the transparent derivative *allowable* preserves both the phonological and the orthographic features of the base word *allow*. Another example of a transparent derivative in Windsor's study was *purist*. Poor readers were generally able to use phonological information to identify the semantic relationship between *pure* and *ist*, even though the orthographic form of *pure* was changed. In contrast, poor readers had more difficulty with opaque derivatives such as *acidic*, which maintained the orthographic form of *acid* but not the phonological form. These findings suggest that good readers had stronger connections between phonological and orthographic processing units because they are able to more flexibly use phonological and/or orthographic information as needed, as mentioned earlier, to "fill in the blanks."

We know that lexical choice and comprehension are also affected by *syntax* (word order). The most common error in oral reading is the substitution of one word for another. Most studies of oral reading errors reveal that readers often substitute words that play the same grammatical roles as the author-intended words (e.g., nouns for nouns, verbs for verbs). For example, Gillam and Carlile (1997) analyzed the oral reading and story retelling of 14 school-age children with language impairments who were between the ages of 8 and 11 years. These children presented expressive language difficulties with syntax and inflectional morphology. Gillam and Carlile matched the children with language impairments to younger, normally achieving students according to their single-word decoding skills. All the children were asked to read and retell stories that were approximately one grade level above their reading level.

Gillam and Carlile (1997) found that the younger, normally achieving children's substitutions were more similar to the printed words, their reading errors were less likely to cause sentences to be ungrammatical, and their story retellings were more complete. Despite the fact that the two groups were matched on the ability to read words from a list, children with language impairments were less likely to produce reading errors that retained the grammatical acceptability of the sentence, probably because they had more grammatical problems. In this group of children, difficulties with morphosyntactic ability had an affect on the lexical units that children accessed during reading. Therefore, lexical decisions affect and are affected by the activation of morphosyntactic networks, which also play a role in creating interpretations of the entire text.

Semantic Processing Units

There is also conclusive evidence that semantic processing units influence word identification and contribute to the creation of the proposition networks required for text interpretation. This has been demonstrated repeatedly by studies that investigate how words that are presented together affect the speed and accuracy of reading (known as "semantic priming effects"). For example, Meyer and Schvaneveldt (1971) showed students pairs of words that were semantically related (e.g., *bread–butter*, *doctor–nurse*) or unrelated (*bread–doctor*, *nurse–butter*). Students read words faster and reached decisions about the relatedness of words much faster when they were presented in related sets as compared to unrelated sets or in isolation. This finding is completely consistent with a dynamic model of reading. When a word like *bread* is activated, its lexical network would automatically spread activation to neighboring related nodes, which likely would include the word *butter* but not the word *nurse*. Because *butter* is close in the semantic neighborhood, it will be read faster than an unrelated word (like *nurse*) that would not be activated before attending to the letters.

Notice the arrows running between the morphosyntactic and semantic processing units in Figure 3.1. These arrows represent the spreading activation between these types of knowledge networks. Rumelhart (1994) provides examples of the way semantics can affect the reader's apprehension of the syntax of sentences like:

1. They are eating apples.
2. The children are eating apples.
3. The juicy red ones are eating apples.

In each of these sentences, the first noun phrase ("They," "The children," "The juicy red ones") could be thought to be acting on ("eating") the apples. The first noun phrase could also be a member of a type of apple, namely, "eating apples." The readers' knowledge networks surrounding the concept of "apples" would activate nodes relating to actions on apples or types of apples. In this way, semantic networks help the reader figure out the grammatical structure of the sentence.

Contextual Processing Units

We have just shown how morphosyntactic knowledge networks and semantic networks can influence reading. Reading is also influenced by the readers' knowledge of the general context and the nature of the discourse (e.g., conversation, narration, or explanation) that commonly occurs within a context. This knowledge is represented in Figure 3.1 by the box labeled "Contextual Processing Units." Readers create contexts as they read by determining what the important concepts are in a text and building association networks that link the important concepts together (Goldman & Rakestraw, 2000). Readers use their prior knowledge and experience to help them mentally create a general context that is consistent with what they are reading. This general context consists of connections between the words they are reading in the moment (*local text*), what they have already read (*global text*), and prior contextual knowledge. When readers come to words and sentences that do appear to fit into the general context that they are building, they reinterpret what they had already read (Graesser et al., 1997), or they make inferences that enable them to fill in the inconsistencies (Graesser, Singer, & Trabasso, 1994). This type of reading is known as "knowledge-driven processing."

Because of knowledge-driven processing, readers who draw on different experiences may interpret a story they are reading in various ways.

For example, Anderson and his colleagues (Anderson, Reynolds, Schallert, & Goetz, 1977) created passages like the following:

> Tony slowly got up from the mat, planning his escape. He realized things were not going well for him. He hated being held, especially since the charge against him was weak. The lock felt strong, but he thought he could break it with the right timing. As he waited, the situation became more frustrating. As his anger increased, he realized he had to make his move. He knew his success or failure would depend on what he did in the next few seconds.

Most college students thought this passage was about a prisoner planning his escape from jail. However, young men on the wrestling team all thought this passage referred to the sport of wrestling. This example shows how readers mix their prior knowledge with the words, phrases, and sentences in a reading passage to interpret what they are reading. Readers with different life experiences come to the reading with different mind-sets, which they use to create different contexts.

Children in the elementary grades often find themselves in the position of having incomplete knowledge of topics contained in the texts they read in school. For example, students in Detroit who were assigned to read a chapter about the Alamo may have had very little prior knowledge about Texas and Mexico to draw on. Students who have less previous knowledge about the content of a text must rely on cognitive, metacognitive, and self regulatory strategies to create their understanding of the larger context of a reading passage (Alexander & Jetton, 2000). This process, known as "text-based processing" (Goldman & Rakestraw, 2000), requires strategies such as slower reading rate, increased rehearsal, and greater attention to headers, topic sentences, and linguistic cues within the text that is being read. These strategies are necessary to create the general context and to recall important content (Brown & Campione, 1990).

Summary

We have shown that word identification is a dynamic process that draws upon numerous linguistic and discourse components. Readers bring a great deal of knowledge about letters, sound sequences, words, grammar, and discourse contexts to the word identification process, and they integrate that knowledge with the information in the text as they read. The remainder of this chapter concerns children who have difficulties with word identification, how to measure word identification as an integral part of the reading system, and how to help young readers who are having difficulty with word identification and reading.

IMPLICATIONS FOR
COLLABORATIVE PRACTICES

There are a number of reasons why children may have difficulty identifying words during reading. Children may have limited knowledge of one or more of the phonological, morphological, semantic, syntactic, and/or contextual aspects of oral and written language. In addition, children may have difficulty integrating limited semantic, morphosyntactic, and contextual knowledge to create a complete understanding of the text they are attending to (Gillam, 1990; Gillam & Carlile, 1997). We believe children benefit when regular classroom teachers, special educators, and speech–language pathologists work together in collaborative teams to assess the dynamic processes that contribute to reading and language difficulties, to plan instruction that focuses on those dynamic processes that are the most critical for educational success, and to support students as they learn, practice, and transfer new skills to classroom contexts. Scientific, evidence-based educational decisions should be guided by a complete description of the nature of the child's difficulty, selection of teaching strategies that well-conducted research has shown to be successful with children who are similar to the child being assessed, participation of the child's family in decision making, and attention to applicable theory.

We agree with Ehri and McCormick (1998) that instruction offered as early intervention or after a special education diagnosis can be equally successful if teachers and specialists use appropriate instructional strategies. Unfortunately, strategies that work for most children may not be sufficient for children who are experiencing reading difficulties. Educational research has consistently shown that poor readers respond well to clear, well-sequenced, systematic instruction that teaches specific reading skills, includes ample practice in supportive contexts, provides strategies for using new skills, and supports children as they apply their new skills and strategies in classroom contexts. Some successful instructional strategies are summarized in this chapter. Many more approaches to reading instruction that have been shown to be effective are summarized in a report by the National Reading Panel (2000).

A few studies have provided evidence for the effectiveness of collaborative intervention teams. Farber and Klein (1999) investigated the outcomes of a collaborative intervention program implemented in several schools in Philadelphia with diverse student populations. Of 12 classrooms chosen to participate, one kindergarten and one first-grade classroom in each of six schools were randomly assigned to an experimental group in which speech–language pathologists collaborated with teachers to develop literature-based lessons on vocabulary, cognitive language concepts, and critical thinking skills. Speech–language pathologists provided instruction in their designated classrooms using a split-class or whole-class format for three sessions totaling 2 hours and 25 minutes each week. There were an additional 233 students in kindergarten and first-grade classrooms in which teachers implemented the regular curriculum that served as the control group. To help reduce possible effects of teacher bias, 46 students from the control classrooms made up a second experimental group. These students regularly attended an experimental classroom during the three collabora-tive intervention lessons each week. At the end of the academic school year, children's performance in writing, listening, speaking, and reading skills was measured using a curriculum-based test. Results indicated that chil-dren in the collaborative classrooms achieved significantly higher total test scores. Specifically, children in the collaborative classrooms made greater gains on a listening task and on a writing task as compared to children who were exposed only to the regular curriculum.

In another study, Hadley, Simmerman, Long, and Luna (2000) dem-onstrated the effectiveness of a classroom-based intervention model in increasing kindergarten and first-grade students' vocabulary and phono-logical awareness skills. This particular language-focused curriculum was designed to meet the educational needs of children with normal language development, children with language impairments, and children who were learning English as a second language. The principle components of the collaborative model included the teaming of experienced teachers with a speech-language pathologist, joint curriculum planning and weekly meet-ings, and naturalistic language facilitation embedded into classroom ac-tivities. Four classrooms in an ethnically and linguistically diverse inner-city school district in Phoenix participated. The classroom-based intervention model was implemented in one kindergarten classroom and one classroom with kindergartners and first graders combined. The speech-language pathologist taught in these classrooms 2½ days a week and also helped the teachers modify their language use to make it more comprehensible for students with language impairments and students learning English as a second language. The regular curriculum was followed in another kinder-garten classroom and a combined kindergarten and first-grade classroom designated as the control group. Analysis of children's pre- and posttest scores on vocabulary tests and phonological awareness measures revealed that children in the experimental group made significant gains in recep-tive vocabulary, expressive vocabulary, phonological awareness, and letter-sound association after 6 months of intervention compared to stu-dents in the nonexperimental group.

While classroom collaboration may be helpful, the results of at least one study suggest that reading instruction for poor readers is even more effec-tive when it is provided in small groups. Schumm, Moody, and Vaughn (2000) found that poor readers receiving 1:1 instruction and instruction in groups of 3:1 made similar gains in reading. Students in these small groups made significantly more progress than students who received the same types of reading instruction in groups of 10:1. Therefore, we suggest that teachers, speech–language pathologists, and special educators should collaborate on assessing children's reading and planning appropriate interventions. Then speech–language pathologists and special educators should teach new skills and provide practice using those skills in intensive small-group instruction that is provided inside or outside of the classroom. When students are using their new skills well in small-group instructional contexts, the collaborative team should work together to support the students' transition back into large-group instruction in the regular classroom. The next two sections provide information about using collaborative practices in assessing and treating reading difficulties.

Collaborative Practices in Authentic Assessment

As noted by Evans (2002), one implication of a dynamic characterization of learning is that each child brings a unique language-learning history, unique ways of organizing prior knowledge, and unique language-processing strategies to the moment of reading. One way to discover how the intrinsic nature of each child's unique language and literacy system affects reading is to look for reading contexts in which the child's reading process becomes unstable. Teachers, special educators, and speech–language pathologists can work together in collaborative teams to collect the data that are needed to determine whether a child has a reading disorder and the extent to which language impairments may be contributing to reading problems.

We believe that assessment of word identification abilities should reflect the definition of reading that is inherent in the model presented in Figure 3.1. If reading is a dynamic process in which phonological, orthographic, lexical, morphosyntactic, semantic, and discourse processes impact on each other, then teachers and clinicians should gather information about children's language knowledge at each level. They should also observe how knowledge at each level interacts in real reading.

In many school settings, speech–language pathologists play a vital role in assessing reading and writing, identifying children who are at risk for reading and writing problems, and providing intervention that helps children with language impairments and reading disorders profit from the instruction they receive in regular classrooms (American Speech–Language–Hearing Association, 2001). Speech–language pathologists have special knowledge of the ways that deficits in phonological processing, morphosyntatic processing, semantic processing, and contextual processing affect spoken language development. Special educators have special knowledge of the way deficits in these processing systems affect written language development. Working together as a collaborative team, specialists in these two areas and classroom teachers can determine why children may be experiencing reading difficulty and can create effective strategies to remediate problems they may find.

Standardized Testing

Traditional tests of reading accuracy and rate can be used to compare a child's performance on orthographic awareness, phonological awareness, and word recognition tasks to that of other children his or her age. Educators who plan to give standardized tests of reading should be aware of recent research by Catts, Fey, Zhang, and Tomblin (2001). These authors administered a battery of language and reading measures to 604 children who were participating in a large epidemiological study in Iowa. Catts and his colleagues followed these children from kindergarten to second grade, and used a procedure called "logistic regression analysis" to examine the relationship between performance on tests during kindergarten and second-grade reading outcomes. The research team identified five measures that were useful for predicting which children had reading difficulty in second grade. The Letter Identification subtest of the *Woodcock Reading Mastery Test—Revised* (Woodcock, 1987), the Sentence Imitation subtest on the *Test of Language Development—Primary* (Newcomer & Hammill, 1997), the mother's education level, and sound deletion and rapid-naming tasks (Catts, 1993) turned out to be good predictors of later reading difficulties. Catts and his colleagues (Catts et al., 2001) provide a formula and a step-by-step explanation for creating an Excel spreadsheet that can be useful for determining the probability that a kindergartner will have reading difficulties in second grade. Readers should be cautioned that the identification of "probable risk" does not automatically mean that a child should be "labeled" with a disability. The focus should be on actions that regular and special educators could take to prevent future reading difficulties.

With respect to the dynamic processes involved in the lower half of Figure 3.1, we recommend three standardized tests. The *Test of Silent Word Reading Fluency* (Mather, Hammill, Allen, & Roberts, 2004) can be administered to a group of students in 3 minutes. Students are presented with a sheet of paper that contains rows of words, ordered by reading difficulty. There are no spaces between the words on the page. The students' job is simply to draw lines between as many word boundaries as possible within 3 minutes. This task quickly and effectively measures interactions between orthographic processing units, phonological processing units, and lexical units.

To assess the critical components of phonological and lexical processing units, we recommend that clinicians administer the age-appropriate phonological awareness subtests on the *Comprehensive Test of Phonological Processing* (Wagner, Torgesen, & Rashotte, 1999) together with the Word Identification and Decoding subtests on the *Woodcock Reading Mastery Test—Revised* (Woodcock, 1987). Children who score 1 or more standard deviations from the mean on two or more of these subtests should be considered to be at risk for significant word identification problems.

With respect to the dynamic processes involved in the upper half of Figure 3.1, there are standardized tests that evaluate children's lexical knowledge, morphosyntactic knowledge, and semantic knowledge. Gillam and Hoffman (2001) recommend that assessment teams limit themselves to administering one global language test because the items on most standardized language tests are far removed from real language use. The three most commonly used tests of general language skills in school-age children are the *Comprehensive Assessment of Spoken Language* (Carrow-Woolfolk, 2001), the *Test of Language Development—Primary: 3rd Edition* (Newcomer & Hammill, 1997), and the *Clinical Evaluation of Language Fundamentals—4th Edition* (Semel, Wiig, & Secord, 2003).

The *Test of Narrative Language* (TNL; Gillam & Pearson, 2004) is different from other standardized tests of oral language because it was designed to examine interactions between the components of oral language within a functional discourse context. To perform the story comprehension tasks, children must listen to stories told by examiners, remember the content, and respond to literal and inferential information questions about the stories. To perform the story production tasks, children must formulate interrelated ideas about characters, their goals, their actions, and the outcomes of those actions. Then they must weave strings of words, phrases, and sentences together in ways that represent sequential and causal relationships between characters, actions, and outcomes. Therefore, this test can provide assessment teams with information about a child's ability to integrate morphosyntactic, semantic, and contextual processing aspects of discourse. We believe that the TNL is a natural complement to other standardized tests that use contrived formats to assess the components of language, and that it provides the assessment team with important information about dynamic language processing in spoken language contexts. Gillam and Pearson found that performance on the TNL correlated moderately ($r = .45$) with performance on a reading comprehension measure. This is consistent with Scarborough's (1998) findings. Children who have difficulty with comprehending and producing stories on the TNL may also present difficulties integrating morphosyntactic, semantic, and contextual knowledge during reading comprehension tasks.

Oral Language Samples

Language analysis has long been a mainstay of language assessment by speech–language pathologists. Guidelines for collecting and analyzing language samples have been described in depth by a number of authors (see Dollaghan & Campbell, 1992; Dunn, Flax, Sliwinski, & Aram, 1996; Evans, 1996; Evans & Craig, 1992; Johnston, Miller, Curtiss, & Tallal, 1993). To analyze language use within school-like discourse contexts, we recommend that clinicians adopt Hadley's (1998) useful step-by-step procedures (adapted from McCabe & Peterson, 1991) for collecting language samples from school-age children. In Hadley's protocol, clinicians tell short personal narratives and then prompt children to talk about their own related experiences. For example, a clinician might tell a short story about the time when she and her friend got lost in a shopping mall. Then children are prompted to tell a story about something that happened with one of their friends. Our research (Gillam, Loeb, Friel-Patti, Hoffman, & Brandel, 2004) suggests that clinicians can routinely collect 100 child utterances or more in a 20-minute conversation with school-age children utilizing this type of a procedure.

Computer language analysis systems have been developed to assist in the laborious and tedious process of analyzing language samples. After keying in and coding a language sample transcript, these programs quickly calculate analyses that would otherwise require a considerable length of time. We recommend using *Systematic Analysis of Language Transcripts* (SALT; Miller & Chapman, 1998), which comes with a database for comparing results of numerous language measures to same-age children from Wisconsin. Assessment teams should pay particular attention to four measures: (1) mean length of utterance in morphemes, a measure of language productivity that relates to morphosyntactic development; (2) total number of different words, a measure of language productivity that relates to lexical knowledge and use; (3) percentage of words in mazes, which measures language fluency; and (4) number of words per turn, which reflects pragmatic and contextual processes in conversational discourse. The SALT profiler provides information about the mean and standard deviation for each measure, as well as a z-score, which reveals how many standard deviations the child's score on each measure falls from the mean of the comparison group. Clinicians who do not have the resources to purchase the SALT program can still compute one or more of these measures by hand and can compare a child's language sample measures to the SALT database, which is published in *Language Sample Analysis: The Wisconsin Guide* (Leadholm & Miller, 1992). As with standardized testing, two or more measures that fall 1.25 standard deviations or more from the mean would suggest that children's language abilities place them at risk for social educational difficulties.

Oral Reading Samples

Children's oral reading can reveal a great deal about the integration of children's language and reading processes. One useful procedure for collecting and analyzing samples of oral reading is the *Reading Miscue Inventory* (RMI; Goodman, Watson, & Burke, 1987; Laing, 2002; McKenna & Stahl, 2003). In this procedure, children read stories aloud and then retell them. Examiners analyze the nature of the discrepancies between the author's text and the words the child reads to determine how children integrate orthographic, phonological, semantic, and syntactic knowledge as they read stories. Story retelling is also part of the RMI procedure. Story retelling provides students with the opportunity to use their own language to reflect on and repeat the story they read aloud. Retellings reveal how students modify and integrate the story's vocabulary, language, and propositions into their own narratives.

Examiners begin the task by asking children to read short stories that are approximately one grade level above their word identification level. Students are given a book that is opened to a story and are asked to read the story aloud. Examiners encourage children to continue when they stop, lose their place, or perseverate on a particular word. Each reading and retelling is audio-recorded for later analysis. Typed scripts of the texts of the stories are marked for reader substitutions, omissions, insertions, repetitions, and corrections.

The children's word substitutions can be judged for their graphophonemic similarity to the author-intended word using the criteria established by Goodman et al. (1987) and validated for children with language impairments by Gillam and Carlile (1997). Readers who present many difficulties with phonics and sound blending often have high percentages (30% or higher) of substitutions with some or little graphophonic similarity (Gillam & Carlile, 1997; Laing, 2002).

- A substitution that retains between 66 and 100% of the phoneme sequence of the original word is classified as "high" in graphophonemic similarity (e.g., *sheep* for *sheet*).
- A substitution that retains between 33 and 65% of the phoneme sequence of the original word is classified as having "some" graphophonemic similarity (e.g., *ship* for *sheet*).
- A substitution that retains less than 33% of the phonemes in the original word is classified as having "little" graphophonemic similarity (e.g., *string* for *sheet*).

Sentences containing one or more uncorrected substitutions, omissions, or additions are evaluated for syntactic acceptability. Sentences without errors are not included in the analysis because the intent is to determine the extent to which reading errors interfere with syntax. Sentences containing substitutions that interfere with grammaticality (e.g., *The boy fell doing* for *The boy fell down*) are judged to be syntactically unacceptable. Children with language impairments often have reading errors that make 20% or more of their sentences ungrammatical (Gillam & Carlile, 1997).

Sentences containing uncorrected reading errors are also judged according to their semantic similarity to the original sentences. Sentences with no meaning change are semantically and pragmatically related to the author's sentences. Sentences with partial meaning changes are those in which minor concepts, events, or characters are omitted or altered (e.g., *The boy fell doing* for *The boy fell down*). Note that this example demonstrates both syntactic and semantic errors. Sentences with significant meaning changes are those in which important concepts, events, or characters have been omitted or altered. For example, if the author's text was "The horse crossed the road," but the student read *The car covered the road*, the sentence would be scored as syntactically acceptable because *car* and *horse* are both nouns, and *covered* and *crossed* are both verbs. If the sentence was part of a story about horses, and crossing the road was an important event in the story, this miscue would represent an important change to the author's intended meaning and would be classified as a significant meaning change. Children with language impairments who have difficulty integrating morphosyntactic and semantic information while they are reading offer partial or significant meaning changes in 20% or more of the sentences in a story (Gillam & Carlile, 1997).

After reading a story aloud, students retell the story in their own words. Four measures can be calculated that pertain to dynamic relationships between text-processing units. Contextual processes can be evaluated by assigning a holistic score to the child's retelling (see Table 3.1; also see McFadden & Gillam, 1996, for step-by-step instructions for holistic scoring). Semantic processing units can be evaluated by calculating the percentage of story constituents (setting, initiating events, internal responses, plans, attempts, consequences, reactions, and endings) that were retained in the retelling. Morphosyntactic processes can be evaluated by determining the subordination index. This measure is calculated by dividing the total number of clauses by the total number of T-units (the main clause and all clauses subordinate to it) in the story. Teachers and speech-language pathologists should refer to Hughes, McGillivray, and Schmidek's (1997) excellent summary of narrative analysis techniques for step-by-step instructions for determining the subordination index.

In summary, teachers, special educators, and speech-language pathologists should collaborate on assessments that provide information

TABLE 3.1. Holistic Scoring Criteria

Category 1: Poor retelling

- General references to characters (the boy or the girl); no characters are named
- No critical goal-directed actions
- More than two unclear referents
- Poorly organized with no clear sequences of events
- Two or more utterances do not make sense with reference to the original story
- No ending or confusing ending

Category 2: Weak story

- Only one character is named correctly
- Inconsistent references leading to some confusion
- Only the most critical goal-directed actions are included
- Unclear relationships between the actions and the resolution of the story
- No mention of character motivations, reactions, and/or feelings
- Basic ending with no elaboration

Category 3: Good story

- All major characters are named correctly
- Consistent references to characters
- Critical goal-directed actions are included with some elaboration; little mention of secondary goal-directed actions
- Critical complications are included in the retelling
- Some mention of character motivations, reactions, and/or feelings
- Clearly stated resolutions and ending

Category 4: Strong story

- All the characters are named correctly
- Consistent reference to characters
- Elaboration on the critical and secondary goal-directed actions
- Critical and secondary complications are included
- Elaboration on character motivations, reactions, and/or feelings
- Literate-like language is retained in the retelling

about children's basic phonology, orthography, vocabulary, morphology, syntax, semantics, and contextual processing units. Standardized tests and language samples can provide basic information about the knowledge and processes that underlie reading. However, it is the integration of basic knowledge and processes that is critical to reading. Standardized measures like the *Test of Narrative Language* (Gillam & Pearson, 2004), language sample analyses, and informal reading measures, like the *Reading Miscue Inventory* (Gillam & Carlile, 1997; Laing, 2002), are useful for providing educators with meaningful information about dynamic interactions in reading.

Implications for Intervention Practices

A dynamic model of reading has several implications for intervening with students who are experiencing reading difficulties. Based on evidence supporting collaborative models of instruction that was summarized at the beginning of this section, we recommend that teachers, special educators, and speech–language pathologists work together in collaborative teams to integrate oral language and reading instruction. We believe intervention that combines direct instruction and strategy instruction holds considerable promise for helping children who have spoken language and literacy difficulties.

Based on our review of effective instructional practices with low-achieving students, we advise collaborative teams to focus their teaching on specific reading processes and then to include opportunities for students to practice integrating new knowledge and processes into real classroom contexts such as listening to and reading stories, answering questions about stories, and telling and writing stories. This can be done in the five-step process listed in Table 3.2.

As we noted earlier in the chapter, teachers, special educators, and speech–language pathologists should base specific educational decisions on treatment practices that have been proven to be effective. A number of studies have demonstrated successful approaches to assisting children who are experiencing difficulties with word recognition. The general approach to instruction provided in Table 3.2 has not been validated empirically in any one study. We suggest it here as a framework for guiding future educational research with poor readers. The next section of the chapter summarizes a variety of procedures that have been used with poor readers.

Phonological and Orthographic Processes in Word Identification

Some children experience difficulty with word identification processes because they are poor at processing phonological and/or orthographic information. A number of studies have tested methods for teaching phonological and orthographic processes to children who are at risk for reading difficulties.

Van Kleeck, Gillam, and McFadden (1998) conducted a study in which speech–language pathologists ran "sound centers" in prekindergarten and kindergarten classrooms twice each week for a year. The center activities lasted approximately 10 minutes, and were conducted with small groups of three or four children who had speech and language disorders. The speech–language pathologists focused on rhyming during the first semester and on phonemic awareness during the second semester. After one

TABLE 3.2. A Four-Step Process for Establishing New Processing Units and for Practicing Their Use in Authentic Classroom Discourse

Step 1

Focus the child's attention on the goal of the lesson and the reason why it is important. For example, tell the child, "Today we're going to learn how to ___ because it will help you read better." Return to this step throughout the lesson to remind children what they are learning about.

Step 2

Demonstrate an activity that requires knowledge and use of a language process or the interaction between language processes.

Step 3

Provide multiple opportunities for the child to practice activities like the one that was demonstrated and support the child when he or she struggles.

Step 4

Work with the student on strategies for remembering to use newly learned skills. Graham and Harris (1996) suggest that teachers and students discuss the benefits of newly acquired skills, plan a way for the student to remember how to apply the new skills, and plan self-instructions for carrying out the strategy. Then students memorize the strategy steps, practice using the strategy, and self-assess their success.

Step 5

Provide an opportunity for the child to transfer new knowledge to classroom activities with less teacher support.

semester of rhyming training, children improved on rhyming tasks, but not on phoneme awareness tasks. However, after a semester of working phonemic awareness tasks that included attention to phoneme identification ("What's the first sound in *sat*?"), phoneme segmentation ("What are all the sounds in *sat*?"), and phoneme blending ("What is this word: s—*a*—t?"), children with speech and language disorders were better at a series of phonemic awareness tasks than a group of first graders who had participated in the same classrooms (without the collaborative centers) during the previous school year.

Training phonological and orthographic processing elements together may result in more dramatic gains than teaching phonological awareness alone (Fuchs et al., 2001). For example, Gillon (2000) compared the effects of three different intervention conditions on children's gains in reading. Participants included 61 English-speaking children in New Zealand with spoken language impairment and 30 with normal speech and language, ranging from backgrounds of low to high socioeconomic status, and all of normal nonverbal intelligence. These children were receiving reading instruction in their regular classrooms that generally followed a whole language approach.

Gillon divided the children into three groups. One group received an experimental phonological awareness intervention program for two individual sessions each week totaling 20 hours. These children received training that included rhyming, identifying phonemes, phonological segmentation, and blending sounds to create words. Additional activities focused on children's awareness of the sound structure of spoken language, their ability to link speech to print, and their ability to articulate sounds correctly in words and sentences. The second group of children received traditional speech therapy designed to improve articulation of target sounds in isolation, syllables, words, phrases, and sentences. Children in the control group received very little additional help. They were seen a maximum of one time per month by a speech–language pathologist to improve speech production skills.

Analysis of pre- and posttest measures of speech production, literacy skills, and phonological awareness indicated that the children who received a mixture of phonological awareness and literacy intervention made more improvements in word recognition, reading, text comprehension, nonword decoding, and articulation of single words than children in the traditional speech therapy or children in the control group. By the end of the intervention, even the most impaired children in the phonological awareness group appeared to catch up to children with less severe impairment on measures of phonological awareness and reading skills. In addition, these children demonstrated phonemic awareness skills similar to controls with typical speech and language development. Gillon (2000) concluded that phonological awareness intervention integrated with reading practice may be necessary for children with language and reading disorders to make accelerated literacy growth.

It is important to remember that children with relatively poor language and preliteracy skill levels appear to benefit most from early instruction in phonemic and orthographic awareness. In a number of studies, children with disabilities and those who were judged to be at risk for reading problems outperformed their peers when they received extra training on phonological awareness (O'Connor, Notari-Syverson, & Vadasy, 1996; Schneider, Roth, & Ennemoser, 2000). Poor readers in the experimental groups retained their advantages over poor readers in the control groups for up to 2 years. However, children who functioned in the average or high-average range did not maintain their gains over time.

Morphological Processes in Word Recognition

There is unequivocal evidence that phonemic and orthographic awareness has a robust role in the development of the alphabetic principle, which drives early decoding (for further discussion, see Ehri & McCormick, 1998, and Troia, Chapter 4, this volume). Current research elucidates additional contributing roles, such as morphological awareness and semantic processing, when children begin reading multisyllabic words. Ehri and McCormick (1998) have hypothesized that many poor readers get caught in a "partial" alphabetic stage in which they know letter–sound correspondences but fail to read accurately because they do not process all the letters in a word. Knowledge of morphological connections and how to combine word forms may be especially useful for helping older children who are having trouble reading multisyllabic words.

There are several treatment studies that support targeting morphological awareness as part of a comprehensive intervention plan. For example, Arnbak and Enbro (2000) conducted a study with 33 fourth- and fifth-grade Danish students with dyslexia to see if students with severe reading deficits could be trained in morphological awareness using oral training. If so, they also wanted to examine whether the gains in morphological awareness in spoken language would result in improved reading and spelling skills. The intervention focused heavily on the meaning of morphemes. Targets progressed from the most to the least semantically transparent morphemes in Danish: root words, prefixes, suffixes, and inflections. For each morpheme class, the training activities included segmenting words into morphemes, analyzing the semantic relationship between the root word and an additional morpheme, and finally producing real and new words by changing or adding different morphemes to root words. Postintervention results indicated that the students did indeed make gains in morphological awareness. Gains in word-decoding skills were slight, but not statistically significant. Students did, however, make significant gains in reading comprehension and in their ability to spell morphologically complex words. Arnbak and Enbro suggested that, perhaps, students with dyslexia needed direct training in written language as well as spoken language to develop greater awareness of morphemes.

Berninger, Abbott, Billingsley, and Nagy (2001) compared the effects of morphological versus phonological intervention that linked spoken language to print. Both treatment approaches focused on word building, word generating, unit finding, and transfer activities. In the phonological treatment, children counted syllables and phonemes in spoken words, generated new words containing target phonemes, underlined and wrote spelling units, and sounded out words unit by unit. Then children practiced transferring their skills via oral reading of new words. For the morphological treatment, children built new words from a list of root words and affixes, generated new words containing the targeted affixes, and practiced finding morphemic units by underlining base words and circling affixes. Finally, children read a different set of words out loud with the same affixes to encourage the transfer of skills to reading. Overall results indicated that morphological treatment resulted in greater gains in word learning and changes in brain activation on phoneme mapping (as indicated by functional magnetic resonance imaging [fMRI]). The investigators reported that morphological treatment contributed to the formation of semantic–phonological mappings and orthographic phonological mappings, which resulted in improved reading efficiency and rate. They suggested that training in the alphabetic principle may not be sufficient to help later struggling readers, but that a multifaceted approach including morphological training may also be necessary.

Integrating Phonological, Orthographic, and Morphological Processing

Collaborative teams may wish to focus not only on teaching phonemic and morphological awareness, but also on the phonological and semantic changes that inflected and derived words undergo. To help children attend to these changes, the clinician should initially choose base words whose meanings are familiar to the child.

Lenz and Hughes (1990) developed a word recognition strategy to help students integrate phonemic and morphological knowledge during decoding. The strategy, known as DISSECT, includes the following seven steps: (1) *D*iscover the context, (2) *I*solate the prefix, (3) *S*eparate the suffix, (4) *S*ay the stem, (5) *E*xamine the stem, (6) *C*heck your accuracy with another person, and (7) *T*ry to find the word in a dictionary. Lenz and Hughes found that adolescents learned the strategy accurately after 6 weeks of three 20-minute sessions per week.

Integrating Syntactic, Semantic, and Contextual Processes

In our own practice, we have found that short lessons that focus on specific kinds of cue integration problems have been useful for helping children learn how to integrate information across multiple cue systems. The basic procedure is rather simple. The speech–language pathologist creates overheads of "cloze" sentences that are "gated," which means that each sentence provides successively more information than the sentence before it. All the sentences are covered except the first one. As each sentence is uncovered in succession, students brainstorm answers that fit the cues that are provided. All the words that fit the available cue constraints are written on the chalkboard. After each new sentence, the group discusses which words no longer fit the cues and the reasons why these words are no longer appropriate. When the final sentence is uncovered, the entire group sees what word the author had intended. Sentences can be found in students' reading assignments.

To demonstrate the integration of orthographic, semantic, and textual cues, create sentences like the following:

   a. It was cold outside so I put on my __.
   b. It was cold outside so I put on my __. It made my head warm.
   c. It was cold outside so I put on my c_ . It made my head warm.
   d. It was cold outside so I put on my <u>cap</u>. It made my head warm.

To demonstrate the integration of orthographic, semantic, syntactic, and contextual reading processes, we have created sets of sentences like the following:

   a. Our whole class went on a field trip. __ got lost. When we found ___ said, "Where have you guys been all this time?"
   b. Our whole class went on a field trip. S_ got lost. When we found h <u>s</u> said, "Where have you guys been all this time?"
   c. Our whole class went on a field trip. <u>Sus</u> got lost. When we found <u>he</u> , <u>sh</u> said, "Where have you guys been all this time?"
   d. Our whole class went on a field trip. <u>Susan</u> got lost. When we found <u>her</u> <u>she</u> said, "Where have you guys been all this time?"

These activities can be implemented with the entire classroom or in small groups outside the classroom. The benefit to small-group instruction is that children receive more individual attention and each child has more opportunities to practice. The value of whole-class instruction is the children who are experiencing reading difficulty have the opportunity to benefit from peer models. However, teachers, special educators, and speech–language pathologists need to make sure that they follow large-group instruction with multiple opportunities for low-performing children to practice the processing skills that are being taught. We believe this happens best when special educators and speech–language pathologists provide short lessons to small groups of children who are at risk for reading failure either inside or outside the classroom. These lessons should focus children's attention on a specific reading process, demonstrate how to perform that process successfully, provide multiple opportunities for children to practice, and show children how to transfer their new knowledge to the types of reading contexts that they will experience in their regular classrooms.

CONCLUSION

We have presented a dynamic model of reading in which multiple language processes interact to support word recognition and text interpretation. As children attend to printed letters, they combine phonological processing and orthographic processing to access words. As they work their way through sentences, they use morphosyntactic processing, semantic processing, and contextual processing to narrow the possible options for the next word that they encounter. They also integrate what they are reading with what they know about the world to build an interpretation of the text. The main point of this model is that word recognition is completely interconnected with higher levels of linguistic and cognitive processing during reading.

Children who are experiencing difficulty learning to read frequently have problems integrating phonological processing, orthographic processing, lexical retrieval, morphosyntactic processing, semantic processing, and contextual processing. Teachers should work closely with special educators and speech–language pathologists in collaborative teams to conduct assessments that combine standardized testing, language sample analysis, and analyses of real reading. When assessment reveals areas of weakness that contribute to reading failure, collaborators should work together to plan instruction that teaches language and reading processes that are critical for accessing the curriculum and to support children during the learning process. We have provided examples of activities that are designed to foster dynamic interactions between various reading processes. These activities should be part of an integrated approach to instruction in which educators and speech–language pathologists focus children's attention on the learning goal, demonstrate how to complete the activity successfully, provide ample opportunities for children to practice the activity, and then support transfer of the newly learned skills and strategies into classroom learning contexts.

REFERENCES

Aarnoutse, C., Leeuwe, J. Van, Voeten, M., & Oud, H. (2001). Development of decoding, reading comprehension, vocabulary and spelling during the elementary school years. *Reading and Writing, 14*(1–2), 61–89.

Alexander, P. A., & Jetton, T. L. (2000). Learning from text: A multidimensional and developmental perspective. In M. L. Kamil, P. B. Mosenthal, P. D. Pearson, & R. Barr (Eds.), *Handbook of reading research* (Vol. 4, pp. 285–310). Mahwah, NJ: Erlbaum.

American Speech–Language–Hearing Association. (2001). Roles and responsibilities of speech–language pathologists with respect to reading and writing in children and adolescents (Position Statement, Executive Summary of Guidelines, Technical Report). *ASHA Supplement, 21*, 17–28.

Anderson, R. C., Reynolds, R. E., Schallert, D. L., & Goetz, E. T. (1977). Frameworks for comprehending discourse. *American Educational Research Journal, 14*, 367–382.

Arnbak, E., & Enbro, C. (2000). The effects of morphological awareness training on the reading and spelling skills of young dyslexics. *Scandinavian Journal of Educational Research, 44*(3), 229–251.

Badian, N. A. (1998). A validation of the role of preschool phonological and orthographic skills in the prediction of reading. *Journal of Learning Disabilities, 31*(5), 472–481.

Berninger, V. W., & Abbott, R. D. (2002). Modeling developmental and individual variability in reading and writing acquisition: A developmental neuropsychological perspective. In D. L. Molfese & V. J. Molfese (Eds.), *Developmental variations in learning: Applications to social, executive function, language, and reading skills* (pp. 275–308). Mahwah, NJ: Erlbaum.

Berninger, V. W., Abbott, R. D., & Alsdorf, B. J. (1997). Lexical- and sentence-level processes in comprehension of written sentences. *Reading and Writing, 9*(2), 135–162.

Berninger, V. W., Abbott, R. D., Billingsley, F., & Nagy, W. (2001). Processes underlying timing and fluency of reading: Efficiency, automaticity, coordination, and morphological awareness. In M. Wolf (Ed.), *Dyslexia, fluency, and the brain* (pp. 383–413). Timonium, MD: York.

Brown, A. L., & Campione, J. C. (1990). Communities of learning and thinking: Or, a context by any other name. *Human Development, 21*, 108–125.

Buchanan, L., Hildebrandt, N., & MacKinnon, G. E. (1999). Phonological processing reexamined in acquired deep dyslexia. In R. M. Klein & P. McMullen (Eds.), *Converging methods for understanding reading and dyslexia* (pp. 191–220). Cambridge, MA: MIT Press.

Bus, A. G., & van IJzendoorn, M. H. (1999). Phonological awareness and early reading: A meta-analysis of experimental training studies. *Journal of Educational Psychology, 91*(3), 403–414.

Carlisle, J. F. (1995). Morphological awareness and early reading achievement. In L. B. Feldman (Ed.), *Morphological aspects of language processing* (pp. 189–209). Hillsdale, NJ: Erlbaum.

Carlisle, J. F. (2000). Awareness of the structure and meaning of morphologically complex words: Impact on reading. *Reading and Writing: An Interdisciplinary Journal, 12*(3–4), 169–190.

Carlisle, J. F., & Nomanbhoy, D. M. (1993). Phonological and morphological awareness in first graders. *Applied Psycholinguistics, 14*(2), 177–195.

Carrow-Woolfolk, E. (2001). *Comprehensive assessment of spoken language.* Circle Pines, MN: American Guidance Service.

Catts, H. W. (1993). The relationship between speech–language impairments and reading disabilities. *Journal of Speech and Hearing Research, 36*, 948–958.

Catts, H. W., Fey, M. E., Zhang, X., & Tomblin, J. B. (1999). Language basis of reading and reading disabilities: Evidence from a longitudinal investigation. *Scientific Studies of Reading, 3*(4), 331–361.

Catts, H. W., Fey, M. E., Zhang, X., & Tomblin, J. B. (2001). Estimating the risk of future reading difficulties in kindergarten children: A research-based model and its clinical implementation. *Language, Speech, and Hearing Services in the Schools, 32*(1), 38–50.

Catts, H. W., & Kamhi, A. G. (1999). *Language and reading disabilities.* Needham Heights, MA: Allyn & Bacon.

Cunningham, A. E., Perry, K. E., Stanovich, K. E., & Share, D. L. (2002). Orthographic learning during reading: Examining the role of self-teaching. *Journal of Experimental Child Psychology, 82*(3), 185–199.

Dollaghan, C. A., & Campbell, T. F. (1992). A procedure for classifying disruptions in spontaneous language samples. *Topics in Language Disorders, 12*(2), 56–68.

Dunn, M., Flax, J., Sliwinski, M., & Aram, D. (1996). The use of spontaneous language measures as criteria for identifying children with specific language impairment: An attempt to reconcile clinical and research incongruence. *Journal of Speech and Hearing Research, 39*(3), 643–654.

Ehri, L. C., & McCormick, S. (1998). Phases of word learning: Implications for instruction with delayed and disabled readers. *Reading and Writing Quarterly: Overcoming Learning Difficulties, 14*, 135–163.

Elman, J. L. (1993). Learning and development in neural networks: The importance of starting small. *Cognition, 48*, 71–99.

Elman, J. L. (1995). Language as dynamical system. In S. Port & T. van Gelder (Eds.), *Mind in motion* (pp. 154–187). Cambridge, MA: MIT Press.

Ericsson, K., & Kintsch, W. (1995). Long-term working memory. *Psychological Review, 102*(2), 211–245.

Evans, J. L. (1996). Plotting the complexities of language sample analysis: Linear and nonlinear dynamical models of assessment. In P. S. Dale, K. N. Cole, & D. J. Thal (Eds.), *Assessment of communication and language* (Communication and language intervention series, Vol. 6, pp. 207–256). Baltimore: Brookes.

Evans, J. L. (2001). An emergent account of language impairments in children with SLI: Implications for assessment and intervention. *Journal of Communication Disorders, 34*, 39–54.

Evans, J. L. (2002). Variability in comprehension strategy use in children with SLI: A dynamical systems account. *International Journal of Language and Communication Disorders, 37*(2), 95–116.

Evans, J. L., & Craig, H. K. (1992). Language sample collection and analysis: Interview compared to freeplay assessment contexts. *Journal of Speech and Hearing Research, 35*(2), 343–353.

Farber, J. G., & Klein, E. R. (1999). Classroom-based assessment of a collaborative intervention program with kindergarten and first-grade students. *Language, Speech, and Hearing Services in Schools, 30*, 83–91.

Fowler, A. E., & Liberman, I. Y. (1995). The role of phonology and orthography in morphological awareness. In L. B. Feldman (Ed.), *Morphological aspects of language processing* (pp. 157–188). Hillsdale, NJ: Erlbaum.

Fuchs, D., Fuchs, L. S., Thompson, A., Otaiba, S. A., Yen, L., Yang, N. J., Braun, N., & O'Connor, N. E. (2001). Is reading important in reading-readiness programs?: A randomized field trial with teachers as program implementers. *Journal of Educational Psychology, 93*(2), 251–267.

Gernsbacher, M. A. (1995). The structure building framework: What it is, what it might also be, and why. In B. K. Britton & A. C. Graesser (Eds.), *Models of text understanding* (pp. 289–311). Hillsdale, NJ: Erlbaum.

Gillam, R. B. (1990). An investigation of the oral language, reading, and written language competencies of language-learning impaired and normally achieving school-age children. *Dissertation Abstracts International, 50*(12-A, Pt. 1), 3918.

Gillam, R. B., & Carlile, R. M. (1997). Oral reading and story retelling of students with specific language impairment. *Language, Speech, and Hearing Services in the Schools, 28*(1), 30–42.

Gillam, R. B., & Hoffman, L. M. (2001). Language assessment during childhood. In D. Rosello (Ed.), *Tests and measurements in speech–language pathology* (pp. 77–118). Newton, MA: Butterworth Heinemann.

Gillam, R. B., Loeb, D. F., Friel-Patti, S., Hoffman, L. M., & Brandel, J. (2004). *Randomized clinical comparison of three language intervention programs.* Unpublished manuscript, Austin, TX.

Gillam, R. B., & Pearson, N. (2004). *Test of Narrative Language.* Austin, TX: PRO-ED.

Gillon, G. T. (2000). The efficacy of phonological awareness intervention for children with spoken language impairment. *Language, Speech, and Hearing Services in the Schools, 31*(2), 126–141.

Goldman, S. R., & Rakestraw, J. A. (2000). Structural aspects of constructing meaning from text. In M. L. Kamil, P. B. Mosenthal, P. D. Pearson, & R. Barr (Eds.), *Handbook of reading research* (Vol. 3, pp. 311–335). Hillsdale, NJ: Erlbaum.

Goodman, Y. M., Watson, D. J., & Burke, C. L. (1987). *Reading Miscue Inventory: Alternative procedures.* New York: Owen.

Graesser, A. C., Gernsbacher, M. A., & Goldman, S. R. (1997). Cognition. In T. A. van Dijk (Ed.), *Discourse as structure and process. Discourse studies: A multidisciplinary introduction* (Vol. 1, pp. 292–319). London: Sage.

Graesser, A. C., Singer, M., & Trabasso, T. (1994). Constructing inferences during narrative text comprehension. *Psychological Review, 101*(3), 371–395.

Graham, S., & Harris, K. R. (1996). Addressing problems in attention, memory, and executive functioning: An example from self-regulated strategy development. In G. R. Lyon & N. A. Krasnegor (Eds.), *Attention, memory, and executive function* (pp. 349–366). Baltimore: Brookes.

Hadley, P. A. (1998). Language sampling protocols for eliciting text-level discourse. *Language, Speech, and Hearing Services in Schools, 29*, 132–147.

Hadley, P. A., Simmerman, A., Long, M., & Luna, M. (2000). Facilitating language development for inner-city children: Experimental evaluation of a collaborative, classroom-based intervention. *Language, Speech, and Hearing Services in the Schools, 31*(3), 280–295.

Hammill, D. D. (2004). What we know about correlates of reading. *Exceptional Children, 70*, 453–468.

Hughes, D. L., McGillivray, L., & Schmidek, M. (1997). *Guide to narrative language.* Eau Claire, WI: Thinking Publications.

Inhoff, A. W., Starr, M., & Shindler, K. L. (2000). Is the processing of words during eye fixations in reading strictly serial? *Perception and Psychophysics, 62*(7), 1474–1484.

Jenkins, W. M., Merzenich, M. M., Ochs, M. T., Allard, T., & Guic-Robles, E. (1990). Functional reorganization of primary somatosensory cortex in adult owl monkeys after behaviorally controlled tactile stimulation. *Journal of Neurophysiology, 63*(1), 82–104.

Johnston, J. R., Miller, J. F., Curtiss, S., & Tallal, P. (1993). Conversations with children who are language impaired: Asking questions. *Journal of Speech and Hearing Research, 36*(5), 973–978.

Kintsch, W. (1994a). The role of knowledge in discourse comprehension: A construction–integration model. In R. B. Ruddell, M. R. Ruddell, & H. Singer (Eds.), *Theoretical models and processes of reading* (4th ed., pp. 951–995). Newark, DE: International Reading Association.

Kintsch, W. (1994b). Text comprehension, memory, and learning. *American Psychologist, 49*(4), 294–303.

Kintsch, W. (1998). The representation of knowledge in minds and machines. *International Journal of Psychology, 33*(6), 411–420.

Kintsch, W. (2000). The control of knowledge activation in discourse comprehension. In W. J. Perrig & A. Grob (Eds.), *Control of human behavior, mental processes, and consciousness: Essays in honor of the 60th birthday of August Flammer* (pp. 137–146). Hillsdale, NJ: Erlbaum.

Laing, S. P. (2002). Miscue analysis in school-age children. *American Journal of Speech–Language Pathology, 11*, 407–416.

Leadholm, B., & Miller, J. (1992). *Language sample analysis: The Wisconsin guide.* Madison: Wisconsin Department of Public Instruction.

Lenz, B. B., & Hughes, C. A. (1990). A word identification strategy for adolescents with learning disabilities. *Journal of Learning Disabilities, 23*, 149–163.

Lundberg, L., Frost, J., & Petersen, O. (1988). Effects of an extensive program for stimulating phonological awareness in preschool children. *Reading Research Quarterly, 23*(3), 264–284.

Manis, F. R., Doi, L. M., & Bhadha, B. (2000). Naming speed, phonological awareness, and orthographic knowledge in second graders. *Journal of Learning Disabilities, 33*(4), 325–333.

Mather, N., Hammill, D. D., Allen, E. A., & Roberts, R. (2004). *Test of Silent Word Reading Fluency.* Austin, TX: PRO-ED.

McCabe, A., & Peterson, C. (1991). Getting the story: A longitudinal study of parental styles in eliciting narratives and developing narrative skill. In A. McCabe & C. Peterson (Eds.), *Developing narrative structure* (pp. 217–253). Hillsdale, NJ: Erlbaum.

McFadden, T. U., & Gillam, R. B. (1996). An examination of the quality of narratives produced by children with language disorders. *Language, Speech, and Hearing Services in Schools, 27*, 48–56.

McKenna, M. C., & Stahl, S. A. (2003). *Assessment for reading instruction.* New York: Guilford Press.

Merzenich, M. M. (1990). Development and maintenance of cortical somatosensory representations: Functional "maps" and neuroanatomical repertoires. In K. E. Barnard & T. B. Brazelton (Eds.), *Touch: The foundation of experience: Fully revised and expanded proceedings of the Johnson & Johnson Pediatric Round Table X Clinical Infant Reports* (pp. 47–71). Madison, CT: International Universities Press.

Meyer, D. E., & Schvaneveldt, R. W. (1971). Facilitation in recognizing pairs of words: Evidence of a dependence between retrieval operations. *Journal of Experimental Psychology, 90,* 227–234.

Miller, J. F., & Chapman, R. S. (1998). *Systematic analysis of language transcripts.* Madison, WI: Language Analysis Laboratory, Waisman Research Center.

Nation, K., & Hulme, C. (1996). The automatic activation of sound–letter knowledge: An alternative interpretation of analogy and priming effects in early spelling development. *Journal of Experimental Child Psychology, 63*(2), 416–435.

National Reading Panel. (2000). *Teaching children to read: An evidence-based assessment of the scientific research literature on reading and its implications for reading instruction.* Washington, DC: National Institute of Child Health and Human Development.

Newcomer, P. L., & Hammill, D. D. (1997). *Test of Language Development—Primary* (3rd ed.). Austin, TX: PRO-ED.

O'Connor, R.E., Notari-Syverson, N., & Vadasy, P. (1996). Ladders to literacy: The effects of teacher led phonological activities for kindergarten children with and without disabilities. *Exceptional Children, 63,* 117–130.

Plaut, D. C., McClelland, J. L., Seidenberg, M. S., & Patterson, K. (1996). Understanding normal and impaired word reading: Computational principles in quasi-regular domains. *Psychological Review, 103,* 56–115.

Rawson, K. A., & Kintsch, W. (2002). How does background information improve memory for text content? *Memory and Cognition, 30*(5), 768–778.

Reichle, E. D., Rayner, K., & Pollatsek, A. (1999). Eye movement control in reading: Accounting for initial fixation locations and refixations within the E-Z Reader model. *Vision Research, 39*(26), 4403–4411.

Rumelhart, D. E. (1994). Toward an interactive model of reading. In R. B. Ruddell, M. R. Ruddell, & H. Singer (Eds.), *Theoretical models and processes of reading* (4th ed., pp. 864–894). Newark, DE: International Reading Association.

Scarborough, H. S. (1998). Predicting the future achievement of second graders with reading disabilities: Contributions of phonemic awareness, verbal memory, rapid naming, and IQ. *Annals of Dyslexia, 48,* 115–136.

Schneider, W., Roth, E., & Ennemoser, M. (2000). Training phonological skills and letter knowledge in children at risk for dyslexia: A comparison of three kindergarten intervention programs. *Journal of Educational Psychology, 92,* 284–295.

Schumm, J., Moody, S. W., & Vaughn, S. (2000). Grouping for reading instruction: Does one size fit all? *Journal of Learning Disabilities, 33,* 477–488.

Semel, E., Wiig, E., & Secord, W. (2003). *Clinical evaluation of language fundamentals* (4th ed.). San Antonio: TX: Psychological Corporation.

Thelen, E., & Smith, L. B. (1994). *A dynamic systems approach to the development of cognition and action.* Cambridge, MA: MIT Press.

Torgesen, J. K., Alexander, A. W., Wagner, R. K., Rashotte, C. A., Voeller, K. K., & Conway, T. (2001). Intensive remedial instruction for children with severe reading disabilities: Immediate and long-term outcomes from two instructional approaches. *Journal of Learning Disabilities, 34*(1), 33–58.

Torgesen, J. K., Wagner, R. K., Rashotte, C. A., Rose, E., Lindamood, P., Conway, T., et al. (1999). Preventing reading failure in young children with phonological processing disabilities: Group and individual responses to instruction. *Journal of Educational Psychology, 91*(4), 579–593.

van Kleeck, A. (2003). Research on book sharing: Another critical look. In A. van Kleeck, S. A. Stahl, & E. Bauer (Eds.), *On reading books to children: Parents and teachers* (pp. 271–320). Mahwah, NJ: Erlbaum.

van Kleeck, A., Gillam, R. B., & McFadden, T. (1998). Teaching rhyming and phonological awareness to preschool-aged children with language disorders. *American Journal of Speech–Language Pathology, 7,* 66–77.

Wagner, R. K., Torgesen, J. K., & Rashotte, C. A. (1999). *Comprehensive Test of Phonological Processing.* Austin, TX: PRO-ED.

Whitehurst, G. J., & Fischel, J. E. (2000). Reading and language impairments in conditions of poverty. In D. V. M. Bishop & L. B. Leonard (Eds.), *Speech and language impairments in children: Causes, characteristics, intervention, and outcome* (pp. 53–71). Philadelphia: Psychology Press.

Windsor, J. (2000). The role of phonological opacity in reading achievement. *Journal of Speech Language and Hearing Research, 43*(1), 50–61.

Woodcock, R. W. (1987). *Woodcock Reading Mastery Tests—Revised.* Circle Pines, MN: American Guidance Service.

Xerri, C., Merzenich, M. M., Jenkins, W., & Santucci, S. (1999). Representational plasticity in cortical area 3b paralleling tactualmotor skill acquisition in adult monkeys. *Cerebral Cortex, 9*(3), 264–276.

4

🍃

Building Word Recognition Skills through Empirically Validated Instructional Practices

Collaborative Efforts of Speech–Language Pathologists and Teachers

GARY A. TROIA

Although the ultimate goal of reading is to derive meaning from text, it is well established that recognizing individual words is the sine qua non of reading achievement. For beginning readers, as well as for most children who struggle with reading, learning to decode print and acquiring a large sight vocabulary are their greatest challenges. In fact, the chief problem encountered by children identified with reading disabilities (RD) is slow and inaccurate word recognition (Liberman & Shankweiler, 1985; Rack, Snowling, & Olson, 1992; Stanovich, 1988; Vellutino & Scanlon, 1987). Prevention and intervention efforts are crucial to avoiding the potentially chronic and debilitating effects of poor word recognition skills. Without such efforts, an alarming number of children are likely to fail to achieve a level of reading proficiency that accords them the benefits of competent and routine reading. These benefits include a strong vocabulary, a wealth of declarative and procedural knowledge, the ability to meaningfully participate in a democratic society and contribute to a global economy, and pleasure from indulging personal interests written about in books, magazines, newspapers, and other print media (Cunningham & Stanovich, 1991,

1997; Stanovich, 1986; Stothard, Snowling, Bishop, Chipchase, & Kaplan, 1998; West, Stanovich, & Mitchell, 1993). It is well established that a majority of children who are identified early as poor readers continue to perform poorly in reading for the remainder of their school careers and beyond (Catts, Fey, Zhang, & Tomblin, 1999; Cunningham & Stanovich, 1997; Francis, Shaywitz, Stuebing, Shaywitz, & Fletcher, 1996; Scarborough, 1998; Torgesen, Wagner, Rashotte, Alexander, & Conway, 1997). For instance, Juel (1988) reported nearly a 90% probability that children identified as poor readers at the end of first grade would be classified as students with RD by the end of fourth grade. Consequently, our efforts must begin early, when children's literacy-related oral language skills and beginning reading skills are developing, and must be maintained with sufficient intensity to avert these dismal outcomes.

The purposes of this chapter are to (1) identify the key principles of effective basic reading skills instruction that have emerged from the research literature; (2) describe how various educators and speech–language pathologists can and do work together to make these principles visible in preschool and elementary classrooms; and (3) recommend ways in which professionals can enhance their instructional efforts through student assessment. Throughout, examples of interdisciplinary teamwork are documented in which clinicians and teachers have combined their talents in innovative ways for teaching basic reading skills. The chapter is organized around five guiding principles, each of which is essential for maximizing the collaborative work of educators and speech–language pathologists who are concerned with children's reading. Before discussing these principles, I offer a brief review of the development of word recognition skills and the related problems encountered by children who are poor readers.

THE DEVELOPMENT OF ACCURATE AND FLUENT WORD RECOGNITION

There are two primary means by which a child can read a word. For example, a child might recognize *painfully* by "sight" when connections between its orthographic structure (i.e., spelling) and its phonological structure (i.e., pronunciation) are fully specified in long-term memory. These connections extend beyond a simple association between how the word looks and how it is uttered. Specifically, multiple levels of information are stored (Ehri, 1998; Perfetti, 1992), including (1) grapheme–phoneme correspondences (*p* is associated with /p/); (2) graphological and phonological rime patterns (*pain* shares the same spelling pattern with *train*, *main*, and *rain*, and simultaneously rhymes with *plane*, *stain*, and *vein*);

(3) syllable and morphological structure (*pain-ful-ly*); and (4) a whole-word representation. Orthographic word identification exemplifies skilled reading; words are recognized virtually instantaneously with little conscious effort. On the other hand, a child might "sound out" the unfamiliar word *painfully* using a phonological recoding strategy, converting the letters and letter strings into their corresponding sounds and then reassembling the sounds to pronounce the word (Torgesen et al., 2001; Torgesen, Wagner, & Rashotte, 1997). Alphabetic reading is a slower, less efficient approach to word recognition often taken by inexperienced readers who have yet to develop sufficient orthographic representations of words in memory.

How is the transition from alphabetic to orthographic reading accomplished? According to Share (1995; Share & Stanovich, 1995), children's early encounters with words provide them with a self-teaching mechanism for developing spontaneous recognition. With each successful attempt to decode a new word, larger bits of word-specific orthographic information are layered upon smaller bits. As they decipher other words with similar orthographic features, children generalize their knowledge of spelling patterns, thereby giving rise, for example, to an aptitude for reading novel words by analogy (*gainfully* can be read because it is similar to the recognized word *painfully*). Although it is little wonder that words such as *the*, *is*, and *and* become sight words, given the frequency with which they are seen in text, most words read orthographically appear only occasionally in text.

Apparently, most children do not require many repetitions before acquiring strong orthographic representations for words. A laboratory study by Reitsma (1983) illustrates this point. Children were able to significantly decrease reading times for words they had been shown as few as four times, but only after the midpoint of first grade; younger students were not able to reduce their reading times for the same set of words, presumably because they lacked sufficient graphophonemic knowledge to capitalize on repeated exposures. Thus, students who were unable to decode well were unable to acquire word-specific spelling knowledge, a finding paralleled by sizable correlations between early alphabetic reading and later orthographic reading (Compton, 2000; Shankweiler et al., 1999). Even more persuasive evidence of the role of decoding in sight word recognition comes from studies in which exception words (e.g., *yacht*, *aisle*, *sword*) are used as stimuli. Exception words, or irregular words, cannot be read strictly by applying graphophonemic knowledge (although they do possess some letter–sound regularities); irregular orthographic patterns must be memorized as multiletter units. Nevertheless, only accomplished decoders are also proficient at exception word reading (Gough & Walsh, 1991; Tunmer & Chapman, 1998).

There are two sorts of knowledge that appear to be of utmost importance in decoding: graphophonemic relations and phonemic awareness. Knowledge of letter–sound associations permits children to map phonemes onto their matching graphemes, the quintessential attribute of alphabetic reading (Adams, 1990; Catts, 1989; Juel, Griffith, & Gough, 1986; Liberman & Shankweiler, 1985, 1991). But to take full advantage of the alphabetic principle (i.e., English orthography systematically represents English phonology), children must appreciate the segmental nature of speech: that speech is comprised of discrete subsyllabic units of sound (Liberman & Shankweiler, 1991). They need to come to understand, for example, that the spoken words *fell, after,* and *loaf* all contain the /f/ sound, and that this sound corresponds to the letter *f* in the printed word *fish;* otherwise, the letter itself is meaningless.

That phonemic awareness plays a prominent role in the development of basic reading skills is indisputable. Children's performance on phonological awareness tasks administered in kindergarten, before they have learned how to read, is the single best predictor of first- and second-grade reading achievement (Perfetti, Beck, Bell, & Hughes, 1987; Torgesen, Wagner, & Rashotte, 1994; Wagner & Torgesen, 1987). This predictive relationship is evident even when controlling for initial IQ, vocabulary, verbal memory, and socioeconomic status (Bryant, MacLean, Bradley, & Crossland, 1990; MacLean, Bryant, & Bradley, 1987; Wagner & Torgesen, 1987; Wagner, Torgesen, & Rashotte, 1994). Unfortunately, phonemic awareness is not conferred simply by learning to speak a language, because speech is not phonemically segmented as it is perceived. Rather, speech is heard as a succession of syllables, each of which has an energetic vowel nucleus that envelopes the surrounding consonants, rendering them virtually imperceptible as distinct sounds (Liberman, 1982). Phonemic awareness appears to emerge primarily as a product of typically developing children's early exposure to print and print-related concepts, language and word play, and excellent reading instruction (Ehri, 1987; Perfetti et al., 1987; Scarborough & Dobrich, 1994; Snow, Burns, & Griffith, 1998; Torgesen et al., 1994; van Kleeck & Schuele, 1987).

WORD RECOGNITION PROBLEMS IN POOR READERS

Not surprisingly, children with RD manifest significant weaknesses in all components of word recognition, including phonemic awareness, graphophonemic knowledge, decoding accuracy, speed, and orthographic knowledge (e.g., Felton & Wood, 1992; Juel, 1988; Rack et al., 1992; Shankweiler et al., 1999; Wagner, Torgesen, Laughon, Simmons, & Rashotte, 1993; Mody, 2003). It is generally assumed that these weaknesses are attributable to a core phonological processing deficit (Lyon, 1995; Stanovich, 1988; Stanovich & Siegel, 1994). A consequence of this deficit is inferior performance, regardless of IQ, in one or more skills that utilize phonological processing, including phonological awareness (e.g., Stanovich, 1986; Vellutino & Scanlon, 1987; Wagner & Torgesen, 1987), rapid naming (e.g., Badian, 1993; Wolf & Bowers, 1999), and serial memory (e.g., Rapala & Brady, 1990; Torgesen et al., 1994).

The precise nature of the relationships among these various skills and their associations with word recognition have yet to be determined. For example, the assumption that rapid naming tasks are representative of phonological processing (see Schatschneider, Carlson, Francis, Foorman, & Fletcher, 2002; Torgesen & Burgess, 1998) is contested among researchers, in part because there is growing evidence that phonemic awareness and rapid naming contribute unique variance to word reading proficiency (Allor, 2002; Bowers, 1995; Cornwall, 1992; Felton & Brown, 1990; Manis, Seidenberg, & Doi, 1999; McBride-Chang & Manis, 1996; Torgesen, Wagner, Rashotte, Burgess, & Hecht, 1997). Some argue that these findings demonstrate that rapid naming primarily taps nonphonological processes important to word recognition, such as attention, visual recognition, lexical retrieval, and information-processing speed (e.g., Wolf, Bowers, & Biddle, 2000). In other words, naming speed deficits may independently contribute to reading difficulties and, when present, may exacerbate reading problems that arise from limited phonemic awareness. Those children who demonstrate such a double deficit (Bowers & Wolf, 1993; Wolf & Bowers, 1999) do tend to be the worst readers and are more resistant to reading interventions (Allor, Fuchs, & Mathes, 2001; Bowers, 1995; Bowers & Wolf, 1993; Torgesen et al., 1994; Vellutino et al., 1996). According to Manis, Doi, and Bhadha (2000), children with a double deficit are disadvantaged in both decoding (because they lack sufficient sensitivity to speech sounds to capitalize on an alphabetic script) and sight word recognition (because they are unable to process information rapidly enough to efficiently store and retrieve orthographic patterns). Schatschneider et al. (2002) counter that, due to a moderate positive correlation between rapid naming and phonemic awareness, children who exhibit a double deficit are bound to demonstrate lower scores on phonemic awareness measures (and consequently on word recognition measures) than children who exhibit only a deficit in phonemic awareness. Presumably, this is because of the shared attributes of rapid naming and phonemic awareness (i.e., phonological processing) that are more profoundly impaired rather than an independent contribution of slow naming speed.

CHARACTERISTICS OF EXEMPLARY WORD RECOGNITION INSTRUCTION AND FIVE PRINCIPLES TO GUIDE COLLABORATIVE EFFORTS

Obviously, word recognition instruction requires much more than teaching children how to "sound out" words. Word recognition instruction should possess four characteristics to be effective. First, instruction should be multifaceted to address both alphabetic and orthographic reading and the funds of knowledge that support them. Second, instruction should be explicit and intensive, as research suggests that these features are associated with better reading outcomes, especially for poor readers (e.g., Torgesen et al., 1997). Third, instruction should begin early in order to (1) prevent limited reading achievement among children who enter school without the benefits of substantive early literacy experiences; (2) ameliorate the reading problems of children whose disabilities have genetic or neurobiological origins; (3) avert negative attitudes and avoidance of reading; and (4) lessen the likelihood that poor reading skills become intractable and unresponsive to intervention (Lyon & Moats, 1997). Fourth, instruction should be coordinated among all those who are concerned with reading and its associated skills, including classroom teachers, special educators, speech–language pathologists, reading teachers, and families. These individuals can bring unique perspectives, knowledge, and talents to bear to plan comprehensive and intensive instruction that supports children's early development of accurate and fluent word recognition.

Speech–language pathologists are well suited for informing the creation of high-quality reading programs for at least two reasons. One, they possess critical expertise in speech and language development and disorders and the connections between oral and written language. Many classroom teachers may lack this knowledge and may be insufficiently prepared for teaching children to read using evidence-based practices (McCutchen et al., 2002; Moats, 1994; Moats & Lyon, 1996). For instance, Moats (1994) found that only 20% of previously certified teachers enrolled in graduate education programs demonstrated adequate knowledge of language structure and of how to apply it in the classroom. Two, they are often the first professionals to encounter children who are at risk for RD, and consequently are in a position to coordinate and provide early intervention services. The cognitive and linguistic underpinnings of reading are securely in place when children begin school, and preschoolers with language impairments are frequently destined to become poor readers even if their communication disorders appear to resolve (Bishop & Adams, 1990; Fey, Catts, & Larrivee, 1995; Lonigan, Burgess, Anthony, & Barker, 1998;

Scarborough, 2001; Stothard et al., 1998). This highlights the importance of early language intervention as well as continuing involvement by speech–language pathologists as children transition to the demands of beginning literacy. Five instructional principles to guide this kind of collaborative work are described below:

1. Target the linguistic foundations of literacy.
2. Immerse students in print-rich environments.
3. Ground children in the alphabetic principle.
4. Teach students to use a variety of strategies to decode words.
5. Build reading accuracy and fluency.

Principle 1: Target the Linguistic Foundations of Literacy

Is Instruction in Phonological Awareness Worthwhile?

There is compelling evidence that sensitivity to the phonological structure of language can be increased through explicit instruction, often with simultaneous improvements in word reading and spelling (e.g., Bhat, Griffin, & Sindelar, 2003; Foorman, Francis, Novy, & Liberman, 1991; O'Connor, Jenkins, & Slocum, 1995; Tangel & Blachman, 1992; Torgesen & Davis, 1996; Torgesen, Morgan, & Davis, 1992; but see Troia, 1999, for concerns about the methodological rigor of this body of work). Even greater gains in literacy achievement are obtained when phonemic awareness training is coupled with instruction in graphophonemic knowledge (Byrne & Fielding-Barnsley, 1991; Cunningham, 1990; Hatcher, Hulme, & Ellis, 1994). However, not all children benefit equally from such training, as up to 30% fail to make appreciable gains in either phonemic awareness or literacy (Foorman et al., 1991; Torgesen & Davis, 1996; Torgesen et al., 1992; Torgesen et al., 1994). Moreover, positive treatment effects on reading often attenuate in as few as 18 months (Bus & van IJzendoorn, 1999). It is unclear why some children fail to respond to excellent phonemic awareness treatments such as those designed by researchers. Attention, motivation, degree and type of language impairment, instructional history, training materials and procedures, and other moderating variables probably exert a strong influence on how well children learn to blend and segment sounds, and ultimately to read (Castiglioni-Spalten & Ehri, 2003; McCardle, Scarborough, & Catts, 2001; Troia, 2004; Troia, in press). These variables require more intensive scrutiny and thoughtful integration in future research and dissemination efforts so that more children are enabled to benefit from phonemic awareness instruction.

A series of recent intervention studies (Fuchs & Fuchs, 2001; Fuchs et al., 2001; Mathes, Torgesen, & Allor, 2001) disputes the added value of phonemic awareness instruction when kindergarten and first-grade children are provided with explicit and systematic decoding instruction. In these investigations, students who received sound manipulation training plus peer-mediated decoding instruction did not accrue greater benefits than students who just received decoding instruction. Apparently, strong phonics instruction may implicitly teach phonemic awareness and render deliberate sound sensitivity training superfluous (Perfetti et al., 1987).

Early Intervention Is the Key

While probable that decoding instruction designed and monitored by researchers mitigates the need for separate phonemic awareness training, it is likely that mediocre beginning reading instruction is more the norm than the exception. Explicit teaching of sound segmentation and blending, coupled with letter–sound correspondence instruction, may serve to inoculate youngsters against the adverse effects of weak phonics instruction. Roth, Troia, Worthington, and Dow (2002) contend that to maximize the positive influence of metaphonological competence on subsequent literacy achievement in at-risk populations (e.g., children who live in poverty, those from culturally and linguistically divergent homes, those with developmental disabilities, and those whose parents are illiterate), explicit instruction in phonological awareness should begin during preschool.

To this end, Roth et al. (2002) have developed a comprehensive program for one of the largest populations of at-risk preschoolers: children with speech and language impairments. Their program, Promoting Awareness of Sounds in Speech (PASS), has three components: (1) scripted lessons for progressively more challenging rhyming, blending, and segmentation tasks, presented in stand-alone modules; (2) appealing, developmentally appropriate activities, such as singing songs, chants, and nursery rhymes that accentuate the phonological properties of words, playing sound manipulation games, and reading children's books that feature sound play; and (3) multisensory grapheme–phoneme association training. Additionally, the program incorporates features of direct instruction (Carnine, Silbert, & Kame'enui, 1997), including sequenced objectives, carefully selected training stimuli, extensive modeling, immediate feedback, a brisk instructional pace, positive reinforcement, and clear performance criteria. In as few as 8 weeks, after about 12 hours of intervention with the PASS program, preschoolers with communication disorders, who frequently exhibit weak phonological awareness skills (Catts, 1993; Magnusson & Naucler, 1993; Scarborough, 1998, 2001; Webster & Plante, 1992, 1995), have been taught to rhyme and blend phonemes with nearly a 90% success rate (Roth et al. are currently evaluating the efficacy of their segmentation training module).

These findings, in conjunction with those of other researchers (van Kleeck, Gillam, & McFadden, 1998), suggest that teaching preschoolers who are likely to become poor readers how to detect and manipulate the phonological properties of speech is a viable goal, one that may best be accomplished with the assistance of knowledgeable practitioners like speech–language pathologists. A myriad of assessment and intervention resources are available to support this kind of work, many of which have been compiled by Torgesen and Mathes (2000). Likewise, Yopp and Yopp (2000) describe a variety of phonological awareness activities for children. Intervention guidelines culled from the literature are reviewed by Troia, Roth, and Graham (1998) and are summarized in Table 4.1.

The Role of Speech–Language Pathologists

Speech–language pathologists can and do play a prominent role in the development of metaphonological competence in children with and without disabilities, sometimes more indirectly than directly. For example, after attending a district-sponsored workshop on phonological awareness assessment and instruction, a small group of school clinicians and resource room teachers established a network of special education service providers, reading specialists, classroom teachers, and university faculty interested in language and literacy. The members meet once a month and communicate via e-mail to discuss recent research, evaluate intervention materials, plan lessons, and grapple with perplexing cases. The group continues to grow in size and has managed to secure funds from their school district to accomplish two goals: (1) to launch a website that will serve as an information resource and interactive discussion forum for school personnel and families concerned with, primarily, phonological awareness and beginning reading instruction; and (2) to conduct professional development seminars and follow-up activities in each elementary school in the district to help more teachers gain a better understanding of the relationships between oral and written language and integrate phonological awareness activities into their literacy instruction. In this instance, the collaborative efforts of speech–language pathologists and special education teachers were pivotal in brokering relationships between interested parties and in leveraging financial support for the important work of this community of educators.

Of course, the traditional responsibilities of speech–language pathologists offer added opportunities for more directly influencing children's phonological awareness and other literacy-related skills. Many speech–

TABLE 4.1. Instructional Guidelines for Teaching Phonological Awareness Skills

- Engage children in activities that can help them shift their attention away from the meaning of language to its form, such as reciting finger plays and nursery rhymes, singing songs and chants, viewing educational programming (e.g., *Between the Lions*), reading books that invoke sound play, and writing.

- Use direct instruction methods, including sequenced objectives, carefully selected training stimuli, extensive modeling, immediate feedback, positive reinforcement, and clear performance criteria.

- Begin with the easiest phonological awareness skill (rhyming < blending < segmentation) in which children require instruction and progress to more difficult skills, or combine skills; in either case, segmentation must be achieved.

- Move from cognitively less demanding exercises (matching, elimination, and judgment) to more demanding exercises (segmental representation such as clapping syllables; simple production, such as blending sounds; and compound production, such as phoneme deletion, substitution, or reversal).

- For blending and segmentation exercises, begin instruction with larger linguistic units (words and syllables) and advance to smaller units (onset–rimes and phonemes); simultaneously, progress from two to more units.

- For blending and segmentation exercises, use words that contain continuant consonant sounds (e.g., /s/, /m/, /f/) before those with noncontinuant sounds (e.g., /t/, /b/, /k/).

- Initially, use words that are concrete and familiar to children (e.g., compound words and children's names) because low-frequency words tend to be more difficult to manipulate.

- Provide temporary scaffolding by making segmental features more salient (e.g., exaggerating pronunciation of continuants and iterating noncontinuants), accompanying stimuli with illustrations, using place holders such as squares and markers to facilitate sequencing, etc.

- Help children connect speech–motor patterns to phoneme perception and manipulation.

- Synchronize phonemic awareness, letter recognition and naming, and letter–sound association instruction.

- Train for generalization, recognizing that improvement in one skill may not spontaneously transfer to other skills.

language pathologists who work with young children in educational settings appreciate the value of phonological awareness instruction for improving literacy outcomes and therefore teach rhyming, blending, and segmentation to children who lack these skills either during individual or small-group therapeutic sessions or while providing services in the classroom. There also is growing evidence that therapy for expressive phonology impairments can simultaneously improve phonological awareness (Gillon, 2000). Finally, the prominence of oral language abilities other than

phonological awareness in literacy achievement, such as vocabulary knowledge, listening comprehension, and expressive syntax (e.g., Scarborough,
1998), suggests that intervention in these areas, a responsibility often assumed by clinicians, will have a positive influence on children's reading
and writing skills.

Principle 2: Immerse Students in Print-Rich Environments

The Importance of Preschool Literacy Experiences

There is little doubt that the environment in which children are raised
profoundly affects their readiness for school and their academic progress.
Not surprisingly, then, children from impoverished homes perform more
poorly on measures of oral language (Lonigan & Whitehurst, 1998), phonological and orthographic processing (Bowey, 1995; MacLean et al., 1987),
and reading (Juel et al., 1986; Smith & Dixon, 1995). Likewise, children who
do not speak English as their first language and children whose parents
are poor readers are predisposed to reading failure (Scarborough, 1991,
1998; Snow et al., 1998). There are numerous reasons why family socioeconomic status, native language of the home, and parental reading achievement have such a strong relationship with children's oral and written
language skills, but two stand out. First, children from culturally, linguistically, and socioeconomically diverse families often do not have the same
early oral language experiences that promote emergent literacy as their
peers from mainstream families (Marvin & Mirenda, 1993; Scarborough,
1991; Whitehurst & Lonigan, 1998). Second, children from poor families
or from homes in which English is not spoken or the parents do not
read are less likely to be exposed to the same types and number of print
and literacy-oriented artifacts as children reared in middle- and upper-
income English-speaking homes (Chaney, 1994; Marvin & Mirenda, 1993;
McCormick & Mason, 1986).

When children's home experiences are not optimized for promoting
emergent literacy, there are likely to be negative consequences for later
reading achievement. A number of studies suggest that preschoolers' adult-
mediated interactions with print predict future literacy skills. For instance,
children's encounters with rhyming patterns through nursery rhymes and
language play influence their sensitivity to rhyme, which in turn affects
their early reading performance (Baker, Fernandez-Fein, Scher, & Williams,
1998). Likewise, frequency of storybook and, most notably, alphabet book
reading exerts a powerful influence on beginning word recognition (Baker
& Mackler, 1997; Crain-Thoreson & Dale, 1992). Those youngsters from
homes where these interactions occur infrequently often end up being dis-

advantaged in learning to read. They are ill-equipped for acquiring concepts about print (e.g., reading conventions such as directionality and book handling and literacy-related vocabulary such as *word* and *letter*), learning to recognize and name letters, and assuming a positive motivational stance toward reading.

One means of counteracting these effects is to make sure that children are surrounded by all kinds of print materials. These include a variety of children's books, encompassing alphabet books, storybooks, predictable books, and nursery rhymes; literacy artifacts such as alphabet blocks, magnetic letters, and other such toys; and tools for writing. Of course, transacting meaningfully with these materials is of greatest importance, as is participating in other customary literacy-enhancing experiences, such as reading environmental print (e.g., restaurant logos and traffic signs) during family outings and following recipes to make birthday treats. Roth and Baden (2001) provide a list of such experiences in which children and adults can engage that demonstrate to youngsters that reading and writing are used for multiple purposes. Print needs to be woven not only into the fabric of children's home lives, but also into their school lives. Classrooms in which literature is the focal point of instruction display and make use of myriads of books, magazines, comics, newspapers, and reference guides, word walls, children's writing, computers with Internet access, and the like.

The Role of Speech Language Pathologists

Recently, a reading specialist and a clinician working at an inner-city school with few instructional resources and virtually no recent book acquisitions paired up to secure funding for classroom libraries. Recognizing the importance of access to authentic reading materials for children, teachers, and parents, the pair convinced the grantor that each classroom required its own set of books for teachers to use during instructional activities and for parents to read at home with their sons and daughters. The reading specialist and the speech–language pathologist also arranged to have interested parents and their children meet at the school on Saturday mornings for shared reading time. At each gathering, the speech–language pathologist and the reading teacher first modeled joint predictable book reading with small groups, hoping to positively influence the way parents and children interacted around text. They showed parents how to assume the role of an active listener by asking questions about a story, adding information about the events, and prompting elaboration while the child read or attempted to read a familiar book (see Whitehurst & Lonigan, 1998). Then each parent–child dyad selected a book to read together, and afterwards received informal feedback from the educators about the quality of the episode. In time, they saw many parents appropriate a conversational approach to shared reading in which children were taking more responsibility for handling books and reading texts with support from their parents in the form of dialogue about the story events, characters, and their personal reactions. Previously, parents had done almost all of the reading and book handling and rarely engaged their children in extended discourse about texts. Although this endeavor met with success, it is important for educators to keep in mind that, to achieve successful reading outcomes, literacy materials and activities need to align with parents' frames of reference for understanding how children learn to read (e.g., DeBaryshe, 1995).

Principle 3: Ground Children in the Alphabetic Principle

Teaching Letters and Sounds

To read an alphabetic writing system such as English, children must be able to recognize letters, name the letters, and associate the letters with their corresponding sounds. The importance of letter recognition and graphophonemic knowledge in mastering the alphabetic principle is rather straightforward, but that of letter names is somewhat more ambiguous, in part because, although many letter names match more or less the sounds with which the letters are associated (e.g., *a*, *m*, *t*), others do not (e.g., *h*, *w*, *y*). In fact, some instructional programs (e.g., Reading Mastery) avoid teaching letter names, at least initially, to avoid potential confusion. Nevertheless, knowledge of letter names in kindergarten is a strong predictor of word recognition ability in the primary grades, even more robust than graphophonemic knowledge, and has an enduring relationship with phonological awareness (e.g., Adams, 1990; Burgess & Lonigan, 1998; Kaminski & Good, 1996; Scarborough, 1998; Stahl & Murray, 1994; Wagner et al., 1994). Knowledge of letter names may help children associate phonemes with graphemes because so many letter names contain the relevant sounds (Ehri, 1987), or it may serve as a proxy for other cognitive skills important for reading. At any rate, letter naming should receive instructional focus and be practiced for automaticity (Adams, 1990).

Multisensory approaches to teaching letter recognition, letter names, and letter–sound correspondence are commonplace; many preschool and kindergarten teachers can be found asking their students to trace, feel, discriminate, copy, or write letters while hearing and saying their names. The Orton–Gillingham and Slingerland methods are two of the most popular visual–auditory–kinesthetic–tactile (VAKT) direct instruction programs. A more implicit but effective approach to teaching the alphabetic principle involves encouraging children to use invented spelling. Clarke (1988) found that, in comparison to classes in which children were not encouraged to use invented spelling, first graders in classes where teachers encouraged them to invent spellings for words they did not know how to spell demonstrated significantly greater progress in decoding and spelling. Asking children to encode sound–symbol relationships to spell words they wish to use in order to communicate their ideas forces them to struggle with the representation of sounds in longer and more phonetically complex words, which affords them even greater insight into the alphabetic principle (see Apel & Masterson, 2001; Templeton, Chapter 10, this volume).

The Role of Speech–Language Pathologists

One way that speech–language pathologists can become involved with teaching the alphabetic principle is to help teachers make informed decisions about the order in which they teach letters. Although it is traditional to introduce letters in alphabetic order (because children often are already familiar with the alphabet), this may not be the best approach. Some letters occur more frequently in children's reading materials, some sounds associated with letters are easier for young children to articulate, some letters are less easily confused, and some grapheme–phoneme associations are more consistent than others (see Table 4.2 for specific examples).

While working at a preschool for children with developmental disabilities, a speech–language pathologist helped a teacher develop the scope and sequence for her alphabet instruction. The teacher had become dissatisfied with her traditional approach for two reasons. First, children had to wait too many weeks before they could begin to use the letters they had learned to read or to write words associated with objects in the classroom. Second, children often confused letters that resembled each other, which just happen to appear close to each other in alphabetic order (e.g., $b/d, m/n, p/q$). Based on his knowledge of developmental phonology and direct instruction principles, the clinician worked with the teacher to create a new sequence of letter introduction: $a, m, s, o, t, p, i, f, n, d, u, k, g, l, e, b, r, j, v, h, c, q, w, x, y, z$. This sequence permitted the instructors to capitalize on children's prior knowledge of the alphabet (e.g., the letter a was introduced first) while accounting for visual properties of each letter and related sound (e.g., many of the contiguous letters and letter sounds are visually distinct), frequency of occurrence, and ease of articulation. Also, in this sequence, only a handful of letters needed to be introduced before children could begin to read phonetically transparent words.

The teacher and the clinician devised and cotaught a set of three half-hour lessons for each letter consisting of phonological awareness activities, multisensory letter–sound instruction, review of previously taught letters, vowel–consonant (VC) and consonant–vowel–consonant (CVC) decoding and spelling practice, and reading of books that featured the

TABLE 4.2. Instructional Guidelines for Teaching Grapheme–Phoneme Correspondence and Decoding

- Separate visually or phonetically similar letters (e.g., *p*/*b*, *e*/*i*) and patterns (*sh*/*ch*, *ar*/*ir*).

- Introduce upper- and lowercase letters that are similar (e.g., *C*/*c*, *O*/*o*, *S*/*s*) before those that are dissimilar (e.g., *A*/*a*, *D*/*d*, *G*/*g*); otherwise, introduce lowercase letters first.

- Letters that are associated with a single sound (e.g., *s*, *m*, *f*) should be taught before those associated with multiple sounds (e.g., *c*, *g*, *y*).

- Begin instruction with letters that are more common and that are easier to articulate.

- Introduce a new letter once every few days to help children quickly acquire enough knowledge to begin decoding.

- Teach letter–sound correspondences that can be used to build a variety of words and be sure to introduce continuant sounds (e.g., /s/, /f/) before obstruent (e.g., /ʃ/, /dʒ/) or stop (e.g., /k/, /d/) sounds.

- Incorporate recently taught letters and sounds into decoding activities as soon as possible.

- Progress from simple vowel–consonant, consonant–vowel, consonant–vowel–consonant, and consonant–vowel–consonant–silent *e* decoding to decoding of words that contain consonant blends (e.g., *st*, *pl*, *fr*), consonant digraphs (e.g., *th*, *sh*, *ph*), vowel digraphs (e.g., *ea*, *oa*, *ee*), and diphthongs (e.g., *oy*/*oi*, *au*/*aw*, *ou*/*ow*).

- Teach common phonograms (e.g., *-at*, *-eat*, *-op*) to build orthographic reading skills.

- Teach structural analysis as a strategy for decoding polysyllabic words (i.e., compound words, base words with inflected endings or derivational affixes, and root words with derivational affixes).

- Use script adaptations, such as marking long versus short vowels and using colored or differently sized letters to indicate silent letters, to support students' decoding efforts.

- Combine texts that exploit word recognition instruction (e.g., predictable books, decodable books, high interest-low vocabulary leveled books) and authentic reading materials.

- Monitor students' progress in letter recognition, letter naming, letter–sound knowledge, and decoding proficiency through frequent (e.g., weekly) assessment.

target letter. They also developed an assessment matrix to evaluate and record each child's performance of discrete skills (recognize letter, name letter, write letter, give letter sound) after each set of lessons was completed. In this way, they were able to closely monitor each child's progress and determine which children needed additional instruction. Every few weeks, after five or so letters had been introduced, the children added the new letters to their personal alphabet books and the class alphabet strip designed by the students.

Principle 4: Teach Students to Use a Variety of Strategies to Decode Words

Phonics Instruction

Obviously, for children to take full advantage of the alphabetic principle, they need to apply it when trying to read unfamiliar words. Consequently, beginning readers should be taught to convert graphemes to phonemes and to blend the resulting sequence of sounds—to "sound out" unknown words—with ample opportunities to practice this strategy with isolated words so as to facilitate the stabilization of graphophonemic knowledge. Traditional synthetic phonics instruction such as this is but one approach to teaching decoding skills; others include traditional analytic phonics (sets of known words are deconstructed to identify phonic rules and generalizations), contemporary spelling-based approaches, and contemporary analogy-based approaches (see Stahl, 2001, for review).

Although no single type of phonics instruction appears to be substantially more advantageous than another, explicit and systematic instruction has been shown to produce greater effects on decoding performance (as measured by reading nonsense words) than less explicit forms of instruction, at least for beginning readers (Blachman, Tangel, Ball, Black, & McGraw, 1999; Foorman, Francis, Fletcher, Schatschneider, & Mehta, 1998; National Reading Panel, 2000; Stahl, Duffy-Hester, & Stahl, 1998; Torgesen et al., 1999). For older readers, either form of instruction appears equally effective (Torgesen et al., 2001). This does not mean that decoding practice should occur only within the context of skills-based instruction; graphophonemic conversion tactics also should be encouraged when children read whole texts. The type of text in which this practice occurs should be carefully considered. There is evidence that decodable texts, those that are linguistically valid and engaging but contain an accumulation of letter–sound associations being taught (some irregular words are included as well to maintain text coherence), are more beneficial for improving decoding skills than less phonetically transparent texts (Juel & Roper-Schneider, 1985). However, teachers should supplement these texts with authentic children's literature to help students develop a strong sense of narrative structure and comprehension of complex semantic and syntactic relations.

Moving Beyond Symbol–Sound Correspondence

Identifying unknown words by analogous comparison with known words is another powerful decoding strategy that children should learn to use (Goswami, 1986). When reading by analogy, children draw comparisons between phonograms, or orthographic rimes, in words. So a child who is familiar with the phonogram (and word) *eat* can, by analogy, read the words *seat, cheat, beat, heat,* and *meat*. The phonogram provides a consistent mapping between orthography and phonology, especially with respect to vowel pronunciation, which is notoriously unpredictable (Treiman & Zukowski, 1996). Because the mapping is beyond the level of simple letter–sound association, it enables children to decode words more efficiently and to develop orthographic word recognition. Three instructional techniques are often used to help children learn to read by analogy: explicit teaching of anchor words for common phonograms (see Gaskins et al., 1988), self-directed word sorts to facilitate discovery of spelling patterns (Bear, Invernizzi, Templeton, & Johnston, 2000), and guided spelling with predetermined sets of letters that are part of pattern words (Cunningham & Cunningham, 1992). Though effective by itself, phonogram instruction should be combined with instruction in graphophonemic conversion for the best results (Lovett et al., 2000).

Children also need to know how to decode polysyllabic words through graphomorphemic, or structural, analysis. The words *transport, portable, report,* and *export* all contain the same root, *port,* which means to carry or take, plus a derivational affix that modifies the meaning of the root. Similarly, the words *plays, played,* and *playing* all contain the same base word, *play,* plus inflectional affixes marking verb tense. Children can use this information not only to recognize words more efficiently (roots, base words, and affixes are often, but not always, stable with respect to pronunciation), but to determine the meanings of the words and their functions in sentence contexts. In fact, Nagy and Anderson (1984) estimate that about 70% of English words have meanings that can be predicted, to some degree, from the meanings of their parts. This is an aspect of decoding instruction in which collaboration between speech–language pathologists and teachers may be exceptionally beneficial, because clinicians possess expertise in morphology whereas teachers typically do not. Professional development activities organized by the school clinician are a potential vehicle for communicating this type of information and its usefulness in literacy instruction to a large number of teachers at one time.

Students and teachers grow frustrated when poor readers continue to struggle year after year with "sounding out" increasingly longer and more phonetically opaque words. Consequently, a shift in instructional emphasis from symbol–sound conversion tactics to analogy detection and structural analysis is likely to be beneficial for older children and youth with reading difficulties. This does not imply that the alphabetic principle becomes superfluous for these students; all children, regardless of age, must possess an explicit awareness of the phonological structure of language and know how to map graphemes onto phonemes in order to read an alphabetic orthography. For older students, however, these skills should be embedded within age-appropriate literacy activities, in particular spelling exercises. As children learn to spell and read common orthographic rimes, roots, base words, and affixes, teachers can help students decompose these larger units so that they gain a better understanding of how speech sounds are represented by various orthographic patterns.

The Role of Speech–Language Pathologists

The joint efforts of a special education teacher and a speech–language pathologist at a suburban elementary school illustrate how a remedial reading program might coordinate instruction in advanced decoding strategies and help children continue to develop phonemic awareness and graphophonemic knowledge. At this particular school for children in grades three through six, approximately 6% of the students were identified as children with language-learning disabilities, almost all of whom displayed markedly inferior reading achievement. Seeing the need for a more integrative and developmentally responsive approach to reading instruction for these older students with limited word recognition, the special educator and the speech–language pathologist devised a program in which spelling activities were the centerpiece of their intervention.

The special educator and the speech–language pathologist collaboratively developed and taught weekly word study units in which common phonograms or roots/base words, often derived from the students' reading materials, were introduced. At the beginning of the week, words containing a new orthographic pattern were added to a class word wall. For example, one week the phonogram *ight* was introduced. An anchor word for this pattern, *light*, was selected and printed on the word wall. Children generated other words containing this pattern, including *plight*, *frightening*, and *mightily*, that also were added to the word wall under the anchor word. The teacher made sure that these words were placed near another pattern and its examples that shared the same underlying phonological structure, in this case *ite*, as in *rite* and *spiteful*, and pointed this out to the students. Children then searched their texts for other examples of the new pattern and related patterns and recorded them on their personal copies of the word wall.

During the next 2 days, students performed word pattern sorts. For example, one week children were learning about the root *sign*. Each child was given a set of index cards and asked to (1) sort the cards into as many different "words" as possible; (2) record all of the "words" on a separate sheet; (3) determine if each "word" was an acceptable English word; and (4) if an acceptable word, write the word in a sentence to demonstrate understanding of its meaning. For this particular root word, children were given cards on which *sign*, *de*, *re*, *as*, *s*, *ed*, *ing*, *er*, *ate*, *al*, *ment*, *ify*, and *ation* were printed. Thus, they were able to create words such as *designate*, *assignment, resignation,* and *signify.* Students discovered how various affixes could be combined with the root to form different words, how affixes influenced meaning, and how pronunciation changed while spelling of the root remained the same. On the fourth day, students participated in a guided spelling activity using letter tiles. They combined the tiles to spell many of the words containing the target root, base word, or phonogram they had been studying. The teacher then conducted a mini-lesson focusing on the meaning and spelling of a few affixes with which students had been working (e.g., *re, ing, ify*). At the end of the week, children read texts that contained the relevant spelling patterns and monitored their ability to recognize and define the words.

There are numerous ways in which the three basic decoding strategies can be effectively and creatively taught to children with and without reading problems, but describing them all is far beyond the scope of this chapter. The reader is encouraged to consult three superb resources for instructional ideas: *Phonics They Use: Words for Reading and Writing* by Patricia Cunningham (2000), *From Phonics to Fluency: Effective Teaching of Decoding and Reading Fluency in the Elementary School* by Rasinski and Padak (2001), and *Words Their Way: Word Study for Phonics, Vocabulary, and Spelling Instruction* by Bear et al. (2000). In addition, a brief list of recommendations is provided in Table 4.2.

Principle 5: Build Reading Accuracy and Fluency

Fluency Is Just as Important as Accuracy

To achieve the ultimate goal of reading, comprehension, children need to be able to recognize words not only accurately but also quickly. Slow word identification hinders comprehension because the reader must devote finite cognitive resources to decoding, leaving few resources available for comprehension monitoring and repair (e.g., Chard, Vaughn, & Tyler, 2002; Kuhn & Stahl, 2003; Tyler & Chard, 2000). The oral reading of children with RD is frequently slow, halting, and replete with miscues. Fortunately, there are a number of effective ways to increase the reading fluency of children with and without reading problems.

Ways to Increase Oral Reading Fluency

A long-standing, empirically validated approach is *repeated reading*, which improves overall reading performance both for passages that are practiced and novel ones (Rasinski, 1990; Vaughn et al., 2000). Repeated reading can take many forms. For example, in paired reading (Topping, 1989), a fluent reader first reads a passage at a moderate pace while a less fluent reader "shadows" by trying to read at the same or a trailing pace. Then the weaker reader reads the same passage alone. In shared reading, a more fluent child or adult reads a passage to the student, modeling good fluency, then the student reads the text along with the partner (as in paired reading), and finally the student reads the text to the partner. In paired repeated reading (Koskinen & Blum, 1986), the less fluent reader reads a passage several times while receiving feedback and assistance from a more competent peer, then the roles are reversed. Students also can be partnered with younger children. In this case, the struggling reader selects a relatively easy text that is more appropriate in content for the younger child (which provides an authentic reason for reading simpler texts), practices the text, and then reads it to the younger child. Paired reading also can be accomplished using audio-tape recordings of passages, which has the added benefit of permitting fluency practice in or out of school.

Readers' theater is another means of improving children's reading rate and prosody (Martinez, Roser, & Strecker, 1999; Rasinski, 2000; Tyler & Chard, 2000). It also serves as an authentic reason for reading a text multiple times. Children can select poems, famous speeches, lyrics, or other such materials to practice for presentation to the class, or, more typically, can rewrite a favorite story as a play to rehearse and present. Readers' theater offers an opportunity for speech–language pathologists and teachers to work together because oral language skills (e.g., narration, grammar, pragmatics) and reading skills can be nurtured simultaneously.

Children should be shown how to monitor and record their reading fluency progress, which may serve as an additional incentive to improve their performance. After counting the number of words in a passage, they can time each other when doing partner reading (or time themselves after tape-recording an oral reading sample) and record either the amount of time it took to read the selection or the number of words read per unit of time (e.g., 1 minute) on a personal graph. Then, with the teacher's guidance, each child can establish a reading rate goal to work toward (grade-level norms are provided in Rasinski & Padak, 2001). Once the goal has been met, the children select a reward from a menu of possible reinforcers.

Finally, children need to read large amounts of text to encounter words frequently enough to build word-specific orthographic representations. To encourage wide reading, materials should be selected that match students' interests and that are at an independent reading level. Providing books on tape or compact disc alongside print versions gives children a model of fluent reading and permits them to tackle more challenging texts. Closed captioning combined with lowered volume can motivate students to read quickly to follow their favorite television programs, which they undoubtedly watch for long periods of time. Although reading fluency can be improved through practice with words printed on flash cards (Tan & Nicholson, 1997), such instruction is likely to be less motivating for students. Typically, word recognition drills use high-frequency words, such as those from the Dolch basic reading vocabulary lists.

The Role of Speech–Language Pathologists

A speech–language pathologist and a special education teacher employed at an urban, low-income elementary school worked with many of the same students who exhibited academic difficulties. Believing that engaging and authentic texts offered a focal point for addressing students' communication difficulties and reading deficiencies, they collaborated on a unit of instruction that incorporated famous speeches and popular song lyrics selected by the students to be presented at a schoolwide talent show. This venue provided a strong motivation for their students to be well prepared, so they reread their chosen texts many times and rehearsed them in front of small groups.

The students worked with partners in daily paired, repeated reading sessions over two weeks. During each session, the students timed their partner and then graphed the amount of time required to read the speech or song lyrics. The students had reading rate goals that permitted them to finish in the two minutes each was given on stage. When students read aloud to partners or to small groups, the speech–language pathologist coached them to maintain eye contact with their audience, to use adequate vocal intensity and inflection, and to show enthusiasm and confidence with their facial expressions. She also pointed out how the lyrics and poems used vocabulary and grammar in unique ways and contrasted these with students' typical ways of speaking.

Because this single unit was not likely to have a lasting effect on the students' reading accuracy and fluency, the special education teacher and the clinician also worked together to identify a common core vocabulary for language intervention and reading remediation (a number of these words were found on published reading vocabulary lists). They printed the words on flash cards so students could practice reading, spelling, defining, and using them in spoken utterances. With the help of the school librarian, they also identified trade books that contained many of the core vocabulary words and color coded the books by approximate reading levels so the students would know which books were "just right" for them. Some of the books also were on compact disc or audiotape, so the students could have fluent reading models when they attempted to read more challenging texts.

CONCLUDING REMARKS

This chapter has described five principles of effective word recognition instruction derived from the extant research literature. Each can guide the collaborative efforts of professionals who work with poor readers and children who are at risk for developing reading problems. The impact of these efforts must be evaluated so that professionals can remain responsive to the changing needs and performance of individual readers as they acquire the linguistic underpinnings of literacy, come to understand the alphabetic principle, learn to use a broad array of decoding strategies, and develop word recognition fluency in print-rich environments. Continuous progress monitoring in basic reading skills can and should inform the decisions that educators make as they plan, implement, and modify their reading interventions. Although many standardized instruments are available for assessing phonological awareness, graphophonemic knowledge, orthographic processing, and reading fluency, most of these are designed for one of two purposes: to determine if a delay is evident (i.e., norm-referenced tests) or to ascertain the absolute level of skill mastery (i.e., criterion-referenced tests). These instruments are limited in their capacity for appraising student learning and instructional efficacy. Curriculum-based measures, on the other hand, are well suited for determining if a child falls below growth rate expectations and if modification of an intervention is warranted to accelerate growth (Deno, 1997). The *Dynamic Indicators of Basic Early Literacy Skills* (DIBELS; Good & Kaminski, 1996, 2002; Kaminski & Good, 1996) serve as an example of a systematic approach to curriculum-based literacy assessment.

The DIBELS help practitioners (1) identify children who are likely to struggle with acquiring early literacy skills; (2) select clear and meaningful instructional objectives; (3) use reliable, valid, and economical measures to regularly monitor students' progress in attaining performance benchmarks at specified time points; and (4) evaluate the effectiveness of reading interventions. Presently, DIBELS are available for children in kindergarten through sixth grade. For kindergartners, four tasks are administered: (1) initial sound fluency (number of initial sounds correctly identified in spoken words per minute) and (2) phoneme segmentation fluency (number of sounds correctly segmented from spoken words per minute) serve as indicators of phonemic awareness; (3) letter naming fluency (number of upper- and lowercase letters correctly named in 1 minute) serves as an indicator of graphophonemic knowledge; and (4) nonsense word fluency (number of letter sounds correctly identified in pseudowords in 1 minute) serves as a measure of decoding. For first graders, all but one of these measures (initial sound fluency) are used for measuring general reading outcomes. In addition, oral reading fluency (average number of correct words per minute read aloud in a series of leveled reading passages) is evaluated. For students in second through sixth grade, only oral reading fluency is measured.

Good and his colleagues (Good, Kaminski, Shinn, Bratten, & Laimon, in press) report that the DIBELS are reliable predictors of general outcomes in beginning reading. Alternate-form reliability estimates for the group of measures range from .72 (initial sound fluency) to .88 (letter naming fluency). Predictive validity of kindergarten and first-grade DIBELS with first- and second-grade Woodcock–Johnson Psycho-Educational Battery Total Reading Cluster scores range from .36 (initial sound fluency) to .68 (phoneme segmentation fluency). Reliable and valid tools such as the DIBELS hold great promise for achieving the seamless integration of assessment and instruction for improving the word recognition skills of children with and without reading problems.

REFERENCES

Adams, M. J. (1990). *Beginning to read: Thinking and learning about print*. Cambridge, MA: MIT Press.

Allor, J. H. (2002). The relationships of phonemic awareness and rapid naming to reading development. *Learning Disability Quarterly, 25*, 47–57.

Allor, J. H., Fuchs, D., & Mathes, P. G. (2001). Do students with and without lexical retrieval weaknesses respond differently to instruction? *Journal of Learning Disabilities, 34*, 264–275.

Apel, K., & Masterson, J. J. (2001). Theory-guided spelling assessment and intervention: A case study. *Language, Speech, and Hearing Services in the Schools, 32*, 182–195.

Badian, N. A. (1993). Phonemic awareness, naming, visual symbol processing, and reading. *Reading and Writing: An Interdisciplinary Journal, 5*, 87–100.

Baker, L., Fernandez-Fein, S., Scher, D., & Williams, H. (1998). Home experiences related to the development of word recognition. In J. L. Metsala & L. C. Ehri (Eds.), *Word recognition in beginning literacy* (pp. 263–287). Mahwah, NJ: Erlbaum.

Baker, L., & Mackler, K. (1997, April). Contributions of children's emergent literacy skills and home experiences to grade 2 word recognition. In R. Serpell, S. Sonnenschein, & L. Baker (Chairs), *Patterns of emerging competence and sociocultural context in the early appropriation of literacy*. Symposium presented at the meeting of the Society for Research in Child Development, Washington, DC.

Bear, D. R., Invernizzi, M., Templeton, S., & Johnston, F. (2000). *Words their way: Word study for phonics, vocabulary, and spelling instruction* (2nd ed.). Upper Saddle River, NJ: Prentice-Hall.

Bhat, P., Griffin, C. C., & Sindelar, P. T. (2003). Phonological awareness instruction for middle school students with learning disabilities. *Learning Disability Quarterly, 26*(2), 73–87.

Bishop, D. V. M., & Adams, C. (1990). A prospective study of the relationship between specific language impairment, phonological disorders, and reading retardation. *Journal of Child Psychology and Psychiatry, 31,* 1027–1057.

Blachman, B. A., Tangel, D. M., Ball, E. W., Black, R., & McGraw, C. K. (1999). Developing phonological awareness and word recognition skills: A two-year intervention with low-income, inner-city children. *Reading and Writing: An Interdisciplinary Journal, 11,* 239–273.

Bowers, P. G. (1995). Tracing symbol naming speed's unique contributions to reading disabilities over time. *Reading and Writing: An Interdisciplinary Journal, 7,* 189–216.

Bowers, P. G., & Wolf, M. (1993). Theoretical links among naming speed, precise timing mechanisms and orthographic skill in dyslexia. *Reading and Writing: An Interdisciplinary Journal, 5,* 69–85.

Bowey, J. A. (1995). Socioeconomic status differences in preschool phonological sensitivity and first-grade reading achievement. *Journal of Educational Psychology, 87,* 476–487.

Bryant, P. E., MacLean, M., Bradley, L. L., & Crossland, J. (1990). Rhyme and alliteration, phoneme detection, and learning to read. *Developmental Psychology, 26,* 429–438.

Burgess, S. R., & Lonigan, C. J. (1998). Bidirectional relations of phonological sensitivity and pre-reading abilities: Evidence from a preschool sample. *Journal of Experimental Child Psychology, 70,* 117–141.

Bus, A. G., & van IJzendoorn, M. H. (1999). Phonological awareness and early reading: A meta-analysis of experimental training studies. *Journal of Educational Psychology, 91,* 403–414.

Byrne, B., & Fielding-Barnsley, R. (1991). Evaluation of a program to teach phonemic awareness to young children. *Journal of Educational Psychology, 83,* 451–455.

Carnine, D. W., Silbert, J., & Kame'enui, E. J. (1997). *Direct instruction reading.* Upper Saddle River, NJ: Merrill.

Castiglioni-Spalten, M. L., & Ehri, L. C. (2003). Phonemic awareness instruction: Contribution of articulatory segmentation to novice beginners' reading and spelling. *Scientific Studies of Reading, 7,* 25–52.

Catts, H. W. (1989). Phonological processing deficits and reading disabilities. In A. G. Kamhi & H. W. Catts (Eds.), *Reading disabilities: A developmental language perspective* (pp. 101–132). Boston: Allyn & Bacon.

Catts, H. W. (1993). The relationship between speech–language impairments and reading disabilities. *Journal of Speech and Hearing Research, 36,* 948–958.

Catts, H. W., Fey, M. E., Zhang, X., & Tomblin, J. B. (1999). Language basis of reading and reading disabilities: Evidence from a longitudinal investigation. *Scientific Studies of Reading, 3,* 331–361.

Chaney, C. (1994). Language development, metalinguistic awareness, and emergent literacy skills of 3–year-old children in relation to social class. *Applied Psycholinguistics, 15,* 371–394.

Chard, D. J., Vaughn, S., & Tyler, B. (2002). A synthesis of research on effective interventions for building reading fluency with elementary students with learning disabilities. *Journal of Learning Disabilities, 35,* 386–406.

Clarke, L. K. (1988). Invented versus traditional spelling in first graders' writings: Effects on learning to spell and read. *Research in the Teaching of English, 22,* 281–309.

Compton, D. L. (2000). Modeling the response of normally achieving and at-risk first-grade children to word reading instruction. *Annals of Dyslexia, 50,* 53–84.

Cornwall, A. (1992). The relationship of phonological awareness, rapid naming, and verbal memory to severe reading and spelling disability. *Journal of Learning Disabilities, 25,* 532–538.

Crain-Thoreson, C., & Dale, P. S. (1992). Do early talkers become early readers?: Linguistic precocity, preschool language, and emergent literacy. *Developmental Psychology, 28,* 421–429.

Cunningham, A. E. (1990). Explicit versus implicit instruction in phonemic awareness. *Journal of Experimental Child Psychology, 50,* 429–444.

Cunningham, A. E., & Stanovich, K. E. (1991). Tracking the unique effects of print exposure in children: Associations with vocabulary, general knowledge, and spelling. *Journal of Educational Psychology, 83,* 264–274.

Cunningham, A. E., & Stanovich, K. E. (1997). Early reading acquisition and its relation to reading experience and ability 10 years later. *Developmental Psychology, 33,* 934–945.

Cunningham, P. M. (2000). *Phonics they use: Words for reading and writing* (3rd ed.). New York: Addison Wesley Longman.

Cunningham, P. M., & Cunningham, J. W. (1992). Making words: Enhancing the invented spelling–decoding connection. *The Reading Teacher, 46,* 106–115.

DeBaryshe, B. D. (1995). Maternal belief systems: Linchpin in the home reading process. *Journal of Applied Developmental Psychology, 16,* 1–20.

Deno, S. L. (1997). Whether thou goest. . . . Perspectives on progress monitoring. In J. W. Lloyd, E. J. Kame'enui, & D. Chard (Eds.), *Issues in educating students with disabilities* (pp. 77–99). Mahwah, NJ: Erlbaum.

Ehri, L. C. (1987). Learning to read and spell words. *Journal of Reading Behavior, 19,* 5–31.

Ehri, L. C. (1998). Grapheme–phoneme knowledge is essential for learning to read words in English. In J. L. Metsala & L. C. Ehri (Eds.), *Word recognition in beginning literacy* (pp. 3–40). Hillsdale, NJ: Erlbaum.

Felton, R. H., & Brown, I. S. (1990). Phonological processes as predictors of specific reading skills in children at risk for reading failure. *Reading and Writing: An Interdisciplinary Journal, 2,* 39–59.

Felton, R. H., & Wood, F. B. (1992). A reading level match study of nonword reading skills in poor readers with varying IQ. *Journal of Learning Disabilities, 25,* 318–326.

Fey, M. E., Catts, H. W., & Larrivee, L. S. (1995). Preparing preschoolers for the academic and social challenges of school. In M. E. Fey, J. Windson, & S. F. Warrent (Eds.), *Language intervention: Preschool through the elementary years* (pp. 3–37). Baltimore: Brookes.

Foorman, B. R., Francis, D. J., Fletcher, J. M., Schatschneider, C., & Mehta, P. (1998). The role of instruction in learning to read: Preventing reading failure in at-risk children. *Journal of Educational Psychology, 90,* 37–55.

Foorman, B. R., Francis, D. J., Novy, D. M., & Liberman, D. (1991). How letter–sound instruction mediates progress in first-grade reading and spelling. *Journal of Educational Psychology, 83,* 456–469.

Francis, D. J., Shaywitz, S. E., Stuebing, K. K., Shaywitz, B. A., & Fletcher, J. M. (1996). Developmental lag versus deficit model of reading disability: A longitudinal, individual growth curve analysis. *Journal of Educational Psychology, 88,* 3–17.

Fuchs, D., & Fuchs, L. S. (2001, June). *The respective contributions of phonological awareness and decoding to reading development in Title 1 and non-Title 1 schools.* Paper presented at the annual meeting of the Society for the Scientific Study of Reading, Boulder, CO.

Fuchs, D., Fuchs, L. S., Thompson, A., Yen, L., Otaiba, S. A., Nyman, K., Yang, N., & Svenson, E. (2001, April). *A randomized field trial to explore the effectiveness of a beginning reading program that excludes phonological awareness training.* Paper presented at the annual meeting of the American Educational Research Association, Seattle, WA.

Gaskins, I. W., Downer, M. A., Anderson, R. C., Cunningham, P. M., Gaskins, R. W., Schommer, M., & Teachers of Benchmark School (1988). A metacognitive approach to phonics: Using what you know to decode what you don't know. *Remedial and Special Education, 9,* 36–41.

Gillon, G. T. (2000). The efficacy of phonological awareness intervention for children with spoken language impairment. *Language, Speech, and Hearing Services in Schools, 31,* 126–141.

Good, R. H., & Kaminski, R. A. (1996). Assessment for instructional decisions: Toward a proactive/prevention model for decision making for early literacy skills. *School Psychology Quarterly, 11,* 1–11.

Good, R. H., & Kaminski, R. A. (Eds.). (2002). *Dynamic indicators of basic early literacy skills* (6th ed.). Eugene, OR: Institute for the Development of Educational Achievement. Available online at: *http://dibels.uoregon.edu.*

Good, R. H., Kaminski, R. A., Shinn, M. R., Bratten, J., & Laimon, L. (in press). *Technical adequacy and decision making utility of DIBELS* (Technical Report). Eugene: University of Oregon.

Goswami, U. (1986). Children's use of analogy in learning to read: A developmental study. *Journal of Experimental Child Psychology, 42,* 73–83.

Gough, P. B., & Walsh, M. (1991). Chinese, Phoenicians, and the orthographic cipher of English. In S. A. Brady & D. Shankweiler (Eds.), *Phonological processes in literacy: A tribute to Isabelle Y. Liberman* (pp. 199–209). Hillsdale, NJ: Erlbaum.

Hatcher, P. J., Hulme, C., & Ellis, A. W. (1994). Ameliorating early reading failure by integrating the teaching of reading and phonological skills: The phonological linkage hypothesis. *Child Development, 65,* 41–57.

Juel, C. (1988). Learning to read and write: A longitudinal study of 54 children from first through fourth grades. *Journal of Educational Psychology, 80,* 437–447.

Juel, C., Griffith, P. L., & Gough, P. B. (1986). Acquisition of literacy: A longitudinal study of children in first and second grade. *Journal of Educational Psychology, 78*, 243–255.

Juel, C., & Roper-Schneider, D. (1985). The influence of basal readers on first grade reading. *Reading Research Quarterly, 20*, 134–152.

Kaminski, R. A., & Good, R. H. (1996). Toward a technology for assessing basic early literacy skills. *School Psychology Review, 25*, 215–227.

Koskinen, P. S., & Blum, I. H. (1986). Paired repeated reading: A classroom strategy for developing fluent reading. *The Reading Teacher, 40*, 70–75.

Kuhn, M. R., & Stahl, S. A. (2003). Fluency: A review of developmental and remedial practices. *Journal of Educational Psychology, 95*, 3–21.

Liberman, I. Y. (1982). A language-oriented view of reading and its disabilities. In H. Myklebust (Ed.), *Progress in learning disabilities* (Vol. 5, pp. 81–101). New York: Grune & Stratton.

Liberman, I. Y., & Shankweiler, D. (1985). Phonology and the problems of learning to read and write. *Remedial and Special Education, 6*, 8–17.

Liberman, I. Y., & Shankweiler, D. (1991). Phonology and beginning reading: A tutorial. In L. Rieben & C. A. Perfetti (Eds.), *Learning to read: Basic research and its implications* (pp. 3–17). Hillsdale, NJ: Erlbaum.

Lonigan, C., Burgess, S. R., Anthony, J. L., & Barker, T. A. (1998). Development of phonological sensitivity in 2– to 5–year-old children. *Journal of Educational Psychology, 90*, 294–311.

Lonigan, C. J., & Whitehurst, G. J. (1998). Examination of the relative efficacy of parent and teacher involvement in a shared-reading intervention for preschool children from low-income backgrounds. *Early Childhood Research Quarterly, 13*, 263–290.

Lovett, M. W., Lacerenza, L., Borden, S. L., Frijters, J. C., Steinbech, K. A., & De Palma, M. (2000). Components of effective remediation for developmental reading disabilities: Combining phonological and strategy-based instruction to improve outcomes. *Journal of Educational Psychology, 92*, 263–283.

Lyon, G. R. (1995). Toward a definition of dyslexia. *Annals of Dyslexia, 45*, 3–27.

Lyon, G. R., & Moats, L. C. (1997). Critical conceptual and methodological considerations in reading intervention research. *Journal of Learning Disabilities, 30*, 578–588.

MacLean, M., Bryant, P. E., & Bradley, L. L. (1987). Rhymes, nursery rhymes, and reading in early childhood. *Merrill-Palmer Quarterly, 33*, 255–282.

Magnusson, E., & Naucler, K. (1993). The development of linguistic awareness in language-disordered children. *First Language, 13*, 93–111.

Manis, F. R., Doi, L. M., & Bhadha, B. (2000). Naming speed, phonological awareness, and orthographic knowledge in second graders. *Journal of Learning Disabilities, 33*, 325–333.

Manis, F. R., Seidenberg, M. S., & Doi, L. M. (1999). See Dick RAN: Rapid naming and the longitudinal prediction of reading subskills in first and second grades. *Scientific Studies of Reading, 3*, 129–157.

Martinez, M., Roser, N. L., & Strecker, S. (1999). "I never thought I could be a star": A reader's theater ticket to fluency. *The Reading Teacher, 52*, 326–334.

Marvin, C., & Mirenda, P. (1993). Home literacy experiences of preschoolers enrolled in Head Start and special education programs. *Journal of Early Intervention, 17,* 351–367.

Mathes, P. G., Torgesen, J. K., & Allor, J. H. (2001). The effects of peer-assisted literacy strategies for first-grade readers with and without additional computer-assisted instruction in phonological awareness. *American Educational Research Journal, 38,* 371–410.

McBride-Chang, C., & Manis, F. R. (1996). Structural invariance in the associations of naming speed, phonological awareness, and verbal reasoning in good and poor readers: A test of the double deficit hypothesis. *Reading and Writing: An Interdisciplinary Journal, 8,* 323–339.

McCardle, P., Scarborough, H. S., & Catts, H. W. (2001). Predicting, explaining, and preventing children's reading difficulties. *Learning Disabilities Research and Practice, 16,* 230–239.

McCormick, C. E., & Mason, J. M. (1986). Intervention procedures for increasing preschool children's interest in and knowledge about reading. In W. H. Teale & E. Sulzby (Eds.), *Emergent literacy: Writing and reading* (pp. 90–115). Norwood, NJ: Ablex.

McCutchen, D., Abbott, R. D., Green, L. B., Beretvas, S. N., Cox, S., Potter, N. S., Quiroga, T., & Gray, A. L. (2002). Beginning literacy: Links among teacher knowledge, teacher practice, and student learning. *Journal of Learning Disabilities, 35,* 69–86.

Moats, L. C. (1994). The missing foundation in teacher education: Knowledge of the structure of spoken and written language. *Annals of Dyslexia, 44,* 81–102.

Moats, L. C., & Lyon, G. R. (1996). Wanted: Teachers with knowledge of language. *Topics in Language Disorders, 16*(2), 73–86.

Mody, M. (2003). Phonological basis in reading disability: A review and analysis of evidence. *Reading and Writing: An Interdisciplinary Journal, 16,* 21–39.

Nagy, W., & Anderson, R. C. (1984). How many words are there in printed school English? *Reading Research Quarterly, 19,* 304–330.

National Reading Panel. (2000). *Report of the National Reading Panel.* Washington, DC: National Institute of Child Health and Development.

O'Connor, R. E., Jenkins, J. R., & Slocum, T. A. (1995). Transfer among phonological tasks in kindergarten: Essential instructional content. *Journal of Educational Psychology, 87,* 202–217.

Perfetti, C. A. (1992). The representation problem in reading acquisition. In P. B. Gough, L. C. Ehri, & R. Trieman (Eds.), *Reading acquisition* (pp. 145–174). Hillsdale, NJ: Erlbaum.

Perfetti, C. A., Beck, I., Bell, L., & Hughes, C. (1987). Phonemic knowledge and learning to read are reciprocal: A longitudinal study. *Merrill-Palmer Quarterly, 33,* 283–319.

Rack, J. P., Snowling, M. J., & Olson, R. K. (1992). The nonword reading deficit in developmental dyslexia: A review. *Reading Research Quarterly, 27,* 29–53.

Rapala, M. M., & Brady, S. A. (1990). Reading ability and short-term memory: The role of phonological processing. *Reading and Writing: An Interdisciplinary Journal, 2,* 1–25.

Rasinski, T. V. (1990). Effects of repeated reading and listening-while reading on reading fluency. *Journal of Educational Research, 83,* 147–150.

Rasinski, T. V. (2000). Speed does matter in reading. *The Reading Teacher, 52,* 146–151.

Rasinski, T. V., & Padak, N. D. (2001). *From phonics to fluency: Effective teaching of decoding and reading fluency in the elementary school.* New York: Addison Wesley Longman.

Reitsma, P. (1983). Printed word learning in beginning readers. *Journal of Experimental Child Psychology, 36,* 321–339.

Roth, F. P., & Baden, B. (2001). Investing in emergent literacy intervention: A key role for speech–language pathologists. *Seminars in Speech and Language, 22,* 163–173.

Roth, F. P., Troia, G. A., Worthington, C. K., & Dow, K. A. (2002). Promoting Awareness of Sounds in Speech (PASS): An initial report of an early intervention program for children with speech and language impairments. *Applied Psycholinguistics, 23,* 535–565.

Scarborough, H. S. (1991). Antecedents to reading disability: Preschool language development and literacy experiences of children from dyslexic families. *Reading and Writing: An Interdisciplinary Journal, 3,* 219–233.

Scarborough, H. S. (1998). Early identification of children at risk for reading disabilities: Phonological awareness and some other promising predictors. In B. K. Shapiro, P. J. Accardo, & A. J. Capute (Eds.), *Specific reading disability: A view of the spectrum* (pp. 75–119). Baltimore: York Press.

Scarborough, H. S. (2001). Connecting early language and literacy to later reading (dis)abilities: Evidence, theory, and practice. In S. B. Neuman & D. K. Dickinson (Eds.), *Handbook of early literacy research* (pp. 97–110). New York: Guilford Press.

Scarborough, H. S., & Dobrich, W. (1994). On the efficacy of reading to preschoolers. *Developmental Review, 14,* 245–302.

Schatschneider, C., Carlson, C. D., Francis, D. J., Foorman, B. R., & Fletcher, J. M. (2002). Relationship of rapid automatized naming and phonological awareness in early reading development: Implications for the double-deficit hypothesis. *Journal of Learning Disabilities, 35,* 245–256.

Shankweiler, D., Lundquist, E., Katz, L., Stuebing, K. K., Fletcher, J. M., Brady, S. A., Fowler, A. E., Dreyer, L. G., Marchione, K. E., Shaywitz, S. E., & Shaywitz, B. A. (1999). Comprehension and decoding: Patterns of association in children with reading disabilities. *Scientific Studies of Reading, 3,* 69–94.

Share, D. L. (1995). Phonological recoding and self-teaching: Sine qua non of reading acquisition. *Cognition, 55,* 151–218.

Share, D. L., & Stanovich, K. E. (1995). Cognitive processes in early reading development: Accommodating individual differences into a model of acquisition. *Issues in Education: Contributions from Educational Psychology, 1,* 1–57.

Smith, S. S., & Dixon, R. G. (1995). Literacy concepts of low- and middle-class four-year-olds entering preschool. *Journal of Educational Research, 88,* 243–253.

Snow, C. E., Burns, S., & Griffith, P. (Eds.). (1998). *Preventing reading difficulties in young children.* Washington, DC: National Academies Press.

Stahl, S. A. (2001). Teaching phonics and phonological awareness. In S. B. Neuman

& D. K. Dickinson (Eds.), *Handbook of early literacy research* (pp. 333–347). New York: Guilford Press.

Stahl, S. A., Duffy-Hester, A. M., & Stahl, K. A. (1998). Everything you wanted to know about phonics (but were afraid to ask). *Reading Research Quarterly, 33,* 338–355.

Stahl, S. A., & Murray, B. A. (1994). Defining phonological awareness and its relationship to early reading. *Journal of Educational Psychology, 86,* 221–234.

Stanovich, K. E. (1986). Matthew effects in reading: Some consequences of individual differences in the acquisition of literacy. *Reading Research Quarterly, 21,* 360–407.

Stanovich, K. E. (1988). Explaining the difference between the dyslexic and the garden-variety poor reader: The phonological–core variable–difference model. *Journal of Learning Disabilities, 21,* 590–604.

Stanovich, K. E., & Siegel, L. S. (1994). Phenotypic performance profiles of children with reading disabilities: A regression-based test of the phonological–core variable difference model. *Journal of Educational Psychology, 86,* 25–53.

Stothard, S. E., Snowling, M. J., Bishop, D. V. M., Chipchase, B. B., & Kaplan, C. A. (1998). Language-impaired preschoolers: A follow-up into adolescence. *Journal of Speech, Language, and Hearing Research, 41,* 407–418.

Tan, A., & Nicholson, T. (1997). Flashcards revisited: Training poor readers to read words faster improves their comprehension of text. *Journal of Educational Psychology, 59,* 276–288.

Tangel, D. M., & Blachman, B. A. (1992). Effect of phoneme awareness instruction on kindergarten children's invented spelling. *Journal of Reading Behavior, 24,* 233–261.

Topping, K. (1989). Peer tutoring and paired reading: Combining two powerful techniques. *The Reading Teacher, 42,* 488–494.

Torgesen, J. K. Alexander, A. W., Wagner, R. K., Rashotte, C. A., Voeller, K. S., & Conway, T. (2001). Intensive remedial instruction for children with severe reading disabilities: Immediate and long-term outcomes from two instructional approaches. *Journal of Learning Disabilities, 34,* 33–58.

Torgesen, J. K., & Burgess, S. R. (1998). Consistency of reading related phonological processes throughout early childhood: Evidence from longitudinal-correlational and instructional studies. In J. L. Metsala & L. C. Ehri (Eds.), *Word recognition in beginning literacy* (pp. 161–188). Mahwah, NJ: Erlbaum.

Torgesen, J. K., & Davis, C. (1996). Individual difference variables that predict response to training in phonological awareness. *Journal of Experimental Child Psychology, 63,* 1–21.

Torgesen, J. K., & Mathes, P. G. (2000). *A basic guide to understanding, assessing, and teaching phonological awareness.* Austin, TX: PRO-ED.

Torgesen, J. K., Morgan, S., & Davis, C. (1992). The effects of two types of phonological awareness training on word learning in kindergarten children. *Journal of Educational Psychology, 84,* 364–370.

Torgesen, J. K., Wagner, R. K., & Rashotte, C. A. (1994). Longitudinal studies of phonological processing and reading. *Journal of Learning Disabilities, 27,* 276–286.

Torgesen, J. K., Wagner, R. K., & Rashotte, C. A. (1997). Prevention and remediation of severe reading disabilities: Keeping the end in mind. *Scientific Studies of Reading, 1,* 217–234.

Torgesen, J. K., Wagner, R. K., Rashotte, C. A., Alexander, A. W., & Conway, T. (1997). Preventative and remedial interventions for children with severe reading disabilities. *Learning Disabilities: A Multidisciplinary Journal, 8,* 51–62.

Torgesen, J. K., Wagner, R. K., Rashotte, C. A., Burgess, S., & Hecht, S. (1997). Contributions of phonological awareness and rapid automatic naming ability to growth of word-reading skills in second- to fifth-grade children. *Scientific Studies of Reading, 1,* 161–185.

Torgesen, J. K., Wagner, R. K., Rashotte, C. A., Rose, E., Lindamood, P., Conway, T., & Garvan, C. (1999). Preventing reading failure in young children with phonological processing disabilities: Group and individual responses to instruction. *Journal of Educational Psychology, 91,* 579–593.

Treiman, R., & Zukowski, A. (1996). Children's sensitivity to syllables, onsets, rimes, and phonemes. *Journal of Experimental Child Psychology, 61,* 193–215.

Troia, G. A. (1999). Phonological awareness intervention research: A critical review of the experimental methodology. *Reading Research Quarterly, 34,* 28–52.

Troia, G. A. (2004). Phonological processing and its influence on literacy learning. In C. A. Stone, E. R. Silliman, B. J. Ehren, & K. Apel (Eds.), *Handbook of language and literacy: Development and disorders* (pp. 271–301). New York: Guilford Press.

Troia, G. A. (in press). Phonological awareness acquisition and intervention. *Current practice alerts.* Reston, VA: Council for Exceptional Children.

Troia, G. A., Roth, F. P., & Graham, S. (1998). An educator's guide to phonological awareness: Assessment measures and intervention activities for children. *Focus on Exceptional Children, 31*(3), 1–12.

Tunmer, W. E., & Chapman, J. W. (1998). Language prediction skill, phonological recoding ability, and beginning reading. In C. Hulme & R. M. Joshi (Eds.), *Reading and spelling: Development and disorders* (pp. 33–67). Hillsdale, NJ: Erlbaum.

Tyler, B. J., & Chard, D. J. (2000). Using readers theater to foster fluency in struggling readers: A twist on the repeated reading strategy. *Reading and Writing Quarterly: Overcoming Learning Difficulties, 16,* 163–168.

van Kleeck, A., Gillam, R. B., & McFadden, T. U. (1998). A study of classroom-based phonological awareness training for preschoolers with speech and/ or language disorders. *American Journal of Speech–Language Pathology, 7*(3), 65–76.

van Kleeck, A., & Schuele, C. M. (1987). Precursors to literacy: Normal development. *Topics in Language Disorders, 7*(2), 13–31.

Vaughn, S., Chard, D. J., Pedrotty-Brynat, D., Coleman, M., Tyler, B., Linan-Thompson, S., & Kousekanani, K. (2000). Fluency and comprehension interventions for third-grade students. *Remedial and Special Education, 21,* 325–335.

Vellutino, F. R., & Scanlon, D. M. (1987). Phonological recoding, phonological awareness, and reading ability: Evidence from a longitudinal and experimental study. *Merrill-Palmer Quarterly, 33,* 321–363.

Vellutino, F. R., Scanlon, D. M., Sipay, E. R., Small, S. G., Pratt, A., Chen, R., & Denckla, M. B. (1996). Cognitive profiles of difficult to remediate and readily remediated poor readers: Early intervention as a vehicle for distinguishing between cognitive and experiential deficits as basic causes of specific reading disability. *Journal of Educational Psychology, 88,* 601–638.

Wagner, R. K., & Torgesen, J. K. (1987). The nature of phonological processing and its causal role in the acquisition of reading skills. *Psychological Bulletin, 101,* 192–212.

Wagner, R. K., Torgesen, J. K., Laughon, P., Simmons, K., & Rashotte, C. A. (1993). Development of young readers' phonological processing abilities. *Journal of Educational Psychology, 85,* 83–103.

Wagner, R. K., Torgesen, J. K., & Rashotte, C. A. (1994). The development of reading-related phonological processing abilities: New evidence of bi-directional causality from a latent variable longitudinal study. *Developmental Psychology, 30,* 73–78.

Webster, P. E., & Plante, A. S. (1992). Effects of phonological impairment on word, syllable, and phoneme segmentation and reading. *Language, Speech, and Hearing Services in Schools, 23,* 176–182.

Webster, P. E., & Plante, A. S. (1995). Productive phonology and phonological awareness in preschool children. *Applied Psycholinguistics, 16,* 43–57.

West, R. F., Stanovich, K. E., & Mitchell, H. R. (1993). Reading in the real world and its correlates. *Reading Research Quarterly, 28,* 34–51.

Whitehurst, G. J., & Lonigan, C. J. (1998). Child development and emergent literacy. *Child Development, 69,* 848–872.

Wolf, M., & Bowers, P. G. (1999). The double-deficit hypothesis for the developmental dyslexias. *Journal of Educational Psychology, 91,* 415–438.

Wolf, M., Bowers, P. G., & Biddle, K.. (2000). Naming speed processes, timing, and reading: A conceptual review. *Journal of Learning Disabilities, 33,* 387–407.

Yopp, H. K., & Yopp, R. H. (2000). Supporting phonemic awareness development in the classroom: Playful and appealing activities that focus on the sound structure of language support literacy development. *The Reading Teacher, 54,* 130–143.

5

Reading Comprehension Instruction for All Students

CHRISTINA PENNINGTON WHITAKER
LINDA B. GAMBRELL
LESLEY MANDEL MORROW

Reading is recognized as a skill basic for virtually all learning. Most students are successful at learning to read during the primary and elementary grades, and that success lays the foundation for the high-level reading comprehension that is expected of them during the middle- and high-school grades. Some students, and especially those with language and learning disabilities, experience frustration because reading is difficult and the meaning of the text message often eludes them. It is clear that failure to learn to read well can severely limit a student's capacity to obtain an education and enjoy the full benefits of life (Donahue, Voelkl, Campbell, & Mazzeo, 2002). Reading comprehension instruction needs to support the acquisition of strategies that will enhance students' understanding of text and independence as learners.

This chapter discusses several components of effective reading comprehension instruction. First, we discuss several definitions of reading comprehension and comprehension strategies instruction. Second, we review historical perspectives of reading comprehension. Third, we present recent insights about comprehension instruction. Fourth, we explore the results of two studies: one study focused on what teachers report they do when they teach reading comprehension, while the other focused on what classroom observations reveal about what exemplary teachers do during comprehension strategy instruction. Finally, we present recommendations for effective comprehension instruction.

READING COMPREHENSION AND COMPREHENSION STRATEGIES INSTRUCTION: DEFINITIONS

Reading comprehension is generally defined as the ability to acquire meaning from written text. Written text can take many forms, such as that found in traditional books, signs on the highway, the print on cereal boxes, and the print that appears on computer screens. During the process of reading comprehension, the reader interacts with the print and is involved in making meaning from the message.

Reading comprehension is an interactive process involving the reader, the text, and the context. Reading comprehension is acknowledged to be a highly interactive process. During the reading comprehension process the reader attends to the text-based information and relates to the text in terms of his or her own experiences. In other words, proficient readers use information from the text (print) and their background knowledge to make meaning from text. Reading comprehension is a fluid process. Sometimes, the text dominates with respect to meaning making, while other times the prior knowledge of the reader dominates.

In addition, the social context influences what one reads, how one reads, and why one reads. *What* a person reads may be influenced by the social context of the home or school environment. For example, in a classroom the text to be read might be assigned by the teacher, while at home the reader may choose a book by a favorite author to read for pleasure. Membership in social groups is another example of how context can influence what one reads. If the reader is a member of a chess club or a garden club, he or she will probably be drawn to books about that specific topic. *How* one reads is also affected by the context. If a reader is looking for information that he or she needs quickly, skimming the text might be the most appropriate approach. If the reader is reading for pleasure, deep and thoughtful reading would probably occur. *Why* one reads is also associated with the social context. Think of being in the grocery store—if you have made a shopping list you will probably read the list many times as you go down the various aisles of the store to make sure you have all the items on your list. If you are trying to figure out how to put together a toy, you may need to read the directions for assembly repeatedly. If you have free time on your hands, you may want to settle down with a good book for relaxation and pleasure. The social context in which reading occurs plays a significant role in determining how the reader comes to understand the message in the text (Almasi, 2003).

The characteristics of the text also influence reading comprehension. The reader's comprehension may be affected by the length of the text, the density of the concepts it presents, the number of difficult or unknown words in the text, the author's style of writing, and the text genre. These are only a few of the features of any text that can influence the reader's ability to comprehend its message.

Readers comprehend text by acquiring meaning, confirming meaning, and creating meaning. In sum, reading comprehension is the process of meaning making (Gambrell, Block, & Pressley, 2002). Children are taught to read via comprehension strategies so that they can better understand what is in a text (Pressley, 2000). Reading comprehension is usually a primary focus of instruction in the postprimary grades, after word recognition skills have been largely mastered, though comprehension of text should also be an integral part of reading instruction with beginning readers as well (RAND Reading Study Group, 2001).

There is clear research evidence that many students, and especially those with language and learning disabilities, have difficulty understanding what they read (Montgomery, 2002). There is also ample evidence that with appropriate comprehension strategy instruction students can make significant gains in their ability to understand and learn from text (Pressley, Johnson, Synmons, McGoldrick, & Kurita, 1990).

According to Paris, Wasik, and Turner (1991), there are five research-based reasons for teaching students to become strategic comprehenders:

1. Strategies enhance the reader's ability to elaborate, organize, and evaluate information contained in the text.
2. As students become more strategic readers, they learn strategies for enhancing attention, memory, communication, and learning.
3. Acquiring a larger repertoire of strategies enables students to be more independent in their own learning.
4. Strategic processing supports metacognitive development and motivation because students need both in order to become proficient at strategy implementation.
5. Strategy use helps students be more successful across all areas of the curriculum.

READING COMPREHENSION INSTRUCTION: A BRIEF HISTORY

Research on reading comprehension instruction is relatively new. Most authorities agree that Durkin's (1978–1979) classic study that revealed the lack of comprehension instruction in elementary classrooms heralded the advent of research on reading comprehension instruction. However, very early research viewed reading comprehension through the lens of assessment (Singer, 1970). In 1921, Gates administered a battery of tests to assess oral and silent reading (speed and comprehension), vocabulary knowledge, and intelligence in grades 3–8. He found that the results did not justify the conclusion that reading is a construct composed of a group of functions bound by some general factor. Furthermore, he found that there is a useful distinction between ability to comprehend and rate of reading. In McCullough's (1957) study of second graders, correlation of comprehension scores for tests of main ideas, details, sequence, and creative reading were low. Second graders could score high on one type of comprehension and low on another, and vice versa. In 1978–1979, Dolores Durkin published a landmark study on comprehension instruction in the upper elementary grades. Durkin, who observed reading lessons and focused particularly on comprehension instruction, found that very little reading comprehension *instruction* actually took place. Instead, she discovered that a great deal of comprehension *testing* (i.e., teachers asked students questions about what they had read after they had gone through a text) occurred under the guise of instruction (Durkin, 1978–1979).

Reading Comprehension Assessment

The history of reading comprehension assessment is short. In one of the first reading tests, Daniel Starch (1915) measured (1) comprehension of the material read, (2) speed of reading, and (3) correctness of pronunciation. Starch considered comprehension and speed to be the most important of the three elements. The first systematic attempts to index reading ability by measuring comprehension date back to World War I. Thorndike (1917) offered the first professional glimpse into the mind of the reader; he tried to characterize what must go on in the mind to produce the sorts of answers readers come up with in response to questions about what they have read.

During the 1970s, according to Sarroub and Pearson (1998), three important facets of reading comprehension assessment were used: (1) standardized multiple-choice tests, (2) criterion-referenced assessments of specific skills, and (3) informal classroom assessments of comprehension. Both the multiple-choice tests and the informal comprehension assessments had a long history in our schools, but criterion-referenced assessments were something new.

By the late 1980s, constructivist approaches to reading assessment included children's need to rely on resources, such as prior knowledge, environmental clues, the text itself, and the key players involved in the reading process. According to Sarroub and Pearson (1998), the most significant advances in classroom comprehension assessment tools during this period came from cognitive science. Reading comprehension tests began to include longer text passages, more challenging questions, and different question formats (such as multiple choice, with more than one right answer; open-ended questions; and response-to-literature formats). Retelling and think-alouds began to increase as ways to assess and measure comprehension.

In addition to witnessing changes made in test formats, the late 1980s and early 1990s saw performance assessments and portfolios become useful classroom tools. These classroom-based assessments were important for two reasons (Sarroub & Pearson, 1998): (1) students were to be evaluated on what they actually did in the classroom, and (2) both teachers and students could hold positions of power as they became key players in the evaluation process. The application of these new assessments did not always take root. Today, within the political arena, educators seem to be searching for a compromise position that preserves some of the features of the reforms of the late 1980s and early 1990s while acknowledging that those efforts may have gone too far (Sarroub & Pearson, 1998).

Overall, reading comprehension assessment has improved in two significant ways: in the nature of the reading tests themselves and in the variety of types of reading assessment (Barry, 1998). Reading assessment today emphasizes comprehension and gives test takers examples of "real" text (Barry, 1998). Educators now believe that assessment should serve a dual role: it should provide measurement of reading comprehension performance and it should improve the teaching and learning of reading comprehension. Getting to the fundamental processes of comprehension as they occur in the mind has remained a sort of "holy grail" for comprehension researchers throughout this century (Sarroub & Pearson, 1998).

Comprehension Strategies Instruction

Gaffney and Anderson (2000) conducted a historical review of the trends in reading research in the United States across three decades, 1966–1996. They found that the term "comprehension" peaked in references in the literature during the early 1980s. From about 1986 to 1996, the most frequently used term was "reading strategies," thus indicating the shift from general comprehension to an emphasis on comprehension instruction that included strategy instruction. Some of the influential studies reported during this period included the work on reciprocal teaching (predict, question, clarify, summarize) by Palincsar and Brown (1984), the work on direct explanation and modeling of comprehension strategies by Duffy (1997), and the work on transactional strategies instruction by Pressley and his colleagues (Pressley et al., 1992; see also Pressley & Hilden, Chapter 6, this volume).

Since research during the 1980s revealed the significant positive effects of teaching students to use specific comprehension strategies, researchers' attention has shifted to include a focus on combined comprehension strategy use. Research on comprehension strategies instruction conducted in actual classrooms (Palincsar & Brown, 1984; Paris & Oka, 1986) encouraged teachers to implement comprehension strategies instruction in their literacy curriculum. Researchers began to focus on the effects of combined comprehension strategies instruction, teaching students to use a variety of strategies. Evidence from verbal report studies (Pressley & Afflerbach, 1995) supports the notion that good readers use a variety of strategies, use different strategies for different kinds of reading tasks (e.g., use of imagery for vivid prose, rereading for difficult text), and are fluid in their use of strategies throughout the reading of a text. A number of studies on combined comprehension strategies instruction have revealed significant positive effects on measures related to reading comprehension for elementary-age students. Block (1993) found that combined strategies instruction increased reading comprehension, transfer, and critical and creative thinking. Dole, Brown, and Trathen (1996) compared combined strategies instruction, story content instruction, and a basal control, and found significant positive effects in favor of the strategies instruction group on reading comprehension. In a qualitative study, Baumann and Ivey (1997) investigated two approaches to reading instruction: immersion in literature and embedded (combined) strategies instruction. They reported significant positive effects for the combined strategy instruction group on children's reading and writing performance.

This brief history of reading comprehension reveals that, while much of the early research focused on how to assess reading comprehension, today's research emphasizes effective models of reading comprehension instruction. A number of recent national reading reports that have focused on effective reading instruction support the conclusion that effective reading comprehension is a highly complex and multifaceted endeavor.

NATIONAL READING REPORTS: INSIGHTS ABOUT COMPREHENSION INSTRUCTION

While reading comprehension has been a focal point in reading research for decades, several recent national reports have revealed insights about the process of reading comprehension as well as necessary reading comprehension skills. Three of these reports have been the focus of much discussion about effective comprehension instruction. These three reports are the National Assessment of Educational Progress (NAEP; Donahue et al., 2002), compiled by the National Center for Educational Statistics, the report of the National Reading Panel (NRP) (2000), and the report of the RAND Reading Study Group (2001).

National Assessment of Education Progress

The NAEP is the only nationally representative and continuing assessment of student achievement in specific subject areas in the United States. One of the subject areas assessed is reading. The Reading Framework for the NAEP (1992–1998) (Donahue et al., 2002) has two major goals: first, to reflect current educational and assessment practices, and second, to measure change in reading achievement reliably over time. Since 1969, NAEP has provided results for student achievement in grades 4, 8, and 12 on reading achievement, instructional experiences, and environment. The NAEP must administer reading and mathematics assessments for grades 4 and 8 every other year in all states. In addition, the NAEP must test these subjects on a nationally representative basis at grade 12 at least as often as it has done in the past, or every 4 years. The NAEP does not provide scores for individual student or school achievement. The most recent NAEP technical report was published by the U.S. Department of Education, Office of Educational Research and Improvement, in 2003. Table 5.1 offers findings from NAEP 1998.

National Reading Panel Report

The second report was issued by the NRP in 2000. In 1997, Congress asked the director of the National Institute of Child Health and Human Development to convene a national panel on reading. The NRP was asked to assess the status of research-based knowledge about reading, including the effectiveness of various approaches to teaching children to read. Many of the panel members were leading scientists in reading research, representatives of colleges of education, teachers, educational administrators, and parents. The NRP used three ways to gather information. First, they reviewed a variety of public databases to determine what research had already been conducted. Second, they gathered information from the public about their needs and understanding of reading research. Third, they consulted with leading edu-

---

TABLE 5.1 Major Findings from the NAEP 1998 Reading Assessment

---

- Overall average scale score results for the nation were mixed.
- Female students had higher average reading scores than male students.
- Student eligible for the free/reduced price lunch program had lower average scores than students not eligible for this program.
- Students who reported reading more pages daily in school and for homework had higher average scores than students who reported reading fewer pages.
- Students who reported more frequent writing of long answers on tests or assignments that involved reading had higher scores than students who reported less frequent writing.

---

cation organizations that had an interest in reading issues. The findings of the NRP were reported in *Teaching Children to Read*.

In carrying out its study of reading comprehension, the NRP noted three main themes in the research on the development of reading comprehension skills. First, reading comprehension is a complex cognitive process that cannot be understood without a clear description of the role that vocabulary development and vocabulary instruction play in the understanding of what has been read. Second, comprehension is an active process that requires an intentional and thoughtful interaction between the reader and the text (i.e., text comprehension instruction). Third, the preparation of teachers to better equip students to develop and apply reading comprehension strategies to enhance understanding is intimately linked to students' achievement in this area.

RAND Reading Study Group Report

The third, and most recent report, was published by the RAND Reading Study Group in 2001. RAND is a contraction of the term "research and development." Created in 1946, RAND was the first organization in the United States to be referred to as a "think tank." RAND's work is diverse, but focuses on social and international issues. It is a nonprofit institution that helps improve policy and decision making through research and analysis. RAND has studied such topics as K–12 assessment and accountability, school reform evaluation, teachers and teaching, and challenges in higher education. In 2001, the RAND Reading Study Group published *Reading for Understanding: Toward an R&D Program in Reading Comprehension* as a technical report for the Office of Educational Research and Improvement.

There are common themes across the reports issued by the NAEP, the NRP, and the RAND Reading Study Group about what constitutes effective reading instruction. Perhaps the most predominant theme is an appreciation that reading comprehension is a complex cognitive process that requires intentional and thoughtful interaction between the reader and the text. Taken together, the NAEP, the NRP, and the RAND Reading Study Group reports focus on six characteristics of good readers that distinguish them from less-proficient readers.

These six characteristics of good readers are directly related to and contribute to effective comprehension (See Table 5.2.). In addition, the NRP emphasized that research on reading comprehension indicates that vocabulary development and vocabulary instruction play an important role in understanding what has been read. The NRP also noted that the preparation of teachers to better equip students to develop and apply reading comprehension strategies to enhance understanding is linked to students' reading achievement.

TABLE 5.2. Characteristics of Good Readers

Good readers . . .

- Have positive habits and attitudes about reading.
- Are fluent enough to focus on understanding what they read.
- Use their world knowledge to understand what they read.
- Develop an understanding of what they read by extending, elaborating, and evaluating the meaning of the text.
- Use a variety of effective strategies to enhance and monitor their understanding of text.
- Can read a variety of texts and can read for a variety of purposes.

Across these three reports (NAEP, NRP, RAND), a number of features that are key to skilled reading comprehension emerged: vocabulary, world knowledge, motivation, purposes and goals, cognitive/metacognitive strategies, linguistic knowledge, discourse knowledge, and fluency. These areas and their relationship to reading comprehension are briefly reviewed next.

COMPONENTS OF SKILLED READING COMPREHENSION

Vocabulary

The importance of vocabulary knowledge has long been recognized in the development of reading skills. As early as 1925, researchers noted that growth in reading power means continuous growth in word knowledge (Whipple, 1925). The larger the reader's vocabulary (oral or print), the easier it is for him or her to make sense of the text. The NRP (2000) reported findings from studies on vocabulary with specific implications for teaching reading:

- Vocabulary should be taught both directly and indirectly.
- Repetition and multiple exposures to vocabulary items are important.
- Learning in rich contexts, incidental learning, and use of computer technology all enhance the acquisition of vocabulary.
- Direct instruction should include task restructuring as necessary and should actively engage the student.
- Dependence on a single vocabulary instruction method will not result in optimal learning.

The RAND Reading Study Group (2001) report refers to vocabulary as knowledge of word meanings. Analyses of vocabulary instruction show that explicit vocabulary instruction produces gains in comprehension.

Current practice deemphasizes vocabulary instruction, in part because traditional, definition-based approaches to vocabulary instruction are not very effective, either for increasing vocabulary or for improving reading comprehension (RAND Reading Study Group, 2001).

World Knowledge

Research suggests that text comprehension is enhanced when readers actively relate the ideas represented in print to their own knowledge and experiences and construct mental representation in memory (National Reading Panel, 2000). World knowledge comes from experience and from texts previously read. Researchers have found that most children from middle-class families enter school with more world knowledge about school-related topics than do most children from poor families (RAND Reading Study Group, 2001).

Motivation

According to the RAND Reading Study Group (2001) report, *motivation* is defined as encompassing intrinsic motivation, extrinsic motivation, self-efficacy, social goals, and experience with reading. Because reading is an effortful activity that involves choice, motivation is fundamentally important to reading comprehension. Most children initially are positively motivated toward reading. Unfortunately, many lose their motivation as they go through school. As Paris and Oka (1986), have emphasized, it is imperative that our students develop the skill and the will to read.

Purposes and Goals

Students who are expert readers are purposeful. They have specific goals for reading, such as gaining knowledge, enjoying literature, locating specific information, and learning from text in order to solve problems (RAND Reading Study Group, 2001). Skilled readers appear to view reading as a meaning-getting process. Less-skilled readers appear to be more content to decode a text, with little regard for meaning (Rubman & Waters, 2000). Students with clear goals are better comprehenders than students with vague goals (RAND Reading Study Group, 2001).

Cognitive/Metacognitive Strategies

The NRP found that comprehension strategies instruction enhanced comprehension. The NRP identified a number of strategies that positively affect the comprehension of text. Teaching students to use a small repertoire of research-based strategies independently was given a strong endorsement by the panel. *Strategies* are processes and procedures that readers use in comprehending text (RAND Reading Study Group, 2001). Although there is little knowledge available about the prerequisites for effective strategy instruction (RAND Reading Study Group, 2001), the NRP identified seven instructional strategies that have a solid scientific basis:

1. *Comprehension monitoring*, where readers learn how to be aware of their understanding of the material.
2. *Cooperative learning*, where students learn reading strategies together.
3. *Use of graphic and semantic organizers* (including story maps), where readers make graphic representations of the material to assist comprehension.
4. *Question answering*, where readers answer questions posed by the teacher and receive immediate feedback.
5. *Question generation*, where readers ask themselves questions about various aspects of the story.
6. *Story structure*, where students are taught to use the structure of the story as a means of helping them recall story content in order to answer questions about what they have read.
7. *Summarization*, where readers are taught to integrate ideas and generalize from the text information.

In general, the evidence suggests that teaching a combination of reading comprehension techniques is the most effective method. Significant differences have been found between good and poor readers and between younger and older readers in the effective use of overall comprehension monitoring strategies (Paris et al., 1991).

Linguistic Knowledge

Linguistic knowledge encompasses oral language capacities, both production and comprehension, and the capacity to reflect on one's knowledge of language. Successful reading depends on extensive knowledge at all linguistic levels: phonology, morphology, and syntax, as well as higher level discourse structures (RAND Reading Study Group, 2001).

Discourse Knowledge

Expert readers use discourse knowledge to connect text elements in a coherent fashion and to relate the content to the messages of the author. Discourse knowledge includes the structure of different text genres, the distinction between given and new information in the discourse context, the points that the author intends to convey, the topic structure, the pragmatic goals/plans of the communicative exchange, and the function of speech acts (RAND Reading Study Group, 2001).

Fluency

Fluency is defined as effortless reading with ease and expression. Fluency includes accuracy and automaticity of word identification, ease in decoding, and expressiveness in reading connected text. Several instructional methods have been shown to be effective in improving reading fluency. One method is repeated reading, where a single text is reread several times. A second method is guided oral reading with feedback (RAND Reading Study Group, 2001). Research also suggests that rereading is a useful strategy for increasing fluency (Bossert & Schwantes, 1995–1996) (For further discussions, see Troia, Chapter 4, this volume.)

The NAEP, the NRP, and the RAND Reading Study Group converge in their findings and recommendations with respect to the characteristics of good readers and the key features of skilled reading comprehension. Current research suggests that reading strategies instruction promotes comprehension and the extraction of meanings from text, and that successful instruction depends on a teacher's understanding of the components of skilled reading and strategic reading behaviors.

WHAT DO TEACHERS DO WHEN THEY TEACH READING COMPREHENSION?

Good teaching matters for all students, and particularly for those students who have language and learning disabilities. A number of recent studies indicate that student's reading proficiency rests largely on the ability of the classroom teacher to provide expert, exemplary reading instruction (Block & Mangieri, 2003; Allington & Johnson, 2001; Darling-Hammond, 1999; Pressley, 2000; Sanders, 1998). These studies suggest that effective teachers produce better achievement regardless of which instructional materials, pedagogical approach, or reading program they use. To assure reading achievement for all children, teachers must use research-based strategies and best practices (Allington, 2002). Clearly, a child's preparedness to handle the task of reading comprehension is shaped by home, school, and personal life experiences, as well as by the teacher's ability to provide high-quality reading comprehension instruction (Ivey, 2002, 2003; Pressley, 2001).

In the following sections, we describe two studies that explore exemplary comprehension instruction in elementary classrooms: a questionnaire study and an observational study. The questionnaire study was conducted with teachers to determine what they consider to be effective reading comprehension instruction and what comprehension strategies they teach their students. Then we move to an observational study on exemplary reading instruction (Morrow, Tracey, Woo, & Pressley, 1999). Exemplary classroom teachers identified by administrators, peers, parents, and students were selected to participate in the study. In addition, the students in these rooms scored well on tests of comprehension over a 5-year period. The observations were conducted to explore what exemplary comprehension practice looked like in elementary classrooms. Specifically, we wanted to know what practicing teachers did when they taught reading comprehension.

WHAT TEACHERS REPORT THEY DO DURING COMPREHENSION STRATEGY INSTRUCTION

In our questionnaire study, 25 teachers enrolled in a graduate program to obtain a master's degree as a reading specialist filled out a questionnaire to determine their knowledge and beliefs about comprehension instruction. When readers comprehend text, strategies are the processes and procedures they use (RAND Reading Study Group, 2001). The teachers were asked to respond to three questions:

1. Describe the most effective comprehension lesson you have taught in the last couple of months.
2. What comprehension strategies do you think are the most important to use in order to teach children how to comprehend text?
3. What comprehension strategies have you taught during the last 3 weeks?

When teachers responded to the question about "the most effective comprehension lesson you have taught in the last couple of months," lessons were described with 10 features:

- Shared reading in a Directed Reading and Thinking Format
- Discussion involving comparing and contrasting
- Story retelling after reading a story
- Drawing illustrations to reflect the meaning of the text
- Use of a Venn diagram to see relationships
- Use of a story web for building vocabulary about the text
- Dramatizations after reading
- Repeated reading to gain further insight

- Providing background information before reading
- Discussion after reading

The responses of these teachers suggested that they are well aware of the features of a good comprehension strategy instruction lesson and they were all able to describe a "most effective reading comprehension lesson" they had conducted with their students.

When teachers were asked the question, "What comprehension strategies do you think are the most important to use in order to teach children how to comprehend text?," they responded with seven strategies:

- Ask children to make predictions.
- Ask children to retell text in sequence.
- Ask children to compare and contrast ideas in the text.
- Ask children to use visual imagery.
- Build vocabulary.
- Ask children to make inferences.
- Build on informational background knowledge.

What is especially interesting here is that the responses to this question were more focused. Several of these strategies map on to the comprehension strategies that were identified by the National Reading Panel (2000) as being supported by research: use of graphic and semantic organizers, story structure (retelling), summarization (retelling), and question answering (predicting, comparing and contrasting, making inferences). The teachers appeared to respond to this question in terms of specific instructional strategies, while the RAND (RAND Reading Study Group, 2001) report listed more general instructional strategies such as comprehension monitoring and cooperative learning.

Teachers responded to the question about what comprehension strategies they have taught during the last 3 weeks with the following answers:

- Questioning students
- Asking students to summarize the text
- Having students retell the story in sequence, including story structure elements
- Having students look at differences between fact and fiction
- Asking students to compare and contrast
- Asking students to make predictions
- Building background knowledge
- Repeated readings
- Asking students to make visual images
- Asking students to make inferences

All the teachers were able to describe in detail reading comprehension lessons that they had recently taught. Again, these lessons appeared to focus on specific strategies and techniques that support independent strategy use. The teachers specifically identified two additional strategies identified by the RAND Reading Study Group (2001) as being research based: question answering and summarizing.

As mentioned earlier, the teachers who responded to this questionnaire were experienced and also pursuing graduate study in the field of reading. There is clearly much overlap in their responses. They selected a group of strategies that both check comprehension and provide students with independent skills to help them comprehend on their own. They are very much aware of some of the strategies that were discussed by the National Reading Panel (2000) and the RAND Reading Study Group (2001). In summary, the teachers mentioned three types of strategy instruction:

- Building background knowledge
- Teaching vocabulary
- Teaching multiple strategies for independent comprehending such as: predicting, mapping, and webbing, using a Venn diagram to illustrate relationships, making inferences, using visual imagery, retelling, repeated reading, comparing and contrasting

While the RAND Reading Study Group (2001) and the National Reading Panel (2000) both emphasize the importance of comprehension monitoring, the teachers who responded to our questionnaire did not specifically report lessons designed for helping student to self-evaluate and monitor their comprehension. Furthermore, teachers did not make any reference to supporting students in developing the ability to generate their own questions.

CLASSROOM OBSERVATIONS ABOUT WHAT EXEMPLARY TEACHERS DO DURING COMPREHENSION STRATEGY INSTRUCTION

As part of a study on literacy instruction, classroom teachers were identified as exemplary by administrators, peers, parents, and students. These exemplary teachers were invited to participate in the study. In addition, the students in these classrooms scored well on tests of comprehension over a 5-year period. The teachers were observed to see what exemplary comprehension practice looked and sounded like in their classrooms.

The comprehension instruction we observed took place in highly successful classrooms. In brief, these classrooms exuded positive climates characterized by unusually high levels of student engagement, motivation, time on task, and self-regulation, and usually low levels of classroom management problems. Additionally, the classrooms had exceptionally rich literacy environments. These classroom environments were created deliberately and thoughtfully by master teachers with many years of teaching experience, a high degree of graduate level training, and clear values and beliefs about literacy learning. It is from within these powerful classroom communities that the two scenarios depicting the ways in which exemplary teachers foster reading comprehension were selected (Morrow et al., 1999).

Comprehension and Vocabulary Instruction in Ms. Linda Keefe's First-Grade Classroom

Ms. Keefe turns the class's attention to two pieces of literature, one of which was read the previous day, "First Woman and the Strawberry," and one of which they would read that day, "The First Strawberry: A Cherokee Story." Ms. Keefe addresses the students: "Yesterday we read the story, 'First Woman and the Strawberry.' Who can tell me what it was about?" After the children have responded, Ms. Keefe asks one of them to place a marker on the classroom map showing the southwest region of the country. This is where both stories took place.

Ms. Keefe prints the word *strawberry* vertically on a fresh piece of chart paper and says to the students, "Let's think a little bit about strawberries before we start our new story. We know this spells "*strawberry*," right? I'd like you to tell me some describing words for the word *strawberry* using its letters." The children begin with the word *sweet* and then add *tasty*, *red*, *amazing*, and so on. Ms. Keefe prints the words that the students generate.

Ms. Keefe says, "As I read the story I want you to remember the setting, theme, plot episodes, and resolution of the story. When I finish reading I will use a story map for us to plot out the story elements I just mentioned to help you organize these in your mind."

Ms. Keefe then reads a section of the new piece of literature to the students. She stops periodically to discuss key ideas and important vocabulary words with the students. She asks questions to link the content of the story with the children's own backgrounds.

At the conclusion of the brief oral reading, Ms. Keefe drew the map or graphic organizer on a sheet of chart paper, printing the title of one book at the top. The students were familiar with the task and began naming the story elements and the part of the story that fit with the element. When they needed help, Ms. Keefe prompted the students with questions, such as asking what was the goal of the main character, and what was her problem, and how was the problem solved.

Comprehension Instruction in Ms. Veronica Gebesi's Fourth-Grade Classroom

Ms. Gebesi begins her lesson by orienting the students to the specific language arts literacy standards which their work will address that day:

> "Good afternoon, boys and girls. Today we're going to take a look at our objective: students will be able to analyze characters' traits, compare characters, and understand characters' point of view in a fantasy tale. This work coincides with New Jersey State Standards for the Language Arts, Literacy Standards 3.1, 3.3, and 3.4.
>
> "We have already read the story "Mufaro's Beautiful Daughters" and there were two main characters in the story, Manyara and Nyasha. What I want to do today is to take a look at their character traits, their personalities, the way they behave, and the way they act. We're going to find out about the characters' feelings—how the characters felt at different points in the story. We're going to find out about the characters' motives—why the characters behaved as they did."

Ms. Gebesi takes out a piece of chart paper with the characters' names underlined, points to Manyara's name, and continues: "Raise your hand if you can tell me a little bit about Manyara. What type of person was she?" Jamal raises his hand and answers, " She was selfish." "Yes, good, selfish," Ms. Gebesi responds and then asks, "At what point of the story was she selfish?" After the students reply, she continues, "What was another of Manyara's characteristics?" A student replies, "Impatient." Again, Ms. Gebesi praises the student, and then asks when Manyara was impatient. The activity continues until several characteristics have been generated for both Manyara and Nyasha.

After separate lists of personality traits have been created for both Manyara and Nyasha, Ms. Gebesi turns to a new page of chart paper containing a Venn diagram. "OK, we have some character traits of each character. Let's take a look at both of them together. Let's take a look at our Venn diagram. Were they the same in any way?" The students respond that both of the daughters were beautiful and both were excited. As the students continue, Ms. Gebesi completes the Venn diagram, filling in the personality traits that the characters shared in the overlapping section of the diagram and filling in the unique traits of each character in the nonintersecting sections. As each defining characteristic is added to the diagram, she discusses with the class the ways in which the personality trait was shared, or not shared, by the characters.

Ms. Gebesi then turns to a third piece of chart paper and tells the class that they will now be working on their story starters. She reviews a previous assignment that part of the class had already completed in which the students had assumed the character role of either Manyara or Nyasha. Ms. Gebesi continues:

> "Some of you wrote very good story beginnings with this story starter, *My name is (Manyara or Nyasha). Some people feel that I am* _____, _____, *and* _____. *I am this way because* _____. Some of you are going to continue to work with this story starter and some of you are going to work on our second story starter, the part when the story is over, the part that we didn't see, the part that we're going to imagine."

Ms. Gebesi points to the second starter on the chart paper and reads, "After the wedding I felt. . . ." She then questions the class: "Who's going to write from Manyara's point of view?" Students raise their hands. "What did Manyara think and feel at the end of the story? Remember, she didn't get the prize. She wasn't the queen. Who's going to write from Nyasha's point of view?" The remainder of the students raise their hands. "How did she feel after the wedding?" Ms. Gebesi then assigns students to one of three groups for writing workshop: one group still needs to finish the beginning of their stories using the first story starter. The second group has finished the beginning of their stories but needs to elaborate their Venn diagrams. The third group has finished both their story beginnings and their Venn diagrams and are ready to write the next portion of their story.

Ms. Gebesi circulates through the class as the children work on their writing tasks. She stops to respond to students' individual needs and to praise their efforts. The students write for approximately 15 minutes. At the conclusion of the writing workshop the class moves to the rug to hear three students read their stories. Clapping is heard after each child reads.

Analysis of the Classroom Observations

The analysis of the observations of these classrooms revealed that these teachers had clear and specific goals to enhance students' reading comprehension. They were aware of the importance of building vocabulary and background knowledge to aid in comprehension. They both use questioning and summarizing as part of their interactions with the students. Graphic organizers were used to clearly illustrate the elements emphasized in the lesson. These graphic organizers teach comprehension and are independent strategies for students to use when trying to comprehend on their own (see Singer & Bashir, Chapter 9, this volume, for further discussion of graphic organizers). The lessons are all about meaning and making meaning based on the text and what children know from their own experiences. The instruction provided by these teachers was direct but within a motivating environment. The children were frequently asked to evaluate and reflect upon their thoughts and ideas. Clearly, the portraits of these two classrooms illustrate how effective teachers provide exemplary comprehension strategy instruction for their students.

CONCLUSION: RECOMMENDATIONS FOR EFFECTIVE COMPREHENSION STRATEGIES INSTRUCTION

In making recommendations for effective comprehension instruction for all students, and particularly those with language and learning disabilities, we believe that the work on comprehension strategies instruction and the work on effective teaching has much to offer (Pressley & El-Dinary, 1997). We offer five recommendations for implementing effective comprehension strategies instruction.

First, effective comprehension strategies instruction is not easy. It requires a long-term commitment. Comprehension strategies instruction needs to occur over the course of months and years rather than over a number of lessons. Second, effective comprehension strategies instruction for students, particularly those with language and learning disabilities, at a minimum will require much direct explanation and modeling of strategy use, as well as scaffolded student practice. Third, comprehension strategies instruction must be conducted in concert with decoding and other skills instruction. Fourth, comprehension strategies instruction needs to occur across the curriculum. Fifth, according to Pressley and El-Dinary (1997), comprehension strategies instruction requires giving up some teacher control because the goal is to produce independent, self-regulated readers.

In closing we offer an insightful perspective from Villaume and Brabham (2002) about the importance of comprehension strategies instruction:

> We do not want to teach comprehension strategies because it is in vogue or even because it is what the research says to do. We want to teach these strategies because we have a great desire to share with our students the empowering potential of reading experiences. We know that the only way students can tap into this potential is to develop strategies that allow them to become actively and intensely involved in their reading. Through strategic reading, students gain access to the rights, responsibilities and benefits afforded to skillful readers (pp. 672–673)

REFERENCES

Allington, R. L. (2002, June). What I've learned about effective reading instruction from a decade of studying exemplary elementary classroom teachers. *Phi Delta Kappan*, pp. 740–747.

Allington, R. L., & Johnson, P. H. (2001). What do we know about effective fourth-grade teachers and their classrooms? In C. Roller (Ed.), *Learning to teach read-*

ing: Setting the research agenda (pp. 150–165). Newark: International Reading Association.

Almasi, J. F. (2003). *Teaching strategic processes in reading.* New York: Guilford Press.

Barry, A. L. (1998). The evolution of reading tests and other forms of educational assessment. *The Clearing House, 71,* 231–236.

Baumann, J. F., & Ivey, G. (1997). Delicate balances: Striving for curricular and instructional equilibrium in a second grade, literature/strategy based classroom. *Reading Research Quarterly, 32*(3), 244–275.

Block, C. C. (1993). Strategy instruction in a literature-based reading program. *Elementary School Journal, 94,* 139–151.

Block, C. C., & Mangieri, J. N. (2003). *Exemplary literacy teachers: Promoting success for all children in grades K–5.* New York: Guilford Press.

Bossert, T. S., & Schwantes, F. M. (1995–1996). Children's comprehension monitoring: Training children to use rereading to aid comprehension. *Reading Research and Instruction, 35,* 109–121.

Darling-Hammond, L. (1999). *Teacher quality and student achievement: A review of state policy evidence.* Seattle: University of Washington, Center for Teaching Policy.

Dole, J. A., Brown, K. J., & Trathen, W. (1996). The effects of strategy instruction on the comprehension performance of at-risk students. *Reading Research Quarterly, 31,* 62–88.

Donahue, P. L., Voelkl, K. E., Campbell, J. R., & Mazzeo, J. (2002). *Reading framework for the National Assessment of Educational Progress, 1992–1998.* Technical report for the U.S. Department of Education, Office of Educational Research and Improvement. Washington, DC: National Center for Education Statistics.

Duffy, G. G. (1997). Powerful models or powerful teachers?: An argument for teacher-as-entrepreneur. In S. Stahl & D. Hayes (Eds.), *Instructional models in reading* (pp. 331–365). Mahwah, NJ: Erlbaum.

Durkin, D. (1978–1979). What classroom observations reveal about reading comprehension instruction. *Reading Research Quarterly, 16,* 515–544.

Gaffney, J. S., & Anderson, R. C. (2000). Trends in reading research in the United States: Changing intellectual currents over three decades. In M. Kamil, P. Mosenthal, P. D. Pearson, & R. Barr (Eds.), *Handbook of reading research* (Vol. 3, pp. 53–77). Mahwah, NJ: Erlbaum.

Gambrell, L. B., Block, C. C., & Pressley, M. (2002). Improving comprehension instruction: An urgent priority. In C. Collins, L. B. Gambrell, & M. Pressley (Eds.), *Improving comprehension instruction: Rethinking research, theory, and classroom practice* (pp. 3–16). San Francisco: Jossey-Bass.

Gates, A. I. (1921). An experimental and statistical study of reading and reading tests. *Journal of Educational Psychology, 12,* 303–314, 378–391, 445–464.

Ivey, G. (2002). Getting started: Manageable literacy practices. *Educational Leadership, 60*(3), 20–23.

Ivey, G. (2003). The teacher makes it more explainable and other reasons to read aloud in the intermediate grades. *Reading Teacher, 56*(8), 812–814.

McCullough, C. M. (1957). Responses of elementary school children to common types of reading comprehension questions. *Journal of Educational Research, 51,* 65–70.

Montgomery, J. W. (2002). Information processing and language comprehension in children with specific language impairment. *Topics in Language Disorders, 22*(3), 62–84.

Morrow, L. M., Tracey, D. H., Woo, P. G., & Pressley, G. M. (1999). Characteristics of exemplary first-grade literacy instruction. *The Reading Teacher, 52,* 462–476.

National Reading Panel. (2000). *Teaching children to read: An evidence-based assessment of the scientific research literature on reading and its implications for reading instruction.* Washington, DC: National Institute of Child Health and Human Development.

Palincsar, A. S., & Brown, A. L. (1984). Reciprocal teaching of comprehension fostering and monitoring activities. *Cognition and Instruction, 1,* 117–175.

Paris, S. G., & Oka, E. R. (1986). Children's reading strategies, metacognition, and motivation. *Developmental Review, 6,* 25–56.

Paris, S. G., Wasik, B. A., & Turner, J. C. (1991). The development of strategic readers. In R. Barr, M. L. Kamil, P. B. Mosenthal, & P. D. Pearson (Eds.), *Handbook of reading research* (Vol. 2, pp. 815–860). New York: Longman.

Pressley, M. (2000). What should comprehension instruction be the instruction of? In M. Kamil, P. Mosenthal, P. D. Pearson, & R. Barr (Eds.), *Handbook of reading research* (Vol. 3, pp. 545–561). Mahwah, NJ: Erlbaum.

Pressley, M. (2001). Comprehension instruction: What makes sense now, what might make sense soon. *Reading Online, 5*(2).

Pressley, M., & Afflerbach, P. (1995). *Verbal protocols of reading: The nature of constructively responsive reading.* Hillsdale, NJ: Erlbaum.

Pressley, M., & El-Dinary, P. (1997). What we know about translating comprehension-strategies instruction research into practice. *Journal of Learning Disabilities, 30*(5), 486–488, 512.

Pressley, M., El-Dinary, P. B., Gaskins, I., Schuder, T., German, J., Almasi, J., & Brown, R. (1992). Beyond direct explanation: Transactional instruction of reading comprehension strategies. *The Elementary School Journal, 92,* 511–554.

Pressley, M., Johnson, C. J., Synmons, S., McGoldrick, J. A., & Kurita, J. (1990). Strategies that improve children's memory and comprehension of text. *The Elementary School Journal, 90,* 3–32.

RAND Reading Study Group. (2001). *Reading for understanding: Toward an R&D program in reading comprehension* (Technical report for the Office of Educational Research and Improvement). Washington, DC: Author.

Rubman, C. N., & Waters, H. S. (2000). A, B seeing: The role of constructive processes in children's comprehension monitoring. *Journal of Educational Psychology, 92,* 503–514.

Sanders, W. L. (1998). Value-added assessment. *School Administrator, 55,* 101–113.

Sarroub, L., & Pearson, P. D. (1998). Two steps forward, three steps back: The stormy history of reading comprehension assessment. *The Clearing House, 72,* 97–106.

Singer, H. (1970). Research that should have made a difference. *Elementary English, 41,* 27–34.

Starch, D. (1915). The measurement of efficiency in reading. *Journal of Educational Psychology, 6,* 1–24.

Thorndike, E. L. (1917). Reading as reasoning: A study of mistakes in paragraph reading. *Journal of Educational Psychology, 8,* 323–332.

Villaume, S. K., & Brabham, E. G. (2002). Comprehension instruction: Beyond strategies. *The Reading Teacher, 55*(7), 672–675.

Whipple, G. M. (1925). *The twenty-fourth yearbook of the National Society for the Study of Education: Part I.* Bloomington, IL: Public School Publishing Company.

6

Toward More Ambitious Comprehension Instruction

MICHAEL PRESSLEY
KATHERINE HILDEN

Recently, we were involved with a school attempting to increase its students' reading comprehension. As external experts in the process, we came to a fortunate situation. The principal had done extensive reading about effective comprehension instruction, as had the language arts coordinator. One teacher had read deeply on the topic and had reformed her own teaching to make it more consistent with comprehension strategies instruction as depicted in the literature (e.g., Keene & Zimmermann, 1997). Several other teachers were committed to mastering comprehension instruction. These teachers, working with the principal and us to pilot changes in instruction, hoped to share the new system with the entire school if it proved to be successful.

Another positive was that the school is in an excellent school district, one located in a university town in a state that takes pride in the fact that its schools produce high achievement. This is one of those school districts that is always looking toward the cutting edge, always motivating its instructional leaders to be thinking about what is required to maximize reading achievement in the district. The school's principal is well respected in the district, as is its language arts director. As such, they have been instrumental in working with the distict's elementary language arts director, who has state-of-the-science knowledge of comprehension instruction. In short, the school is in a context that is strongly supportive of efforts to improve reading comprehension, with that support extending from the state department of instruction, to the school district's central offices, to the principal's office.

Something that was very notable to us, as we worked in the school, is that our efforts were not just supported by the school district's infrastructure but also informed the district somewhat. During our consultation with the school, the district was in the midst of a basal adoption decision process. Various players in the district who were interested in assuring that the new adoption maximally supported comprehension development in students looked to us for input to their thinking. Our ideas, even ideas sometimes offered on the run, entered district conversations as the decision-making process took place. In the end, the quality of support for comprehension instruction was a key determinant of the district's adoption decision, which increased our confidence that our work with this particular school might go easier in subsequent years because there would likely be greater materials support the following year and beyond for teaching students how to process texts so as to maximize their understanding of what they read.

As we worked in this school, we were struck by the idea that despite the strong support we had from a number of teachers, there would be many others who would have to be brought onboard, all of whom would have to learn a great deal and become committed to substantial change. First, there were the teachers in the school who were not part of the pilot project this year, that is, those teachers who were not so enthusiastic about comprehension instruction that they volunteered to be in the first round. Fortunately, many of these teachers decided to come onboard the following year after they saw the success of the pilot project. However, some other teachers were still very reluctant about changing their current ways of teaching; their feelings ranged from indifference to feeling threatened. Also, there were Chapter 1 and special education teachers who could either do pull-out instruction or be incorporated into the classroom as assistants to classroom teachers. There were speech–language specialists, who, in this school, worked only with students who had severe speech and language difficulties, and who only occasionally touched on students' reading comprehension. And there were parent volunteers as well as the many parents who do not volunteer at school but who do work with their children at home. In short, there was really a village of folks who could be interacting in a curriculum reform effort, such as increasing comprehension instruction in the school.

SOURCES OF SUPPORT

Distal Supporters

The distal participants in the process included state department of education officials who support high comprehension as a goal and state-of-the-science comprehension instruction as the means of achieving that goal (e.g., in contrast to a philosophy that if children simply read a great deal, they will learn how to comprehend). Publishers were distal participants as well. Their representatives, who visited the state, the school districts, and individual schools increased local understanding about how a published product can make a difference in a school's efforts to improve—in this case, with respect to comprehension instruction. We were lucky that current market pressures had stimulated publishers to include much more information about comprehension instruction in their manuals. This, in part, reflected another distal influence, the federal government, informed by the National Reading Panel (2000), which exerted various pressures into the system to increase comprehension instruction. Previous federal administrations have had no understanding that comprehension instruction matters; not so long ago, there was little to no information in publisher's manuals about how to increase comprehension skills in children.

The Principal

A prime mover in the village, however, was the local principal. Although she interacted with the district, both affecting district policies and selecting relevant district resources for the school, the principal's most obvious role was impacting the teachers in her school. She highlighted the accomplishments of teachers who bought into the reform. The principal reflected about how a reform such as comprehension instruction could do the most good in every classroom in the building (i.e., from one headed by a teacher too shy to do the direct instruction and modeling demanded by comprehension instruction to another who boldly asserted that the methods she has used for years continue to be good enough).

Classroom Teachers

The teachers, in turn, were the main contact points for most students with respect to comprehension instruction, although the classroom teachers also needed to work with resource teachers (i.e., special education teachers and aides, speech–language professionals) to coordinate what is happening in the classroom with what occurs during one-on-one work with the special service providers. It helps if the principal has worked hard to fold the resource personnel into the curriculum reforms, including making certain that they participate in workshops and professional development activities that promote understanding about how to deliver excellent comprehension instruction. The teachers were also the main point of contact with parents to encourage their support of instruction occurring in the classroom.

Special Education Resource Teachers

We have to admit that we really had little insight about how to work with other professionals in the school to stimulate teaching of comprehension in school. The easiest group to work with was the special education resource teachers, for special educators often know more about comprehension instruction than do regular education teachers. In fact, the most extensive deployment of state-of-the-science comprehension instruction is in special education, because of the work of Donald Deshler and his associates (e.g., Deshler, Ellis, & Lenz, 1996). Deshler's network now includes more than 100,000 special educators who have been educated about how to teach cognitive strategies, with comprehension strategies one of the more prominent strategies in the Deshler quiver. (Deshler's work had definitely impacted the school described earlier in this chapter.) The challenge is to figure out how to mesh the special educators with the comprehension instruction going on in the regular classrooms. We sensed that the principal and regular teachers would like to see the special education teachers working in the regular classroom, targeting the neediest students. We did not know quite how to make certain that meshing of special education and regular education would be best encouraged.

Speech–Language Professionals

We were even less certain about how to work with other adults who come in contact with the students. While it is clear that speech–language professionals generally have an excellent background in the psychological foundations of the instructional approaches we favor (i.e., they are familiar with information-processing theory), they typically have not been asked to teach comprehension skills and strategies to students. We continue to seek ways to work with these speech–language specialists, since they are as yet a valuable but untapped resource, at least in the schools where we have consulted.

Parents

Then there are the parents. Parents differ in so many ways. They are as diverse as the middle-American town where the school is located. As this chapter was being written, we were completely beside ourselves about how to teach the teachers to work with the parents to reinforce the comprehension instruction occurring in the classroom.

Rather than close on such a pessimistic point, we emphasized that the principal in the building and the administrators in the district really did have a good understanding of comprehension instruction and how it could be accomplished. Yes, they were still learning, which was one of the reasons we were working with the school. But these administrators were wonderfully open to our input, ready for it largely because they had already been working on encouraging comprehension in the district for a few years. The current effort was meant to ratchet up a direction that seemed more and more attractive to these educators with every additional encounter. We felt lucky to be working with these individuals because, in the past, we have encountered many district-level staff and principals who know nothing about comprehension instruction and do not even realize that comprehension skills in students are most likely to develop only when students are taught strategies.

Without a doubt, the most prominent instructional element to promote comprehension skills is comprehension strategies instruction. Hence, more attention will be given to this element of instruction than others in this chapter. That said, we foreshadow the chapter's concluding section by pointing out here that comprehension strategies instruction is just one element among many that should be included in comprehension teaching at every grade level and across grade levels.

COMPREHENSION STRATEGIES INSTRUCTION

When Pressley (1976) first began studying comprehension in the mid-1970s, few others were interested in the topic. There was little teaching of comprehension skills in school (Durkin, 1978–1979). Instead, there was a great deal of testing of comprehension—usually in the form of questions following a reading, either questions delivered orally by the teacher (Mehan, 1979) or printed at the end of a text as comprehension checks (e.g., Rothkopf, 1966). The assumption seemed to be that the demand *to comprehend* would somehow lead readers to discover *how to comprehend*.

A great deal happened in the concluding quarter of the 20th century that dramatically increased the options available to educators who wanted to increase student learning from text. This was an arena where theoretical advances certainly stimulated applied research that could be translated into realistic classroom instruction. (See also Whitaker, Gambrell, & Morrow, Chapter 5, this volume.) In particular, cognitive psychologists proposed and studied many ways that humans can represent texts (Adams, Treiman, & Pressley, 1998): the mature mind processes the many small ideas in text but manages to condense across these ideas to retain the gist (e.g., van Dijk & Kintsch, 1983). When reading narratives, good readers especially seem to understand and remember parts of the story consistent with the typical structure of stories. That is, setting and character information is encoded, as are the problems encountered by the protagonists in the story and their means for solving those problems (e.g., Mandler, 1984; Stein & Glenn, 1979). Skilled readers often translate the verbal ideas in text into mental images representing the ideas expressed in words by the author (Clark & Paivio, 1991). In short, a number of ways for representing the ideas in text were considered by cognitive psychologists in the 1970s, 1980s, and 1990s.

Educational psychologists, in particular, were inspired by the theoretical work on representation to devise interventions intended to encourage readers to create text representations as they read. That is, educational psychologists devised comprehension strategies, including summarization, attention to story grammar elements, and construction of mental images. There was a great deal of this type of work in the 1970s and 1980s. We touch on some of the better known studies in what follows.

Summarization

Since good readers abstract the gist of text (Kintsch & van Dijk, 1978), it made sense to a number of cognitive psychologists to teach all children to do so, with the assumption that such summarization instruction would improve their comprehension of text. The catch is that children need to be taught how to summarize, for they experience difficulties doing it on their own (Brown & Day, 1983; Brown, Day, & Jones, 1983).

By the upper elementary grades, children can be taught to carry out processes similar to the ones skilled adult readers seem to use as they read text (Kintsch & van Dijk, 1978). This can be accomplished by teaching students a series of rules for producing a summary of a piece of text (Brown & Day, 1983):

- Delete trivial information.
- Delete redundant information.
- Substitute superordinate terms for lists of items.
- Integrate a series of events with a superordinate action term.
- Select a topic sentence.
- Invent a topic sentence if there is none.

In general, such summarization improves recall of text summarized, and such instruction seems to produce generalized improvements in comprehension (e.g., as assessed with standardized tests; see Bean & Steenwyk, 1984; Taylor & Beach, 1984).

Rinehart, Stahl, and Erickson (1986) used a similar approach, but simplified it. The simplified approach emphasized deleting trivial and redundant information and looking for main ideas (i.e., find the most important information):

- Identify main information.
- Delete trivial information.
- Delete redundant information.

As they processed each paragraph, students were encouraged to use a series of questions to facilitate their processing:

- Have I found the overall idea of the paragraph?
- Have I found the most important information that tells more about the overall idea?
- Have I any information that is not about the overall idea?
- Have I used any information more than once?

The students practiced these questions with increasingly longer paragraphs and then with multiple-paragraph texts. To summarize a multiple-paragraph text, Rinehart et al. (1986) instructed students to carry out three steps as part of summarization training:

- Write summaries of each paragraph.
- Create a summary of the paragraph summaries.
- Apply the four summarization rules to this paragraph (i.e., identify the main information, delete trivial information, delete redundant information, relate main idea and supporting ideas).

Rinehart et al. (1986) provided explicit explanation about summarization to their students as they modeled the processes for them. Students were provided substantial practice with feedback. The task was made increasingly demanding both by increasing the length of passages processed and by fading out teacher support. That is, with practice, students took greater and greater self-control of the processing. Elementary-school students who experienced this training, in fact, could remember a good deal more from text than students not receiving such training.

Summarization instruction sometimes includes teaching students to draw spatial diagrams as a way of representing relationships expressed in text. Thus, children can be taught to summarize by putting the main idea of a text in the center of a diagram with supporting big ideas in the text surrounding the center (i.e., construct semantic maps). Details supporting each of the big ideas can be placed under the big idea. Such semantic mapping improves recall of passages (Berkowitz, 1986).

Summarization instruction can also improve student memory of expository texts. Armbruster, Anderson, and Ostertag (1987) taught fifth graders that many social studies texts have a problem–solution structure. The students were taught to summarize a text by placing a summary of the problem in a box at the top of a diagram and summaries of potential solutions in boxes underneath the problem box. Children's recall of social studies texts was improved by such summarization training, which again was a form of semantic mapping.

In short, a variety of approaches to teaching elementary-school students to summarize text improved their later recall of text, which presumably depends on understanding of text. Quite a bit was learned about summarization training in these studies, including that such instruction takes awhile. Rapid training does not produce much benefit for students (e.g., Taylor, 1982). At least by the end of the elementary-school years, students can learn to find the gist in text.

Story-Grammar Instruction

Mature, good readers note the important parts of a story: the setting, the characters, initiating events, problems encountered by characters, solution attempts to problems, solutions to problems, and story closings (Mandler, 1984; Stein & Glenn, 1979). That is, they notice the *grammar* of the stories, with material related to the main elements of story grammar encoded as a story is processed. But weaker readers often fail to note the story grammar elements (Rahman & Bisanz, 1986).

More positively, weak child readers can be taught to notice story grammar elements; when they are taught to do so, their comprehension improves. Perhaps the best known study of this type was conducted by Short and Ryan (1984). They trained fourth graders to use a series of questions to guide their reading of stories:

- Who is the main character?
- Where and when did the story take place?
- What did the main characters do?
- How did the story end?
- How did the main character feel?

At first the instructors modeled and explained the use of the questions to guide reading, but they gradually required the children to increasingly use the questions on their own. This training increased the student's memory of what occurred in the stories.

Story grammar can be taught as a form of semantic mapping. Idol (1987) and Idol and Croll (1987) taught children in the upper elementary grades to construct a story map, with the beginning of the story represented at the top of the map and its end at the bottom of the map. That is, information about the setting and characters is placed in a top box. Below are more boxes with a summary of the problems encountered by the characters, followed by information about the characters' goals in the story, followed by summaries of the actions taken by characters to resolve their problems and meet their goals.

Mental Imagery

Good child readers sometimes construct mental images depicting the ideas represented in text that they read (e.g., Sadoski, 1983, 1985). When middle- and upper-elementary students do not generate such images on their own, they can be taught to do so rather easily. With a little practice, children are able to make pictures in their heads of ideas in concrete stories, with generation of such images improving recall of text and enhancing understanding, as reflected by children recognizing when ideas in text do not make sense (Gambrell & Bales, 1986; Pressley, 1976).

Other Individual Strategies

Researchers developed and demonstrated the efficacy of a number of other strategies for improving students' understanding and memory of text. One of the most prominent of these was *self-questioning,* that is, teaching students to generate questions as they read (Rosenshine, Meister, & Chapman, 1996). Encouraging students to *activate their prior knowledge about the topic of a text is another strategy* that improves understanding of the text (e.g., Hansen & Pearson, 1983). Teaching students to *monitor whether what they are reading makes sense* is also an integral strategy. Only if students are aware of when they are experiencing difficulties in comprehending will they adjust their reading to improve their comprehension (Baker, 2002).

In summary, there was quite a bit of work in the 1970s and 1980s that made clear that there were individual strategies that could be taught to students to increase what they learned when reading text. The problem with the teaching of individual strategies, however, is that good readers do not use just one approach when they read, but rather they coordinate a variety of strategies (Pressley & Afflerbach, 1995). That is, good readers make predictions about what might be in text as they read, pay attention to the important elements of the text (e.g., story grammar elements for fiction; key structural elements in expository texts, such as problem and solution information), generate questions, construct mental images representing the ideas in the text, monitor whether they are understanding what is being read—changing strategies or seeking clarification when they are not understanding—and summarize the ideas in the text. Mature, excellent readers are very, very active as they read. Moreover, there is nothing rigid about the active comprehension process—for example, with both predictions and summaries generated throughout reading.

In part, because of analyses that made clear that good readers used multiple strategies as they read text, instructional researchers developed interventions to encourage the use of multiple strategies. This work began in the 1980s.

MULTIPLE STRATEGIES INSTRUCTION

Reciprocal Teaching

Annemarie Palincsar and Ann Brown (1984) created an approach to multiple strategies instruction that they dubbed "reciprocal teaching." In their first investigation of the approach, they studied grade-7 readers who could read the words of text but who had problems comprehending what they read—that is, they studied a type of troubled reader that is very common in the upper-elementary and middle-school grades. The participants in the treated condition were taught four comprehension strategies: prediction based on prior knowledge, generating questions about ideas encountered in text, seeking clarification when confused, and summarizing. In the initial lessons, the teacher extensively explained and modeled the strategies, but very quickly the students were practicing use of the strategies in small groups, with the students taking turns leading the group through the application of the four strategies to short texts. There were 20 instruction and practice sessions.

The strategies-instructed students in Palincsar and Brown (1984) were taught the value of the strategies they were learning. In particular, the students were explicitly informed that predicting, questioning, seeking clarification, and summarizing were strategies that improved comprehension. They also were encouraged to use the strategies when they read on their own. For example, teachers emphasized that being able to summarize passages and predict the questions on upcoming tests were good ways to assess whether what was read was understood.

Reciprocal teaching impacted several different measures of comprehension, from responding to short-answer questions to passage retellings. The Palincsar and Brown (1984) study inspired many replications, which were reviewed by Rosenshine and Meister (1994). Across investigations, there was clear evidence that children can learn to carry out the cognitive processes that are part of the reciprocal teaching package. There was also clear evidence of improvement on measures such as standardized tests of comprehension, although sometimes the effects were not particularly large. More positively, the more direct teaching of the four strategies by the teacher, the greater the effects on standardized comprehension measures. Improved performance on measures such as standardized tests is important, for, at a minimum, such gains as a function of reciprocal teaching are evidence of strategy transfer (i.e., students were not trained with standardized tests).

Reciprocal teaching was an important starting point for many educators who decided to teach packages of comprehension strategies to their students. Even so, many educators who were inspired by Palincsar and Brown (1984) ended up teaching multiple comprehension strategies very differently than they were operationalized in the original experiment on the approach (Marks et al., 1993). In particular, the use of strategies was not quite as rigid. In the original formulation, the strategies were always executed in the order of prediction, questioning, clarification, and summarization. Marks et al. (1993) observed teachers encouraging students to use the strategies as demanded by the text (e.g., summaries whenever they made sense, questions whenever they made sense). In addition, Marks et al. (1993) observed multiple strategies instruction that was occurring over many more lessons than occurred in Palincsar and Brown (1984)—in many cases, over the entire school year or for several years. In fact, what Marks et al. (1993) observed was so very different from the original Palincsar and Brown (1984) formulation that it came to be formally known as "transactional strategies instruction," a name that captures one of this instructional approach's most important characteristics.

Transactional Strategies Instruction

Transactional strategies instruction begins with teacher modeling and explanation of comprehension strategies. Although the teacher's goal is to develop readers who use a repertoire of comprehension strategies (e.g., prediction, questioning, imagery, relating to prior knowledge, monitoring and seeking clarification, summarization), she or he typically begins with one strategy. Quite often, the first strategy taught is prediction based on prior knowledge. The teacher explains to students that good readers often make guesses about what will occur in a text. She or he then models making predictions, perhaps as part of a picture walk through the story, making predictions based first on the title of the story and then based on the pictures. Once reading of the story begins, the teacher models awareness of whether the predictions, in fact, occurred in the story. Over the course of a few weeks, the teacher encourages students to make predictions, continuing to do so until the students are regularly making predictions on their own.

Then it is time for the teacher to introduce a second strategy, perhaps imagery. Again, the teacher explains and models the strategy, often during read-alouds. The teacher progressively demands more of the students, including that they use both predictions and imagery together while processing text. Once the teacher senses that the students are comfortable using the two strategies together, it is time for her or him to introduce a third strategy . . . and then a fourth . . . until the entire repertoire of strategies is introduced.

It can take awhile for a teacher to introduce the full repertoire of comprehension strategies—perhaps most of a year. Even then, it is far from certain that all students will be using the strategies fluently (Pressley et al., 1992). Nonetheless, a semester to a year of transactional strategies instruction produces clear comprehension benefits, as assessed in a variety of ways by well-controlled validation studies, including standardized reading test data (Anderson, 1992; Brown, Pressley, Van Meter, & Schuder, 1996; Collins, 1991).

Much of the transactional strategies instruction takes place in small reading groups, ones resembling guided reading groups. As students take turns reading, they are encouraged to report which strategies they are using as they experience a text. Usually, there is a poster in the small-reading-group corner of the room that summarizes the repertoire of strategies, a simple listing of the strategies, such as this:

- Predicting
- Questioning
- Constructing images representing text meaning
- Relating to prior knowledge
- Monitoring
- Seeking clarification
- Summarizing

If students are not reporting strategies, the teacher might prompt them: "Make certain that you let us know what strategies you are choosing and using"; "Good readers are active when they read"; "I hope you choose to use our strategies as you read." That is, the teacher consistently sends the message that students should choose to be cognitively active, for the goal is self-regulated strategy use. If students fail to display appropriate strategy use, the teacher can create need-based groups consisting of a handful of invited students to practice troubling strategies (Keene & Zimmermann, 1997). Self-regulation is all about students "doing it on their own," not about students responding to explicit prompts to use strategies. Thus, the transactional strategies instruction teacher never says to a student, "It's time to makes images" or "This is where you should summarize."

What transactional strategies instruction is really about is encouraging young readers to be active cognitively as they read, just the way that mature, excellent readers are active cognitively. Transactional strategies instruction is so named because readers are encouraged to actively use strategies to interpret text (Rosenblatt, 1978), with the expectation that even students who have been taught the same strategies will use them differently. That is, if five different students read a text, they will employ five different combinations of strategy use. Thus, as some students report what they do as they read ("I have an image"), other students compare and discuss the strategies they use ("I made a summarization instead"). The result is real interpretive conversations about text, transactions between readers in the very best sense of the term (Rosenblatt, 1978).

Consistent with a Vygotskian perspective (Vygotsky, 1978), transactional strategies instruction begins with input from a more knowledgeable other, the teacher who models and explains use of comprehension strategies. Then students practice using strategies with other students, with the many exchanges providing students practice in using strategies and feedback about their use of strategies (e.g., when a student makes a ridiculous association to text, other students in the group let her or him know). Gradually students come to use the strategies on their own, both when they are reading with one another (e.g., during pair reading) and when they are reading on their own. What were once processes carried out *interpersonally* are now processes carried out *intrapersonally*, consistent with the Vygotskian perspective on the internalization of cognitive processes (Vygotsky, 1978).

While a year or more of practice is required to be fluent in use of comprehension strategies (Pressley et al., 1992), even children in the early elementary grades benefit greatly from transactional strategies instruction (e.g., Brown et al., 1996). In our present study, discussed at the beginning of this chapter, our most successful comprehension teacher teaches first grade! Her whole-group read-alouds are noisy conversations with excited students vying to share their predictions, images, and other strategies.

Flexibility in Transactional Strategies Instruction

A hallmark of the transactional approach to comprehension strategies instruction is that it is flexible. One way that it is flexible is that there is no particular set of strategies that must be taught. Yes, the strategies mentioned thus far seem to occur more often than other strategies, but not all the strategies need to be taught for there to be a real increase in cognitive activity due to strategies use. Moreover, teachers can teach other strategies besides the ones on the main list.

For example, Pressley, Gaskins, Wile, Cunicelli, and Sheridan (1992) documented how a teacher (Deborah Wile) at Benchmark School taught her students to use text analysis strategies. Benchmark School is a private school dedicated to improving the reading abilities of children who have not had success learning to read elsewhere. Benchmark was one of the schools that invented transactional strategies instruction (Pressley et al., 1992). Ms. Wile's students already knew and used a large number of comprehension strategies, having learned them during their first several years at Benchmark School. She wanted her students to expand their strategic repertoire, specifically, by acquiring the habit of analyzing expository texts for their structures—to determine whether a passage was mostly descriptive, about cause and effect, or a specification of a temporal sequence.

The teacher introduced the text analysis strategy through direct explanation and lots of modeling, with modeling continuing for a long time, well after students had begun to try using the strategies on their own. One clear indication of flexibility in the teaching was that the students were attempting to use the text analysis strategies all the time, during reading group, when reading *Weekly Reader*, and when tackling texts read in social studies. At first, the teacher scaffolded use of the strategies in new situations, but after awhile, students were using the text analysis strategies on their own.

As this new strategy was being taught, students continued to use and to be taught to use the other comprehension strategies they had learned. The teacher modeled use of the new strategy in conjunction with the previously acquired strategies. She prompted students to use all of their strategies as they were working through text, sometimes by providing gentle reminders.

The teacher taught the students to use the text analyses strategies as interpretive tools, emphasizing that different people sometimes detected different structural elements in expository texts. As part of the teaching of the strategy, students made semantic maps representing ideas in text. The teacher emphasized that very different maps could all capture the meaning in a text. She also made the point that sometimes massive revision of maps was called for when a reader changed her or his interpretation of the text midway through it. The teacher consistently sent the message that the strategy was to encourage student thinking about the ideas in the text, not a formula for discovery of the one "right" interpretation of the text.

Strategy instruction was completely integrated with content learning in this classroom. It was not an add-on in the curriculum, but rather was an integral part of the ongoing curriculum. The same texts that would have been read otherwise were read as part of strategies instruction. The difference, of course, was that students got more out of each encounter with text as a function of using the strategies being taught (see especially Brown et al., 1996).

Affective Dimensions of Transactional Strategies Instruction

Something that cannot be missed in transactional strategies instruction classrooms is that they are engaging places, environments where students are very motivated. Certainly, it is encouraging to students to be learning approaches to text that permit them to get much meaning from their reading. That said, strategies use requires real effort. When students construct images of the ideas in text, they have to get beyond the meaning of individual words to grasp the overall sense of the text; summarization similarly forces consideration of how ideas in text relate to one another and make sense together. Such integration is anything but automatic for many elementary readers (e.g., Wiener & Cromer, 1967).

Because strategies use is effortful, transactional strategies instruction teachers must do much to ensure that students are motivated to try hard. They can do so through a variety of means, with the potential result a very positive instructional situation. Some instructional tactics include the following (Pressley, El-Dinary, Marks, Brown, & Stein, 1992):

- Extensive scaffolding (Wood, Bruner, & Ross, 1976) can be provided to students, which increases the likelihood of student success and decreases student frustration.
- As part of scaffolding, the teacher should have students practice strategies with texts that are appropriately difficult for the students, ones that are a bit challenging, neither too easy nor so far beyond the students' ability that there is no hope of understanding them.
- Transactional strategies instruction teachers reinforce student use of strategies by providing a great deal of praise when students evidence the comprehension strategies being taught. This translates into reinforcement for the effort exerted to carry out comprehension strategies.
- There is little criticism in transactional strategies instruction classroom. Rather, teachers encourage academic engagement, and when students have the cognitive tools to do so (i.e., the strategies), they engage, which provides opportunity for lots of reinforcement.
- Transactional strategies instructional teachers emphasize the usefulness of the strategies being taught by constantly pointing out that students are learning skills that are really important in life.
- Rather than emphasizing how well students are doing relative to one another, the transactional strategies instruction teacher emphasizes how much the individual student's reading comprehension is improving. *Doing better than before* is emphasized rather than *doing better than others*, in contrast to what occurs in many classrooms (Nicholls, 1989).
- Transactional strategies instruction teachers have students practice strategies with authentic texts, ones that are interesting to students.
- Student choice is emphasized. Students learn that they can choose to be active and can choose how they are active in engaging text.

For some, this will mean a great deal of use of imagery. For others, it will mean a great deal of summarization.

This is not one-size-fits-all instruction. Rather, the message is that good comprehenders make their own interpretations, using the powerful cognitive skills that are comprehension strategies to process texts in ways that are comfortable and meaningful for them.

Summary Comment

As was the case a quarter of a century ago, there is still little comprehension instruction in schools (Pressley, Wharton-McDonald, Hampson, & Echevarria, 1998; Taylor, Pearson, Clark, & Walpole, 2002). More positively, much has been learned in the past quarter century about how to teach elementary students to comprehend better, in particular by teaching them to use comprehension strategies when they read, including summarization, story grammar analysis, and imagery. In recent years the focus of comprehension strategies instruction research has been the development of young readers who are taught to use a repertoire of strategies, who are taught to be diversely active as they read in the ways that good readers are diversely active as they read. In particular, when students are taught a repertoire that includes predicting based on prior knowledge, questioning, imagery, monitoring, seeking clarification when confused, and summarization, there are striking improvements in their level of comprehension. Development of such a repertoire requires long-term teaching (i.e., a semester to a year).

What is most striking about transactional strategies instruction classrooms is that they are exceptionally positive environments characterized by high learner engagement. This is because transactional strategies instruction emphasizes a variety of positive motivational mechanisms. Transactional strategies instruction teachers are always "stroking" student efforts and improvement as they read appropriately challenging and interesting materials. That the approach produces success in reading helps as well, for nothing motivates like success.

It is also striking that some of the most impressive impacts of transactional comprehension strategies instruction have been with students who are experiencing reading and learning disabilities (Anderson, 1992; Brown et al., 1996). Possibly the most impressive and extensive implementation of the approach is at Benchmark School, a school with a long track record of transforming failing elementary-level readers into academically capable graduates who do well in high school and go on to college (Pressley et al., 1992). Transactional strategies instruction can dramatically impact struggling readers with comprehension disabilities (Deshler et al., 1996).

HOW ELSE CAN COMPREHENSION
BE IMPROVED?

Although most work on comprehension instruction has involved study of comprehension strategies instruction, other elements of instruction also enjoy some empirical validation for promoting comprehension (National Reading Panel, 2000; Pressley, 2002; RAND Reading Study Group, 2002).

Decoding Instruction

Except for picture books with little or no text, comprehension of text is logically impossible when the reader cannot read the words. Thus, it is critical that readers learn how to decode (i.e., recognize words). One of the most prominent conclusions of the National Reading Panel (2000) was that young readers benefit from systematic phonics instruction when they are first learning to read words. There is a great deal of accumulated evidence that learning to sound out words is a good start on reading. That said, sounding out words is just a start on word recognition, a way station that needs to be moved through as quickly as possible. When young readers sound out words, they have to devote a lot of mental effort to the activity. In the process, they have little mental capacity left over for comprehending either the individual word that is being sounded out or other words in the text (LaBerge & Samuels, 1974). Fortunately, what begins as sounding out and blending often becomes more automatic recognition of word chunks (e.g., *log* is at first sounded out as three sounds, then sounded out as two, the *l* sound and the sound of the chunk *-og* which has been encountered previously in *dog*, *log*, and *pog* [Goswami, 2000]). Recognition of chunks is easier than blending one sound at a time.

The ultimate goal of word recognition instruction, however, is fluent recognition of whole words, that is, recognition of words as sight words. The correlation between fluent reading and comprehension is well established (e.g., National Reading Panel, 2000). Even more important, when fluency is developed through instruction and practice, comprehension improves (e.g., Tan & Nicholson, 1997; see also Breznitz, 1997a, 1997b). Instruction that develops fluent word recognition should be part of every reading program, for without fluent word recognition comprehension will be compromised.

Vocabulary Instruction

The correlation between good reading and extensive vocabulary is common knowledge among reading researchers. What is more impressive is that teaching students vocabulary increases their comprehension skills (National Reading Panel, 2000; RAND Reading Study Group, 2002). An effective comprehension instructional program must include vocabulary instruction.

Developing Students' World Knowledge

One great contribution of the 35 years of the Center for the Study of Reading at the University of Illiniois was that Richard Anderson and his colleagues established very well that world knowledge matters: the more one knows, the better and more certain comprehension will be (Anderson & Pearson, 1984). A recent demonstration of the power of worthwhile world knowledge comes from work inspired by E. D. Hirsch's (1996) conception of cultural literacy: Hirsch believes that schools should explicitly teach significant scientific and social scientific knowledge as well as the best of literature and mathematics. Some schools are doing this, attempting to emphasize the knowledge he identified as appropriate in each of the elementary grades (Core Knowledge Foundation, 1998). These Core Knowledge Schools, about 800 of them, have now been operating long enough for at least some preliminary data to emerge. So far, the Core Knowledge approach seems to lead to small but significant gains in reading achievement (Datnow, Borman, & Stringfield, 2000).

The obvious question is how to build excellent world knowledge. Most emphatically, most kids are not enrolled in Core Knowledge programs. What every kid can do, however, is to read, and, in particular, to choose to read worthwhile books, ones that are informative about important social scientific, scientific, literary, and mathematical contents. This is a controversial stance, however, for it means favoring such worthwhile books over other books that many kids prefer. Although a case can be made that the reading of purely entertaining books positively affects fluency, no reasonable case can be made that reading such books will result in important shifts in world knowledge.

Something else that kids can do is to watch worthwhile television. Informative television in general, such as the fare on the Discovery Channel, impacts literacy positively (Koolstra, van der Voort, & van der Kamp, 1997; Wright et al., 2001). Moreover, the effects of watching such child-informative programming during the preschool years carry over at least into adolescence, with heavier preschool viewers of child-informative programming doing better in school than other children, even controlling for alternative variables that might produce boosts in literacy achievement (Anderson, Huston, Schmitt, Linebarger, & Wright, 2001; Rosengren & Windahl, 1989). Informative television also provides an opportunity for the literacy-rich to get richer: for example, 5-year-olds who are more advanced with respect to literacy are more likely to watch informative television than less literacy-advanced 5-year-olds (Wright et al., 2001). In doing so, they gain more opportunities to learn information and skills that can affect literacy development positively. Getting children to turn on something other than the Cartoon Network or reruns of situation comedies should be a high priority for all teachers.

In addition to building prior knowledge, it is also essential to encourage students to make use of the prior knowledge they already have. My students and I provided many demonstrations of underuse of prior knowledge (Pressley, Wood, et al., 1992; see esp. Martin & Pressley, 1991). For example, when we asked Canadian students to read about events that occurred in each of the Canadian provinces, they often failed to use their prior knowledge to situate the events sensibly in the provinces where they occurred. In one situation, when reading about baseball first being played in Ontario, they did not automatically infer why it made sense that the event occurred in Ontario rather than elsewhere in Canada (Martin & Pressley, 1991; Woloshyn, Pressley, & Schneider, 1992). More positively, when students were prompted to ask themselves why it made sense for the events to occur where they did in Canada (e.g., Why would Ontario have been the place where baseball was first played in Canada?), they did use their prior knowledge, with huge increases in memory of what they read. When it comes to factual text, it is often very helpful for students to be taught to ask themselves why the facts they are presented are sensible, for often readers will be able to explain the facts by relating the new information to their prior knowledge. Otherwise, students often do not use what they know to understand new material.

Read, Read, Read

One of the most common signs posted in elementary classrooms is "Read, Read, Read." Sadly, during the early 1990s, when whole language approaches dominated reading instruction, there was a belief that skilled comprehension would be a natural by-product of large doses of reading a variety of texts and genres. Indeed, massive reading does do much good for the developing reader, and in ways that affect comprehension positively. It promotes fluency at the word level, increases vocabulary, and permits opportunities to apply comprehension strategies being learned, including monitoring and relating new information encountered in text to prior knowledge. Massive reading is an essential part of elementary comprehension development, even though it is not sufficient to develop skilled comprehension.

We now know that it makes a great deal of sense also to teach word recognition skills, vocabulary, and comprehension strategies and monitoring, as well as to encourage habits of life that develop worthwhile world knowledge (e.g., encourage broad reading, viewing of worthwhile television, habitual reflection on why facts as stated in text make sense based on prior knowledge). While quality and quantity of reading characterize the habits of good readers, more is needed to develop skilled student comprehenders.

Summary Comment

Skilled comprehension involves the addition and interaction of word recognition, vocabulary, comprehension strategy, and world knowledge components. That is why skilled comprehension requires years to develop, and why really skilled comprehension is only seen in very mature readers, typically individuals who are past the K–12 years (Pressley & Afflerbach, 1995). Fortunately, all components that contribute to comprehension *can* be taught, and they *should* be!

Imagine a classroom that incorporates all of these individual components. For example, if such a classroom were to study a unit on butterflies, we would expect to see student-created lists of vocabulary words, like *cocoon*, with their definitions on the wall. The teacher might also have the class take a trip to the library where students could check out stories and expository texts on butterflies or even look for information on the migration patterns of monarch butterflies on the Internet. The class would then meet later to discuss and share what they learned with one another. In addition, we might find the teacher reading a big book on the life cycle of butterflies. She would often stop to model strategies and listen to students discuss the strategies they actively use. Later in the day, she would meet with small, needs-based groups to work on word recognition and strategy skills as they read stories and books about butterflies. Obviously such a classroom is a busy, well-planned, integrated classroom.

CONCLUDING REFLECTION

We plan to be back again at the school discussed at the beginning of the chapter, working with the principal and all of the teachers to foster the entire faculty as transactional strategies instruction teachers. That's what we know how to do. Even so, we will also be looking for ways to fold the other players in the school into the instruction: the special education teachers and aides who will be working with students in classrooms, the speech and language specialists, and the parents. In addition, we will be working hard to encourage the administration, teachers, and others to work on the development of fluent word recognition in students (although this school already has much instruction targeting this goal), teach more vocabulary, and encourage the development of significant world knowledge through worthwhile reading and other experiences. In short, we will be working on the development of comprehension instruction that includes more players and more instructional components than our past work.

REFERENCES

Adams, M. J., Treiman, R., & Pressley, M. (1998). Reading, writing, and literacy. In I. Sigel & A. Renninger (Eds.), *Handbook of child psychology: Vol. 4. Child psychology in practice* (pp. 275–355). New York: Wiley.

Anderson, D. R., Huston, A. C., Schmitt, K. L., Linebarger, D. L., & Wright, J. C. (2001). Early childhood television viewing and adolescent behavior. *Monographs of the Society for Research in Child Development, 66* (Serial No. 264).

Anderson, R. C., & Pearson, P. D. (1984). A schema-theoretic view of basic processes in reading. In P. D. Pearson (Ed.), *Handbook of reading research* (pp. 255–292). New York: Longman.

Anderson, V. (1992). A teacher development project in transactional strategy instruction for teachers of severely reading-disabled adolescents. *Teaching and Teacher Education, 8,* 391–403.

Armbruster, B. B., Anderson, T. H., & Ostertag, J. (1987). Does text structure/summarization instruction facilitate learning from expository text? *Reading Research Quarterly, 22,* 331–346.

Baker, L. (2002). Metacognition in comprehension instruction. In C. C. Block & M. Pressley (Eds.), *Comprehension instruction: Research-based best practices* (pp. 77–95). New York: Guilford Press.

Bean, T. W., & Steenwyk, F. L. (1984). The effect of three forms of summarization instruction on sixth graders' summary writing and comprehension. *Journal of Reading Behavior, 16,* 297–306.

Berkowitz, S. J. (1986). Effects of instruction in text organization on sixth-grade students' memory for expository reading. *Reading Research Quarterly, 21,* 161–178.

Breznitz, Z. (1997a). Effects of accelerated reading rate on memory for text among dyslexic readers. *Journal of Educational Psychology, 89,* 289–297.

Breznitz, Z. (1997b). Enhancing the reading of dyslexic children by reading acceleration and auditory masking. *Journal of Educational Psychology, 89,* 103–113.

Brown, A. L., & Day, J. D. (1983). Macrorules for summarizing texts: The development of expertise. *Journal of Verbal Learning and Verbal Behavior, 22,* 1–14.

Brown, A. L., Day, J. D., & Jones, R. S. (1983). The development of plans for summarizing texts. *Child Development, 54,* 968–979.

Brown, R., Pressley, M., Van Meter, P., & Schuder, T. (1996). A quasi-experimental validation of transactional strategies instruction with low-achieving second grade readers. *Journal of Educational Psychology, 88,* 18–37.

Clark, J. M., & Paivio, A. (1991). Dual coding theory and education. *Educational Psychology Review, 3,* 149–210.

Collins, C. (1991). Reading instruction that increases thinking abilities. *Journal of Reading, 34,* 510–516.

Core Knowledge Foundation. (1998). *Core knowledge sequence: Content guidelines for grades K–8*. Charlottesville, VA: Author.

Datnow, A., Borman, G., & Stringfield, S. (2000). School reform through a highly specified curriculum: Implementation and effects of the core knowledge sequence. *Elementary School Journal, 101,* 167–191.

Deshler, D., Ellis, E. S., & Lenz, K. (1996). *Teaching adolescents with learning disabilities: Strategies and methods*. Denver, CO: Love.

Durkin, D. (1978–1979). What classroom observations reveal about reading comprehension instruction. *Reading Research Quarterly, 15,* 481–533.

Gambrell, L. B., & Bales, R. J. (1986). Mental imagery and the comprehension-monitoring performance of fourth- and fifth-grade poor readers. *Reading Research Quarterly, 21,* 454–464.

Goswami, U. (2000). Phonological and lexical processes. In M. Kamil, P. B. Mosenthal, P. D. Pearson, & R. Barr (Eds.), *Handbook of reading research* (Vol. 3, pp. 251–267). Mahwah, NJ: Erlbaum.

Hansen, J., & Pearson, P. D. (1983). An instructional study: Improving the referential comprehension of good and poor fourth grade readers. *Journal of Educational Psychology, 75,* 821–829.

Hirsch, E. D. (1996). *The schools we need and why we don't have them*. New York: Doubleday.

Idol, L. (1987). Group story mapping: A comprehension strategy for both skilled and unskilled readers. *Journal of Learning Disabilities, 20,* 196–205.

Idol, L., & Croll, V. J. (1987). Story-mapping training as a means of improving reading comprehension. *Learning Disability Quarterly, 10,* 214–229.

Keene, E. O., & Zimmermann, S. (1997). *Mosaic of thought: Teaching comprehension in a reader's workshop*. Portsmouth, NH: Heinemann.

Kintsch, W., & van Dijk, T. A. (1978). Toward a model of discourse comprehension and production. *Psychological Review, 85,* 363–394.

Koolstra, C. M., van der Voort, T. H. A., & van der Kamp, L. J. T. (1997). Television's impact on children's reading comprehension and decoding skills: A 3-year panel study. *Reading Research Quarterly, 32,* 128–152.

LaBerge, D., & Samuels, S. J. (1974). Toward a theory of automatic information processing in reading. *Cognitive Psychology, 6,* 293–323.

Mandler, J. M. (1984). *Stories, scripts, and scenes: Aspects of schema theory*. Hillsdale, NJ: Erlbaum.

Marks, M., & Pressley, M., with Coley, J. D., Craig, S., Gardner, R., Rose, W., & DePinto, T. (1993). Teachers' adaptations of reciprocal teaching: Progress toward a classroom-compatible version of reciprocal teaching. *Elementary School Journal, 94,* 267–283.

Martin, V. L., & Pressley, M. (1991). Elaborative interrogation effects depend on the nature of the question. *Journal of Educational Psychology, 83,* 113–119.

Mehan, H. (1979). *Social organization in the classroom*. Cambridge, MA: Harvard University Press.

National Reading Panel. (2000). *Teaching children to read: An evidence-based assessment of the scientific research literature on reading and its implications for reading instruction: Reports of the subgroups*. Washington, DC: National Institute of Child Health and Development.

Nicholls, J. G. (1989). *The competitive ethos and democratic education.* Cambridge, MA: Harvard University Press.

Palincsar, A. S., & Brown, A. L. (1984). Reciprocal teaching of comprehension-fostering and monitoring activities. *Cognition and Instruction, 1,* 117–175.

Pressley, G. M. (1976). Mental imagery helps eight-year-olds remember what they read. *Journal of Educational Psychology, 68,* 355–359.

Pressley, M. (2002). *Reading instruction that works: The case for balanced teaching* (2nd ed.). New York: Guilford Press.

Pressley, M., & Afflerbach, P. (1995). *Verbal protocols of reading: The nature of constructively responsive reading.* Hillsdale, NJ: Erlbaum.

Pressley, M., El-Dinary, P. B., Gaskins, I., Schuder, T., Bergman, J. L., Almasi, J., & Brown, R. (1992). Beyond direct explanation: Transactional instruction of reading comprehension strategies. *Elementary School Journal, 92,* 511–554.

Pressley, M., El-Dinary, P. B., Marks, M. B., Brown, R., & Stein, S. (1992). Good strategy instruction is motivating and interesting. In K. A. Renninger, S. Hidi, & A. Krapp (Eds.), *The role of interest in learning and development* (pp. 333–358). Hillsdale, NJ: Erlbaum.

Pressley, M., Gaskins, I. W., Wile, D., Cunicelli, B., & Sheridan, J. (1991). Teaching literacy strategies across the curriculum: A case study at Benchmark School. In J. Zutell & S. McCormick (Eds.), *Learner factors/teacher factors: Issues in literacy research and instruction. Fortieth yearbook of the National Reading Conference* (pp. 219–228). Chicago: National Reading Conference.

Pressley, M., Wharton-McDonald, R., Hampson, J. M., & Echevarria, M. (1998). The nature of literacy instruction in ten grade-4/5 classrooms in upstate New York. *Scientific Studies of Reading, 2,* 159–191.

Pressley, M., Wood, E., Woloshyn, V. E., Martin, V., King, A., & Menke, D. (1992). Encouraging mindful use of prior knowledge: Attempting to construct explanatory answers facilitates learning. *Educational Psychologist, 27,* 91–110.

Rahman, T., & Bisanz, G. L. (1986). Reading ability and the use of a story schema in recalling and reconstructing information. *Journal of Educational Psychology, 78,* 323–333.

RAND Reading Study Group. (2002). *Reading for understanding: Toward an R&D program in reading comprehension.* Arlington, VA: Author.

Rinehart, S. D., Stahl, S. A., & Erickson, L. G. (1986). Some effects of summarization training on reading and studying. *Reading Research Quarterly, 21,* 422–438.

Rosenblatt, L. M. (1978). *The reader, the text, the poem: The transactional theory of the literary work.* Carbondale: Southern Illinois University Press.

Rosengren, K. E., & Windahl, S. (1989). *Media matter: TV use in childhood and adolescence.* Norwood, NJ: Ablex.

Rosenshine, B., & Meister, C. (1994). Reciprocal teaching: A review of nineteen experimental studies. *Review of Educational Research, 64,* 479–530.

Rosenshine, B., Meister, C., & Chapman, S. (1996). Teaching students to generate questions: A review of the intervention studies. *Review of Educational Research, 66,* 181–221.

Rothkopf, E. Z. (1966). Learning from written materials: An exploration of the control of inspection of test-like events. *American Educational Research Journal, 3,* 241–249.

Sadoski, M. (1983). An exploratory study of the relationship between reported imagery and the comprehension and recall of a story. *Reading Research Quarterly, 19,* 110–123.

Sadoski, M. (1985). The natural use of imagery in story comprehension and recall: Replication and extension. *Reading Research Quarterly, 20,* 658–667.

Short, E. J., & Ryan, E. B. (1984). Metacognitive differences between skilled and less skilled readers: Remediating deficits through story grammar and attribution training. *Journal of Educational Psychology, 76,* 225–235.

Stein, N. L., & Glenn, C. G. (1979). An analysis of story comprehension in elementary school children. In R. O. Freedle (Ed.), *New directions in discourse processing* (Vol. 2, pp. 53–120). Norwood, NJ: Ablex.

Tan, A., & Nicholson, T. (1997). Flashcards revisited: Training poor readers to read words faster improves their comprehension of text. *Journal of Educational Psychology, 89,* 276–288.

Taylor, B. M. (1982). Text structure and children's comprehension and memory for expository material. *Journal of Educational Psychology 74,* 323–340.

Taylor, B. M., & Beach, R. W. (1984). The effects of text structure instruction on middle-grade students' comprehension and production of expository text. *Reading Research Quarterly, 19,* 134–146.

Taylor, B. M., Pearson, P. D., Clark, K., & Walpole, S. (2002). Effective schools and accomplished teachers: Lessons about primary-grade reading instruction in low-income schools. In B. M. Taylor & P. D. Pearson (Eds.), *Teaching reading: Effective schools, accomplished teachers* (pp. 3–72). Mahwah, NJ: Erlbaum.

van Dijk, T. A., & Kintsch, W. (1983). *Strategies of discourse comprehension.* New York: Academic Press.

Vygotsky, L. S. (1978). *Mind in society: The development of higher psychological processes.* Cambridge, MA: Harvard University Press.

Wiener, M., & Cromer, W. (1967). Reading and reading difficulty: A conceptual analysis. *Harvard Educational Review, 37,* 620–643.

Woloshyn, V. E., Pressley, M., & Schneider, W. (1992). Elaborative interrogation and prior knowledge effects on learning of facts. *Journal of Educational Psychology, 84,* 115–124.

Wood, S. S., Bruner, J. S., & Ross, G. (1976). The role of tutoring in problem solving. *Journal of Child Psychology and Psychiatry, 17,* 89–100.

Wright, J. C., Huston, A. C., Murphy, K. C., St. Peters, M., Piñon, M., Scantlin, R., & Kotler, J. (2001). The relations of early television viewing to school readiness and vocabulary of children from low-income families: The early window project. *Child Development, 72,* 1347–1366.

Yager, S., Johnson, D. W., & Johnson, R. T. (1985). Oral discussion, group-to-individual transfer, and achievement in cooperative learning groups. *Journal of Educational Psychology, 77*(1), 60–66.

7

🍂

Integration of Language
and Discourse Components
with Reading Comprehension

It's All About Relationships

MAVIS L. DONAHUE
SHARON K. FOSTER

Relationships among oral language and written language abilities are still not well understood, as illustrated by other chapters in this volume. This is a surprising gap, given that the wide variations among current models of reading instruction can be largely explained by differences in beliefs about how aspects of oral and written language development interact. For example, whole language models assume that oral and written discourse support each other from the very onset of literacy development. Yet from a historical perspective, this is a recent and radical belief. In fact, the early Greeks viewed written language not only with a great deal of suspicion, but actually as a potential detriment to the mission of oral discourse.

In a paper titled "If Socrates Had E-Mail," Nugent (1997) drew intriguing analogies between modern-day anxieties about technology, and the fear and distrust that ancient Greeks felt about their new technology: written language. These qualms are exemplified by the first reference to writing in the Western tradition in Homer's *Iliad*, itself originally a work created in the oral tradition. A character named Bellerophon, who cannot read, is given a tablet with print on it and ordered to deliver it to a king in another country. The print was "Kill the bearer of this message." This tale illustrates how print was perceived as a tool for those who wish to deceive and destroy the unsuspecting illiterate. This attitude undoubtedly persists among many students in the new millennium as they struggle to comprehend written text!

Similarly, Nugent (1997) highlighted Socrates' arguments in the *Phaedrus* that reading and writing would undermine the fundamental nature of social interaction, especially the give-and-take of conversation. For example, "written words . . . seem to talk to you as though they were intelligent, but if you ask them anything about what they say, from a desire to be instructed, they go on telling you just the same thing forever" (Socrates, as cited by Nugent, 1997, p. 4). In essence, Socrates criticized writing and writers for their inability to engage in Socratic dialogue, when ideas can be immediately questioned, challenged, extended, and refuted, through talk.

Yet we contend that Socrates was wrong. Reading *is* social discourse. Expert reading comprehension is crowded with other people and noisy with overlapping conversations. Depending on their purpose for reading, readers form relationships with the text, the author, and the characters. They also discern and evaluate the relationships among the characters in the text. (Some readers even form relationships with the physical book, as illustrated by the Harry Potter books that take up permanent residence in many children's backpacks.)

The purpose of this chapter is to explore the notion that reading comprehension depends on many of the social cognitive processes that underlie oral dialogue. First, we describe theories that have acknowledged the overlapping aspects of social knowledge and reading comprehension. Second, we propose that a model of social information processing designed for understanding "online" social interaction may be useful for posing questions about the social cognitive underpinnings of reading comprehension. Third, we illustrate some of the social cognitive strategies that readers bring to the task of understanding the Shirley Jackson story "Charles" (we recommend that you read this short story now [see Appendix 7.1], and notice the rich social and discourse knowledge base that you apply to the comprehension process). Finally, we highlight the implications of these interactions among social cognitive and reading comprehension processes in the collaborative activity of enhancing literacy in students with language learning disabilities.

DIALOGUING WITH TEXT

As other authors in this volume indicate (Whitaker, Gambrell, & Morrow, Chapter 5; Pressley & Hilden, Chapter 6), reading comprehension is a remarkably complex cognitive activity that develops across the lifespan, in the same way that oral discourse abilities evolve as social/political contexts, roles, and agendas change. Raising a serious dilemma for educators, November (1998) described the reading comprehension experience of Zack, a 14-year-old student who was assigned a history research project on a "unique topic." In Zack's Internet search, he was surprised to come across a webpage claiming that the Holocaust had never taken place. Given that he found this information on the website of a professor at a well-known university, Zack decided that this was a credible source. He was also persuaded by the text, which claimed to have new evidence that refuted previous reports. His parents and teachers were undoubtedly taken aback when he chose the topic "How the Holocaust Never Happened" for his research paper.

This case clearly illustrates that expert reading comprehension is not a simple by-product of reaching mastery on decoding, vocabulary, and fluency skills, but must involve an understanding of social relationships. What can explain Zack's interpretation of the text in the Holocaust-denying website? At first glance, this incident seems to support Socrates' point that written text offers no opportunity for the reader to question its meaning. Text read without knowledge of the author's discourse goals or social context may be difficult to evaluate. Clearly, if this website author had been in the oral marketplace of ideas, perhaps on Speakers' Corner in London's Hyde Park, or even on talk radio, his status as a prominent member of a hate group would have been immediately uncovered through the dialogue.

However, as expert readers stumble on ideas that contradict their own knowledge base, they respond as any good conversationalist would. They immediately pose questions to the author/conversational partner. The first questions may be "What is this author's purpose? Should I believe him or her? Why?" This is the point where Zack's novice reading abilities became apparent: although he attempted to evaluate the author's credibility, his social/cognitive experiences could not provide him with any plausible explanation for why an educated professional would tell such lies. Therefore, he assumed that the author's arguments must be accurate.

For more experienced and critical readers, however, the reading task becomes a search for the answers to their questions in the rest of the text. They may reread to confirm their initial interpretations. Expert readers also check their own goal for reading the text—for example, "Am I looking for information? Or for entertainment?" They then retrieve from long-term memory previous strategies for being a critical evaluator. Because of this sense of self-efficacy, readers might ask: "Should I choose not to read this website? Should I check Internet links to find out this author's agenda?" At every step of this process, readers filter their decision making and conclusions through a rich database of memories of past social experiences and schemas. The ultimate outcome of this process is comprehension. Notice that these strategies for discourse processing mirror the cognitive activities that have been identified as key to reading comprehension, loosely grouped along three dimensions (e.g., Pearson & Fielding, 1991; Pressley, 2000): recruiting prior knowledge to make sense of characters and key events; using strategies to organize ideas in the text (e.g., summarizing, "finding the main idea"); and self-monitoring the comprehension process, in order to identify and clarify confusing concepts.

In sum, describing reading comprehension as a dialogue with text is at least a useful metaphor for highlighting the social understandings that relate to comprehending written texts. More optimistically, this metaphor may shed light on the processes by which readers create discourse with written text, and how to make these processes explicit for struggling comprehenders.

READING THEORIES THAT ACKNOWLEDGE SOCIAL RELATIONSHIPS

The notion that reading is a social process is by no means a new one (see, e.g., Dewey, 1906). In fact, several theories have converged on this idea, even when starting from rather different assumptions. These theories create a kind of "French braid" around three kinds of relationships that expert readers establish: with the text, with the author, and with the characters (Donahue & Foster, 2004). (Although not discussed in this chapter, other theorists [e.g., Beach, 2000; Lewis, 1998; Moller & Allen, 2000] have highlighted a critical fourth dimension—the social context in which the text is read, discussed, and transformed.)

Relationships with the Text

Constructivist theories, like schema theory and reader-response theory (Fish, 1980; Marshall, 2002; Rosenblatt, 1995), focus on how the meaning of a text is created anew by each reader, and at each reading. Given that every text (oral or written) has gaps, every reader must fill in those gaps to construct ideas that make sense, using prior knowledge and text structure. This approach assumes that meaning does not reside in the text by itself, but instead in the "transaction" between the ideas in the text and the experiences that the reader brings.

Of course, this transactional model raises the possibility that the same text read by readers with different experiences will result in as many interpretations as there are readers. Although most reader-response theorists would agree that no one interpretation is "correct," they are likely to disagree about the relative importance of the text versus the reader in how meaning is constructed. Some privilege the reader's personal response, and others tip the balance toward the text. Yet Hynds and Appleman (1997) suggest that Rosenblatt's reader-response perspective "has clearly liberated generations of students and teachers from a one-correct answer approach to literary reading" (p. 275).

In a rare study that actually assessed the social cognitive processes that underlie readers' responses to text, Hynds (1985) asked 83 typically achieving 11th-grade readers to describe a liked and a disliked peer, and then a favorite and a least favorite character in an assigned short story. The complexity with which these students described the social and psychological traits of their peers significantly predicted the richness with which personalities of story characters were interpreted. This was especially true for students who reported that they read widely outside the classroom. Interestingly, this measure of peer understanding was not correlated with students' ability to answer literal comprehension questions, but did predict scores on inferential questions. Further, in an intriguing measure called "response preference," students were given a list of 20 questions and asked to identify the five questions that were most important to understanding the story. Students with higher levels of social cognitive ability were more likely to select questions that reflected interest in people, that is, a concern for the actions and motivations of the author, the characters, and people in the students' own social experiences (e.g., "What is the writer's attitude toward the people in the story? How can we explain the way people behave in the story? Are any of the characters in the story like people I know?"). In contrast, students with less social cognitive ability preferred the question "Does the story succeed in getting me involved in the situation?," suggesting that a motivating plot about topics of personal interest may be more salient to these readers.

Hynds (1989) extended this exploration of how social cognitive abilities are used to interpret and respond to literature in case studies of four adolescent readers. Although all four students showed the prerequisite social cognitive abilities, they differed in the degree to which they applied their understandings about people to reading comprehension. Both motivational and classroom factors seemed to play a role. One reader did not realize that his own social experiences were even applicable to literary texts. Two students were likely to disengage if the text was not congruent with their social scripts. Another student, an avid reader outside the classroom, showed sophisticated links between her social cognitive knowledge and her understanding of story characters, but this skill emerged only in written work, not during oral discourse. These patterns suggest that engaging their social cognitive processes in text comprehension is not automatic for all students, and that this ability seems to be unrelated to typical measures of school achievement.

Relationships with the Author

Engaging in discourse with an author would undoubtedly be a difficult notion for Socrates to grasp. Yet implicit in constructivist models of literacy instruction is the communicative mission of reading and writing, that is, that students realize that readers and authors are involved in a dialogue. Therefore, students' personal and social responses to the author are critical components of reading comprehension. These assumptions are key to literature-based approaches to reading comprehension like "literature circles" and "book clubs" (e.g., Raphael & Au, 1998).

One straightforward approach to initiating this author–reader dialogue could have been helpful to Zack in his website reading task. Called "Questioning the Author," this model encourages students to respond to deceptively simple questions like "What is the author trying to say?" and "What do you think the author means by that?" As Beck, McKeown, Sandora, Kucan, and Worthy (1996) explain, "the intent of interrogating the ideas in a text through dialogue with the author is to 'depose' the authority of the text by actualizing the presence of an author as a fallible human being "(p. 387). Approaches that invite readers to envision and question the author's perspective and agenda have been found to improve reading comprehension, even with fourth-grade at-risk readers (e.g., Beck et al., 1996). In particular, this approach dramatically enhanced the collaborative nature of teacher and student discourse in the classroom, an outcome that Socrates would have undoubtedly predicted and applauded.

Relationships with the Characters

It is no surprise that readers can form intense relationships with characters in text, involving the ability to understand, evaluate, and predict their beliefs, goals, and actions. Whether theorists use terms like "empathy," "perspective taking," "overcoming egocentrism," "intersubjectivity," or "theory of mind," it is clear that expert readers actively strive to "get inside the heads" of characters.

Several studies suggest that readers' emotional ties to characters actually influence their decoding and interpretation of text (e.g., Campbell & Williams, 2000; Gardner & Smith, 1987; Gaskins, 1996; Hynds, 1989). For example, one study asked eighth graders to read and retell a passage about a fight during a basketball game between a Boston team (presumably the Celtics) and a Philadelphia team (presumably the 76ers). The readers were from Boston or Philadelphia, and were selected only if they declared themselves to be avid fans of their hometown basketball team. The text itself was neutral in terms of how valid the referees' calls were and which team started the fight. Interestingly, the readers' interpretations of the text were directly and dramatically biased by their emotional involvement in the teams. This was especially apparent in comparison to other readers' responses to a control passage of the same story with fictional teams.

Other studies have found that readers' interpretations of text differ according to their social values, attitudes, and even personalities (e.g., Campbell & Williams, 2000; Dole & Sinatra, 1994). This notion is similar to the assumptions of the bibliotherapy approach. From a psychodynamic point of view, it is believed to be therapeutic for readers to identify with the characters, share in their dilemmas and emotions, and transfer these ideas to their own lives (e.g., Sridhar & Vaughn, 2002).

In summary, the process of reading comprehension seems to engage a variety of social cognitive processes in forming relationships with text, author, and characters. Although the three domains are likely to be intertwined, each may activate different aspects of social and discourse knowledge.

HOW CAN A MODEL OF SOCIAL INFORMATION PROCESSING BE USED TO UNDERSTAND READING COMPREHENSION?

Despite the many theorists who acknowledge the social nature of reading comprehension, none of their models seems sufficiently detailed, complex, and interactive to explain how a reader interprets texts about social discourse. Fortunately, research on the development of social information processing that underlies "online" social behaviors seems to hold great promise for illuminating this process. In particular, a model proposed by Crick and Dodge (1994; see Figure 7.1) tries to capture the multiple and overlapping factors that may explain individual differences in social understandings and relationships.

Using dozens of studies of children's social cognition and interaction, Crick and Dodge (1994) defined six steps related to actual social behaviors and adjustment. In their model, individuals approach any social situation with a database of memories of past social experiences and schemas, represented by the inner circle. They then receive a particular set of social cues as input. The actual response to an interaction (Step 6) is an outcome of the ways in which these cues are processed through five steps: (1) encoding, through perceiving and attending to internal and external cues; (2) representing and interpreting the cues; (3) selecting a goal for the situation; (4) retrieving possible responses from long-term memory; and (5) evaluating these responses and their outcomes and selecting one conclusion. Step 6 is the behavioral enactment of that response. Although this model is presented as a sequence, one of its key aspects is the presence of

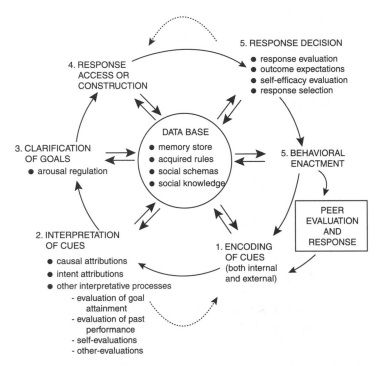

FIGURE 7.1. Social information-processing model. From Crick and Dodge (1994, p. 76). Copyright 1994 by the American Psychological Association. Reprinted by permission.

feedback loops connecting all previous steps. As the five steps influence each other, they continue to be filtered through the database of stored social experiences and knowledge.

One small incident illustrates the usefulness of this model for understanding the complexities of social interactions. Sean, a senior in high school, was enrolled in a required physical education class in tap dancing. At 6 feet 2 inches tall and 200 pounds, he was not a star tap dancer. According to his own database and social schemas, this was the last context where he would expect to meet potential dates. Therefore, he was very startled when an attractive girl, Danielle, initiated a conversation with him. A few days later, she gave him a note suggesting that they get together after class. Given that she had met him when he was in the embarrassing position of wearing gym shorts and size-12 tap shoes, Sean interpreted all those cues as clear evidence that she was interested in dating him (Steps 1 and 2). Selecting a goal of getting to know her better (Step 3), and accessing the response to call her (Step 4), he evaluated the response of making this phone call by consulting with other friends (Step 5). Finally, he invited her on a date (Step 6). In the peer evaluation and response phase, Danielle accepted his invitation.

How did Sean then encode and interpret this set of cues from Danielle? Again, filtered through his database of memories and social schemas, he remained baffled about this appealing girl's interest in him, the school's worst tap dancer. Reencoding and reinterpreting the cues from that perspective (Steps 1 and 2), he became uneasy. This led him to clarify his goal (Step 3): he wanted to get to know her, but he also wanted to avoid the humiliating experience of being alone with a girl who was "out of his league," and having no shared interests to keep the conversation going. This possibility was exacerbated by the realization that he would then see her every day in tap dancing class. Now the goal of "avoiding humiliation" took priority. Again recruiting his database in order to construct a solution, Sean moved on to Step 4, and retrieved a social script that many of his friends had used for first dates. This social script could be called "There's safety in numbers," in which boys invite other friends along on the date! He evaluated this response, especially in light of his low sense of self-efficacy at being "cool" enough to go on a date with Danielle, in Step 5. Finally, at Step 6, he called her back to finalize the plans for the date, suggesting that they go to the movies. He also casually mentioned that three or four of his friends would accompany them. This time he received a different peer response: Danielle suddenly remembered that she had to baby-sit that evening!

Suppose Sean had read a narrative about a high school boy meeting a girl in a tap dancing class? Would he have used the same lens and database to interpret the text and make a prediction about the boy's actions? Would a reader with more self-efficacy about his tap dancing skills come to a different conclusion? The Crick and Dodge (1994) model may be useful in exploring readers' comprehension of text about social interaction. If the description of the five steps of the Crick and Dodge model of social information processing was modified to replace the word "individual" with "reader," and "social cues" with "text," it would be apparent that oral and written discourse comprehension share critical social cognitive processes.

If these shared dimensions could be identified, then an important piece of the puzzle in working with students with language learning disabilities could be put in place: Why do so many students struggle with reading comprehension even after they have mastered word- and sentence-level reading skills? Could these inferential reading difficulties reflect underlying differences in social information processing? Although there are no reading research studies that directly address this question, the research literature on social cognition in students with learning disabilities provides some support for this notion. Motivated by the well-known findings that many students with language learning disabilities have difficulty with peer acceptance and peer interaction (Kavale & Forness, 1996; Pearl & Donahue, 2004; Rice, 1993; Wong & Donahue, 2002), a number of studies have attempted to identify the social information-processing components that underlie their social competence (Tur-Kaspa, 2002).

While social cognition studies are not substitutes for reading comprehension research, they may provide insights about the perceptions that students bring to a reading task. Typical stimulus materials have examined comprehension of brief scenarios or problem situations. These scenarios lack the shifts across time and place, cast of secondary characters, and subplots that enrich literature selections. However, they do follow a format familiar to written text that includes setting and character, introduction of problem or conflict, attempts to resolve conflict, and resolution or outcome. For example, using audiotaped conflict scenarios featuring children interacting with peers, teachers, or siblings, Tur-Kaspa and Bryan (1994) assessed students' ability to encode, interpret, search for a response, decide which response to choose, evaluate that response, and enact that response decision (Crick & Dodge, 1994). Students listened to this sample vignette: "One free period Bill has nothing to do. He walks outside and sees two of his classmates playing a game. Bill really wants to play with them. He walks up to them but they just keep playing."

Using stories like that one, students have been asked to identify goals, interpret characters' words and actions, and predict consequences. Findings clearly suggest that some individuals with learning disabilities differ from typical students in their comprehension of linguistic and situational cues. Whether scenes were enacted on videotape or read aloud with accompanying written scripts, students with learning disabilities generated less sophisticated and less accurate interpretations of the social scenarios before them. They also were more likely to rate neutral or friendly scenes as "unfriendly." Other studies have found that students with learning disabilities chose different social goals than other students, usually preferring goals that avoided conflict or were less assertive. The finding that students with learning disabilities are more likely to add extraneous details when retelling problem scenarios suggests that they may rely more on their own social script and databases than on the text or discourse when interpreting information (Williams, 1993). In short, students with learning disabilities have been found to differ from typical classmates at every step of the Crick and Dodge (1994) model, suggesting that they may also struggle to comprehend and interpret the desires, plans, and courses of action undertaken by authors and characters (see Tur-Kaspa, 2002, for a review).

In summary, the Crick and Dodge (1994) model may hold the potential to frame our thinking about how social cognitive processes come to light during reading comprehension. In particular, the assumption that processing of every social cue is filtered through an individual's database of social experiences and schemas elucidates how readers vary in their responses to text. Although these notions seem most applicable to the comprehension of written narratives, it is likely that expository and persuasive genres also require readers to recruit their social cognitive abilities, for example, as the reader assesses the credibility and goals of the author.

READING "CHARLES"

To explore the idea that social information-processing deficits may resurface in comprehending text about social interaction, we selected the Shirley Jackson (1948) short story about a child starting kindergarten, "Charles" (included in Appendix 7.1). Although this text has a traditional readability level of only about fourth grade, it is obviously crammed with complex social understandings and misunderstandings.

An example of the use of social information-processing strategies in comprehending text is provided by the first author's (Donahue) experience while reading this story. I was completely hooked by the end of the first paragraph. Of course, the story is written from a mother's perspective, so I had a rich database of prior knowledge. Having experienced sending three children off to kindergarten, I immediately detected the first telltale sign of a mother "in denial" when the narrator in the first paragraph generously suggests that Laurie just "forgot" to wave good-bye to her. I then chose the goal to confirm my suspicion that Laurie's mother had some lurking qualms about her own as well as Laurie's adjustment to kindergarten. In the next several paragraphs, I noted three incidents of Laurie's mildly rebellious behavior, ignored by his parents.

In the fourth paragraph, the first direct discourse in the text is *"How was school today?" I asked, elaborately casual.* I immediately used an author-questioning strategy: "Why did the author write that the mother felt the need to be 'elaborately casual'? Was it because she was afraid to know the truth? Or that she didn't want Laurie to know how important his answer was to her?" At this turning point, Laurie offered stories about Charles as a window to life in kindergarten; the parents' immediate and intense fascination with these stories confirmed to me that they were very relieved that it was somebody else's child who was causing all the problems! Checking against my own database, I evaluated my hypotheses and drew my conclusions. They were corroborated throughout the rest of the story, but the narrator's overwhelming desire to meet Charles's mother was an important tip-off. Of course, that person turned out to be herself, an irony that I found delicious.

Clearly, in constructing this conclusion, I drew upon my own social experiences to create a relationship with the text, with the author, and with the main character. Of course, not every reader would construct the same meanings. In fact, based on our experiences reading this story with middle-school and high-school students, we were startled at the variability across students in their ability to solve the mystery of Charles's identity. A few students would begin to grin halfway through reading the story. Others were still puzzled by the end of the story, wondering "So what happened to Charles?" Intriguingly, this variability in comprehension seemed to be unrelated to students' decoding, fluency, or discussion skills. Two secondary English teachers who had read the story many times with their students confirmed our observations; one commented that she often assigned the story at the beginning of the year as a means of assessing the range of inferential comprehension abilities in her classes.

Below we highlight the social information processing that social interaction and written text comprehension may share, through examples from the oral responses to Charles of some middle-school and high-school students with a wide range of reading abilities. The claim that readers invoke their database of memories and social schemas to detect incongruities in text was immediately apparent. In fact, we were compelled to modify the story because of this tendency. In the original Shirley Jackson story, published in 1948, the punishment for Charles's transgressions was spanking. The notion that teachers would strike a child was so discrepant from our readers' school schemas that they were distracted from the story line. At the risk of interfering with the authenticity of the text, we ultimately "updated" the story, to replace spanking with "time-outs" as the consequence for Charles's misbehavior.

Discussions were organized around three open-ended questions:

1. What happened at the end of the story?
2. What did Laurie and the children at school think about Charles?
3. Why didn't Laurie's parents ever suspect that Laurie was making up a story?

Their interpretations illustrate how so-called wrong answers shed light on readers' relationships with the text, the author, and the characters.

What Happened at the End of the Story?

Even though all students decoded the basic, literal message of the text, their interpretations were unpredictable and wide-ranging. Some students made no social inferences, and formed no relationships with the characters. They simply recalled the literal final events.

"The teachers have a PTA meeting with Laurie's mother. The teacher said that Laurie adjusted very slowly."

"Laurie's mom was looking for Charles's mom, but no one was looking like she said."

Other readers inferred that there was no Charles, but did not understand why. These interpretations seemed to reflect a basic faith that all of the author's words were sincere and true. However, readers clearly struggled to use prior knowledge to reconcile the mystery and generate some hypotheses.

"Charles was there and then he wasn't."

"I didn't get that at all. First Charles was in the story and then he wasn't. Maybe he moved away."

"I didn't get this. Maybe they kicked him out."

"Maybe the teacher made a mistake. Maybe he was there, and then he moved or something."

Another student who himself was sometimes victimized by peers focused on the theme of Charles as a bully. His interpretation may have reflected "wishful thinking."

"There was a Charles in the first part and then they took him away and no one knew where."

A few readers inferred that Laurie had invented Charles, but did not make the inferential leap that Laurie *was* Charles. This reflected a lack of insight into the character's goals or agendas—for example, why Laurie may have felt the need to lie.

"Maybe Laurie had an imaginary friend."

Finally, some readers, although not necessarily the best decoders, "got it" immediately.

"I think Laurie's mother finds out that Laurie was lying about Charles doing all these things and it was really Laurie doing the things."

"Charles is really Laurie and Laurie did all the stuff and told his mom that Charles did it, but it was really him. So when his mom went to the PTA meeting she found out Charles is not real."

Of those students who inferred that Charles did not really exist, only a few students became suspicious in the middle of the story. Most students pointed to the last sentence, the teacher's statement, "We don't have any Charles in the kindergarten," to indicate when they knew that Charles was not real.

What Did Laurie and the Children at School Think of Charles?

Of course, there is no explicit text-based answer to this question. As readers never meet Charles, they must invent him in the same way that Laurie did. Note that there was one critical detail in the story that itself led to several different interpretations of this question: Laurie reported to his parents that when Charles was punished by being kept after school, all the children stayed after school with him. For readers who "get" the story, of course, this is often the bit of incongruity that triggers their first suspicion that Charles is actually Laurie. Three different patterns of interpretations of this detail seemed to emerge, all clearly filtered through the readers' personal memory and scripts.

Taking the reports of Charles's misbehavior at face value, most readers imposed their own opinions, or perhaps the opinion that they assumed adults would endorse (e.g., Campbell & Williams, 2000), and claimed that nobody approved of Charles.

"Laurie didn't like him at all."

"Maybe he's a troubled child."

"A mean kid."

"They didn't like him."

"Bully."

In musing about this question, however, several readers brought up the "children staying after school" anomaly and tried to shoehorn it into their schemas. Some thought that Charles's behavior must have caused the other children to get into trouble as well, and therefore they also were forced to stay after school. Some were puzzled, or changed their ideas midstream.

"Laurie thought he was a troublemaker. All the kids had to stay after school. [Why?] They were probably aware of the situation. I'm not sure. I read that they had to stay after."

"He was horrible. [Why did they stay after school with Charles?] They had to. [Why?] No idea."

"I don't know. But I think they *had to* stay after school."

"Mean. Whenever he has time-out, they stay with him. [Why?] To see what he would do. [Do you think they like him?] I think."

The student for whom Charles' bullying was salient reconciled the mystery of why other children would choose to stay after school with him as "the need for vigilance"!

"They had to watch him to make sure he wouldn't do anything else."

Finally, some readers picked up on textual cues that suggested that the other children approved of Charles, including the notion that they stayed after school with him "in solidarity."

"They liked him cause they stayed after school. They thought he was really cool."

"Laurie likes seeing him get in trouble."

"Laurie thinks Charles is cool. In another place, the teacher said 'Don't play,' and they did anyways."

"Laurie laughed at the things Charles did. He liked it when Charles does bad stuff."

Why Didn't Laurie's Parents Ever Suspect That Laurie Was Making Up a Story?"

Most interpretations were tied to the text, assuming that the parents could only have suspected if the text and the teacher had explicitly told them.

"Because the baby got sick [i.e., therefore the mother could not attend the first PTA meeting]."

"Because they hadn't met the teacher yet, and they hadn't met anyone in the class."

Other students did show some insight into the beliefs and reasoning of the parents.

"Because Laurie mentioned it when he had dinner every night."

"Because that could happen. There could be a kid that had bad behavior. [Why didn't they think that Laurie could be bad at school?] He was good at home? And the teacher don't say anything. They thought he was a good kid. He would never do it."

"His parents were blinded by love."

"Because they could have gone to the teacher and found out if he was telling the truth or not [i.e., in other words, the parents would infer that Laurie would have known that it would be too easy for the lie to be discovered; note the complex layering of social cognitive processing and perspective taking that this response entailed]."

Finally, a response from a fifth-grade student makes the point that reading comprehension involves a consideration of multiple social perspectives. This remark was made after a heated group discussion that left the answer to this question still unresolved.

> WILLIAM: Oh, I know. I get it now. I know. And you guys are gonna really laugh when I say it. Why they didn't suspect? Well, look at how long it took *us* to figure out who Charles was!
>
> CLASSMATES: (*Silence*)
>
> TJ: I'm not laughing.

Notice that William's insight shows how the reader is juggling social relationships through multiple lenses:

1. A prediction of how his classmates and fellow readers will respond (which turns out to be wrong, as his classmates do not understand his point).
2. An awareness of his own difficulty as a reader, struggling to understand the mind of characters with a complicated social relationship with another character, that is, the parents and their son Laurie.
3. Most importantly, a recognition that the reader *still* had an advantage over the parents in figuring out the mind of their own child.

What is that advantage? As predicted by our model of social information processing, unlike fast-fading social interaction, reading offers the time to freeze the interaction, reread the text, reinterpret the social cues, filter those cues through the reader's prior knowledge and schemas, reflect on the characters' goals, question the possible social responses, and think about the characters' decision making.

In summary, these responses illustrate how a text well within readers' word recognition and vocabulary abilities can still be interpreted in multiple ways. Understanding how these responses reflect social experiences and cognitive processes in individual children may elucidate the complex interactions between oral and written discourse.

IMPLICATIONS FOR INFORMING PRACTICE

As educators and speech–language pathologists, our overriding questions are: If reading comprehension depends on many of the social cognitive processes that underlie oral dialogue, what kinds of social information-processing strategies are needed for a reader to "get" a particular text? Can insights into a student's social cognitive processes help us understand the seemingly "off the wall" interpretations that some readers make? Conversely, can written text about social interaction be used to analyze and scaffold "online" discourse? Clearly, research is needed that addresses the complex developmental relationships among social information processes and the comprehension of oral and written discourse, especially for readers with language and learning disabilities. Although concrete implications for assessment and intervention are premature, we believe that an exploration of these relationships holds great promise for informing the practice of educators and speech–language pathologists.

The notion that reading comprehension depends on a transaction between the text and the reader's own social experiences and processing may seem obvious. However, it invites educators and speech–language pathologists to reflect upon the processes and dialogues that they themselves use as readers. If these transactions are barely discernible to the proficient reader, they are likely to be completely invisible to the struggling comprehender. Socially complex texts like "Charles" are valuable for making explicit the relationships that readers establish with the text, the author, and the characters, for example, through teacher "think-alouds" that highlight the self-questioning dialogues of expert readers (e.g., "Does this make sense? I wonder why the character responded in that way. What did the author mean in this passage?"). In the same way, educators and speech–language pathologists can frame questions from the social information-processing model to analyze student responses that would typically be considered just "wrong." For example, practitioners can assess whether a reader "missed the details" of the text, or simply interpreted them through his or her own lens of prior knowledge and social scripts.

Acknowledging that readers draw from different sources in order to comprehend text also challenges educators and speech–language pathologists to assess and adjust their own discourse styles. At the moment of redirecting a student in order to prompt a "correct" answer, practitioners automatically make choices about the relative priority of the reader/text transaction. Traditional discourse models that correct inaccurate responses, either through a teacher or peer comment, may repair the response, but typically fail to illuminate the social cognitive path that led to that response. Moving toward comprehension instruction that makes explicit the readers' social information-processing decisions may necessitate a conscious adjustment in the manner in which we scaffold student attempts.

One goal of comprehension instruction may be to challenge students to identify their social point of reference for comprehension, and also to evaluate whether that point of reference is sufficient to interpret the text before them. Does a particular response derive from the text or from their own set of experiences and values? If the latter, are those experiences and values congruent with the author's treatment of setting, plot, and character? For example, imagine a die-hard fan of the Chicago Cubs reading a newspaper editorial about how the team should be disbanded. Students could be asked to predict what the fan's biases might be, relative to their own perceptions. This process encourages students to manage their own comprehension skills and analyze their own errors. Students could be invited to switch perspectives and then to reread to identify the correct or relevant information. Students may become aware that comprehension comes from the written page, from their own set of experiences and values, or from an intersection of text and reader expectations.

More ambitious, perhaps, is the possibility that written texts about social interaction may be valuable sites for scaffolding the development of oral discourse (e.g., Donahue, 1997; Donahue, Szymanski, & Flores, 1999). Given the subtle and fast-fading nature of social cues, it is difficult for students with social cognitive deficits to get accurate "data" for analyzing interaction. However, unlike face-to-face social interaction, the characters in written text do not walk away before the student can process their comments, catch the sarcasm, or think of an effective "comeback" line. Further, there is no social risk to reinitiating the interaction, by rereading, questioning, and thinking aloud about social cues, goals, relationships, and outcomes.

Fortunately, assessment and intervention approaches that highlight the relationships among social information-processing strategies and reading comprehension are entirely consistent with literature-based models of reading instruction. New materials, expensive kits for teaching "stand-alone" social skills, or a dramatic restructuring of the curriculum are not required. These approaches also offer a natural opportunity for classroom teachers and speech–language pathologists to work together to analyze the social information-processing demands of written texts, adapt their own discourse styles to enable students to make reader and text relationships explicit, and integrate oral and written discourse goals.

In short, Socrates was wrong. Reading comprehension is inherently social discourse, as readers form relationships with the text, the author, and the characters. The very fact that writers are dialoguing with Socrates' ideas in 2004 proves our point that written text enables discourse across the centuries. What would happen if Socrates had e-mail? We predict that he would be spending his time in Internet chat rooms, questioning, clarifying, challenging, and refuting the viewpoints of other writers, engaged in true Socratic dialogue.

APPENDIX 7.1: A SHORT STORY, "CHARLES," FROM *THE LOTTERY* BY SHIRLEY JACKSON

The day my son Laurie started kindergarten he renounced corduroy overalls with bibs and began wearing blue jeans with a belt; I watched him go off the first morning with the older girl next door, seeing clearly that an era of my life was ended, my sweet-voiced nursery-school tot replaced by a long-trousered, swaggering character who forgot to stop at the corner and wave goodbye to me.

He came home the same way, the front door slamming open, his cap on the floor, and the voice suddenly become raucous shouting, "Isn't anybody *here*?"

At lunch he spoke insolently to his father, spilled his baby sister's milk, and remarked that his teacher said we were not to take the name of the Lord in vain.

"How *was* school today?" I asked, elaborately casual.

"All right," he said.

"Did you learn anything?" his father asked.

Laurie regarded his father coldly. "I didn't learn nothing," he said.

"Anything," I said. "Didn't learn anything."

"The teacher spanked a boy, though," Laurie said, addressing his bread and butter. "For being fresh," he added with his mouth full.

"What did he do?" I asked. "Who was it?"

Laurie thought. "It was Charles," he said. "He was fresh. The teacher spanked him and made him stand in a corner. He was awfully fresh."

"What did he do?" I asked again, but Laurie slid off his chair, took a cookie, and left, while his father was still saying, "See here, young man."

The next day Laurie remarked at lunch, as soon as he sat down, "Well, Charles was bad again today." He grinned enormously and said, "Today Charles hit the teacher."

"Good heavens," I said, mindful of the Lord's name, "I suppose he got spanked again?"

"He sure did," Laurie said. "Look up," he said to his father.

"What?" his father said, looking up.

"Look down," Laurie said. "Look at my thumb. Gee, you're dumb." He began to laugh insanely.

"Why did Charles hit the teacher?" I asked quickly.

"Because she tried to make him color with red crayons," Laurie said. "Charles wanted to color with green crayons so he hit the teacher and she spanked him and said nobody play with Charles but everybody did."

The third day—it was Wednesday of the first week—Charles bounced a see-saw onto the head of a little girl and made her bleed, and the teacher made him stay inside all during recess. Thursday Charles had to stand in a corner during story-time because he kept pounding his feet on the floor. Friday Charles was deprived of blackboard privileges because he threw chalk.

On Saturday I remarked to my husband, "Do you think kindergarten is too unsettling for Laurie? All this toughness, and bad grammar, and this Charles boy sounds like such a bad influence."

"It'll be all right," my husband said reassuringly. "Bound to be people like Charles in the world. Might as well meet them now as later."

On Monday Laurie came home late, full of news. "Charles," he shouted as he came up the hill; I was waiting anxiously on the front steps. "Charles," Laurie yelled all the way up the hill, "Charles was bad again."

"Come right in," I said, as soon as he came close enough. "Lunch is waiting."

"You know what Charles did?" he demanded, following me through the door. "Charles yelled so in school they sent a boy from first grade to tell the teacher she had to make Charles keep quiet, and so Charles had to stay after school. And so all the children stayed to watch him."

"What did he do?" I asked.

"He just sat there," Laurie said, climbing into his chair at the table. "Hi, Pop, y'old dust mop."

"Charles had to stay after school today," I told my husband. "Everyone stayed with him."

"What does this Charles look like?" my husband asked Laurie. "What's his other name?"

"He's bigger than me," Laurie said. "And he doesn't have any rubbers and he doesn't ever wear a jacket."

Monday night was the first Parent–Teachers meeting, and only the fact that the baby had a cold kept me from going; I wanted passionately to meet Charles's mother. On Tuesday Laurie remarked suddenly, "Our teacher had a friend come to see her in school today."

"Charles's mother?" my husband and I asked simultaneously.

"Naaah," Laurie said scornfully. "It was a man who came and made us do exercises, we had to touch our toes. Look." He climbed down from his chair and squatted down and touched his toes. "Like this," he said. He got solemnly back into his chair and said, picking up his fork, "Charles didn't even *do* exercises."

"That's fine," I said heartily. "Didn't Charles want to do exercises?"

"Naaah," Laurie said. "Charles was so fresh to the teacher's friend he wasn't *let* do exercises."

"Fresh again?" I said.

"He kicked the teacher's friend," Laurie said. "The teacher's friend told Charles to touch his toes like I just did and Charles kicked him."

"What are they going to do about Charles, do you suppose?" Laurie's father asked him.

Laurie shrugged elaborately. "Throw him out of school, I guess," he said.

Wednesday and Thursday were routine; Charles yelled during story hour and hit a boy in the stomach and made him cry. On Friday Charles stayed after school again and so did all the other children.

With the third week of kindergarten Charles was an institution in our family; the baby was being a Charles when she cried all afternoon; Laurie did a Charles when he filled his wagon full of mud and pulled it through the kitchen; even my husband, when he caught his elbow in the telephone cord and pulled telephone, ashtray, and a bowl of flowers off the table, said, after the first minute, "Looks like Charles."

During the third and fourth weeks it looked like a reformation in Charles; Laurie reported grimly at lunch on Thursday of the third week, "Charles was so good today the teacher gave him an apple."

"What?" I said, and my husband added warily, "You mean Charles?"

"Charles," Laurie said. "He gave the crayons around and he picked up the books afterward and the teacher said he was her helper."

"What happened?" I asked incredulously.

"He was her helper, that's all," Laurie said, and shrugged.

"Can this be true, about Charles?" I asked my husband that night. "Can something like this happen?"

"Wait and see," my husband said cynically. "When you've got a Charles to deal with, this may mean he's only plotting."

He seemed to be wrong. For over a week Charles was the teacher's helper; each day he handed things out and he picked things up; no one had to stay after school.

"The P.T.A. meeting's next week again," I told my husband one evening. "I'm going to find Charles's mother there."

"Ask her what happened to Charles," my husband said. "I'd like to know."

"I'd like to know myself," I said.

On Friday of that week things were back to normal. "You know what Charles did today?" Laurie demanded at the lunch table, in a voice slightly awed. "He told a little girl to say a word and she said it and the teacher washed her mouth out with soap and Charles laughed."

"What word?" his father asked unwisely, and Laurie said, "I'll have to whisper it to you, it's so bad." He got down off his chair and went around to his father. His father bent his head down and Laurie whispered joyfully. His father's eyes widened.

"Did Charles tell the little girl to say *that*?" he asked respectfully.

"She said it *twice*," Laurie said. "Charles told her to say it *twice*."

"What happened to Charles?" my husband asked.

"Nothing," Laurie said. "He was passing out the crayons."

Monday morning Charles abandoned the little girl and said the evil word himself three or four times, getting his mouth washed out with soap each time. He also threw chalk.

My husband came to the door with me that evening as I set out for the P.T.A. meeting. "Invite her over for a cup of tea after the meeting," he said. "I want to get a look at her."

"If only she's there," I said prayerfully.

"She'll be there," my husband said. "I don't see how they could hold a P.T.A. meeting without Charles's mother."

At the meeting I sat restlessly, scanning each comfortable matronly face, trying to determine which one hid the secret of Charles. None of them looked to me haggard enough. No one stood up in the meeting and apologized for the way her son had been acting. No one mentioned Charles.

After the meeting I identified and sought out Laurie's kindergarten teacher. She had a plate with a cup of tea and a piece of chocolate cake; I had a plate with a cup of tea and a piece of marshmallow cake. We maneuvered up to one another cautiously and smiled.

"I've been so anxious to meet you," I said. "I'm Laurie's mother."

"We're all so interested in Laurie," she said.

"Well, he certainly likes kindergarten," I said. "He talks about it all the time."

"We had a little trouble adjusting, the first week or so," she said primly, "but now he's a fine little helper. With occasional lapses, of course."

"Laurie usually adjusts very quickly," I said. "I suppose this time it's Charles's influence."

"Charles?"

"Yes," I said, laughing, "you must have your hands full in that kindergarten, with Charles."

"Charles?" she said. "We don't have any Charles in the kindergarten."

ACKNOWLEDGMENTS

This chapter is based on a presentation at the conference "Maximizing Students' Language and Literacy Learning," held at Rutgers University and Seton Hall University, April 2002. We are grateful to Elaine Silliman for starting the dialogue, and to the conference organizers and participants for their insights. We also thank Michele Kessler for her contributions.

REFERENCES

Beach, R. (2000). Reading and responding to literature at the level of activity. *Journal of Literacy Research, 32,* 237–251.

Beck, I. L., McKeown, M. G., Sandora, C., Kucan, L., & Worthy, J. (1996). Questioning the author: A year-long classroom implementation to engage students with text. *The Elementary School Journal, 96*(4), 385–414.

Campbell, K., & Williams, J. (2000). Readers' social desirability and text that violates social values: Evidence of an interaction. *Journal of Educational Psychology, 92,* 515–523.

Crick, N. R., & Dodge, K. A. (1994). A review and reformulation of social information-processing mechanisms in children's social adjustment. *Psychological Bulletin, 115,* 74–101.

Dewey, J. (1906). *The child and the curriculum.* Chicago: University of Chicago Press.

Dole, J., & Sinatra, G. (1994). Social psychology research on beliefs and attitudes: Implications for research on learning from text. In R. Garner & P. Alexander (Eds.), *Beliefs about text and instruction with text* (pp. 245–264). Hillsdale, NJ: Erlbaum.

Donahue, M. (1997). Beliefs about listening in students with learning disabilities: "Is the speaker always right?" *Topics in Language Disorders, 17*(3), 441–60.

Donahue, M. L., & Foster, S. K. (2004). Social cognition, conversation, and reading comprehension: How to read a comedy of manners. In C. A. Stone, E. R. Silliman, B. J. Ehren & K. Apel (Eds.), *Handbook of language and literacy: Development and disorders* (pp. 363–379). New York: Guilford Press.

Donahue, M., Szymanski, C., & Flores, C. (1999). "When Emily Dickinson met Steven Spielberg": Assessing social information processing in literacy contexts. *Language, Speech, and Hearing Services in Schools, 30,* 274–284.

Fish, S. (1980). *Is there a text in this classroom?* Cambridge, MA: Harvard University Press.

Gardner, M., & Smith, M. (1987). Does perspective-taking ability contribute to reading comprehension? *Journal of Reading, 30,* 333–336.

Gaskins, R. W. (1996). "That's just how it was": The effect of issue-related emotional involvement on reading comprehension. *Reading Research Quarterly, 31,* 386–405.

Hynds, S. (1985). Interpersonal cognitive complexity and the literary response processes of adolescent readers. *Research in the Teaching of English, 19,* 386–404.

Hynds, S. (1989). Bringing life to literature and literature to life: Social constructs and contexts of four adolescent readers. *Research in the Teaching of English, 23,* 30–61.

Hynds, S., & Appleman, D. (1997, December). Walking our talk: Between response and responsibility in the literature classroom. *English Education,* pp. 272–294.

Jackson, S. (1948). *"The lottery" and other stories.* New York: Farrar, Straus & Giroux.

Kavale, K. A., & Forness, S. R. (1996). Social skill deficits and learning disabilities: A meta-analysis. *Journal of Learning Disabilities, 29,* 226–237.

Lewis, C. (1998). Literary interpretation as a social act. *Journal of Adolescent and Adult Literacy, 42,* 168–177.

Marshall, J. (2000). Research on response to literature. In M. Kamil, P. Mosenthal, P. D. Pearson, & R. Barr (Eds.), *Handbook of reading research* (pp. 381–402). Mahwah, NJ: Erlbaum.

Moller, K., & Allen, J. (2000). Connecting, resisting and searching for safer places:

Students respond to Mildred Taylor's *The friendship. Journal of Literacy Research*, *32*, 145–186.

November, A. C. (1998, September). The Web: Teaching Zack to think. *High School Principal*. Retrieved on October 14, 2002, from http://www.anovember.com/articles/zack.html.

Nugent, S. G. (1997, March). *If Socrates had e-mail*. . . . Paper presented at the symposium, The Transformation of Learning in the Age of Technology, sponsored by Princeton University, Washington, DC.

Pearl, R., & Donahue, M. (2004). Peer relationships. In B. Y. L. Wong (Ed.), *Learning about learning disabilities* (pp. 131–163). New York: Academic Press.

Pearson, P. D., & Fielding, L. (1991). Comprehension instruction. In R. Barr, M. L. Kamil, P. Mosenthal, & P. D. Pearson (Eds.), *Handbook of reading research* (pp. 819–860). New York: Longman.

Pressley, M. (2000). What should comprehension instruction be the instruction of? In M. L. Kamil, P. Mosenthal, P. D. Pearson, & R. Barr (Eds.), *Handbook of reading research* (pp. 545–561). Mahwah, NJ: Erlbaum.

Raphael, T. E., & Au, K. H. (1998). *Literature-based instruction: Reshaping the curriculum*. Norwood, MA: Christopher-Gordon.

Rice, M. (1993). Don't talk to him, he's weird: A social consequences account of language and social interactions. In A. P. Kaiser & D. B. Gray (Eds.), *Enhancing children's communication: Research foundations for intervention* (pp. 139–158). Baltimore: Brookes.

Rosenblatt, L. (1995). *The reader, the text, the poem: The transactional theory of the literary work*. Carbondale: Southern Illinois University Press.

Sridhar, D., & Vaughn, S. (2002). Bibliotherapy: Practices for improving self-concept and reading comprehension. In B.Y. L. Wong & M. Donahue (Eds.), *Social dimensions of learning disabilities: Essays in honor of Tanis Bryan* (pp. 161–187). Mahwah, NJ: Erlbaum.

Tur-Kaspa, H. (2002). Social cognition in learning disabilities. In B. Y. L. Wong & M. Donahue (Eds.), *Social dimensions of learning disabilities: Essays in honor of Tanis Bryan* (pp. 11–31). Mahwah, NJ: Erlbaum.

Tur-Kaspa, H., & Bryan, T. (1994). Social-information processing skills of students with learning disabilities. *Learning Disabilities Research and Practice*, *9*, 12–23.

Williams, J. (1993). Comprehension of students with or without learning disabilities: Identification of narrative themes and idiosyncratic text representations. *Journal of Educational Psychology*, *85*(4), 631–641.

Wong, B. Y. L., & Donahue, M. (Eds.). (2002). *Social dimensions of learning disabilities: Essays in honor of Tanis Bryan*. Mahwah, NJ: Erlbaum.

PART III

*

Writing and Spelling
Perspectives on Instructional and Intervention Practices

8

❧

The Role of Dialogue in Constructing Effective Literacy Settings for Students with Language and Learning Disabilities

CAROL SUE ENGLERT
KAILONNIE DUNSMORE

Students with language and learning disabilities (LLD) are a group for whom educational progress and school success is a challenging goal. Research indicates that students with LLD may possess several difficulties that impact performance, including limited/inflexible vocabulary (Gerber, 1993; Wiig & Secord, 1998), word retrieval difficulties, limited content knowledge, difficulties with pragmatics (nonverbal and verbal), problems with sustained attention (Bos & Vaughn, 2002), inability to employ cognitive and metacognitive strategies (Wong & Jones, 1982; Wong & Wilson, 1984), poor comprehension (Bos & Filip, 1984; Gersten, Fuchs, & Williams, 2001; Wong & Wilson, 1984), and failure to recognize or employ text structure genres (Englert, Raphael, Fear, & Anderson, 1988; Englert & Thomas, 1987; Wong, 1997). These difficulties impact both oral and written communication, since they are language-based (Bos & Vaughn, 2002; Catts, Fey, Zhang, & Tomblin, 1999; Scott & Windsor, 2000). In this chapter, we present instructional snapshots to illustrate what we mean by "best practices" within a language-based perspective, the nature of interactive discourse that promotes students' oral and written language literacy, and particularly, how teachers can address the cognitive, linguistic, metacognitive, and social needs of students with LLD in resource room or inclusion settings.

MAXIMIZING THE POTENTIAL OF LEARNING SETTINGS FOR STUDENTS WITH LANGUAGE AND LEARNING DISABILITIES

The program that informed this work was known as the Literacy Environments for Accelerated Progress (LEAP) project, a multiyear intervention that focused on providing access to the discourses, social practices, tools, and artifacts of readers and writers. We adopted the metaphor of "cognitive apprenticeships" to help teachers understand and employ the pedagogical tools of the project during written literacy instruction (Collins, Brown, & Holum, 1991). A cognitive apprenticeship approach is one "in which interactions between 'experts' and 'novices' support the movement of the novice toward the expert end of the learning continuum" (Hock, Schumaker, & Deshler, 1999, p. 9), and ultimately make visible to students the mature ways of comprehending, producing, reflecting on, and interpreting both spoken and printed texts. There were four features of the approach that informed our design of the apprenticeship model (Englert & Mariage, 2003).

Situated Language Activity

First, we emphasized that language and discourse are important avenues for knowledge acquisition and thought in all disciplinary subjects valued in school. Situated language learning involves the acquisition of language in authentic contexts. Since language is interwoven with the routine processes of knowing, thinking, understanding, and communicating as part of all school-based activities, school subjects offer splendid sites for language instruction. Traditional language interventions have often focused on providing remedial instruction outside the general education classroom; however, we recognized that the acquisition of language and communicative practices could be taught and practiced everyday in the authentic contexts of the academic curriculum.

The implication of this principle is that, ultimately, all teachers can be viewed as language and literacy educators who are responsible for providing students with the language associated with comprehending, communicating, and composing. General education and remedial teachers must not only provide access to, they must apprentice students into, the language of thought, expression, comprehension, and oral/written communication as part of an academic discipline (Englert & Dunsmore, 2002; Hutchins, 1997; Roth, 1998). Rather than pull out students for special instruction, we see that speech–language therapists and general education teachers can support language development in the situated context of the academic curriculum for the betterment of all students.

Apprenticeships to Make Transparent the Invisible

Second, Vygotsky (1978) proposed that the main path of cognitive development lay in social interactions with adults and peers, combined with the provision of mediating tools that support psychological performance. Learning entails mentoring by more experienced or knowledgeable persons (teachers or peers), who engage in the activity by working side-by-side with less experienced persons while providing ongoing support and scaffolding (Lee & Smagorinsky, 2000). At first, mentors make their higher order thinking visible through modeling and thinking aloud, thereby providing access to the discourse and inner speech associated with tool use, as well as to the false starts, waverings, impasses, and corrections that address the situated ebb and flow of problem solving during constructive cognitive activity (Englert & Raphael, 1989; Roth & McRobbie, 1999).

However, Vygotsky (1978) also proposed a developmental shift as novices move from peripheral (observer) to coparticipant (actor) roles in their performance of the discourse-based practices and activities of the discipline. Initially, mentors and students jointly produce the inner thoughts, discourses, and actions on an *intermental or social plane* (e.g., performance is shared or distributed between the two or more participants' minds) (Englert & Mariage, 2003). Over time, students take up the discourse and actions that have been performed by others, and they begin to "ventriloquate" by appropriating the words and actions of mentors and peers (Wertsch, 1991). The discourse may be overtly spoken by students in a form of self-talk known as "egocentric speech," but then the discourse goes underground in the form of inner speech. Ultimately the cognitive processes and practices that were once jointly produced become internalized as the talk is turned inward to guide and influence the students' own thoughts and actions on an intramental plane (i.e., within an individual's mind). Even then, there remains the quality of hidden dialogicality, insofar as the traces of prior conversations, dialogues, and actions still influence the inner talk and behavioral repertoire of the learner (Bakhtin, 1986; Wertsch, 1991). Students anticipate the words previously spoken by mentors and peers, and speak them on a private plane to direct and inform their own performance.

Zones of Proximal Development

A third critical feature of a cognitive apprenticeship that informed the intervention was the emphasis on the mediation of students' performance in the zone of joint or collaborative action (Chaiklin, 2003). Vygotsky (1978) called this the *zone of proximal development*, which he defined as the gap between the level of performance achieved by the student working alone and the level of performance achieved by the student working in collaboration with others or with the scaffolding support and use of mediational tools.

Adults scaffold performance in the zone of proximal development by providing a hierarchy of questions, prompts, or models, or by highlighting critical features (Hogan & Pressley, 1997; Stone, 2002). The hallmark of such guided participation is the calibration of the teachers' prompts to the students' level of understanding, with supports continually added or removed depending upon the students' uptake or response to the adult's prior assisted effort. Teachers simultaneously *step in* to provide supports and scaffolds for skills and strategies that are beyond the child's independent attainment, and *step back* to transfer control to students for other skills and strategies that are within the realm of their growing competence and mastery. Effective scaffolds are always temporary. Teachers must consciously add and withdraw support so that students complete the full cycle of apprenticeship, ending with the development of students' abilities to direct their own mental and physical actions.

Mediational Tools

Finally, a fourth feature of cognitive apprenticeship involves the provision of tools that mediate performance (Kozulin, 2003). Mediational tools include any number of symbolic systems, such as mnemonic techniques, strategic routines, visual or symbolic reminders, graphic organizers, and diagrams, to name but a few (Wong & Berninger, 2004). In reading and writing, tools also include language users' knowledge of text structure genres, the sequential and progressive organization of meanings that help writers engage in text construction and that help readers anticipate and engage in text interpretation and response. Graphic organizers, for example, can help students remember and produce ideas in an organized manner. Knowledge of such structures mediates performance by enabling participants to plan, coordinate, and review their actions (Wells, 2000).

In addition, a primary mediational tool that is used to support language and literacy development is written language. In speech, memory for exact words is extremely short, and, without recourse to a text of what has been said (Wells, 1999), it is difficult for learners to reflect on the meanings and language structures of the spoken text. In contrast, written language offers a permanent record that can be reviewed, rethought, studied, and revised, thereby allowing the text to be the medium for an instructional discourse that can help young language users become conscious of its form and structure. Instructional talk, for example, can move back and forth between an author's lived experience and the transformation of that experience into a written form that can convey precise meanings to an audience that is distant in space and time (Wells, 1999). Simultaneously, the recorded text itself can be reviewed with attention to how the text builds meaning across local (phrases and sentences) units or global (multiparagraph) units. In this manner, both the process of composing (texting) and the artifact itself (text) can be sources of inference and knowledge about the forms, stylistic requirements, and organization of language (Wells, 1999).

The Context of the Study

The purpose of this study was to examine the process of apprenticeship in an effective inclusion classroom. The selection of this classroom was based upon the number of children who were discontinued by school psychologists from special education services in the areas of reading and writing by the end of fifth grade. The teachers also had participated on the literacy project for 4 years, and were considered skilled by researchers and teachers in their implementation of the pedagogical principles of the project. We decided to study their effectiveness in providing a cognitive apprenticeship, and the possible effect of their interactions in moving students from novice to more expert proficiency levels of performance.

The chosen classroom offered a unique vantage point for studying an apprenticeship model because it was an inclusion classroom where a large number of students were identified as having mild disabilities. As a general education multiage classroom (grades 1–4), it included all special education students for the entire school day. The composition of the class was diverse. Of the 28 students, 19 were African American, three were Hispanic, and six were Caucasian. Thirteen of the students had been identified for special education services, including eight students with learning disabilities, two students with behavioral disorders, two students with physical disabilities, and one student with cognitive impairment. Eight of the students received speech and language services. Thus, the classroom problematized the notion of apprenticeship in school settings given the fact that a large number of students (46%) had been identified with learning, language, or cognitive disabilities.

Our study focused on language instruction and development in the context of the writing curriculum. We focused on two activity settings: (1) teacher-mediated whole-class lessons in an activity known as "Personal

News" and (2) partner writing during a thematic unit. These two activity settings permitted the full examination of the nature of the apprenticeship, progressing from the joint or intermental plane of development, with students' participation guided by the teacher or more knowledgeable others, to the intramental plane, reflecting the students' acquisition and growing mastery of writing strategies, tools, and talk. To focus our examination of the apprenticeship and appropriation processes, we examined the participation and performance of a student with LLD as a telling case.

Three questions framed our selection and analysis of the data emerging from the larger study:

1. What teaching practices foster the apprenticeship of students in language tools and writing practices?
2. To what extent do teachers *step in* to lead cognitive development and *step back* to transfer control to students for the problem-solving processes associated with written language?
3. What is the relationship between the discourse practices surrounding the social interactions of teachers and students, and the development of literacy talk and disciplinary knowledge as expressed by students with LLD in their interactions with peers as they jointly construct expository texts?

Case Study Student

The case study student, Joseph, was identified as a 3-year-old for services through the preprimary impairment (PPI) program run by the Intermediate School District. Joseph began receiving services from a speech–language pathologist (for expressive language and articulation disorders), an occupational therapist (for fine and gross motor disabilities), and a learning disabilities specialist as a 3-year-old, and he still received these services when he began elementary school. He entered the multiage inclusion classroom as a kindergartener, because all students with disabilities in the primary grades received services from the special education teacher in the lower elementary inclusion classroom. However, at the time of the case study reported in this chapter, he was a first grader in the multiage classroom.

Since researchers had begun collecting baseline information on students the year prior to this case study, there was some preliminary information about Joseph. In his kindergarten year, his teachers had expressed grave concerns about Joseph's ability to participate in the language-based activities that placed demands on his expressive abilities. They were concerned that the language demands of their multiage classroom might overwhelm him because of his limited language skills. An observation of Joseph during a book discussion in his kindergarten year revealed little or no interaction between Joseph and the other students in the group. In the transcription of a segment of book discussion shown below, Joseph was asked by a peer (Alex) about what part of a picture book he liked.

ALEX: What part do you like, Joseph?

JOSEPH: (*No response*)

TEACHER: Joseph is thinking, and that's OK. What do you think, Joseph? (*to Alex*) What was the question again? Ask him again. He maybe forgot.

ALEX: What part did you like?

JOSEPH: I don't remember.

TEACHER: What happened in the book? What part did you like? I think that's what Alex wants to know.

JOSEPH: I can't remember what I like.

TEACHER: Can't remember?

JOSEPH: (*Shakes head.*)

TEACHER: Need some more time to think?

JOSEPH: (*Nods.*)

ALEX: I like the part where the boy and the girl were hugging the dog.

NICHOLAS: I like that part too.

TEACHER: Can you think of what part you like, Joseph?

JOSEPH: Same as Nicholas.

This segment shows that, as a kindergartener, Joseph had difficulty expressing his views about a picture book that had been read aloud, or even naming the events from the story. He was given five opportunities to comment on the story, but without any success. The teacher did pause to allow Joseph time to think. Finally, on the sixth prompt, he answered: "Same as Nicholas," but Nicholas in his turn had simply concurred with a prior speaker. This shows that Joseph's ability to participate in language events was limited, regardless of the source of his language difficulties. A sample of his writing at the start of his first-grade year confirmed that Joseph was performing at an emergent level of literacy at the start of the case study year, not only in reading but in writing. An example is shown in Figure 8.1. Joseph wrote his first name and the letters "CaB" at the top of the page. At the bottom of the page he has scribbled some text. He told the observer that it says "Joseph went swimming." In the middle of the page is a round-like person without fingers, toes, or hair in a pool of water.

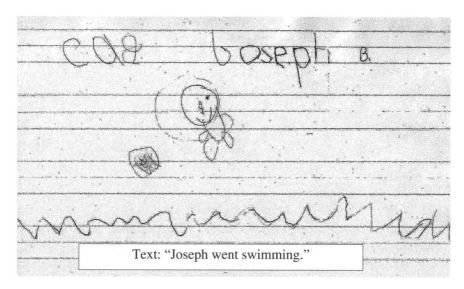

Text: "Joseph went swimming."

FIGURE 8.1. Joseph's September story.

Literacy Context

In the multiage inclusion classroom in the first grade, Joseph was taught by the general and special education teachers who cotaught the entire school day. It was during Joseph's first-grade year that we collected the material that formed the basis of the case study material reported in this chapter. The teachers began their collaboration during the project, which was initiated by the general education teacher because of her respect for the language-based intervention implemented by the special education teacher. At the time of this study, the two teachers strived to teach reading and writing throughout the entire day, using thematic units to extend literacy instruction and language-based activities into the content areas of their curriculum. Through their participation on the LEAP project, the two teachers placed emphases on modeling and fostering students' use of literacy strategies, discourses, and tools in the process of constructing, communicating, and comprehending both narrative and expository texts.

The activity setting in which we undertook the examination of *whole-class writing* instruction was "Morning Message" or "Personal News." In Personal News, a student described a personal experience, which the class transformed into written text by asking questions to gather information from the author, and then transforming the ideas into text that was compatible with the linguistic and symbolic features of the written register. The student featured in the story was designated the author because it was about his or her personal experience. Typically, the author sat in a special chair at the front of the room, and the other students were invited to ask questions of the author. Throughout the activity, the teacher acted as a scribe in recording the group's ideas, although the group jointly negotiated and collaborated to transform the narrative or spontaneous form of oral language into the language of written text. The ideas were progressively refined, as the teacher and students gradually constructed forms of literacy more distant from the immediacy and informality of the grammar of speech (Cope & Kalantzis, 1993). In other words, they had to construct written language that was independent of the contextual clues, meaning interpretations, inquiries, and additional background information that was normally provided by speakers and listeners participating in an interactive and shared context.

The teacher, based on regular interviews and informal conversations with her about her classroom practice, viewed Personal News as a central part of her work in promoting a community of literate students. She highlighted this activity as one in which she modeled many writing skills. She often encouraged students to think of writing as a recursive process involving brainstorming, categorizing or concept map development, paragraph writing (involving a topic sentence, a number of detail sentences, and finally a conclusion sentence), and text editing. For this analysis, a typical Personal News lesson was selected from the latter part of the year (March) to provide information about the potential for oral and written language instruction in the academic curriculum, and the role of the teacher in the language instruction. On this particular day, the special education teacher led the activity, although the lead teaching role did shift between the two teachers.

A second activity setting involved a collaborative context in which two students were engaged in writing a report. The activity typically involved the following process: (1) brainstorming questions about the topic in whole-class contexts; (2) research and inquiry through firsthand (inquiry) and secondhand (reading books) investigations involving note taking and the recording of ideas in symbolic form (using pictures, invented spelling, diagrams, etc.); (3) sharing notes in whole-class discussions and organizing the information in graphic organizers or semantic webs; (4) writing expository papers with peers; (5) conferencing and revising papers with teachers; and (6) producing a final published draft. Throughout the process, students regularly engaged in whole-group, small-group, partner, and independent activity. Many processes were similar to that followed in Personal News, including the generation of topic and detail sentences, paragraphing, mechanics, and so on. As such, it offered a venue for studying the appropriation and internalization of ways of talking about texts, as well as the language and practices associated with writing in situated contexts. We transcribed a videotape of the partner writing activity in which Joseph collaborated with another student with LLD named Dennis to write their joint report. At the time of this study, Dennis was a third grader, and he had just transferred to the inclusion classroom from another school. The partner-writing episode occurred at nearly the same time of year as the Personal News activity.

Methods of Analysis

Because discourse involves an interactive linguistic activity, a primary methodology in this study involved recording, coding, and interpreting classroom discourse. Attention to patterned uses of language helps to explain the ways in which cognitive practices are situated locally by the language participants, as well as linked and transferred to other disciplined-based meanings and practices. This involved the triangulation of multiple data sources (Strauss & Corbin, 1990) to support and extend hypotheses formulated from one data set to create conclusions warranted by a pattern of interpretations in others.

Lesson activities were transcribed with the following conventions. Each speaker was identified and the relevant utterances assigned to him or her. Memos were recorded in a right-hand column to make reference to specific interesting events or related interpretations. When there were specific repeated events or sequences of interactions, we clustered and categorized the events according to their purpose or function. These were then confirmed or disconfirmed through further data analysis. We also interviewed teachers to gather information about their perception of the language events and processes. Through these various data sources, we hoped to gather additional information about how the Personal News activity functioned to support the acquisition and development of literate knowledge and practices in an apprenticeship process.

THE NATURE OF TEACHER PARTICIPATION IN PERSONAL NEWS

We examined the nature of teacher moves in the teacher-guided Personal News activity. This analysis was intended to provide information about how the teacher apprenticed, or positioned, students in the literacy activity. Teacher utterances were clustered, categorized, and then analyzed according to their function. In developing the coding scheme, we sought to identify categories of teacher behavior that were mutually exclusive, that is, an utterance was classified once according to its teaching function. This meant that categories of teacher behavior were defined and coded in ways

that prevented their coclassification in two or more overlapping categories. At the same time, we recognized that teacher behaviors often involved
complex chains of moves that touched upon several types of functions. For
example, a teacher might *reread* a particular segment of written text, which
was coded as *rereading*, but subsequently, if the teacher asked students
to *evaluate* the text that had been reread, this second part of the utterance
was coded according to its evaluative teaching properties. Thus, a single
teaching turn was parsed or segmented when it embodied chains of functions. The coding scheme that emerged through this process is shown
in Table 8.1, which also contains the proportion of teacher moves for each
category.

The findings from this analysis suggested that the lesson of this highly
effective teacher consisted of two main classes of moves: step-in and step-
back moves. In the case of step-in moves, the teacher used a combination
of modeling and prompting behaviors to directly teach and guide students
in the composing and monitoring processes that they needed to acquire in
order to advance as mature writers; and in the case of step-back moves,
she used questions to position her students to take increasing control of
the modeled language and the writing processes. However, the teacher's
greater emphasis on step-back moves was surprising, which we explore
in more depth in the following section.

Step-Back Moves

When we conducted the analysis and clustered the types of teacher's moves
by their function, we found that a large percent of the teacher moves could
be subsumed in a general class of actions involving step-back moves, insofar as the teacher stepped back from the traditional role of the teacher as
the authoritative holder of knowledge regarding text construction and
evaluation (Almasi, 1995), while simultaneously positioning students in
roles of authority involving evaluations or judgments of the text. Nearly
70% of her moves inducted her students into a problem-solving process as
she asked them to evaluate and express opinions about the text, and to direct the efforts to resolve or repair text problems. With these moves, the
teacher repositioned students as the local experts who directed the construction, monitoring, and revision of the language and text construction
process. Within this larger class of moves, we identified three categories
of teacher behavior associated with the teacher's efforts to step back from
authority roles and simultaneously reposition students in roles of agency
or authority associated with decision making and power. These subclasses
included three types of teacher utterances: (1) rereading followed by invitations to problem solve, monitor, evaluate, and express opinions about
the quality of the text; (2) positioning students to explain, justify, teach, or

TABLE 8.1. Percentage of Types of Teacher Moves by Function

Function or purpose of move	Specific category of move	Frequency	Overall %
	Step-back moves		
Launching, problem solving, decision making, and evaluating	Questions that invite evaluations, opinions, and decisions, and that affirm students' opinions	34	47%
	Rereading text	13	
Step-back moves: Positioning student as expert or teacher	"What do we do?"	5	
	"How should we . . . ?"	6	16%
	"Why should we . . . .?"	5	
Moves that followed author's ideas and expertise	Questions of author for background information	5	5%
	Step-in moves		
Teaching moves that offered teacher modeling or explanations	Clarifying questions or ideas	3	
	Prompting and cueing following confusion	5	26%
	Explaining or teaching	2	
	Modeling by demonstrating or thinking aloud	4	
	Factual questions	2	
	Telling answers	1	
	Expansion of students' answers	3	
	Questions that elicit involvement of specific students	4	
Group process: Moves that focus on group process, expectations, or members' responsibilities to helping the group	Group process	5	7%
	Helping responsibility	2	

inform others; and (3) revoicing and following students' ideas, or asking questions to get information about the topic.

Inviting Students to Problem Solve

Nearly 47% of the teacher moves involved the induction of students into a problem-solving process associated with the monitoring and transforming of oral texts into written forms compatible with the written register. The Personal News activity seemed to involve a cycle of activity, flowing from the author's oral text, to the written text recorded by the teacher, to the consideration of the text by the students, to the revisions of the text suggested by students. Typically, the process started with the elicitation of the author's ideas in a narrative first-person form, which were recorded exactly as stated by the student, omitting all written language conventions. By recording oral text in its raw language form, the teacher encouraged students to look back at the text, and invited them to recommend the types of transformations that writers need to employ as they moved back and forth between the oral and the written language register. In this manner, she made it possible for the language forms and the written language conventions to be made visible and accessible.

At the same time, the teacher invited students to participate in a problem-solving process by asking them to reflect on the character of the oral text, the author's intended meaning, and the text's compliance with the requirements of the written register. One simple way that the teacher achieved this goal was by *rereading the text* (13% of teacher moves). Each rereading was followed by a long pause while the teacher waited for students to judge the adequacy of the text based upon their knowledge of the oral or written register, and to suggest needed repairs. To illustrate, Roger began the Personal News message by offering the following text about his visit to his uncle's house: "They want to play the playstation in the basement together." The teacher recorded the text and reread it, as indicated in the following segment:

TEACHER: Let's reread it. (*Leads class in rereading text and points to each word.*) "They want to play the playstation in the basement together." Wow. Risha?

RISHA: Ummm. . . . You could add an adjective.

TEACHER: We could add an adjective (*revoicing speaker's idea*). Where would you like to add that?

RISHA: It's a *Sony* playstation [emphasis of student].

ROGER: It's one of them things that has certain disks and you put the disk in and put the lid down and press "Play" [student explanation].

TEACHER: So do you have a word that could describe playstation?

ROGER: It's the Sony playstation in the basement (*incorporates Risha's suggestion in his dictation.*)

TEACHER: They want to play the Sony playstation in the basement (*rereads text with Roger's suggestion*).

ROGER: Sony playstation (*repeating change*).

TEACHER: Does that help describe it? Do you have a better picture in your head? . . . OK, what do you think of this so far? . . . (*Guides students to reread the text as she points to the words.*)

In this example, the teacher reread and pointed with her finger to the words of the text, and each time she looked to the students to respond or comment. By rereading, the teacher "served up" the evolving ideas for the group's consideration as she invited students to monitor and reflect on its character. As she looked for *comments or disagreement about the quality of the written text*, she encouraged conversations about the problems with the text and the possible repairs to make it comply with the stylistic, conventional, or meaning requirements of a distant reader. By pointing to the words, she mapped the oral onto the written text, accommodating the diverse abilities of the readers and writers in her classroom, as well as supporting the development of language and literacy abilities among emergent readers and writers who needed to learn to track print and associate the oral and the written forms. This also made it possible for students who lacked conventional reading and writing abilities to access meaning by listening, to observe firsthand the reading and writing processes, and to participate in repairing meaning breakdowns as they worked collaboratively to identify and address language ambiguities. When students suggested changes (i.e., Risha's suggestion that they add an adjective), students could see what those changes entailed, how particular language elements functioned, and when those language elements might be employed in a situated language context.

The teacher encouraged students' participation in the evaluation process through a second mechanism: she directly asked students to evaluate the text. In this case, the teacher asked the class for their opinion about the adequacy of the text, such as: "Do you like that?"; "What do you think of this"? Altogether, 34% of the teacher's moves were designed to elicit students' judgments or evaluations. With such an open-ended stance, texts were treated as thinking devices rather than as self-enclosed messages (Gergen, 1995). The teacher prompted her students to engage in executive processes related to ongoing review and reflection, whether there were apparent textual problems or not. This created language sites where students were challenged to take up the responsibility for monitoring meaning as part of a process of text evaluation and reconstruction (Stone, 2002). Ultimately, this might help students develop an understanding of the "relation between the adequacy of the text and the corresponding degree of comprehension on the part of the reader or listener" (Beal, Garrod, & Bonitatibus, 1990, p. 319).

The continual rereading of the text provided the substance and linguistic material for problem solving. In the following segment, Joseph uses
the rereading combined with the meaning resources afforded him by his
knowledge of language to evaluate and repair the text. The segment begins when a first grader with LLD, Charles, adds a period to the text.

TEACHER: "On Friday Roger is going to his Uncle Pat's house in his
  uncle's truck." I've had lots of help from a few of you. I want help
  from more of you. Charles, what do you think? Hmm?

CHARLES: Add a period.

TEACHER: Why do we need that period, Charles?

CHARLES: Because it's the end of the sentence.

TEACHER: You're right. Good job. Ashley?

ASHLEY: On Friday . . . Roger is going to his Uncle Pat's house in his
  truck (*omits the word "uncle's" in "uncle's truck"*).

TEACHER: You want to take "*uncle's*" out. Let's see what it would
  sound like.

ASHLEY: No, keep it in.

TEACHER: Let's see what if would sound like. "On Friday Roger is
  going to his Uncle Pat's house in his truck." Joseph, you've got,
  you put your thumb down right away.

JOSEPH: It wouldn't sound right that way.

TEACHER: How come?

JOSEPH: Because . . . Roger doesn't have his own truck.

TEACHER: We wouldn't know whose truck it is, would we?

JOSEPH: And plus [add] apostrophe s.

TEACHER: How come?

JOSEPH: His *uncle's* truck [emphasis to indicate possession].

In this segment, Ashley tested out her theories about when repetitive
language ("Uncle Pat") was necessary or unnecessary, and submitted her
ideas to critical evaluation and feedback by her peers (Wells, 1999). Although Ashley was quick to try to withdraw her proposal, the teacher gave
weight to her ideas by codifying her proposition in the form of actual
changes made to the text. The re-presentation of Ashley's expressed idea
in a written form created a joint problem space or a "conversational artifact" that allowed students to observe, understand, and repair meaning
(Roth, 1993). Unlike oral texts, written texts provided concrete objects that

could be reviewed, rethought, revisited, and revised in different forms (Wells, 1999). This is why the teacher followed students' tentative ideas and suggestions by making actual and immediate changes to the written text. In this manner, written language was used to mediate performance by helping to bring the components and machinery of spoken and written language into the realm of conscious awareness and volition (Wells, 1999).

Furthermore, although he is a student with LLD, Joseph is clearly developing the metacognitive skills to monitor the relationship between the author's intended meaning and the expression of those meanings in written language. When Ashley, a general education student, proposed her suggestion, it was challenged by Joseph, who offered an explanation that assisted Ashley's performance and understanding. Joseph's explanation revealed his underlying knowledge that a possessive pronoun (*his* truck) must have a clear referent when it appears in a sentence with two subjects (Roger and Roger's uncle). Joseph employed his language skills as part of the comprehension monitoring and construction process. Together Joseph and Ashley constructed a zone of joint action for each other that might be in advance of what either child might manage alone (Wells, 1999). Ashley's suggestion created space for Joseph to exercise his linguistic knowledge, and Joseph's feedback advanced Ashley's understanding of the conditions and the effects of particular writing tools. What was remarkable was that, in the context of problem-centered learning, students with LLD could step into the roles of writing experts, reversing the typical cycle of dependence and nonparticipation found in many classrooms. Joseph's directive performance is especially powerful in light of his earlier silence and nonparticipation in the book discussion. Through the socially organized participation structure of Personal News, students with LLD could gain facility in language and self-monitoring processes, while simultaneously acquiring basic writing skills and participating in the problem-solving and constructive writing processes.

In this manner, Personal News offered a system of interpersonal arrangements in which students with LLD could become more responsible and knowledgeable participants, and the roles of experts and novices could be dynamically renegotiated through each member's participation in the activity. What one student lacked in knowledge, another student could support with his or her own linguistic or cognitive resources. Its structure permitted students with LLD to be "enabled' rather than "disabled," and to come to believe that academic tasks are something other than that which "others can do, but that I need help with" (Biemiller & Meichenbaum, 1998).

Personal News also supported the development of students' knowledge of the graphic symbols of written text. In this segment, both students with LLD, Charles and Joseph, showed a growing mastery of the second-order symbolic system associated with printed texts, since they were able to add diacritical marks (periods, apostrophes) under the appropriate conditions. The fact that neither of these students used diacritical marks at the beginning of the year suggested that they were deepening their awareness of the nature of print, as well as developing their metalinguistic knowledge about print and word conventions (Wells, 1999). Through their involvement with teachers and peers in the process of both texting (writing) and producing texts (artifacts), they were beginning to understand how to reconstitute and distinguish the grammar of their everyday speech from the more abstract and distant written forms required for the written register (Wells, 1999).

Our research has consistently indicated that recording children's ideas in printed forms is an important mediational tool that helps young writers understand the dynamic relationship and differences between the narrative mode of everyday speech and the transformation of narrative experiences into more abstract formal modes of communication (see Wells, 1999). Written texts offered sites for the coordination of talk and gestures, and served as a background against which verbal and nonverbal communication made sense. Yet too often the overreliance on the verbal channel in the absence of written text taxes the memory and cognitive resources of students with LLD (Stone, 2002; Wells, 1999); that is, teachers simply expect students to hold and manipulate the oral text in their heads. However, by recording oral ideas and experiences into a written form, the text became an object-to-think-with and an object-to-talk-with. The teacher's mutual and reciprocal emphasis on oral and written language provided many students with LDD with alternative ways to learn from and to participate in the lesson discourse as they moved toward fuller participation in evaluating the quality of the text in the face-to-face interactions (Forman & McCormick, 1995).

Apprenticeship by Serving as the Apprentice

The second and third most frequent categories of step-back moves involved the teacher's efforts to position students as experts, teachers, and informants. Sixteen percent of the teacher's moves included attempts by the teacher to position students as informants to others. This included invitations to act upon the text by proposing explanations and solutions.

The teacher in this inclusion classroom used two specific types of discourse moves to accomplish this coordinated apprenticeship. One type of utterances served to position students as the experts, while simultaneously repositioning the teacher as the apprentice. These were direct requests of the teacher to students to *direct the writing process*, thereby inducting students into the doing or performing of specific writing practices. These requests were of the order of: "So what do we do?"; "How do we do it?"

TEACHER: So we have a new sentence now that says, "because Roger wants to see him and his uncle wants to see him and because they want to play playstation together and other things." (*Rereads.*) That's still—I need a breath, guys. Brenden?

BRENDEN: Capital *R* on Roger.

TEACHER: How come? . . .

BRENDEN: Capital *R* because it's a name.

TEACHER: OK, now what were you going to say, Roger?

ROGER: You could *list* some of the things that we could do.

TEACHER: *Do you have an idea about how we could do that?*

ROGER: You could put *commas.*

TEACHER: *Do you have an idea of where we could do that?* Come up, scootch around so you can see. (*Rereads.*) "Because Roger wants to see him and his uncle wants to see him and because they want to play playstation together and other things." (*Roger comes up to the board.*)

ROGER: Comma right there, and cross out "and other things." (*Points to the places in the text.*)

TEACHER: Comma, right here? (*Confirms by pointing.*)

ROGER: At "playstation."

TEACHER: At "playstation."

ROGER: Cross out "and other things."

TEACHER: Cross out "and other things."

ROGER: And laser tag.

In this example, the teacher stated, "Do you have an idea how we can do that?" When the student responded, "You could put commas," not only was the student positioned to use the discourse and forms associated with writing, he served to apprentice others in the language and processes of writing. Text breakdowns became instructional sites for students to exercise their language skills and to employ the discourse and practices of writers in the process of solving authentic problems (Roth, 1993). The teacher's multifaceted double moves (e.g., "what can we do?" and "how can we do it") created reversible role relations: it positioned her students as experts who provided direction to the group's actions, and repositioned the teacher in the role of apprentice or novice who listened to and watched the talk and actions of informants and experts (Englert & Dunsmore, 2002). In doing so, the teacher inducted students into the ways of "doing" and "performing" writing, as well as made public their inner speech and thoughts so that others might access information about the internal and external sides of writing activity.

A similar type of step-back move involved teacher solicitations for explanations or justifications of students' positions (e.g., "Why do we to capitalize?"; "Why do we need to add an apostrophe?"). Although these moves might have sounded like the teacher was testing knowledge, in actuality these moves were opportunities for students to communicate their command of the writing process, participate in the writing discourse, and explain the contextual conditions of specific actions. Such moves repositioned students to teach and inform, just as an apprentice might ask the master craftsman to explain why a certain practice or tool should be used. As students shared their inner thoughts, they made their explanations for the conditions of tool use explicit to others. In this way, students actually taught side by side with the teacher, serving as both the apprentice and the expert in a dynamic flow of interactive talk and work. This made it possible for the teacher to use fewer step-in, or direct teaching, moves, because the students were providing the information and knowledge that was necessary for a complete writing explanation.

In the episode above, for example, when the teacher asked Roger to come to the board to show where to make the changes, Roger modeled how and where to use commas in a list. Roger directed the teacher to put a "comma right there, and cross out 'and other things'—thereby making his thoughts and practices transparent to the writing community. Since optimal learning is more likely to result when learners reverse the interactional roles in the typical teaching-learning situation, Personal News offered a laboratory-like setting that engaged the participants in a form of shop talk that brought them more deeply into an intellectual understanding of their writing craft as they gave directions as well as followed them, asked questions as well as answered them, and acted upon text rather than simply observed the teachers' actions (Biemiller & Meichenbaum, 1998; Brown & Palincsar, 1989; Roth, 1993).

In this fashion, Personal News offered a patterned set of discourse and social activities in which the teacher and students participated to get writing talk and work accomplished. Through cyclical turn taking, students circulated language and cognitive resources as they actively shared, borrowed, and built on each other's ideas. Personal News also allowed for the growing autonomy and authority of students as they stepped into leadership roles with respect to particular types of knowledge. What one student didn't know, another student might unlock through his or her questions to support the development of a greater understanding by all the participants. Thus, expertise was distributed throughout the community as the various participants introduced, harvested, and circulated competencies and abilities at different points in time (Roth, 1998). Personal News was not simply focused on the product, it was focused on the production of knowledge to result in learning outcomes that would help the student write on another day.

What was surprising was the striking difference between the Personal News discourse and the traditional discourse found in U.S. schools. Nearly 54% of the students' moves entailed directions or evaluations of text, and only 9% of students' moves entailed answering factual questions posed by the teacher. Correspondingly, 78% of the turns were based upon students' own self-nominations to speak or to participate in the activity. Nearly all of their interactions were focused on text construction and problem-solving activities. In contrast to traditional classrooms, where teachers ask the majority of questions and take up 80% of the classroom interactions (Gergen, 1995), students in Personal News were evaluating texts and taking the lead in challenging the text meaning (Wells, 1998). The teacher's withdrawal from the dominant role that normally left students passive provided an important avenue for the creation of successful apprenticeships. By the teacher's use of step-backs, students were reflexively repositioned to "step in" to employ the literacy tools in judging the appropriateness of the text, and to develop facility in the mental activities and tools in the context of authentic literacy activity (Chang-Wells & Wells, 1993). The teacher ensured that even the lowest readers and writers could participate in shaping the character of the text through the simple technique of rereading and pointing to the words, permitting them to assume active cognitive roles in the literacy activity.

Furthermore, by stepping back to ask students the "what, how, when, and why" of writing, the teacher accomplished several important objectives aligned with a cognitive apprenticeship model (Englert & Dunsmore, 2002), including (1) inducting students into a language and discourse about writing practices, enabling them to use their knowledge in problem-solving activity; (2) positioning students to articulate and defend their thinking; (3) creating opportunities for students to develop expertise and apprentice others; (4) supporting the development of self-regulation by fostering a type of "metaknowledge" associated with the knowledge of what strategies to use and under what conditions; and (5) challenging students to think, but in collaborative enterprise with others. Furthermore, all of these objectives might be reconstituted as language goals, showing the potential of the teacher to offer language instruction as part of the academic curriculum.

Step-In Moves: Acts of Teaching

Prompts to Support Students' Participation

Apprenticeship models always entail instruction by the expert. In this lesson, the teacher also assumed an active role as coach and facilitator when students experienced difficulties or when she anticipated that students might have difficulty participating in the apprenticeship. There were several actions the teacher took that showed remarkable awareness of the complexity of the intellectual work of her students and how she needed to support them in different ways.

First, she gave students a considerable amount of time to think. Routinely, she paused 20 seconds or more to give an individual student time to think when he or she struggled with how to transform the oral into the written register. In one case, a second-grade student with LLD who was called upon sat silent for 12 seconds while he reread the text and sat deep in thought. It was clear that he was engaged in exploratory thought about what change could be made to reduce the repetitious ideas that he had cited as a problem. In contrast to many teachers who would have discouraged such intense reflection to maintain a brisk lesson pace, the teacher encouraged the student to think by saying "Good job rereading, Brenden." By allowing wait-time, she encouraged him to remain an active participant in the language game, and she communicated that his strategic behavior (rereading) was valued. In this classroom, when students asked for the floor, they were allowed the time to construct their thoughts and they were not superseded by "turn sharks," as Erickson (1996) describes those students who lurk to snatch a turn away from a dysfluent or slow speaker.

Second, the teacher valued participation so strongly that she made sure that nearly all the members of the class participated. Of the 25 students that were present in the classroom, 18 students participated in the Personal News activity one or more times. Together, the students took 102 turns in the lessons, which is a high number of turns by any educational yardstick. Special education students took 40 of these turns. Excluding the author, the highest number of student turns were taken by Joseph and Brenden, two students with LLD. If active responding is correlated to achievement, then Personal News seems to be a promising format, especially for students with LLD who might be reluctant to participate. On several occasions, the teacher made specific space for the lowest performers to participate, as indicated in the interactions below:

TEACHER: What else do we need, Matt ?

MATT: The date.

TEACHER: Charles, what do we need here?

CHARLES: Period.

In her interview, the teacher expressed the view that the participation of *all* students was vital, and her actions indicated that she specifically recruited the participation of her youngest and most challenged

group of learners. She explained her thoughts about this matter in the
following way:

> "The scaffolding is just a part of everyone's day, but I think . . . If you
> gave them [something to do]—[put in the] period—and [then] they
> are viewed as doing something. I think that's what makes our inclu-
> sion class work. . . . See, like the lowest writers, when they have their
> hand up, you call on them right away. They need to be viewed as
> people who participate. They need to be viewed like everyone else. . . .
> Those are the kids that need to have the confidence boosters so when
> we do ask them to do more they are going to be willing to take the
> chance. . . . And those are just simple [things], asking the kindergart-
> ner to provide the period. We provide the scaffold. As much fun as
> we make of that word [e.g., scaffold]. That's what we do all day."

The teacher's words also conveyed her belief that participation was at the
root of present and future learning—a belief that has been espoused by
other scholars in activity learning (Wenger, 1998).

A third category of step-in moves involved the teacher's specific efforts to instruct and apprentice students in the specific types of knowledge
that they needed. The teaching moves of the teacher represented 24% of
the total teacher utterances, although this was complemented by the 54%
of the student moves that involved directives, evaluations, and explanations pertaining to specific literacy practices. In fact, the following types
of literate practices and conventions were initiated or implemented by the
students' and/or teacher during the lesson: the use of *question words* (e.g.,
what, how, when, where, why to organize their texts); *dates; indentation* ("Do
you want an arrow to push it over, or do you want us just to add space to
know to push it over?"); *capitalization* (capital *P* on *Pat's*, days of the week);
punctuation marks ("Add a period"); *adjective* ("We could add an adjective"); *apostrophes* (apostrophe *s* on *Pat*); *topic sentence* ("Underline the topic
sentence" because "The whole message is about this"); *commas in a list; closing sentence; editing conventions; rereading; redundancy; clarifying;* and *titles.*
To illustrate the curricular facets covered in the lesson, Roger's Personal
News story is shown in Figure 8.2. The extensive editing changes made
to Roger's text represent sites of classroom conversation about language
forms, meanings, and conventions.

However, unlike the curricular elements normally introduced in a
language arts scope and sequence at the primary-grade level, these language arts elements were modeled and explained in the situated context
of constructing and transforming oral and written texts. Each time the students or teacher identified a problem in the text, their talk was directly
linked to particular language features or symbolic elements that were con-
cretely incorporated into the text. Furthermore, because of the teacher's

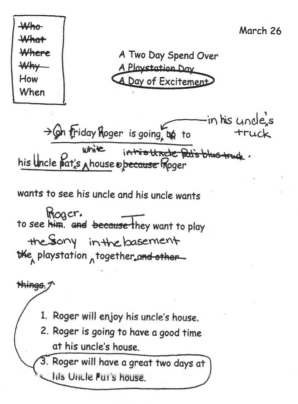

FIGURE 8.2. Roger's Personal News story.

frequent use of Personal News, students had repeated opportunities to acquire the language and monitoring skills on a regular basis, allowing them to develop a deeper understanding and mastery of the language arts curriculum over time.

In addition, of special concern to the teacher in the lesson was the genre of a personal experience. Cope and Kalantzis (1993) recommend a genre approach to literacy instruction. A genre approach "involves being explicit about the way language works to make meaning. It means engaging students in the role of apprentice with the teacher in the role of expert on language system and function. It means an emphasis on content, on structure and on the sequence of the steps that the learner goes through to become literate in a formal educational setting" (Cope & Kalantzis, 1993, p. 1). In the lesson, the teacher sought to teach students about the written genre related to Personal News by informing them their papers needed to answer the *wh-* question words (*who, what, when, where, how, why*). She previewed the question words, listed the question words in the corner of the paper, and then reviewed and crossed off the types of information as they were addressed in their message ("Let's see what we have answered. Do we know *who* we are talking about?"; "Do we know *why*?"; "Do we know *what is happening*?";"Do we know *where*?"). By applying the question words as part of a process of monitoring the written text, students were learning to use these questions as part of a comprehension process to locate and evaluate information; and conversely, by using the question words to question the author, they were learning to use declarative questions as part of a process of communication. The teacher also reminded students about the global, or macrolevel, features of the written text, including the need for a topic sentence, a closing sentence, a title, and so forth. Thus, the teacher called attention to the macrostructure of the text as a basis for composing and evaluating its completeness.

The teacher also apprenticed students through several directed teaching moves. For example, the teacher directly taught specific concepts ("That's not a name. It's just telling us what kind of person he is."), pointed out problems in the text ("How can we. . . . I mean, it just sounds like it is getting kind of wordy?"), thought aloud ("I'm going to cross out 'we' and change it back."), and asked questions to prompt students to use particular types of knowledge ("What do I need here at the end of the sentence?"). In this way, the teacher stepped in to directly cue or instruct students when a skill was beyond their immediate expertise. She provided instruction in the areas in which she perceived they needed assistance, while stepping back in other areas when she felt students could perform the actions independently. There was an inherent tension between leading and following students' development. As students became able to carry out these functions of the written discourse, she distanced herself from an authoritative role to allow them to assume increasing responsibility for directing the writing actions and leading the discussion. This transfer of responsibility was a critical skill in promoting independence and self-regulation.

Community-Building Moves

Finally, a third class of teacher moves involved the teacher's emphasis on the rights and duties of participants in the community. An activity like Personal News depends upon the trust that has been established so that risk-taking behavior is encouraged. Community-building features were evident in the analysis of the lesson. Nearly 7% of the teacher's utterances involved messages about students' responsibility or their personal stake in the activity.

Several instances of community building related to the teacher's expression of respect and appreciation for the hard work and contributions of students to the composition process. Each time a student or several students persisted to mediate especially difficult segments of the text, the teacher expressed her gratitude in an unusual way: she said, "Thank you!" This expression of appreciation is usually reserved for people who bestow favors or share their gifts with others. So her message to students was that she had positioned herself in the subordinate role of one who is the recipient of their intellectual gifts and help. Similarly, she encouraged students to assume their responsibilities to the community during problem solving. Several times she reminded them of their responsibility to share their intellectual resources with the community: "Can anyone help?"; "I need your help."; "We are going to reread and I need everyone's help." When students needed help, she asked them: "Do you want help from the group?"

To summarize, the teacher actively modeled and expressed a deep commitment to the role of community, which was an important foundation for apprenticeships that depended upon social interaction. She positioned her students in interactive and collaborative arrangements and fostered a spirit of cooperation and responsibility to others that was necessary for the performance of the hard cognitive work. Interestingly, the features that characterized the Personal News activity and the teacher's interactions aligned with the features of model programs that take relational approaches to school reform for the development of prosocial character, including emphases on (1) close and caring relationships among children and teachers fostered through cooperative activity; (2) challenging relevant curricula, based on constructivist learning theory; (3) opportunities for children to have voice and choice; and (4) shared responsibility for the caring community (Baker, Terry, Bridger, & Winsor, 1997). In such relationally oriented schools, Baker et al. (1997) noted that teachers use cooperation, encourage participation, ask questions, elicit more critical thinking and student discourse, and use problem-solving approaches. These characteristics typified the interactions in the Personal News activity.

PARTNER WRITING

The second question that we sought to address was the effect of teacher's apprenticeships in the talk and practices of writing. The question that we asked was "What is the relationship between the discourse practices in Personal News, and the discourse practices and disciplinary knowledge expressed by the students with LLD in a joint collaborative writing?" We examined the interactions of Joseph as he collaborated with another student with LLD named Dennis. Of interest in this examination was the extent to which Joseph appropriated the language and literacy practices that had been made available in Personal News.

Prior to this partner-writing activity, the teacher had guided the class in brainstorming and organizing their ideas in a semantic web for a dental unit about teeth that was taught in late February. The two teachers routinely partnered their students in order that they could be more directly involved in using the literacy tools and academic talk related to expository writing. Although the students were in the primary grades, the teachers provided them with a number of scaffolds to ensure their success. In addition to their individual webs, students also had access to a class web as a cognitive resource to help them develop their individual semantic webs containing information about teeth. Then the partners came together to integrate and transform their separate webs into a single written draft of their report. All students were expected to participate in the learning-to-learn process, and the teachers encouraged them to use alternative methods (e.g., invented spellings, pictures) to generate notes, webs, and texts. Thus, they had access to classroom and peer resources to guide them in the writing process, and no student was excused from participation.

At the time of the collaboration, the teacher had asked Joseph and Dennis to cooperate to transform the ideas represented in their semantic webs into a written text. Dennis was new to the school, having just moved to the classroom within the past 3 months. Joseph and Dennis's semantic web for the dental unit is shown in Figure 8.3. Their final draft is shown in Figure 8.4.

Based upon the teacher's participation rules and the norms for collaboration, the two boys assisted each other and took turns in writing portions of the text. In the transcribed segment below, we see Dennis as he is writing about the types of teeth (fourth paragraph), while Joseph is writing the third paragraph about the primary teeth. Although they were writing their separate paragraphs, the oral and written discourse was jointly shaped and constructed.

DENNIS: Yeah, so (*points to fourth category circle on the map*) the topic sentence is gonna be that (*points to category labeled "kinds of teeth"*).

JOSEPH: Kinds?

DENNIS: Kinds of teeth. . . .

JOSEPH: How 'bout, yeah, kinds of teeth!

DENNIS: Push it over (*draws an arrow and begins to write on his paper*).

JOSEPH: (*Writes on his paper.*)

DENNIS: Kinds of teeth. Kinds of teeth. K (*16 seconds while Dennis glances back and forth at the map and writes on his paper*). Put the s in there?

JOSEPH: Yeah, kinds.

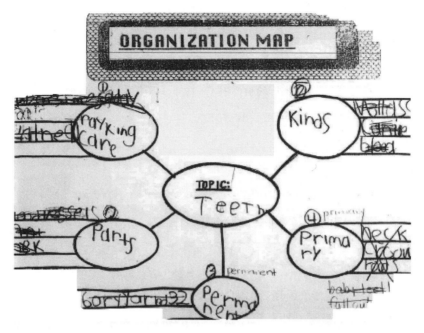

FIGURE 8.3. Joseph and Dennis's map.

DENNIS: Kinds of . . . /o/-/f/ (*sounding out word*).

JOSEPH: *o-f* . . .

DENNIS: *O.* kinds of teeth. I know that. *T-e-e-th. Th.* Kinds, kinds of teeth. Yes!

JOSEPH: Put in a caret. (*He is marking on his paper.*)

DENNIS: OK, give me a sentence I can write.

JOSEPH: How about, um, write every one [e.g., molars, canine, blood vessels] with "We"? [e.g., We have molars. We have canines.]

JOSEPH: Write every one with a *WE* and . . .

DENNIS: Write that (*points to third category of the map, indicating Joseph should work on the third paragraph*).

JOSEPH: Write *WE* (*points to paper Dennis is writing on, to indicate where to write the words*).

DENNIS: I don't know how to spell *We.*

JOSEPH: *W-E.*

DENNIS: *W-E.*

All About Teeth

→ How to take care of your teeth.
You brush your teeth two times a
day. Eat healthy food.

→ Parts of your teeth. Some
teeth have blood vessels. Teeth have
roots to hold teeth in.

→ We have primary teeth.
Primary teeth are your baby teeth.
Baby teeth fall out. When you are 6
months old you get primary teeth.

→ Kinds of teeth. We have
molars. We have canine. We
have blood vessels.

FIGURE 8.4. Joseph and Dennis's story about teeth.

JOSEPH: Have. *H* (*looks at Dennis's paper*). No, *H*.

DENNIS: *H*?

JOSEPH: Make that into an *H*.

DENNIS: Like this?

JOSEPH: Yeah, that's right.

(Dennis writes the sentence: We have molars.)

DENNIS: Done [with first detail].

JOSEPH: I'm not (*looks over and points to Dennis's paper*). Put a period.

DENNIS: I'm done.

JOSEPH: Put a period. [Now] Write "we have" . . . and then use the second one [Joseph underlines the second detail in the map for Dennis].

DENNIS: Second one, like that?

JOSEPH: Yeah. Put "We have" first, OK?

DENNIS: How do you spell *We*?

JOSEPH: Look right there (*leans over and points to the word _we_ in the first sentence*).

In this episode, Joseph stepped into the role of an expert and instructional guide for Dennis. Although the preceding year Joseph sat silently through most of the classroom activities, by now Joseph had developed the executive and discourse skills associated with his growing writing autonomy. He provides expert-like scaffolds for Dennis throughout this episode, as he offers a language structure that Dennis can appropriate and use to generate his own sentences ("start everyone with 'We have' . . . "). Further, he assists him with word spellings (e.g., *we, have*), reminds him of the ending punctuation ("Put a period"), and points out the mediational tools embedded in the language resources around them (e.g., the written text and the map). In many respects, he demonstrates an awareness of the machinery of written language and the discourse that surrounds its generation. Furthermore, like a true apprenticeship, he works side by side with Dennis, to step in and execute whatever aspects of the process is beyond Dennis's immediate grasp and control. Together the two boys accomplish the writing task on an intermental or joint plane. While Dennis cannot perform the task alone, collaboratively the two boys engage in the report writing as a shared enterprise.

Additionally, the presence of Dennis affords many opportunities for Joseph to step into the discourse and technical practices associated with the writing craft. Repeatedly, Joseph thinks aloud and articulates his writing actions. The presence of a peer created a reason and a communicational space for Joseph to explicitly practice the discourse and develop a consciousness about writing. Through such scaffolded opportunities, the possibility existed for Joseph to deepen his own metaknowledge of the "what, how, when, and why" of using particular tools during the writing process. Collaboration with Dennis provided the opportunity for Joseph to exploit resources that he had available, but over which he may not have developed explicit knowledge and control.

The examination of Joseph's written text and discourse showed evidence of his growing awareness of the symbolic tools used in constructing and editing text. A printed copy of Joseph's handwritten fourth paragraph is provided in Figure 8.5. What was interesting about Joseph's text was his appropriation of the editing conventions introduced in Personal News. He uses an arrow at the start of the paragraph to signal the paragraph's indentation. This is very similar to the arrow used by the teacher to insert information in the Personal News story (see Figure 8.2). In his fourth sentence, he used a caret to insert the missing language and subject of the sentence, which suggests that he is rereading and monitoring the quality of his text. As he later explains to Dennis, he also uses an arrow and star to indicate where missing letters and text must be inserted. In this manner, Joseph uses a number of symbol systems (carets, arrows) to signify where text must be inserted and its textual location. Similarly, in Personal News, the teacher often gave students choices about how to signify particular features of the written register (e.g., indentation or arrows), where to locate text additions, and how editorial marks can represent the author's plans. His command and flexibility in using coding symbols shows Joseph's growing confidence in implementing the devices during writing, as he explains his revision plans to Dennis in the transcript segment shown below.

JOSEPH: We're already done with the third. (*Joseph is writing the third paragraph.*)

DENNIS: [Put a] Period [at the end of the sentence].

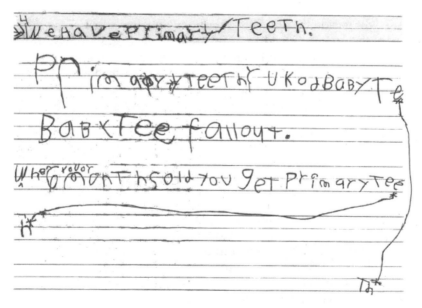

FIGURE 8.5. Joseph's handwritten paragraph.

JOSEPH: H [*writes h, the last letter of teeth, on the next line because he is at the edge of the page*).

DENNIS: No, you can't write right there. You gotta write in these . . . those dots right there. (*trying to explain to Joseph that he cannot put the letters of a word on different lines*).

JOSEPH: Lines, right?

DENNIS: Yeah, right there.

JOSEPH: This is a part of that (*points to the letter h, and then the rest of the word, teeth, at the end of the prior line*). So, I'll put an arrow.

DENNIS: Put a caret, right there. Over there is the end [of the line], so if this is part of that, you gotta put a caret over here somewhere.

JOSEPH: Watch (*draws an arrow from the end of the last line to connect the letter h to the rest of the word*).

DENNIS: You gotta draw an arrow to there?

JOSEPH: And I'll put a star right there (*Joseph puts a star above the line to connect the two parts*). Now we are all done. We are all done now.

What seems evident in this set of interactions is that the partners are communicating about particular symbols and practices. From their mutual perspectives, they monitor and explain what constitutes accepted practices, providing evidence that they have appropriated the editing conventions and talk introduced in Personal News. Joseph and Dennis have borrowed a writing discourse that enables them to communicate with each other about the writing process and the respective actions associated with that process. Particularly remarkable is the fact that Joseph is a first grader, yet he is aware of many higher order skills and writing conventions related to paragraphing, indentation, and editing that might be expected of a more mature writer. Given the fact that at the start of the year Joseph was not aware of sentences, capital letters, periods, or even sound–symbol correspondences, his maturity and metalinguistic growth are remarkable. Joseph also makes available to Dennis the writing tools and practices of the classroom community of which Dennis is less knowledgeable, serving as the more knowledgeable guide who can lead the development of others. Neither student seems to find it remarkable or objectionable that a younger student might be assisting an older student, or vice-versa. Nevertheless, throughout their interactions, it must be remembered that there remains the quality of hidden dialogicality in their speech, because the partners were reenacting the prior social conversations, dialogue, and actions of which they had been prior participants in the social space of Personal News. They have transformed the social conversations in which they have previously participated and turned them inward as a basis for directing their own and others' thoughts and actions. The two partners worked together steadily for over 40 minutes, constructing and engaging in self-regulatory activities related to writing. Unlike many children with learning disabilities, neither Dennis nor Joseph showed evidence of being a passive learner or of demonstrating the "learned helplessness" that so many children with learning disabilities exhibit (Wong, Wong, Perry, & Sawatsky, 1986; Wong, Wong, & Blenkinsop, 1989).

The pride of the students was evident. At different points in the activity, Joseph gives expressions of his own self-esteem and sets high standards for his own performance. Early in the activity, he says to Dennis, nearly out of the blue, "I'm smart, right?" Another time he says, "I'm doing my bestest now. OK. My bestest." Dennis later says to Joseph: "We gotta write good, don't we, Joseph? But we can write messy right now, but when its final copy, let me do all the writing." Their expressions of confidence showed that for these two students with LLD, they felt "enabled" rather than "disabled," and they expressed the belief that writing tasks were not something that "others can do, but that I need help with." The apprenticeship that had been enacted by the teacher led to positions of leadership and competence, and these were reenacted by the partners in reciprocal and dynamic interactions to accomplish the shared and orchestrated work of writing.

Our observations of this and other collaborative writing episodes suggest that partnering students offered a unique acquisition space that did not duplicate what was provided during the teacher-directed lesson. Collaborations extended the potential for students to enact the discourse and practices made available to them during Personal News lessons. For example, whereas Joseph participated 12 times during the Personal News lesson, he participated 157 times during the partner-writing episode. Throughout the partners' collaboration, Joseph was positioned or positioned himself to step into the discourse, actions, and practices of writers. In fact, together Joseph and Dennis enacted talk and action related to each of the following: apostrophe, topic sentences, spellings, meaning, rereading, sentence construction, periods, editing conventions (carets, stars, arrows), first and final drafts, indenting, paragraphing, sequencing, editing, and monitoring. Language permeated their problem-solving activity, becoming the toolkit by which they communicated and acted upon their texts, as well as each other. Many of the skills they employed paralleled those introduced and practiced in the teacher-guided Personal News lesson. The students with LLD had shown a developing competence in using language to achieve literacy ends.

CONCLUSIONS

What was crucial about the participation structure of Personal News was its potential to apprentice students into cognitive processes and skills in actual writing contexts. Teachers did more than merely expose students to a print-rich environment. They explicitly guided and apprenticed students in the language and practices of writers. The teacher seemed to provide this apprenticeship by positioning students as leaders and teachers. By stepping back from the traditional role as the authority figure, she created many writing authorities and local experts in her classroom. Students became more successful and exercised their growing independence in using these practices to direct and revise texts. The discourse of this teacher provided an example of how teachers might socialize students, especially those who are academically challenged, into the collaborative creation of texts (Gover & Englert, 1999).

Ultimately, the goal of Personal News and the other literacy activities was to help children become more competent in using sophisticated language forms and speech genres. However, the apprenticeship did not imply that teachers served as the "more knowledgeable other" and that students simply served as novices. Instead, apprenticeship was represented by the teacher's attempts to distance herself from authoritative positions of "knowing" and "knowledge" so that students could step into the explanatory roles previously occupied by the teacher. This study of apprenticeship proved to be as much about how teachers "stepped back" from teaching roles as it was about how they "stepped into" teaching roles. Through these methods, she allowed her students to become more sophisticated and independent

This study also revealed that the partner-writing task provided another important context for children to apply their knowledge in practical contexts. In the collaborative activity, children had more frequent opportunities to offer ideas and to apply the tools they had been exposed to in the Personal News lesson. As partners, they were able to both observe and use tools in ways that exceeded their own individual levels of performance, since their partners shaped, monitored, and questioned their texts. Partners provided a social space where students transformed their participation by becoming more deeply involved in the discourse and practices of the writing community. If their joint text is compared to the earlier text of Joseph at the start of first grade (see Figures 8.1 and 8.5), the shared text is extraordinarily different in its language sophistication and its symbolic qualities that were reflective of the writers' knowledge of the written register. This acceleration in knowledge would not have been possible without the apprenticeship in Personal News, and the opportunities for intermental practices afforded students during partner writing.

Finally, this study showed the agency of children. In both the teacher-directed and the collaborative activities, children took up powerful positions associated with authority and leadership. From the highest to the lowest achieving student, children were given the authority to "know" and to take risks in expressing their knowledge. That children were so committed to their own agency was clearly reflected in the persistence of children like Joseph and Dennis. Given a voice, these children worked very hard at learning. Given authority, they were able to advocate for themselves. Given access to writing tools and implements, they tried very hard to discover the functions of those tools and to implement those tools in context. They seemed anxious to play in the literacy game as it was negotiated through the social interactions in the teacher-directed and collaborative partner-writing activity. What remains to be determined is whether children who show such willingness to learn and to participate have a more accelerated learning profile than children who hold back and fail to participate. In support of this possibility, Joseph was later discontinued from special education services in 3 years (i.e., at the end of fourth grade), as a result of his continued participation in this inclusion program. For a child identified at the age of 3 years and qualifying for support services in the therapeutic areas of language, gross and fine motor, and learning, this is an incredible story of personal achievement and success. It is as much a story about the teachers' instruction as it is about Joseph enabling himself by accessing the discourse and practices made available to him. Joseph was not alone in this respect. In this classroom, three or four students were discontinued from special education by the end of the elementary years, whereas many school buildings failed to discontinue even one student.

In making recommendations to school personnel, we do believe that the undergirding principles of the project provide a useful framework for developing effective intervention programs. Specifically, we recommend that careful thought be given to the following features:

1. The provision of cognitive apprenticeships in the discourse and tools in the situated context of their use.
2. The provision of socially mediated instruction that progresses from modeling by more knowledgeable others, to the joint performance of the strategies, discourse, and actions, to independent and self-regulated performance.
3. The provision of guided support and mediation in the learners' zone of proximal development.
4. The provision of mediational tools and scaffolds.

The use of authentic problem-solving activities combined with teachers' use of step-back moves can foster apprenticeship by transforming the nature of students' participation from passive to more directed leadership roles. With respect to assessment, both the format of Personal News and partner writing offer teachers insight into children's development as language users, as well as their acquisition of practices and tools.

Language instruction and learning is highly feasible in the situated context of the academic curriculum. From the outset, children and youth undertaking a new academic discipline must confront the machinery of oral and written language as they read, write, think, and communicate (Scribner, 1997). Teachers can model the language of thought and action using think-alouds, but the apprenticeship needs to be completed through the use of discourse-based activities that increase the participation of students in using the language to monitor and direct the problem-solving process. Open-ended language formats, such as that featured in Personal News, can provide critical insight into students' performance, allowing the teacher to step in and step back to guide development on a timely basis. The extension of these formats to encompass partner writing and collaborative projects can yield additional information about children's literacy knowledge, while furthering students' implementation of language in constructive and problem-solving activities in an academic discipline. Language instruction and practice in the situated context of the academic curriculum can further the development of all students, but it is especially valuable for students with LLD. Through careful planning and collaboration, the knowledge of general education and speech–language therapists can intersect to inform and enrich the development of language abilities through explicit instruction and cognitive apprenticeships in situated reading, language, and writing contexts.

ACKNOWLEDGMENTS

This research was part of a larger project, "The Development and Evaluation of an Early Intervention Program for Nonreaders and Nonwriters," funded by a grant from the office of Special Education Programs (No. H023C50089) of the U.S. Department of Education. This research was also partly supported by the Center for the Improvement of Early Reading Achievement, funded by the Office of Educational Research and Improvement. The opinions expressed in this chapter do not necessarily reflect the position, policy, or endorsement of the U.S. Department of Education. We wish to thank the teachers of Lansing School District who participated on the literacy project that led to this work.

REFERENCES

Almasi, J. (1995). The nature of fourth graders' sociocognitive conflicts in peer-led and teacher-led discussions of literature. *Reading Research Quarterly, 30,* 314–351.
Baker, J., Terry, T., Bridger, R., & Winsor, A. (1997). Schools as caring communities: A relational approach to school reform. *School Pyschology Review, 26,* 586–602.

Bakhtin, M. (1986). *"Speech genres" and other late essays* (C. Emerson & M. Holquist (Eds.), V. W. McGee (Trans.). Austin: University of Texas Press.

Beal, C. R., Garrod, A. C., & Bonitatibus, G. J. (1990). Fostering children's revision skills through training in comprehension monitoring. *Journal of Educational Psychology, 82,* 275–280.

Biemiller, A., & Meichenbaum, D. (1998). The consequences of negative scaffolding for students who learn slowly—A commentary on C. Addison Stone's "The metaphor of scaffolding: Its utility for the field of learning disabilities." *Journal of Learning Disabilities, 31,* 365–369.

Bos, C. S., & Filip, D. (1984). Comprehension monitoring in learning disabled and average students. *Journal of Learning Disabilities, 17,* 229–233.

Bos, C. S., & Vaughn, S. (2002). *Strategies for teaching students with learning and behavior problems.* Boston: Allyn & Bacon.

Brown, A. L., & Palincsar, A. S. (1989). Guided, cooperative learning and individual knowledge acquisition. In L. Resnick (Ed.), *Knowing, learning, and instruction* (pp. 393–451). Hillsdale, NJ: Erlbaum.

Catts, H., Fey, M., Zhang, X., & Tomblin, J. B. (1999). Language basis of reading and reading disabilities: Evidence from a longitudinal study. *Scientific Studies of Reading, 3,* 331–361.

Chaiklin, S. (2003). The zone of proximal development in Vygotsky's analysis of learning and instruction. In A. Kozulin, B. Gindis, V. S. Ageyev, & S. M. Miller (Eds.), *Vygotsky's educational theory in cultural context* (pp. 39–64). New York: Cambridge University Press.

Chang-Wells, G. L., & Wells, G. (1993). Dynamics of discourse: Literacy and the construction of knowledge. In E. A. Forman, N. Minick, & C. A. Stone (Eds.), *Contexts for learning: Sociocultural dynamics in children's development* (pp. 58–90). New York: Oxford University Press.

Collins, A., Brown, J. S., & Holum, A. (1991). Cognitive apprenticeship: Making thinking visible. *American Educator, 15,* 6–11, 38–46.

Cope, B., & Kalantzis, M. (1993). The power of literacy and the literacy of power. In B. Cope & M. Kalantzis (Eds.), *The powers of literacy: A genre approach to teaching writing* (pp. 63–89). Pittsburgh, PA: University of Pittsburgh Press.

Engestrom, Y., & Miettinen, R. (1999). Introduction. In Y. Engestrom, R. Miettinen, & R. Punamaki (Eds.), *Perspectives on activity theory* (pp. 1–16). New York: Cambridge University Press.

Englert, C. S., & Dunsmore, K. (2002). A diversity of teaching and learning paths: Teaching writing in situated activity. In J. Brophy (Ed.), *Advances in research on teaching* (Vol. 9, pp. 81–130). Boston: JAI Press.

Englert, C. S., & Mariage, T. (2003). The sociocultural model in special education interventions: Apprenticing students in higher-order thinking. In H. L. Swanson, K. Harris, & S. Graham (Eds.), *Handbook of learning disabilities.* New York: Guilford Press.

Englert, C. S., & Raphael, T. E. (1989). Developing successful writers through cognitive strategy instruction. In J. Brophy (Ed.), *Advances in research on teaching* (Vol. 1, pp. 105–151). Newark, NJ: JAI Press.

Englert, C. S., Raphael, T. E., Fear, K. L., & Anderson, L. M. (1988). Students' metacognitive knowledge about how to write informational texts. *Learning Disability Quarterly, 11,* 18–46.

Englert, C. S., & Thomas, C. C. (1987). Sensitivity to text structure in reading and writing: A comparison of learning disabled and nonhandicapped students. *Learning Disability Quarterly, 10,* 93–105.

Erickson, F. (1996). Going for the zone: The social and cognitive ecology of teacher–student interaction in classroom conversations. In D. Hicks (Ed.), *Discourse, learning and schooling* (pp. 29–62). New York: Cambridge University Press.

Forman, E. A., & McCormick, D. E. (1995). Discourse analysis: A sociocultural perspective. *Remedial and Special Education, 16,* 150–158.

Gerber, A. (1993). *Language related learning disabilities: Their nature and treatment.* Baltimore: Brooks.

Gergen, K. J. (1995). Social construction and the educational process. In L. P. Steffe & J. Gale (Eds.), *Constructivism in education* (pp. 17–40). Hillsdale, NJ: Erlbaum.

Gersten, R., Fuchs, L. S., & Williams, J. P. (2001). Teaching reading comprehension strategies to students with learning disabilities. *Review of Educational Research, 71,* 279–320.

Gover, M., & Englert, C. S. (1999). *Orchestrating the thought and learning of struggling writers:* CIERA Report No. 1-002. Ann Arbor: University of Michigan, Center for the Improvement of Early Reading Achievement.

Hock, M. F., Schumaker, J. B., & Deshler, D. D. (1999). Closing the gap to success in secondary schools: A model for cognitive apprenticeship. In D. D. Deshler, J. Schumaker, K. R. Harris, & S. Graham (Eds.), *Teaching every adolescent every day: Learning in diverse middle and high school classrooms* (pp. 1–52). Cambridge, MA: Brookline.

Hogan, K., & Pressley, M. (1997). Scaffolding scientific competencies within classroom communities of inquiry. In K. Hogan & M. Pressley (Eds.), *Scaffolding student learning: Instructional approaches and issues* (pp. 74–107). Cambridge, MA: Brookline.

Hutchins, E. (1997). Mediation and automatization. In M. Cole, Y. Engestrom, & O. Vasquez (Eds.), *Mind, culture and activity: Seminal papers from the Laboratory of Comparative Human Cognition* (pp. 338–353). New York: Cambridge University Press.

Kozulin, A. (2003). Psychological tools and mediated learning. In A. Kozulin, B. Gindis, V. S. Ageyev, & S. M. Miller (Eds.), *Vygotsky's educational theory in cultural context* (pp. 15–38). New York: Cambridge University Press.

Lee, C. D., & Smagorinsky, L. P. (Eds.). (2000). *Vygotskian perspectives on literacy research: Constructing meaning through collaborative inquiry.* New York: Cambridge University Press.

Roth, W. M. (1993). Construction sites: Science labs and classrooms. In K. Tobin (Ed.), *The practice of constructivism in science education* (pp. 145–170). Hillsdale, NJ: Erlbaum.

Roth, W. M. (Ed.). (1998). *Designing communities.* Boston: Kluwer Academic.

Roth, W. M., & McRobbie, C. (1999). Lifeworlds and the "w/ri(gh)ting" of classroom research. *Journal of Curriculum Studies, 31,* 501–522.

Scott, C., & Windsor, J. (2000). General language performance measures in spoken and written narrative and expository discourse of school-age children with language learning disabilities. *Journal of Speech, Language, and Hearing Research, 43,* 324–339.

Scribner, S. (1997). The cognitive consequences of literacy. In E. Tobach, R. J. Falmagne, M. B. Parlee, L. M. W. Martin, & A. S. Kapelman (Eds.), *Mind and social practice: Selected writings of Sylvia Scribner* (pp. 160–189). New York: Cambridge University Press.

Stone, C. A. (2002). Promises and pitfalls of scaffolded instruction for students with language learning disabilities. In K. G. Butler & E. R. Silliman (Eds.), *Speaking, reading and writing in children with language learning disabilities: New paradigms in research and practice* (pp. 175–198). Mahwah, NJ: Erlbaum.

Strauss, A., & Corbin, J. (1990). *Basics of qualitative research.* Newbury Park, CA: Sage.

Vygotsky, L. S. (1978). *Mind in society: The development of higher psychological processes.* Cambridge, MA: Harvard University Press.

Wells, G. (1999). *Dialogic inquiry: Toward a sociocultural practice and theory of education.* New York: Cambridge University Press.

Wells, G. (2000). Dialogic inquiry in education: Building on the legacy of Vygotsky. In C. D. Lee & L. P. Smagorinsky (Ed.), *Vygotskian perspectives on literacy research: Constructing meaning through collaborative inquiry* (pp. 51–85). New York: Cambridge University Press.

Wenger, E. (Ed.). (1998). *Communities of practice: Learning, meaning and identity.* New York: Cambridge University Press.

Wertsch, J. V. (1991). *Voices of the mind: A sociocultural approach to mediated action.* Cambridge, MA: Harvard University Press.

Wiig, E. H., & Secord, W. A. (1998). Language disabilities in school-age children and youth. In G. H. Shames, E. H. Wiig, & W. A. Secord (Eds.), *Human communication disorders* (pp. 212–247). New York: Merrill.

Wong, B. Y. L. (1997). Research on genre-specific strategies for enhancing writing in adolescents with learning disaiblities. *Learning Disability Quarterly, 20,* 140–159.

Wong, B. Y. L., & Berninger, V. W. (2004). Cognitive processes of teachers in implementing composition research in elementary, middle, and high school classrooms. In C. A. Stone, E. R. Silliman, B. J. Ehren, & K. Apel (Eds.), *Handbook of language and literacy: Development and disorders* (pp. 600–624). New York: Guilford Press.

Wong, B. Y. L., & Jones, W. (1982). Increasing metacomprehension in learning disabled and normally achieving students through self-questioning training. *Learning Disability Quarterly, 5,* 228–240.

Wong, B. Y. L., & Wilson, M. (1984). Investigating awareness of and teaching passage organization in learning disabled children. *Journal of Learning Disabilities, 17,* 447–482.

Wong, B. Y. L., Wong, R., & Blenkinsop, J. (1989). Cognitive and metacognitive aspects of learning disabled adolescents' composing problems. *Learning Disability Quarterly, 12,* 300–322.

Wong, B. Y. L., Wong, R., Perry, N., & Sawatsky, D. (1986). The efficacy of a self-questioning summarization strategy for use by underachievers and learning disabled adolescents in social studies. *Learning Disabilities Focus, 2*(2), 20–35.

9

❧

EmPOWER

*A Strategy for Teaching Students with Language
Learning Disabilities How to Write Expository Text*

BONNIE D. SINGER
ANTHONY S. BASHIR

We all know that moment when the pen hits the paper (or fingers touch the keys) and nothing comes out, not even a word. We sit and stare, trying to organize our thoughts, wondering what to say, searching for language, and trying to communicate with that unseen reader. We work hard, and finally words come with a feeling of "Yes, I said it right! That's what I mean." For some students with language learning disabilities, that feeling is illusive and may never happen. For these students, learning to write, just like learning to speak, poses grave difficulties.

Writing, like speaking, is a complex act that involves a wide range of cognitive, linguistic, motor, affective, and regulatory systems (Hayes, 2000; Levelt, 1989; Singer & Bashir, 1997, 1999). Managing and coordinating these different systems places extensive demands on speakers and writers to allocate cognitive resources effectively in order to successfully produce oral and written language (Lahey & Bloom, 1994). Scardamalia (1981) notes that "To pay conscious attention to handwriting, spelling, punctuation, word choice, syntax, textual conventions, purpose, organization, clarity, rhythm, euphony, and reader characteristics would seemingly overload the infor- mation processing capacity of the best intellects" (p. 81).

Writing poses multiple challenges for everyone because it is a unique social communicative act that requires a specialized medium and a variety

239

of forms through which meanings are constructed with readers. Some students learn to manage these multiple demands admirably. Some find that they can produce only certain kinds of writing (e.g., stories or research reports). Still others struggle inordinately each and every time they have to write.

The purpose of this chapter is threefold. First, a summary of research on the writing abilities of students with language learning disabilities (LLD) is presented. Next, a strategy called EmPOWER™, based on the work of Englert et al. (1988a), is detailed as an approach to helping students with LLD learn to write expository text. Finally, a set of guiding principles for instruction and intervention is presented. These are intended to facilitate collaboration between the teacher and the speech–language pathologist as they work together to address the writing needs of students with LLD.

WHAT DO WE KNOW ABOUT THE WRITING OF STUDENTS WITH LANGUAGE LEARNING DISABILITIES?

Students with LLD are at risk for numerous difficulties with expository text composition. They demonstrate problems with every aspect of both text production and the writing process. For students with LLD, who lack fluency and automaticity in a number of speaking and writing processes (German & Simon, 1991; Scott & Windsor, 2000), an already limited language system can result in a high degree of variability in oral and written language production (Lahey & Bloom, 1994).

The following is a brief review of research that addresses the composing abilities of students with learning disabilities and LLD. In considering this research, a word of caution is in order. The vast majority of reported studies that address writing in children with "learning disabilities" have not specified the linguistic functioning of these students, nor have these studies included information about concomitant deficits (such as memory, visual–spatial skills, or attention) (Singer, 1997). Even when children with language-based learning disabilities are included in studies, the aspects of language that are problematic (e.g., semantic, syntactic, or pragmatic domains of language) are not usually specified. Consequently, we know only a little about the patterns of written language difficulty demonstrated by students with *language* learning disabilities. Whereas the following review refers to studies of students struggling with written *language*, we consider these to reflect the skills and abilities of students with LLD, though we acknowledge that not all subjects included in the studies were identified with primary language disorders. With this in mind, a selected summary of research is presented on various aspects of text production and the writing process.

Text Production

Studies suggest that students with LLD have difficulty instantiating *text schemas*, or mental representations of the underlying structure of a written discourse, to guide their text production (Thomas, Englert, & Gregg, 1987). These students are less proficient than their peers at organizing and producing written compositions that include the essential elements of narrative and expository text structures. Presumably, they lack mental representations of these genres (Englert & Thomas, 1987; Englert, Raphael, Fear, & Anderson, 1988b).

Several studies suggest that students with LLD approach the writing task by producing a linear sequence of utterances, with each sentence triggered associatively by the last. This approach is in contrast to one that constructs overarching goals for the text and crafts content to meet those goals (Englert et al., 1988b; Thomas et al., 1987; Wong, Wong, & Blenkinsop, 1989). Englert and her colleagues (1988b) note:

> Whereas able writers approach the writing process in a top-down fashion, starting with a text structure or organizational plan, LD [learning-disabled] students seemed to be linearly associative, progressing from word to word or from sentence to sentence. They focused on what to say next rather than on text structure as an organizational frame (a) for generating ideas and (b) for tying each succeeding idea back to the major premise. (p. 103)

This style of text production, which Scardamalia and Bereiter (1987) call "knowledge telling," is one that typically developing, yet still immature, writers use. More able writers adopt a "knowledge transforming" approach to producing text, wherein they hold global goals for a text in mind. They write and craft their text by developing subgoals to meet those global goals. (See Table 9.1 for examples of text representing knowledge-telling vs. knowledge-transforming composing strategies.)

McCutchen's (2000) recent model of working memory may help to explain why students with LLD persist in their use of a knowledge-telling strategy. She argues that writing rests upon two foundations. The first is fluent language generation and transcription processes. These allow the writer to manage the constraints imposed by the limited storage capacity of short-term working memory. The second is extensive knowledge of the writing topic and genre. Extensive background knowledge allows the writer to invoke the resources of long-term working memory in order to access text schemas and relevant information stored in long-term memory. Together, fluent language generation processes and knowledge of topic and genre affect what the writer writes. These discourse processes mature with age and experience with text (McCutchen, 1986).

TABLE 9.1. Examples of Student Texts That Reveal Knowledge-Telling versus Knowledge-Transforming (Scardamalia & Berieter, 1987) Styles of Composing

---

Essay on a favorite historical figure, Thurgood Marshall, written by a sixth-grade student with LLD depicting a knowledge-telling style of text production:

Thourd good Marshall, the supreme court judge 1983, was doing the right thing and put people in jail because they was being bad and smoking other things than cigarettes and the other great thing i like is recess going outside to play some basket ball out in the park and some days beat my friends and some day beat me me by cheating but I did not say anything i just let them beat me. I like lunch because you get to see and talk to them but the food is diston to me i rather bring my own food and eat it than eat lunch from the milk and the chips is OK but the food is nasty and I could not take it was so nasty to eat.

Essay on a favorite character in the book Jane Eyre. *Plan for the essay produced by a 10th-grade student with LLD, depicting a knowledge-transforming style of text production:*

Thesis: One of ~~my all time~~ fav. characters in Jane Eyre was Mr. Rochester. This man's ~~will and humor~~ attitude personality ~~failed witout it~~ ~~and humor~~ not only brought him the love of his life, ~~But And~~ but tore her away from him.

Par. One Topic Sentence: Mr. Rochester was a wealthy philanthropist who lived through out Europe courting women and breaking hearts. He lived the life of a king.

Par. Two Topic Sentence: Mr. Rochester had many great and aspiring acts and feelings in his life and yet there would always be one act he wished he had never made.

Par. Three Topic Sentence: Though ~~Jane's~~ Mr. R's heart was broken and tears still come to his eyes, there was no presentiment in this man's future.

Conclusion: Mr. Rochester had to rely on Jane for support and his visual sense. But it is just as for all threw the story Jane had been his eyes. Opening him up to love, hate, envy, true soul intelligence and heart. She also showed him that true sight can never be blinded by the past.

Due to the nature of their language-processing difficulties, students with LLD do not generate language fluently or automatically; they also can have impoverished funds of knowledge. Translating ideas into language is problematic for them due to organization, retrieval, morphosyntactic, and spelling difficulties (Masterson & Apel, 2000; Gillam & Johnston, 1992; German & Simon, 1991; Lahey, 1988). Transcription processes (e.g., handwriting) also are frequently impaired (Graham, 1990). For some students, neither translation nor transcription ever becomes automatic. In addition, decoding and reading comprehension abilities often are impaired (Catts & Kamhi, 1999).

Collectively, deficits in multiple aspects of language knowledge and language production influence writing in numerous ways. Lack of automaticity with language generation is believed to affect the efficiency of short-term working memory processes involved in producing written sentences (McCutchen, 1994; Swanson & Berninger, 1994). Problems in social interaction can limit the extent to which children participate in a discourse community, such as the classroom (Brinton, Fujiki, & Higbee, 1998). Reduced classroom participation can negatively influence the apprenticeship experiences necessary to learn the ways of talking and writing about ideas (Cazden, 2001; Mariage, 2001; Gallas, 1994; Hicks, 1997). Finally, reading impairments result in less exposure to and ability to access information in print, which in turn affects world knowledge, the scope and range of language development, and writing quality (Cox, Shanahan, & Sulzby, 1990).

Considering McCutchen's (2000) model, then, children with LLD are at a considerable disadvantage when it comes to the acquisition of mature composing processes because they struggle with virtually every process that is required for developing and producing text. This may explain why they persist in the use of a knowledge-telling model of production (Englert et al., 1988b) long past their nondisabled peers, and why they struggle inordinately with producing expository genres that require hierarchical thinking, thereby taxing working memory (Scott & Windsor, 2000).

Language Production

The ability to negotiate the writing process is dependent upon a number of factors, of which language production is paramount. What is often most striking about texts written by students with LLD is that they are short. They have fewer words, fewer sentences, and/or fewer propositions than those written by their peers (Barenbaum, Newcomer, & Nodine, 1987). Their writing includes fewer complex sentence structures (Englert & Thomas, 1987), and they have greater difficulty with written morphology in the early grades than their nondisabled peers (Rubin, Patterson, & Kantor, 1991).

Problems with all aspects of language are noted in the written production of students with LLD. For these students, syntax remains problematic well into the school years (Gillam & Johnston, 1992; Scott & Windsor, 2000; Windsor, Scott, & Street, 2000). For example, Gillam and Johnson (1992) found that proficiency with written syntax differentiates students with *language*-based learning disabilities from students with learning disabilities and also distinguishes them from students matched for age and for language ability. Finally, students with LLD are more likely than their nondisabled peers to make language-based errors in writing that involve spelling and punctuation (Kamhi & Hinton, 2000; Moats, 1995; Treimann & Bourassa, 2000).

The Writing Process

Planning and Writing

By and large, students with LLD fail to plan before writing (Englert & Thomas 1987; Graham, 1990). Some argue that their nonreflective approach to production results from their general difficulty with the physical/motor demands of writing, which exhausts them prematurely (Graham, 1990). Others suspect that this reflects their inability to meet the executive function and self-regulatory demands that allow a writer to plan, guide, and monitor text production (Graham, Harris, & Troia, 2000; Zimmerman & Risemberg, 1997). Currently, it is unclear what role deficits in language formulation and flexibility might play in the difficulty that students with LLD exhibit with planning and writing.

Graham's (1990) work reveals that children with LLD often begin essays by responding "yes" or "no" to the essay prompt rather than developing a clear topic or thesis statement. Students then add a few brief reasons for their answer and terminate their essays abruptly. Graham interprets this finding as reflecting their tendency to turn an essay assignment into a question–answer task. He also suggests that students with LLD have yet to transcend dependence on a conversational partner for producing extended text, so they draw upon a cocreated (i.e., conversational) mental representation of discourse rather than a sustained monologue (Bereiter & Scardamalia, 1982). Moreover, this finding suggests that students with LLD have difficulty recognizing their audience and crafting a text that provides their reader with the appropriate type and amount of information.

Some suspect that memory limitations may account for some of the planning and writing difficulties that children with LLD exhibit. McCutchen (1994) and Swanson and Berninger (1994) argue that working memory limitations may leave students without the ability to hold global goals and subgoals for a text in mind while simultaneously chiseling away at achieving those goals. Thus, the student's ability to conceive of and develop a logically organized text may suffer. In addition to difficulty with text production, short-term and working memory limitations can interfere with the development and production of grammatically intact written sentences (Daiute, 1981).

Consequently, it is possible that when students with LLD experience writing difficulties at both the macro- and the microlevel simultaneously, they revert to formulative frameworks that are within their control. The result is that they adopt a writing style that is spontaneous and conversational in nature, rather than planned and hierarchical. These difficulties may also influence all aspects of their written language production.

Revising

With respect to text revision, students with LLD tend not to review what they have written once they complete a text, and they struggle with editing and revising processes (Espin & Sindelar, 1988). Limited research suggests that they attend more to spelling, punctuation, and letter formation than they do to meaning when they revise their texts (McArthur & Graham,1987). Moreover, they rely more on external factors (e.g., teachers) than internal factors (e.g., their own criteria) when making judgments about text they have written (Englert et al., 1988a; Englert et al., 1988b). For example, having failed to develop an internal schema for evaluating and revising their writing, students with LLD rely on the observations, prompts, or comments that their teachers provide rather than their own assessments of their work.

Many students with LLD have difficulty reading (Catts & Kamhi, 1999). They also lack the metalinguisitc and metacognitive strategies needed for revising text (Espin & Sindelar, 1988; McAlister, Nelson, & Bahr, 1999; McNamara, Carter, McIntosh, & Gerken, 1998; Windsor, 1999). As such, deficits in reading or deficits in the capacity to reflect on language and thinking may account for their difficulties with understanding and making judgments about the structure and meaning of what they write.

Alternately, deficits in spoken language processing and production may influence students' ability to judge correct from incorrect structure and meaning. Students with reading problems also come to writing with a paucity of experience with text. They lack ownership of discourse styles, text structures, morphosyntactic rules, and semantic nuances. It is not surprising, then, that the revision process poses such a challenge to them and that they focus their attention primarily on mechanics rather than meaning when revising. Having internalized less effective mental representations of texts, they write and say "I'm done" without evaluating their work in any meaningful or systematic manner.

Summary

Students with LLD are at risk for numerous difficulties with composing text. They demonstrate problems with every aspect of text production and every stage of the writing process. They have difficulty reading their assignments and knowing how to complete their work. They struggle with planning, organizing, and revising their writing. Their texts are short and poorly structured. Their use of language is problematic in terms of syntax, vocabulary diversity, and cohesion, and they make frequent errors in spelling and writing mechanics. They have difficulty making transitions from one step in the writing process to the next. Lacking an inner voice to mediate

their written language production, they often present as overwhelmed by
the multiple demands of writing and appear to have difficulty allocating
sufficient cognitive resources to meet various writing demands (e.g., knowing where to begin, how to stay on and develop a topic, how to represent
their ideas with language, etc.). As a result, they are ineffective and inefficient writers.

In order to support the development of writing in students with LLD,
educators and speech–language pathologists are pressed to develop systematic teaching and intervention approaches. These approaches must adequately support and guide the development of the diverse range of cognitive
and linguistic abilities that must be coordinated to produce written text.
Ample research now shows the positive effect of teaching methods that are
direct and explicit, that model the use of writing strategies for diverse tasks,
and that mentor the student through the writing process (De La Paz & Graham, 2002; Graham & Harris, 2003; Troia, 2002; Troia & Graham, 2002). Such
methods must ensure the full participation of the student within the literate learning community.

THE EmPOWER STRATEGY

Englert et al. (1988a) developed a strategy called POWER that was designed
to teach and scaffold the writing process for students with learning disabilities. POWER stands for *Plan, Organize, Write, Edit, Revise*—the
major stages of the writing process. The POWER strategy specified certain
steps the student should take within each stage of creating a text. For example, in the P(lan) stage, students were prompted to ask themselves,
"What is my topic? Who am I writing for? and What do I already know for
my topic?"

As the work of Englert et al. (1988a) shows, the POWER strategy served
the needs of students with learning disabilities effectively. However, our
observation was that students with weaknesses in language struggled with
it. The original prompts did not provide the linguistic structuring and
mediation that students with LLD required to navigate the strategy or the
writing process successfully. These students appeared to require more
explicit verbal prompts to move them systematically through the steps of
the POWER strategy.

Therefore, the original version of POWER was altered so that it would
reflect the step-by-step conversation that students with LLD need to have
with themselves in order to manage, regulate, and write expository text.
Prompts were developed to mediate and guide students through the steps
of the writing process. Using the feedback and experiences of students,
teachers, and speech–language pathologists, a new version of the strategy

evolved over many years, which differs considerably from the original work of Englert and colleagues (1988a).

The current strategy, called EmPOWER™, is presented in Figure 9.1. This strategy, like its predecessor (Englert et al., 1988), is designed as an instruction and intervention guide to writing that can be used by both the student and the teacher or speech–language clinician to understand and support the writing process. The strategy provides an ideal vehicle for collaboration between speech–language pathologists and teachers who aim to teach students how to develop expository text.

What Is EmPOWER?

EmPOWER approaches writing as a problem-solving task. It is a strategy that guides the writer through the writing process using six fundamental stages of problem solving: *E*valuate, *m*ake a *P*lan, *O*rganize, *W*ork, *E*valuate, and *R*ework. As such, it defines a consistent routine for developing expository text.

Each step of EmPOWER is taught directly using a dialogical approach (Englert, 1992). A coconstructed conversation between the teacher and/or speech–language pathologist and student helps the student understand the demands of each stage of the writing process and the routines for managing those demands successfully. Consequently, EmPOWER aims to make the process of expository writing explicit, opening it up for exploration, discussion, and collaborative problem solving.

EmPOWER evolved from use within individual tutorial/therapeutic settings, general education classrooms providing inclusive services to students with a range of learning needs (e.g., language, visual–spatial processing, attention, and executive function), self-contained classrooms for students with LLD and significant writing difficulties, and whole schools for students with various types of learning disabilities. The strategy has been used by teachers and speech–language pathologists with students in grade 3 and beyond who are learning to write expository text. Its use across these settings has informed the ongoing development of the strategy, leading to its current form and its readiness to be studied empirically. Currently, only case study research has been completed with this version of the strategy, although large-scale exploratory studies are underway that will examine its effect on written language productivity, text structure, and teacher–student dialogue. With this in mind, the strategy is presented below.

Introducing the Strategy

Instruction with the EmPOWER strategy begins with a discussion about the meaning of the word *empower*. Students are asked to offer what they

FIGURE 9.1. The EmPOWER™ approach to teaching expository writing. Copyright 2002 by Innovative Learning Partners, LLC. Reprinted by permission.

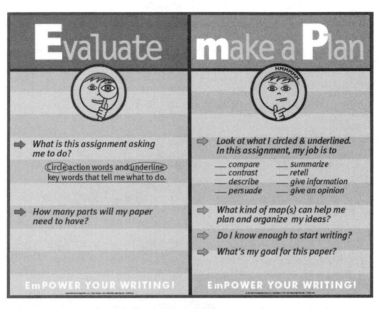

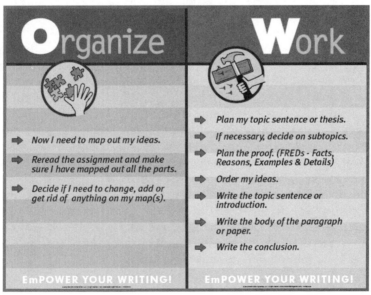

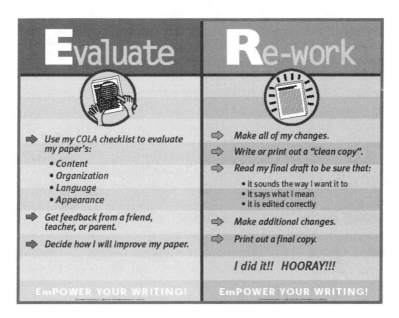

know about that word's meaning and any associations they might have with the word. Many students with LLD do not know what *empower* means, but they do have some understanding of the word *power*. Therefore, instruction begins with brainstorming about what things have power (e.g., cars, remote controls, people in authority roles, etc.). Typically, associations such as *faster*, *easier*, and *in control* emerge. Students are then helped by the teacher or clinician to understand that when a person is "empowered," he or she knows approaches to solving a problem that make him or her feel in control and feel effective. More often than not, students are quite eager to learn more about a strategy that will provide them with these outcomes. With this conceptual framework in place, teachers and clinicians then turn to teaching the individual steps of the strategy.

E = Evaluate

Many expository writing assignments provide students with background information and a context for writing, thus embedding what is being called for within a larger framework. Students with LLD often do not know how to extract what they need to write about from the background and contextual information within an assignment. This can ignite a self-defeating internal voice that says "I can't do this," which in turn causes them to give up before even attempting the task. Lacking strategies for "dissecting" assignments, they do not know how to go about approaching the task and solving the writing problem. To successfully complete an expository writing task, a student first must understand what that task is asking for and what kind of thinking is needed to complete it. These issues are addressed in the E step of EmPOWER using two prompts.

Evaluate the Assignment

To begin with, the strategy first prompts the writer to ask *What is this assignment asking me to do?* This first step is included in the strategy because so many students give up on writing before they have even determined the task, especially when the assignment they are given looks (at first glance) lengthy and/or complicated. Students need an explicit and active strategy for reading an assignment that allows the "trees" to stand apart from the "forest," so this prompt requires the use of a strategy for evaluating assignments. The strategy is to find and then *Circle action words* within the assignment (i.e., the words that tell the writer to take some action) and *underline the key words that tell me what to do* (the information that further defines those actions). For those students who have significant reading problems, the assignment is read to them several times as they listen and read along. Students then identify the words that tell them what action(s) they need to take and details that reveal what they need to do. Consider, for example, the assignment in Figure 9.2. Having completed the first prompt in the E step of EmPOWER, students can now see at a glance what their task is in the essay. What they must do stands out, and this allows them to better consider their approach to the assignment and the writing task.

When applying the circle-and-underline strategy, some students are inclined to merely circle all of the action words (verbs) in the assignment at first; others do not know what an "action word" is. As such, a fair amount of direct instruction and supported practice is often required at this point before students are able to find only those action words that *tell them what to do* in a writing assignment and to identify the words that *clarify* those actions. Such practice can be carried out collaboratively by the speech–language pathologist and the classroom teacher.

Preview the Outcome

Having dissected the assignment, the next prompt is to ask *How many parts will my paper need to have?* This prompt asks students to consciously specify how many actions they must take as a writer to fulfill the requirements of the assignment. This requires a careful reading of what they circled and underlined. Merely counting the number of words that they circled does

Assignment given to a student:

Alexander the Great was an effective and important leader. He quickly won the

love and respect of his people, but did not keep it throughout his time as their

ruler. Discuss what he did to win the devotion of his people and explain

what caused his popularity to decline.

Assignment after a student completes the first step of E (Evaluate):

Alexander the Great was an effective and important leader. He quickly won the

love and respect of his people, but did not keep it throughout his time as their

ruler. Discuss what he did to win the devotion of his people and explain

what caused his popularity to decline.

FIGURE 9.2. Sample assignment with application of the initial step of E (evaluate) in EmPOWER.

not necessarily give them the answer to this question, as some of the circled words might reveal the nature of the writing task (e.g., *write* an essay) rather than the discourse moves they must make within their paper (e.g., *describe* your favorite place). Moreover, some assignments direct students to develop multiple sections in a paper, but do so within one statement (e.g., *Examine* three reasons for Napoleon's demise). Consider the following example. In the assignment "Write an essay and explain why John Smith's leadership helped the Pilgrims survive," students would circle two action words (*write* and *explain*) and underline the information associated with those words. Yet students might determine that their papers would need only one part (i.e., one explanation), or they might determine it would need more than one part (i.e., one paragraph for each major point they want to make about the effects of John Smith's leadership). By acknowledging the various parts or sections of their paper explicitly, students are given preliminary information that will guide their choice of text structure and the various planning strategies aligned with the development of that text structure.

mP = make a Plan

One of the reasons students with LLD may have difficulty reading directions and responding to them is that the words within the directions may not invoke mental representations (or text schemas) related to discourse knowledge or genre. For example, when asked to "discuss" or "argue" a certain point, students do not necessarily conjure a mental representation of how to develop a text accordingly. As such, the next stage of EmPOWER directs students to make a Plan by following four prompts.

Define the Discourse Purpose

The first prompt in step mP is *Look at what I circled and underlined. In this assignment, my job is to . . .* and then provides a list of cognitive–linguistic actions from which to choose (e.g., compare, contrast, give information, describe, etc.). For example, the assignment in Figure 9.2 prompts the student to do two things, discuss and explain, which correspond to several possible rhetorical/discourse moves (depending on how the writer chooses to approach the paper). These include giving an opinion, giving information, summarizing, and/or retelling. Students are taught via mini-lessons how to identify the potential range of discourse moves they might make in their paper by examining the words they circled and underlined in their assignment. Students are given assignments that require them to identify discourse moves with which they are familiar when they use the EmPOWER strategy in class, and their repertoire of rhetorical goals is gradually broadened through systematic instruction.

Choose Graphics

Having acknowledged what discourse moves they need to make in order to develop their paper, students are now well poised for the next prompt of the mP step: *What kind of map(s) will help me plan and organize my ideas?* The goals of a discourse are inextricably linked to an underlying (visual) schema. As such, students need direct instruction in linking various discourse genre words to different visual representations of thought. Here, students choose from a small number of graphics that visually represent the underlying thinking process(es) associated with the rhetorical task at hand (e.g., description, compare/contrast, cause–effect).

A few words about graphics are in order. The use of graphics to facilitate expository writing has been shown to be effective (DiCecco & Gleason, 2002), and graphics are routinely used as prewriting strategies in many schools today. Unfortunately, few schools use the same set of graphics *across all grades*, so many students never internalize them or use them consistently to guide their writing. Furthermore, many teachers use graphics as mere fill-in-the-blanks exercises rather than as tools for conveying thinking and/ or communicative processes (Hyerle, 2000).

Some graphic-organizing strategies better represent text structures and support the drafting process than others. Consider, for example, the graphic shown in Figure 9.3. This graphic was given to Annie by her third-grade teacher to plan a historical fictional story. Annie, a student with language and executive function disabilities, had considerable difficulty with planning, organizing, and generating both oral and written language. Though

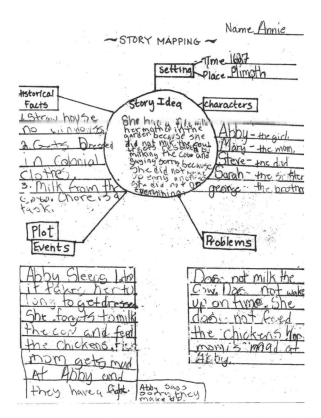

FIGURE 9.3. Graphic given to Annie by her teacher to plan a historical fiction narrative.

she had filled in all of the elements of the graphic in school, she was unable to begin her draft because the graphic did not make it clear to her how her text would unfold and "lay out" in the end. Annie noted that her plan was to randomly choose a box to begin with and simply write down what was in it. But still she was unsure of herself and her ability to complete this task successfully, so she waited until help was available. Once the sequence of narrative elements was reviewed and her ideas were restructured visually so that they reflected the sequential nature of a narrative (see Figure 9.4), Annie was quickly able to write a nicely structured and elaborated story.

In using graphics with EmPOWER, the goal is for students to move fluidly from developing a graphic that represents the structure/patterns of their thinking to drafting the text. For that to happen, students must become flu-

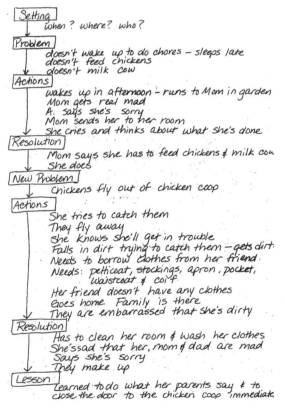

FIGURE 9.4. Reconfiguration of Figure 9.3 graphic into a graphic that visually represents the underlying text structure of a narrative.

ent with only a handful of visual mapping strategies that represent the structure of a range of thinking processes that support expository discourse and that can be used across all academic content areas. Within the mP step of EmPOWER, students identify which of eight graphic representations of fundamental thinking processes will support them in accomplishing the writing job(s) they have set out to do. These graphics are based on the theoretical framework of Hyerle (1996, 2000). Increasing students' familiarity with cognitive schemas leads to increased ease and organization of production, comprehension of content, and more elaborated mental models of meaning (Westby, 1994).

Each graphic mapping strategy is introduced via a four-phase model of instruction (Ellis, 2000). The teacher or speech–language pathologist first introduces the graphic explicitly, modeling how to develop it and when to use it with writing ("I do" phase). If working with a whole class, then the teacher leads students in developing and using the graphic with different content ("We do" phase). Then students practice applying the graphic to new material in small groups ("Y'all do" phase), and finally students apply it independently ("You do" phase).

Two notions are critical for students to understand in these final portions of the mP step. The first is that knowing the purpose of the discourse they are producing as writers is the key to deciphering which graphic(s) to use to organize their ideas. Choosing the wrong graphic for the assigned writing task can be disastrous. The underlying thinking associated with the development of a persuasive essay is quite different from that of a compare/contrast essay. If a student chooses a compare/contrast graphic to represent his or her thinking for a persuasive argument, he or she will embark on a path that will surely lead to frustration and ultimately failure. The task of the teacher or speech–language pathologist in this step is to have students *consciously* understand how the language of an assignment gives the writer cues as to what the discourse purpose is. Knowing this allows the writer to recognize the visual representation of the thought processes underlying that discourse.

In considering these notions, the important influence that reading has in the writing process is quickly apparent. Students who are not exposed to expository text structures through reading and discussion and/or whose teachers do not help them to recognize the text structure devices that are used in texts have considerable difficulty developing a metacognitive understanding of how different texts are structured to accomplish different communicative purposes. Therefore, in addition to explicit work with the mP step, teachers and speech–language pathologists spend much time with their students exploring the work of other authors to examine such notions as text purpose and structure and the discourse devices that reveal and represent them.

Appraise the Knowledge Base

The third prompt of mP asks *Do I know enough to write this paper?* Here, students are prompted to consider whether their current knowledge base on the subject about which they are writing is sufficient. If it is, they may move to the next prompt. If not, they are reminded to consider what information they are lacking and also to consider what source(s) they might turn to in order to learn more. At this point, the teacher and the speech–language pathologist need to collaborate in order to ensure that students with LLD acquire relevant content language as well as strategies for internalizing and accessing that language.

Set Goals

The final prompt of the mP step is *What's my goal for this paper?* Research shows that goal setting is an important part of any task requiring self-regulation (Garavalia & Gredler, 2002; Zimmerman, 1989). Students who set goals for complex tasks perform better than students who embark on a task without a goal in mind. The best performance is seen when students start out by setting process goals and, midway through the task, shift and set goals for the desired outcome. As such, students are prompted at this point in the writing process to set one or two goals for their paper; goals might focus on their successful use of specific strategies, their production of specific text elements, and/or the effect they wish to have on their reader.

Having completed all of the mP (make a Plan) steps in the EmPOWER strategy, students are now ready to move to O: organize.

O = Organize

The third step of EmPOWER prompts students to represent their ideas about their topic on paper and organize those ideas in a logical sequence for writing. In addition to supporting students with organizing their ideas, this step also provides them with an external support for working memory by providing frameworks for storing their ideas for later review. The O step provides three prompts.

Generate Ideas

The first prompt under the O step of EmPOWER is *Now I need to map out my ideas.* At this point, students create a graphic (or set of graphics) to represent the ideas they have about the topic(s) of the writing assignment. For example, a student might brainstorm everything he or she knows about deforestation and gorillas and then select a cause–effect graphic to lay out the ideas showing the causes and effects of deforestation on the world's gorilla population. (See Figure 9.5 for an example of such a graphic.)

For some students with LLD, the task of brainstorming/idea generation is very difficult. At this point, ample scaffolding and/or clinical intervention is necessary to assist students with accessing and retrieving relevant background knowledge and information for their texts. Gradually, teachers and speech–language pathologists fade instructional supports as they help students refine their ability to brainstorm independently.

Reconsider Ideas

The second prompt under step O is *Reread the assignment and make sure I have mapped out all the parts.* This prompt supports students to keep the demands of the task in mind and determine whether the ideas they have mapped out will help them meet those demands. Thus, it provides students who may have difficulty holding assignment demands in working memory long enough to carry them out with an external memory scaffold. The third

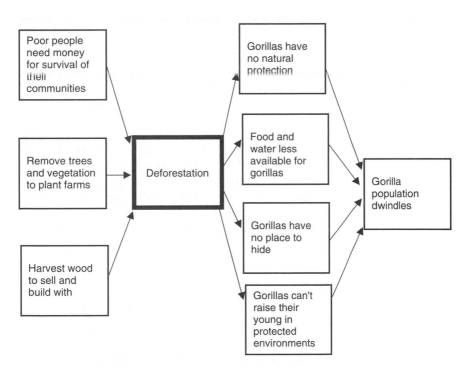

FIGURE 9.5. Graphic to represent cause–effect thinking (based on the work of Hyerle, 1996, 2000).

prompt in step O is *Decide if I need to change, add, or get rid of anything on my map(s)*. This prompt explicitly cues the writer to step back and consider whether each of the ideas he or she has mapped out is relevant and whether he or she has covered the topic thoroughly. Therefore, it prompts the student to *transform* knowledge rather than simply *tell* what he or she knows (Scardamalia & Bereiter, 1987).

W = Work

Having spent considerable time mapping out their thinking and talking about their ideas, students are now ready to begin the task of composing. The transition from planning and organizing to generating language is one that students with LLD may not make easily. Many students find this a daunting task, even when they have worked hard to represent their thinking about their topic visually. Composing involves much more than merely turning planned ideas and words into sentences. The writer must consider a number of variables that shape the tone, format, and style of the language he or she generates. Moreover, writers must "see" how their mapped-out plans translate into a text structure that is represented with language and that captures their ideas. Thus, the W step of EmPOWER explicitly structures and supports the composing process by prompting students to be mindful of those factors that help orient them to the communicative task at hand.

In teaching the W step, consideration of what influence the writer wishes to have on his or her reader is woven through the instruction. Students are reminded to keep the needs of their audience in mind as they write, which allows them to write with a particular style and perspective. For students with pragmatic weaknesses, this aspect of writing can be difficult to establish. Thus, teachers and speech–language pathologists spend a good deal of time via mini-lessons working to build students' ability to take another's perspective and write (and talk) with a particular tone or style that is shaped for various readers. They also closely examine texts being read in class to reveal techniques of specific writing styles and their effect on the reader.

Determine the Point

Without a clear sense of the controlling argument of a paper, it is difficult to create coherent text with ideas that build on one another (Minto, 1995). Accordingly, the first prompt of W is *Plan my topic sentence or thesis*. If students are writing only a single paragraph, the focus is on the topic sentence, whereas the focus turns to the thesis statement if the goal is to write multiparagraph text. Students are taught that a *topic sentence* is a fact or opinion the writer will prove by providing support or explanation. A *thesis state-ment* is a unique opinion or multifaceted fact a writer is presenting to an unseen reader that will be supported with multiple paragraphs. If students aim to write a thesis statement, they are guided at this point through a structured process (adapted from the work of Jeffrey Parker, a teacher at the Norman Howard School in Rochester, NY) for progressing from the topic about which they are writing to a clear statement that they will argue in their paper.

The graphics used in the Organize step assist students with "seeing" what and how they think about a topic, but the graphics themselves do not necessarily look like the structure of a text. For example, the graphic in Figure 9.5 represents cause–effect thinking, but does not look like a paragraph. While some students make the leap from such a graphic to text production intuitively, others do not. Such students are likely to disregard any planning/organizing they might have done and to consider writing as a wholly separate process. To combat this problem, and to support those students who may not be inclined to see such connections between planning, organizing, and writing independently, the EmPOWER strategy specifically prompts students to add their working topic sentence or thesis to a writing template that visually represents the structure of the text. For single paragraphs, the template prompts the student to indent a topic sentence (*fact* or *opinion*), support it with elaborated details, and provide a closing sentence. For multiple paragraphs, a template is used that is similar to the FRAME template developed by Ellis (1998).

Complete the Template

The next prompt is *If necessary, decide on subtopics* and add them to the template. This prompt is essential for students who are composing multi-paragraph text, but is skipped if the goal is to write only a single paragraph. To decide what the subtopics are, students read their working thesis statement and ask themselves what questions a reader would have about that statement (Minto, 1995). The goal here is to help the writer demonstrate his or her understanding of the topic as it relates to the thesis. The questions that students envision a reader having are then shaped into subtopics that will be explored in depth within the body of the paper. Then students determine what fact or opinion they will present about each subtopic that will support their thesis statement. Each statement of fact or opinion becomes a topic sentence for a paragraph the writer must develop fully.

Whether writing a single-paragraph or multiparagraph text, students are now prompted to *Plan the Proof*. Here they refer to the graphics they developed in the *Organize* step and determine the Facts, Reasons, Examples, and Details (FREDs) that support the topic sentence(s) they planned. These are added to their template as well. Teachers and clinicians help children to separate relevant from irrelevant information and to make wise choices about what information to present to their readers. If any FRED does not support the fact or opinion expressed in the topic sentence, it is not included on the template. At this point, the teacher or clinician may need to spend considerable time helping the student to develop the ideas on his or her template so that they are coherent, relevant, and reflect a complete understanding of the topic.

Thus, the goal of the first two W prompts is to help students see how the various ideas they mapped out in the O step fit within a single-paragraph or a multiparagraph text structure.

Consider the Order

By now, if students are writing a paragraph, they have completed a template that includes a topic sentence and the FREDs that support it. If they are writing multiple paragraphs, their template includes a thesis statement, multiple topic sentences that support that thesis, and the FREDs that support each topic sentence. However, students may not always place ideas on their template in an order that will read logically. To help students use a knowledge-transforming (rather than a knowledge-telling) strategy for text production (Scardamalia & Bereiter, 1987), they are prompted to look at the ideas they have included on their template and *Order my ideas*. If they have planned only a single paragraph, they look at the FREDs on their template and decide which should be presented first, second, third, and so on. With multiparagraph text, students are directed to focus on two levels of organization. First, they number the order in which they will present the subtopics/topic sentences. Then they number the FREDs within each subtopic so as to develop a logical progression of thought within each paragraph. Classroom discussion is important here about how sequence makes for an effective paper and affects the reader. Teachers and clinicians may present examples of texts that are effectively versus ineffectively sequenced to build such insights with students.

Write

At this point, students are ready to write. It is here that students with LLD often struggle most with getting started—with getting the first sentence down on paper. The focus begins with developing a clear introduction to the paper, which is an essential component that forms the basis of the whole paper and therefore should not be saved for last (a tactic used by many students who are unclear about how to write an introduction) (Minto, 1995). To achieve this, students are taught a strategy for writing an introduction called BTP, which stands for *Background, Thesis, Preview*. Background statements consist of ideas that hook the reader, orient the reader to the topic, and provide a common ground. These lead the reader to the unique opinion the writer has about the topic, which is presented in the thesis statement. Finally, the writer previews the major subtopics that will be presented in the paper. As a part of teaching the strategy, sample texts are used to help students identify these elements in writing by other authors.

From this introduction, students move on to creating a draft of their paper. They are prompted to *Write the body of the paper*, using their ordered (numbered) templates. Woven alongside this step is explicit instruction on the linguistic underpinnings of sentence and text production. One approach designed to support the development of language for drafting involves "giving students insight into their own composing process and exposing them to a view of what the more mature composing process is like" (Scardamalia & Bereiter, 1987, p. 165). Using a dialogical approach (Englert & Raphael, 1989) with the W step, teachers and speech–language pathologists spend ample time talking about the writing task at hand, providing examples, and using think-alouds for modeling the linguistic formulation of ideas.

Finally, students are directed to *Write the conclusion*. This is often the most difficult portion of the paper for students with LLD. Their difficulty can stem from a number of problems, which include confusion about the purpose of a concluding paragraph, difficulty summarizing and presenting the essential argument(s) of their paper, and determining why their arguments are important to their reader. In keeping with Ellis's (1998) approach, students who are writing a concluding sentence to a single paragraph are taught to reread the topic sentence and body of the paragraph that they have already written and ask themselves, "So what?" The aim is for them to go one step beyond simply paraphrasing the topic sentence by considering what they want the reader to now know and understand about their topic or the implications for the information they presented. To help students with organizing a concluding paragraph, a strategy called PSST is taught. This strategy prompts the student to *Paraphrase the thesis, Summarize the Subtopics*, and leave the reader *Thinking* or feeling. For students with LLD, each part of this strategy is taught explicitly, with examples and ample teacher modeling.

Throughout the W step, as students are developing their texts, teachers and clinicians will want to pay specific attention to several levels of language use and provide scaffolding and explicit instruction as needed. For example, given the difficulty that many students with LLD have with using cohesive ties in writing, teachers and/or speech–language pathologists introduce various types of cohesive devices, and students create purpose-specific word banks to which they refer as they write (e.g., words that add ideas, words that introduce or conclude ideas, words that suggest reasons or outcomes) (see Westby & Clauser, 1999, for examples). Students are taught that connecting words perform specific communicative functions and, as a result, they are commonly used for specific genres of writing. For example, the words *first, next, meanwhile, after that,* and *lastly* are related to the communicative function of sequencing, so they are good choices for connecting ideas in procedural writing. On the other hand, *as a result, because, if, consequently,* and *therefore* have to do with the communicative functions of arguing, so they are good choices for persuasive writing.

Similarly, students may need direct instruction in written sentence formulation. Hillocks (1986) notes that sentence-combining work is an effective approach to developing grammatical complexity. Consequently, sentence structure may be addressed within the classroom and/or in speech–language intervention via systematic sentence-combining exercises (Strong, 1973). Teaching sentence forms and syntax can also be approached using a multisensory program such as Framing Your Thoughts (Green & Enfield, 1998). These competencies are developed via minilessons. When students begin to demonstrate an understanding of each new concept, teachers and/or clinicians gradually cue students to integrate newly learned sentence formulation skills into text production to meet the task's writing requirements.

E = Evaluate

Evaluate Your Work

Having created a draft of a text, students are prompted with the E step of EmPOWER to evaluate what they have written. As Bereiter and Scardamalia (1987) point out, "Significant revision presupposes a system of goals and goal-seeking procedures. Students who lack such a system . . . need more encouragement to revise and guidelines for improving their texts" (p. 156). Prior research has shown that students who are provided with prompts that guide and scaffold their revision process engage in more frequent and more effective revision (Daiute & Kruidenier, 1985; Fitzgerald & Markham, 1987).

In this E step of EmPOWER, then, students are prompted to *Use my COLA checklist to evaluate my paper's Content, Organization, Language, and Appearance.* The COLA strategy guides the revision process by directing the writer's attention to four essential domains within the text. These are:

- *Content* (information included in the text)
- *Organization* (logic of the text's macro- and microstructural elements)
- *Language* (integrity of semantic and morphosyntactic elements)
- *Appearance* (adherence to the linguistic rules regarding mechanics

and spelling as well as overall presentation. Though these rules are linguistic in nature, they are included under *Appearance* because students tend to focus only on these elements of their writing, at the expense of more substantial revisions.)

COLA is designed to provide novice writers with defined revision and editing guidelines, thereby scaffolding the development of metacognitive, text analysis routines. Within each domain of COLA, questions direct the writer's critical reading of a text. The questions on the version of COLA included in Figure 9.6 reflect those aspects of text analysis a group of middle-school teachers believed their students should be able to complete by the time they finished eighth grade. These questions then guided the instructional routines used within their middle-school classrooms. Alternate forms of COLA have also been developed for use at the elementary, high-school, and college levels.

COLA
Reread your paper and ask yourself . . .

		SELF	OTHER
CONTENT	Did I complete all parts of the assignment?		
ORGANIZATION	Did I use my map(s)?		
	Does each paragraph have a topic sentence?		
	Are my ideas ordered logically?		
LANGUAGE	Is each sentence complete? (subject & predicate)		
	Can I use more unusual words?		
	Did I use transition words to connect my ideas?		
APPEARANCE	Does each sentence start with a capital and end with the correct kind of punctuation?		
	Do I use any special words that need to be capitalized?		
	Are any words capitalized that shouldn't be?		
	Are all words spelled correctly?		

FIGURE 9.6. A version of the COLA strategy for revision that is designed for middle-school students with LLD. Copyright 2002 by Innovative Learning Partners, LLC. Reprinted by permission.

Teaching students how to revise offers the opportunity to address many different cognitive–linguistic and learning goals directly. First and foremost, revision is a reading comprehension task (Hayes, Flower, Schriver, Stratman, & Carey, 1987). But, as Hayes and his colleagues point out, reading to revise involves both reading to comprehend and reading to judge and to consciously improve. So the writer must read and comprehend when revising, but also must step back from a text to reflect on the adequacy of its development along many different lines. Thus, reading becomes the vehicle for reflection that writers rely upon to gauge whether what they wrote accurately reflects their goals and intentions and does so in accordance with the conventions of the discourse community.

In teaching students with LLD to read and evaluate their texts, group writing/revising and teacher/clinician modeling are used along with the COLA strategy. Group-writing and group-revising tasks help move students beyond their tendency to only look for spelling and punctuation errors and assist them with developing the ability to respond to (Frank, 1995) and judge text (e.g., Mariage, 2001). Teachers and/or speech–language pathologists model revising and editing processes by rereading text and "thinking aloud" as they consider a range of parameters (e.g., the strength of its arguments, whether or not sentences are complete or make sense, whether the reader will understand what idea they intended to convey, whether or not a word is spelled correctly, etc.). In doing so, they scaffold students' ability to reread text while stepping back to judge aspects of text structure, linguistic style, and elements of language, such as vocabulary, syntax, morphology, and spelling (Hayes et al., 1987). Simultaneously, they reinforce basic concepts about text, paragraph and sentence structure, semantics, and style, as well as spelling and writing mechanics. Most importantly, teachers and/or speech–language pathologists model the internal conversation a competent writer has as he or she rereads and reconsiders the adequacy of the language standing alone on the page. Thus, the instructional aim is to improve students' revising and editing abilities as well as their conscious understanding of texts and writing.

Get Feedback

The second E prompt is *Get feedback from a friend, teacher, or parent.* Incorporating the principles of modeled instruction and traditional writing process methods (e.g., Atwell, 1998; Frank, 1995; Graves & Murray, 1980), teacher conferences and peer review are used to support and direct students as they engage in the reflections necessary for the revision process.

For students with LLD, teacher and peer conferences can be challenging because they require the use of language for social interaction, for making reflective judgments about content, and for deciding what to change. As such, revision and editing processes offer speech–language pathologists an important venue for scaffolding social discourse and social pragmatics, as students need to learn to talk about their writing and offer as well as receive constructive feedback (e.g., see Mariage, 2001).

Make Changes

Having conferred with their peers and teacher or clinician, students are then prompted to *Decide how I will improve my paper*. Here, authors are explicitly empowered to make the final decision about which suggestions for revision to adopt. The aim is for them to sustain a sense of ownership and control over their own writing so that they can look at a text they have written and feel a sense of self-efficacy and pride.

R = Rework

Having planned, organized, written, and revised their texts, students are in the final step of text production: Rework. The first prompt of the R step is *Make all of my changes*. Then students *Write or print out a "clean copy."* To be sure the text reads in accordance with their intentions, students then *Read my final draft to be sure that it sounds the way I want it to, it says what I mean, it is edited correctly*. If they find that corrections are needed, they are directed to *Make additional changes*. Then they *Print out a final copy*. Finally, EmPOWER prompts students to congratulate themselves, offering *I did it! HOORAY!*

GUIDELINES FOR CLASSROOM AND CLINICAL PRACTICE

A number of intervention studies have examined the efficacy of various approaches for teaching writing to students with LLD (De La Paz, 2001; Englert et al., 1988a; Englert, Raphael, Anderson, Anthony, & Stevens, 1991; Wong, 2000; Wong, Butler, Ficzere, & Kuperis, 1996; Troia, Graham, & Harris, 1999). Each approach views writing as a process that requires intention, sustained attention, and the integration of multiple systems (e.g., cognitive, linguistic, motoric, affective, regulatory). Each also uses an explicit and direct approach to teaching writing and teaches student specific strategies for accomplishing the various tasks involved in the writing process (e.g., planning, drafting, revising). Table 9.2 details the various facets of the instructional approaches that research indicates are effective for teaching the writing process to students with LLD. The EmPOWER strategy, presented here and based on the work of Englert et al. (1988a), is designed to reflect those facets

TABLE 9.2. Strategic Approaches to Teaching Expository Writing

- Ensure the supported inclusion of students in a literate learning community.
- Situate students' learning experiences within a dialogical and discourse-rich environment.
- Use systematic and explicit teaching methods.
- Provide extensive modeling and opportunities for apprenticeship.
- Teach various discourse genres.
- Teach planning and organizing strategies.
- Use verbal prompts to support self-regulation of the writing process.
- Use a variety of strategies to address different writing needs.
- Use graphics as a means for displaying and as a vehicle for storing text-relevant information (i.e., language, ideas).
- Integrate oral and written language systems so as to move students from oral to literate written forms in a systematic manner.
- Provide ample opportunity to develop needed communication and language abilities.
- Promote speech–language pathologist and teacher collaboration in mentoring students with LLD as they learn to write.
- Allow for the seamless integration of language intervention and classroom teaching and learning.

of instruction that are known to be effective and that are deemed in education as "best practices."

EmPOWER is designed to be used by students, teachers, and speech–language pathologists alike. For students, EmPOWER provides a series of explicit verbal prompts that guide the production of expository text and foster independence with the writing process. These prompts are carefully designed to reflect the inner dialogue necessary for problem-solving and self-regulated behavior (Vygotsky, 1962). Students who use EmPOWER over time should internalize the language of the strategy as they come to consciously understand all that writing involves and learn a set of flexible strategies and routines for managing its many elements. Teachers and speech–language pathologists can use EmPOWER as a systematic procedure for instructing students in how to go about creating expository text. They can use it to guide and structure their written language curriculum and instruction or intervention practice. EmPOWER can also serve as an authentic assessment tool that allows teachers and clinicians to identify where students encounter difficulty with writing as they work through the writing process. This then allows them to provide individualized interventions that address students' specific writing problems.

The strategy presented here is designed for use with expository writing, although the major steps in the strategy (Evaluate, make a Plan, Organize, Work, Evaluate, Rework) can certainly be applied to narrative writing. However, we have found that the internal script that guides the development of written narratives is slightly different than the one that guides expository text. Thus, to apply EmPOWER to narrative writing, teachers and clinicians would need to work together to develop the verbal prompts that will guide and mediate students' development of a narrative. Likewise, they would need to choose appropriate graphics to support the planning and organizing processes associated with narrative text.

Teachers and speech–language pathologists who have used EmPOWER report that it is not a "quick fix" to any student's writing problem. It takes time to demystify the writing process for students and teach all of its subroutines explicitly. With repeated use, teachers using EmPOWER should find that students acquire a deep appreciation for and mastery of the range of cognitive and linguistic skills that coalesce to support expository writing. Depending on the ability and metacognitive levels of students, some steps of the strategy may require extended periods of teaching and explicit guidance.

SUMMARY

Students with LLD struggle with acquiring the many cognitive–linguistic skills necessary to participate successfully in their classroom communities. With weaknesses in one or more aspect of language content, form, and/or use (Lahey, 1988), they struggle to acquire the oral language skills needed to manage the spoken discourse demands of their classrooms (Brinton et al., 1998). Because oral language foundations inform and constrain written expression, students with LLD are uniquely vulnerable when it comes to expressing what they know and understand in writing.

Language is but one of several systems that must be recruited and juggled simultaneously for text production. Writing demands the integration of diverse cognitive, executive, memory, linguistic, motoric, and affective systems, each of which makes its own unique contribution to the writing process and product. If jugglers focus on how they are throwing and catching only one or two of five balls, they are likely to drop the other three or four. The key to keeping all the balls in the air is to understand and master the many foundational juggling skills so that they can be integrated fluidly. Students with LLD may struggle with virtually all of the skills that support written expression. Lacking an inner dialogue to guide and ease their production process, they may devote precious cognitive resources to managing only some of what needs to be managed for text production. Often, this results in inefficient and ineffective production as well as frustration and a reduced sense of self-efficacy. Effective instruction is critical if students with LLD are to learn to integrate and regulate the various systems that contribute to text production.

Effective writing instruction guides and scaffolds young writers as they move from composing strategies that center on retrieve-and-write (knowledge-telling) approaches to more reflective (knowledge-transforming) strategies (Bereiter & Scardamalia, 1987). To achieve this transition, students must appreciate that writing is a multifaceted, problem-solving process that is mediated internally with language. Students with LLD are vulnerable when it comes to acquiring such insights and learning to write expository text. Therefore, teachers and speech–language pathologists must work together to support such students with literacy learning. EmPOWER, a strategy for teaching expository writing that explicitly teaches students how to self-regulate the writing process, can be used to support students with understanding and internalizing the many steps and routines necessary for expressing themselves in writing.

REFERENCES

Atwell, N. (1998). *In the middle: New understandings about writing, reading, and learning* (2nd ed.). Portsmouth, NH: Heinemann.

Barenbaum, E., Newcomer, P. L., & Nodine, B. (1987). Children's ability to write stories as a function of variation in task, age and developmental level. *Learning Disability Quarterly, 10*(3), 175–188.

Bereiter, C., & Scardamalia, M. (1982). From conversation to composition: The role of instruction in a developmental process. In R. Glaser (Ed.), *Advances in instructional psychology* (Vol. 2, pp. 1–64). Hillsdale, NJ: Erlbaum.

Bereiter, C., & Scardamalia, M. (1987). Two models of the composing process. In C. Bereiter & M. Scardamalia (Eds.), *The psychology of written composition* (pp. 3–30). Hillsdale, NJ: Erlbaum.

Brinton, B., Fujiki, M., & Higbee, L. M. (1998). Participation in cooperative learning activities by children with specific language impairment. *Journal of Speech, Language, and Hearing Research, 41*(5), 1193–1206.

Catts, H., & Kamhi, A. (1999). Causes of reading disabilities. In H. W. Catts & A. G. Kamhi (Eds.), *Language and reading disabilities* (pp. 50–72). Boston: Allyn & Bacon.

Cazden, C. B. (2001). *Classroom discourse: The language of teaching and learning* (2nd ed.). Portsmouth, NH: Heineman.

Cox, B., Shanahan, T., & Sulzby, E. (1990). Good and poor readers' use of cohesion in writing. *Reading Research Quarterly, 25*(1), 47–65.

Daiute, C. (1981). Psycholinguistic foundations of the writing process. *Research in the Teaching of English, 15*(1), 5–22.

Daiute, C., & Kruidenier, J. (1985). A self-questioning strategy to increase young writers' revising processes. *Applied Psycholinguistics, 6*(3), 307–318.

De La Paz, S. (2001). Teaching writing to students with attention deficit disorders and specific language impairment. *Journal of Educational Research, 95*(1), 37–47.

De La Paz, S., & Graham, S. (2002). Explicitly teaching strategies, skills, and knowledge: Writing instruction in the middle school classroom. *Journal of Educational Psychology, 94*(4), 687–689.

DiCecco, V., & Gleason, M. (2002). Using graphic organizers to attain relational knowledge from expository text. *Journal of Learning Disabilities*, 35(4), 306–320.

Ellis, E. (1998). *The framing routine*. Lawrence, KS: Edge Enterprises, Inc.

Ellis, E. (2000, June). *Watering up the curriculum: Information processing accommodations for students with language/learning disabilities*. Presentation at the Emerson College Institute in Language Learning Disabilities, Boston, MA.

Englert, C. S. (1992). Writing instruction from a sociocultural perspective: The holistic, dialogic and social enterprise of writing. *Journal of Learning Disabilities*, 25(3), 153–172.

Englert, C. S., & Raphael, T. (1989). Developing successful writers through cognitive strategy instruction. In J. Brophy (Ed.), *Advances in research on teaching* (Vol. 1, pp. 105–151). Greenwich, CT: JAI Press.

Englert, C. S., Raphael, T. E., Anderson, L. M., Anthony, H. M., Fear, K. L., & Gregg, S. L. (1988a). A case for writing intervention: Strategies for writing informational text. *Learning Disabilities Focus*, 3(2), 98–113.

Englert, C. S., Raphael, T. E., Anderson, L. M., Anthony, H. M., & Stevens, D. D. (1991). Making strategies and self-talk visible: Writing instruction in regular and special education classrooms. *American Journal of Educational Research*, 29(2), 337–372.

Englert, C. S., Raphael, T. E., Fear, K. L., & Anderson, L. M. (1988b). Students' metacognitive knowledge about how to write informational texts. *Learning Disability Quarterly*, 11(1), 18–46.

Englert, C. S., & Thomas, C. C. (1987). Sensitivity to text structure in reading and writing: A comparison between learning disabled and non-learning disabled students. *Learning Disability Quarterly*, 10(2), 90 105.

Espin, C. A., & Sindelar, P. T. (1988). Auditory feedback and writing: Learning disabled and nondisabled students. *Exceptional Children*, 55(1), 45–51.

Fitzgerald, J., & Markham, L. R. (1987). Teaching children about revision. *Cognition and Instruction*, 4(1), 3–24.

Frank, M. (1995). *If you're trying to teach kids how to write . . . you gotta have this book*. Nashville, TN: Incentive Publications.

Gallas, K. (1994). *The languages of learning: How children talk, write, dance, draw, and sing their understanding of the world*. New York: Teachers College Press.

Garavalia, L. S., & Gredler, M. E. (2002). An exploratory study of academic goal setting, achievement calibration, and self-regulated learning. *Journal of Instructional Psychology*, 29(4), 221–230.

German, D., & Simon, E. (1991). Analysis of children's word finding skills in discourse. *Journal of Speech and Hearing Research*, 34(2), 309–316.

Gillam, R. B., & Johnston, J. R. (1992). Spoken and written language relationships in language/learning-impaired and normally achieving school-age children. *Journal of Speech, Language, and Hearing Research*, 35(6), 1303–1315.

Graham, S. (1990). The role of production factors in learning disabled students' compositions. *Journal of Educational Research*, 82(4), 781–791.

Graham, S., & Harris, K. R. (2003). Students with learning disabilities and the process of writing: A meta-analysis of SRDS studies. In H. L. Swanson, K. R. Harris, & S. Graham (Eds.), *Handbook of learning disabilities* (pp. 323–344). New York: Guilford Press.

Graham, S., Harris, K. R., & Troia, G. A. (2000). Self-regulated strategy development revisited: Teaching writing strategies to struggling writers. *Topics in Language Disorders*, *20*(4), 1–14.

Graves, D. H., & Murray, D. M. (1980). Revision: In the writer's workshop and in the classroom. *Journal of Education*, *162*(2), 38–56.

Green, V., & Enfield, M. L. (1998). *Framing your thoughts guide*. Bloomington, MN: Language Circle Enterprises.

Hayes, J. R. (2000). A new framework for understanding cognition and affect in writing. In R. Indrisano & J. R. Squire (Eds.), *Perspectives on writing: Research, theory, and practice* (pp. 6–44). Newark, DE: International Reading Association.

Hayes, J. R., Flower, L., Schriver, K. A., Stratman, J. R., & Carey, L. (1987). Cognitive processes in revision. In S. Rosenberg (Ed.), *Academics in applied psycholinguistics: Vol. 2. Reading, writing and language learning* (pp. 176–240). New York: Cambridge University Press.

Hicks, D. (1997). Working through discourse genres in school. *Research in the Teaching of English*, *31*(4), 459–485.

Hillocks, G. Jr. (1986). *Research on written composition: New directions for teaching*. Urbana, IL: ERIC Clearinghouse on Reading and Communication Skills.

Hyerle, D. (1996). *Visual tools for constructing knowledge*. Alexandria, VA: Association for Supervision and Curriculum Development.

Hyerle, D. (2000). *A field guide to using visual tools*. Alexandria, VA: Association for Supervision and Curriculum Development.

Kamhi, A. G., & Hinton, L. N. (2000). Explaining individual differences in spelling ability. *Topics in Language Disorders*, *20*(3), 37–49.

Lahey, M. (1988). *Language disorders and language development*. New York: Macmillan.

Lahey, M., & Bloom, L. (1994). Variability and language learning disabilities. In G. P. Wallach & K. G. Butler (Eds.), *Language learning disabilities in school-age children and adolescents: Some principles and applications* (pp. 354–372). Needham Heights, MA: Allyn & Bacon.

Levelt, W. J. M. (1989). *Speaking: From intention to articulation*. Cambridge, MA: MIT Press.

MacArthur, C. A., & Graham, S. (1987). Learning disabled students' composing under three methods of text production: Handwriting, word processing and dictation. *Journal of Special Education*, *21*(3), 22–42.

Mariage, T. V. (2001). Features of an interactive writing discourse: Conversational involvement, conventional knowledge, and internalization in "Morning Message." *Journal of Learning Disabilities*, *34*(2), 172–196.

Masterson, J. J., & Apel, K. (2000). Spelling assessment: Charting a path to optimal intervention. *Topics in Language Disorders*, *20*(3), 50–65.

McAlister, K. M., Nelson, N. W., & Bahr, C. M. (1999). Perceptions of students with language and learning disabilities about writing process instruction. *Learning Disabilities Research and Practice*, *14*(3), 159–172.

McCutchen, D. (1986). Domain knowledge and linguistic knowledge in the development of writing ability. *Journal of Memory and Language*, *25*(4), 431–444.

McCutchen, D. (1994). The magical number three plus or minus two: Working memory in writing. In E.C. Butterfield (Ed.), *Children's writing: Toward a process theory of the development of skilled writing* (pp. 1–30). Greenwich, CT: JAI Press.

McCutchen, D. (2000). Knowledge, processing and working memory: Implications for a theory of writing. *Educational Psychologist, 35*(1), 13–24.

McNamara, M., Carter, A., McIntosh, B., & Gerken, L. (1998). Sensitivity to grammatical morphemes in children with specific language impairment. *Journal of Speech, Language, and Hearing Research, 41*(5), 1147–1157.

Minto, B. (1995). *The pyramid principle*. London: Pittman.

Moats, L. C. (1995). *Spelling: Development, disability and instruction*. Baltimore: York Press.

Rubin, H., Patterson, P., & Kantor, M. (1991). Morphological development and writing ability in childen and adults. *Language, Speech and Hearing Services in Schools, 22*(4), 228–235.

Scardamalia, M. (1981). How children cope with the cognitive demands of writing. In C. H. Fredericksen & J. F. Dominic (Eds.), *Writing: The nature, development and teaching of written communication: Vol. 2. Writing: Process, development and communication* (pp. 81–103). Hillsdale, NJ: Erlbaum.

Scardamalia, M., & Bereiter, C. (1987). Knowledge telling and knowledge transforming in written composition. In S. Rosenberg (Ed.), *Advances in applied psycholinguistics: Vol. 2. Reading, writing and language learning* (pp. 142–175). New York: Cambridge University Press.

Scott, C., & Windsor, J. (2000). General language performance measures in spoken and written discourse produced by school-age children with and without language learning disabilities. *Journal of Speech, Language, and Hearing Research, 43*(2), 324–339.

Singer, B. D. (1997). *Parallels between spoken and written syntax in children with language-learning disabilities*. Unpublished doctoral dissertation, Emerson College, Boston, MA.

Singer, B. D., & Bashir, A. S. (1997, November). *Executive functions in the writing performance of students with LLD*. Presentation at the American Speech–Language–Hearing Association Convention, Boston, MA.

Singer, B. D., & Bashir, A. S. (1999). What are executive functions and self-regulation and what do they have to do with language learning disorders? *Language, Speech and Hearing Services in Schools, 30*(3), 265–273.

Strong, W. (1973). *Sentence combining: A composing book*. New York: Random House.

Swanson, H. L., & Berninger, V. W. (1994). Working memory as a source of individual differences in children's writing. In E. C. Butterfield (Ed.), *Children's writing: Toward a process theory of the development of skilled writing* (pp. 31–56). Greenwich, CT: JAI Press.

Thomas, C. C., Englert, C. S., & Gregg, S. (1987). An analysis of errors and strategies in the expository writing of learning disabled students. *Remedial and Special Education, 8*(1), 21–30, 46.

Treimann, R., & Bourassa, D. C. (2000). The development of spelling skills. *Topics in Language Disorders, 20*(3), 1–18.

Troia, G. A. (2002). Teaching writing strategies to children with disabilities: Setting generalization as the goal. *Exceptionality, 10*(4), 249–269.

Troia, G. A., & Graham, S. (2002). The effectiveness of a highly explicit, teacher-directed strategy instruction routine: Changing the writing performance of students with learning disabilities. *Journal of Learning Disabilities, 35*(4), 290–305.

Troia, G., Graham, S., & Harris, K. (1999). Teaching students with learning disabilities to mindfully plan when writing. *Exceptional Children, 65*(2), 235–252.

Vygotsky, L. (1962). *Thought and language.* Cambridge, MA: MIT Press.

Westby, C. E. (1994). The effects of culture on genre, structure, and style of oral and written texts. In G. P. Wallach & K. Butler (Eds.), *Language learning disabilities in school-age children* (pp. 180–218). New York: Merrill.

Westby, C. E., & Clauser, P. S. (1999). The write stuff for writing: Assessing and facilitating written language. In H. W. Catts & A. G. Kamhi (Eds.), *Language and reading disabilities* (pp. 259–324). Needham Heights, MA: Allyn & Bacon.

Windsor, J. (1999). Effects of semantic inconsistency on sentence grammaticality judgements for children with and without language-learning disabilities. *Language Testing, 16*(3), 293–313.

Windsor, J., Scott, C. M., & Street, C. K. (2000). Verb and noun morphology in the spoken and written language of children with language learning disabilities. *Journal of Speech, Language, and Hearing Research, 43*(6), 1322–1336.

Wong, B. Y. L. (2000). Writing strategies instruction for expository essays for adolescents with and without learning disabilities. *Topics in Language Disorders, 20*(4), 29–44.

Wong, B. Y. L., Butler, D. L., Ficzere, S. A., & Kuperis, S. (1996). Teaching low achievers and students with learning disabilities to plan, write, and revise opinion essays. *Journal of Learning Disabilities, 29*(2), 197–212.

Wong, B. Y. L., Wong, R., & Blenkinsop, J. (1989). Cognitive and metacognitive aspects of learning disabled adolescents' composing problems. *Learning Disability Quarterly, 12*(4), 300–322.

Zimmerman, B. J. (1989). A social cognitive view of self-regulated learning. *Journal of Educational Psychology, 81*, 329–339.

Zimmerman, B. J., & Risemberg, R. (1997). Becoming a self-regulated writer: A social cognitive perspective. *Contemporary Educational Psychology, 22*(1), 73–101.

10

❧

Instructional Approaches
to Spelling

The Window on Students' Word Knowledge in Reading and Writing

SHANE TEMPLETON

Over 30 years ago Edmund Henderson, my mentor at the University of Virginia, observed that the way children *spell* words provides the best insight into how they *read* words. At the time this was a relatively radical notion; years later, this perspective is accepted wisdom among researchers who have explored the development of the ability to read words (e.g., Ehri, 1997; Snowling, 1994; Perfetti, 1993, 1997). This relationship is not *exactly* isomorphic; the title of Linnea Ehri's (1997) "Learning to Read and Learning to Spell Are One and the Same—Almost" captures this notion. For most individuals the processes of reading words and the processes of writing words draw upon an underlying core of word, or *orthographic*, knowledge that serves both processes. Analyzing students' spelling of words opens a window into their lexicons, their "dictionaries-in-the-head," affording information about the foundations of their literacy knowledge. The nature of this information determines in significant fashion the quality of students' engagements with texts. Individuals' spellings therefore reveal to us the types of information they use when they read words—the features to which they attend as well as the quality of their lexical access. Do they identify words in reading based only on an alphabetic "scan," or are they also using orthographic and syllabic patterns as well as morphological structure? As Charles Perfetti observed, "Spelling and reading use the same lexical representation" (1993, p. 170), and therefore "spelling is the purest indicator of lexical quality" (1997, p. 30).

The domain and concerns of *spelling*, therefore, are broader than traditionally conceptualized (Templeton, 2003a, 2003b). Spelling is still, of course, a convention of writing and is important in that regard, but spelling is also an indication of knowledge of word structure more generally, and in that capacity it can provide insight into the course and scope of students' word study, guiding teachers' planning of appropriate and effective instruction. This broader conception includes the integration of spelling knowledge into reading as well as writing. Educational practitioners who embrace a narrower conception of spelling, particularly those involved in work with struggling readers and writers, often encourage their students to rely heavily upon spell-check software; unfortunately, spell-check software doesn't help students who don't have enough underlying knowledge about spelling to take advantage of this technology.

All educational practitioners who work with struggling readers and writers should also be involved in facilitating these students' understanding of spelling. Because of the relationship between word knowledge—represented by students' spelling knowledge—and reading, almost all students who struggle with reading also struggle with spelling. Classroom teachers, special education teachers, and speech–language pathologists should all be well grounded in an understanding of how the English spelling system works. Though speech–language pathologists have comprehensive knowledge of the phonology and morphology of English, they often have not made the bridge to understanding how these language systems are represented in orthography. Classroom teachers and special education teachers usually do not study in any depth either spoken or written language systems and how they are learned, inevitably resulting in the belief that spelling doesn't make sense and uncertainty about how to help their students understand the systems. More focused study of these aspects, therefore, is an excellent point at which to begin. There is no gainsaying the fact, though, that a common grounding in process and product among all practitioners who share responsibility for teaching struggling readers and writers is critical and will result in far more consistent, coherent, supportive, motivating, and ultimately successful plans of intervention.

A BRIEF OVERVIEW OF RESEARCH

While linguists have explored the nature of English orthography, psychologists and educators have explored how orthographic knowledge develops. There is a dynamic at work in American English spelling in which the objective of spelling *sounds* consistently is balanced by the objective of spelling *meaning* consistently. In this regard, Venezky (1999) observed that spelling "is not merely a letter-to-sound system riddled with imperfections. Instead, it is a more complex and more regular relationship, wherein phonemes and morphemes share leading roles" (p. ix). Most educators understand that the system attempts to represent phonemes, though the general consensus is that the system performs this task poorly. On the other hand, educators are much less likely to understand—as are most adults—the role that morphemes play (Hughes & Searle, 1997).

Over the course of many years learners can negotiate this balance between spelling sounds and spelling meaning. Their underlying word knowledge will reflect a growth in sophistication of knowledge about letters and sounds, familiarity with letter patterns and syllable patterns, and awareness of how meaning is directly represented through spelling. At the early stages more attention is accorded to the ways in which sound is represented by orthography. In the intermediate school years and beyond, more attention may be accorded to the structural, morphological, or meaning features of the spelling system. Though most adults are not aware of how the spelling system operates at this level, most learners in the intermediate grades and beyond have the necessary language and cognitive foundations to become aware of, appreciate, and explore this facet of spelling.

What are the specific features of the spelling system that learners will explore throughout the course of the elementary and middle-school years—and beyond? In our own work (Bear, Templeton, Helman, & Baren, 2003; Henderson & Templeton, 1986; Templeton & Bear, 1992b; Bear, Invernizzi, Templeton, & Johnston, 2004; Templeton, 2004), we have characterized this exploration in terms of moving from *sound/alphabetic* knowledge, through *pattern*, to *meaning*. The *alphabetic layer* matches sounds and letters in a left-to-right manner—for example, *tip*, *fat*, and *go*. This type of sequential mapping is in accord with the way in which beginning readers expect the spelling system to function. At successive levels of abstraction, the *pattern layer* maps regular sound–spelling correspondences *within* and *between* syllables. Within syllables, a group or pattern of letters functions as a unit that maps to sounds—for example, in the word *cane* the vowel–consonant–silent *e* (VC*e*) spelling pattern represents the "long-*a*" pronunciation—the silent *e* in this spelling pattern functions to distinguish the pattern from the "short-*a*" pronunciation in the word *can*. The pattern layer also reflects the role of *position* on the spelling of sounds. For example, when /ch/ occurs at the end of a syllable *and* follows a short vowel, it is usually spelled *tch* (*catch*, *clutch*). When /ch/ occurs at the end of a syllable *and* follows a long vowel, it is usually spelled *ch* (*teach*, *coach*). Pattern also governs the spelling at the juncture of syllables. Learning about syllable juncture patterns begins with the examination of simple affixation with inflectional suffixes—for example, *clap* + *ing* = *clapping*; *chase* + *ing* = *chasing*. Whether the final consonant is doubled or not depends upon the vowel sound in the base word: if it's short, then double; if it's long, don't double—and drop the final *e*. This fundamental understanding of doubling and *e*-drop (Henderson, 1990) provides the foundation for understanding the vowel–consonant–consonant–vowel (VCCV) syllable pattern and the vowel–consonant–vowel (VCV) syllable pattern. *Syllable patterns* refer to the vowel and consonant letters on both sides of a syllable juncture: words such as *clapping* and *hugging* are examples of the VCCV pattern, illustrated by the underlined italicized letters—*appi* and *uggi*—in each word; *chasing* and *hoping* are examples of the VCV pattern. These patterns are later applied within nonaffixed two-syllable words such as *buggy* and *total*.

The *meaning layer* is captured in the observation that "words that are related in meaning are often related in spelling as well, despite changes in sound" (Templeton, 1991, p. 194). This holds true because meaningful elements, or *morphemes*, tend to be spelled consistently: *crumb–crumble*, *autumn–autumnal*, *please–pleasant*, *legal–legality*, *allege–allegation*, *amnesia–mnemonic*. Spellings that appear illogical when viewed through the lens of sound–letter correspondence, such as the "silent" letters in *autumn*, *crumb*, and *mnemonic*, become quite logical when viewed through the lens of meaning: in the related words *autumnal*, *crumble*, and *amnesia* the spelling visually preserves the meaning relationships shared by these words. "Visual identity of word parts *takes precedence over* letter–sound simplicity" (Venezky, 1999, p. 197, emphasis added); letter–sound simplicity would support the spellings **autum*, **crum*, and **nemonic*.

Investigations of the development of individuals' knowledge of these layers and features of words—their ability to read and to spell words—have reached consensus on the following: With respect to acquisition of orthographic knowledge, there is a common developmental sequence among most learners, though there is variability in the rate at which this knowledge develops. Young children whom we describe as "emergent readers and writers" gradually become aware of the features of sound in spoken language, and, if allowed and encouraged to do so, they attempt to represent these features in their writing. Eventually children become aware of most of the conventional consonant and vowel segments in spoken language—we say they are "phonemically aware"—and map these segments to letters in predictable ways. They have thus acquired knowledge of the alphabetic principle in English and we refer to them as "beginning conventional readers and writers." In time, they will move beyond an alphabetic, left-to-right expectation of the relationship between letters and sounds to the *transitional phase* and understand how letter patterns correspond to sound (Ehri, 1997; Rayner & Polatsek, 1989; Templeton & Bear, 1992a). There is less agreement regarding how the course of development may be characterized beyond this transitional phase, where attention to the morphological aspects of the spelling system may potentially occur.

Coincident with this developmental sequence is the issue of the probability of *qualitative* differences in reading stages or phases. Developmental theories concur with respect to (1) the development of phonemic awareness and the understanding of the alphabetic principle that it affords—the demarcation between emergent and beginning conventional reading; and (2) the movement from *alphabet*ic to *pattern* knowledge. Whether the movement to *meaning*—an understanding and appreciation of the role of morphology—constitutes a qualitative shift as well remains a point of debate (e.g., Gentry, 2000; Templeton, 2003b). More generally, some have argued that developmentalism does not meet the criterion of explanatory adequacy for most cognitive activities (e.g., Baker, 1999). Orthographic development, however, may in fact be an instance where more distinct stages or phases may be suggested (Deese, 1992). Ehri (1997) has suggested that the "key distinguishing capability" between phases or levels of word knowledge rests upon "the approach that predominates at that level" (p. 253); beyond the transitional phase, although readers and writers do indeed marshal alphabetic and orthographic or pattern knowledge in the processes of reading and writing, they also are developing syllabic/morphological knowledge and strategies that may predominate. To argue, as does Gentry (2000), that "there appear to be no qualitative differences between within word, syllable juncture, and derivational constancy invented spellings, and, consequently, no stage that corresponds to these patterns" (p. 325), may lead to the conclusion that there are no qualitative differences between spellings such as STOPING for *stopping* and IRELEVANT for *irrelevant*. The important point that should not get lost in this debate, therefore, is how students' developing word knowledge is indicated in their spelling and how educational practitioners' awareness of this knowledge together with their understanding of the general sequence of word study—from alphabetic through morphological—can inform instruction.

With other investigators, our work has also explored the relationships between word knowledge and other reading and writing behaviors (Templeton & Bear, 1992a). In the next section of this chapter I discuss how this information is applied in the case of three students.

What is the role of *instruction* in developing word knowledge in students? There is consensus among most researchers that words need to be explored outside of running text through focused and sustained word study (e.g., Allal, 1997; Graham, 2000; Templeton, 2003b; Templeton & Morris, 1999; Treiman, 1998). Given this consensus, it is necessary first to assess students' spelling knowledge before instruction begins. It should be a rare classroom indeed in which every student is studying the same spelling words; there is variation in spelling knowledge just as there is variation in reading ability—and not coincidentally. Once instructional groups are set, students should be engaged in active examination of words from a variety of perspectives, comparing and contrasting them as appropriate according to sound, spelling, and meaning characteristics. Word categorization or sorting activities are excellent for this type of inquiry (Bear et al., 2004; Zutell, 1998). Instruction should also include, as appropriate, directed lessons in which features of words are discussed and their function modeled (e.g., Henry, 1993). (See Figure 10.1 for a general scope and sequence for spelling instruction across phases of reading and spelling development.)

MY OWN CORNER OF THE LEARNING AND INSTRUCTIONAL WORLD

A central theme of my own work over the years has been the exploration of the relationship between what students *do* with their word knowledge and what they *think* about what they do: more specifically, how they navigate the terrain between tacit, underlying lexical knowledge and metalinguistic reflection. How do they marshal their word knowledge in the service of strategic online spelling and decoding? Toward this end, together with a number of other educators, I have explored the incorporation of appropriate, effective, and engaging word study into appropriate, effective, and engaging reading and writing instruction. This exploration has included extensive work with classroom teachers in developing a knowledge base about words and word study—exploration that is often given short shrift in teacher preparation programs and in the professional development of experienced teachers.

When I began teaching the primary grades in the early 1970s I learned quickly the futility of *telling* children about word structure rather than *engaging* them in the exploration of that structure. Two early studies (Templeton & Spivey, 1980; Templeton & Thomas, 1984) revealed that young children's performance with respect to writing words tends to run ahead of their reflection upon that performance; this finding was hardly surprising, has been replicated many times over with respect to word knowledge (e.g., Downing, 1986; Templeton, 1989; Sabey, 1997), and is true of most if not all other domains of learning. What remains puzzling and somewhat exasperating has been the persistence of instructional practices that assume a fair degree of metalinguistic expertise as the precondition for learning.

How do we situate appropriate and effective word study within the reading and writing instructional endeavor? We will address this issue by considering three students at different points along a developmental continuum of literacy. Their spelling errors are considered in terms of the in-

Phases of Reading and Spelling Development

Sound/Alphabetic → → Pattern → Meaning

Beginning	Transitional	Intermediate	Skilled/Proficient
Beginning single consonants	Common long vowel patterns	Inflectional suffixes -ed, -ing	Spelling/meaning relationships:
Consonant digraphs	r- and l-influenced vowels	Plural endings	*sign/signal*
Consonant blends	Three-letter consonant blends	Syllable patterns:	*music/musician*
Short vowel patterns	Common spelling for diphthongs /ow/, /oi/	VCCV bas ket rab bit	*mental/mentality*
	Compound words	Open VCV hu man	Greek and Latin Elements:
	Homophones (*mail/male*)	Closed VCV cab in	-phon- aud-
		Less-frequent vowel patterns	-tele- dic-
		Two-syllable homographs:	Assimilated Prefixes:
		PERmit (n.)/perMIT (v.)	*ad- + count = account*
		COMbat (n.)/comBAT (v.)	*in + mediate = immediate*

FIGURE 10.1. General scope and sequence for spelling instruction across phases of reading and spelling development.

sights about word knowledge that their errors reveal, and the type of words and patterns that the students should examine are discussed in the context of their instructional reading levels.

Eric

Eric is a first grader who made the following errors on a qualitative inventory of word knowledge (Bear et al., 2004) in April of the school year:

BAD	(*bed*)
SIP	(*ship*)
WHIN	(*when*)
FLOT	(*float*)
CHRAN	(*train*)

Eric's spelling reveals an alphabetic, or letter-name, understanding of word structure. On an informal reading inventory he was found to be reading on a preprimer level. His teacher was frustrated with his lack of progress. She shared that he usually seemed to get short vowel spellings correct, so she had been working with him on long vowel spellings in an effort to develop his word knowledge, hoping it would help drive his reading ability. He did not seem to be "getting it," however, and the teacher wondered if she should refer him for further evaluation. The reading specialist agreed to work with Eric, but also recommended the continued use of simple patterned texts and suggested the addition of decodable texts that would include a greater proportion of the phonic/spelling patterns Eric would be examining. She also recommended that his word study should take a step back and again go through the examination of short vowels, but instead of revisiting simpler consonant–vowel–consonant patterns such as *bat, sit, tip*, and so forth these sounds and their spellings would be examined in the context of words that included consonant digraphs and clusters (e.g., *flip, step, trap, chin*). His spellings indicated that Eric was attending to these features but that he was inconsistent in his representations of them (SIP, WHIN, FLOT, CHRAN). Because Eric is not including long vowel markers such as silent *e* in his spellings, he is not at the point developmentally where study of long vowel spelling/sound patterns would be beneficial; indeed, such study may in fact have the unintended consequence of sapping his motivation to continue his efforts. Eric should be encouraged to write but should not be expected to revise and edit his writing on a regular basis. This is primarily because during the act of writing Eric's attention must of necessity be allocated to figuring out how to spell the sounds he discriminates in the words he wishes to use at the same time he is trying to maintain some consideration of the topic he is addressing.

Stephanie

Stephanie is a fourth grader who according to her teacher is reading on grade level but whose spelling is lagging far behind this level. Following are a few of the spelling errors she made on a qualitative inventory administered in September and which are representative of the types of errors that appeared in her spontaneous writing:

FLOTE	(*float*)
TRANE	(*train*)
DRAIVE	(*drive*)
SHOPING	(*shopping*)
SPOAL	(*spoil*)
CARESE	(*carries*)

These errors reflect within-word pattern (Henderson, 1990) or consolidated alphabetic (Ehri, 1997) spelling knowledge, more characteristic of second-grade students. We would expect a student reading at grade level at the beginning of fourth grade to have developed knowledge of basic long vowel spelling patterns by this point. There are two common explanations for this apparent paradox. First, Stephanie's less-developed word recognition skill, as evidenced by her spelling, is augmented by the degree of background knowledge she is able to bring to bear during her reading. When her reading includes topics and narratives of interest to her, she seems to enjoy the activity. We would expect that this apparent higher level of comprehension vis-à-vis word knowledge would begin to falter during the year, however, as Stephanie encounters a greater vocabulary load represented by an increasing number of polysyllabic words. The second possibility is that Stephanie is in fact reading on a level closer to that represented by her word knowledge. She has developed sophisticated strategies for compensating and appears to be a better comprehender than she actually is. Such students are often able to "get by" during the primary grades by attending to conversations about the readings as well as by weaving some fairly generic comments into their own responses. As with the first explanation, however, such strategies begin to fall apart as students move into the intermediate school years. The reading specialist resolved Stephanie's paradox by sitting one-on-one with her and asking her to retell what she had just read, exploring her responses to factual and inferential questions by asking her to locate places in the selection that supported her responses. A more focused exploration of Stephanie's reading, in other words, revealed that she was in fact reading at a level closer to that suggested by her word knowledge. The reading specialist suggested that Stephanie's word study should focus on vowel patterns in single-syllable words; most of her instructional-level reading will be at the high-first-/beginning-second-grade level.

Angelica

Angelica is a third grader whose home language is Spanish; she is achieving proficiency in conversational English and is reading on a preprimer level.

BAD	(*bed*)
CHEP	(*ship*)
WAN	(*when*)
LAMP	(*lump*)

Angelica is struggling mightily as a reader in English. After considerable effort she can remember simple short- and long-vowel spellings such as *tag, run, cake,* and *time,* but she cannot apply this knowledge to the spelling or reading of new words. Her performance on the qualitative spelling inventory provides a glimpse into the interaction between her perception and production of sounds in Spanish and her developing sensitivity to English phonology: the short *e* in *bed* and *when,* for example, is a sound that does not occur in Spanish; because of its articulatory proximity to /e/, however, Angelica assimilates it into this sound with which she *is* familiar and uses the letter *a* whose name is /e/. Likewise, because the short-*i* sound in *ship* does not occur in Spanish, Angelica uses the letter *e* whose name is closest in terms of articulation to /I/. Given that Angelica's word knowledge reflects an alphabetic or letter-name perspective, the teacher's expectation that she can learn and apply knowledge of long-vowel pattern words is too ambitious.

We will revisit these conclusions and their implications more specifically for instruction in the next section.

EFFECTIVE WORD STUDY INSTRUCTION FOR STRUGGLING (AND NORMALLY DEVELOPING) READERS AND WRITERS

Most students who are struggling with reading and writing are not doing so because of underlying neurolinguistic/neurophysiological dysfunctions (Vellutino et al., 1996). Rather, there is a mismatch between their place along the continuum of literacy development and instructional expectations for them. Effective assessment and instructional planning will go far to address this mismatch. For those few students whose difficulty does have a biological basis, however, assessing and evaluating their word knowledge will reveal in most cases where they too fall along the continuum. Their spelling errors are usually logical and the scope and sequence of their word study, though progressing more slowly than for most other students, will follow the same developmental progression (Worthy & Invernizzi, 1990).

For most learners, the following principles of word study should guide instruction (Bear et al., 2004):

1. Look for what students "use but confuse."
2. A step backward is a step forward.
3. Use words students can read.
4. Compare words "that do" with words "that don't."
5. Sort by sound, sight, and meaning.
6. Begin with obvious contrasts first.
7. Don't hide exceptions.
8. Avoid rules.
9. Work for automaticity.
10. Return to meaningful texts.

Let's briefly consider each of these in turn:

1. *Look for what students "use but confuse."* Too often we look at what students do not know, what they don't have, and then try to teach whatever that is. In Eric's case, for example, his teacher was emphasizing long vowel patterns when there was no evidence in Eric's spellings that he was attending to and picking up any features of long vowel patterns. Instead the reading specialist looked at what Eric was "using but confusing"—short vowel spellings and consonant clusters—and began word study with those. This focus does not preclude students from acquiring sight words that contain long vowel spellings, and in fact these words will eventually influence Eric's spelling and their features will emerge for conscious and explicit examination.

2. *A step backward is a step forward.* Related to the "using but confusing" principle, taking a step backward helps students *consolidate* their knowledge about a particular feature or pattern before moving ahead. For example, to ground Stephanie comfortably in her word study, the reading specialist began by having Stephanie compare and contrast CVC short vowel words such as *sat*, *lap*, and *bam* with CVe long vowel words such as *lake*, *make*, and *came*. Because Stephanie was familiar with these types of words and patterns, the reading specialist was able to facilitate her reflection and talk about the words, sounds, and spelling patterns.

3. *Use words students can read.* If students do not know what they are looking at, they can hardly be expected to analyze it. All too often we commit this fallacy by using new words in reading as spelling words and compound the problem by trying to get students to analyze the structure of the word to discern a pattern or principle. In contrast, when students know

a word as a sight word, they are much better able to reflect on its structure and to compare and contrast it with other words, and are consequently better able to derive a generalization that may govern the spelling.

4. *Compare words "that do" with words "that don't."* The mind is a marvelous pattern detection device, but it needs appropriate information as input. The reading specialist had this in mind as she engaged Stephanie in comparing and contrasting short-*a* and long-*a* words. Rather than focusing exclusively on long-*a* words and trying to derive a generalization about the function of the silent *e*, this generalization emerges more transparently when the short-*a* pattern words are included for comparison.

5. *Sort by sound, sight, and meaning.* This principle reflects the importance of engaging students in looking at words in different ways. For example, the teacher would ask Stephanie first to sort the following words by sound: *pat, make, have, glad, shade, safe.* In this context *have* would be categorized with words such as *pat* and *glad.* The next sort would be according to sight, in which case *have* is categorized with *shade, safe,* and so forth. In such fashion memory for the spelling of *have* is reinforced in a more deliberate and thoughtful way (which is important, particularly given the fact that it is an "exception"; see No. 7 below).

6. *Begin with obvious contrasts first.* Explorations of consonant doubling and syllable patterns should begin by comparing and contrasting words such as *bag* + *ing* (*bagging*: double final consonant to keep the vowel short) and *make* + *ing* (*making*; *e*-drop) rather than with words such as *cottage* and *pattern* versus *silent* and *crater.*

7. *Don't hide exceptions.* If we try to hide exceptions, students will point them out and ask about them anyway. First of all, there really aren't that many exceptions and in this sense they truly do help the pattern or generalization emerge. It is usually the case that what appears to be an exception at the moment will later be seen to follow a different type of pattern—for example, although *have* does not follow the long-*a* pattern, when compared to other words such as *glove, love,* and *give* students may notice the *v* in all of these words and realize that no word in English can end with a *v.* Having learned about doubling consonants after short vowels, a student may wonder why the spelling of *finish* does not include a double *n.* As the student becomes aware of and understands the role of meaning in the spelling system, however, he will realize that *finish* is related to *final*; the spelling visually preserves the meaning relationships shared by these words.

8. *Avoid rules.* If the rule "use *i* before *e* except after *c*" makes sense to you, it is most likely because you know a lot of words to which that "rule" applies. It is unlikely you learned to spell all of those words by first learning the rule. Of course, this is the nature of learning in general—one has to know a number of examples before the rule that governs those examples can be discerned and appreciated—but in the case of spelling that principle is un-

fortunately too often reversed. Rules do not teach; it is necessary to have some knowledge of the phenomenon to be examined—in this case, words— before rules can make any sense. It is most effective if students explore the words they are comparing and contrasting, discussing them, looking for rules or generalizations. Then, generalizations can help to consolidate understanding of the pattern or patterns being examined. Students may record their sorts in a word study notebook, for example, and write in their own words an explanation (rule) for why they sorted the words as they did.

9. *Work for automaticity.* Over time, as students sort known words according to different criteria, they move from "hesitancy to fluency" (Bear et al., 2004, p. 23). At first they will need to examine each word quite deliberately while determining into which category it should be sorted; with time, this examination becomes more routinized and automatic. For example, as Angelica sorts simple CVC-pattern words according to the short vowel sound she hears within each, over the course of a few days or perhaps a week or two she will become more fluent in her sorting of them. With the other principles of word study guiding her exploration, working toward fluency in sorting assists in concretizing memory for specific words and the abstraction of orthographic patterns that apply to many words.

10. *Return to meaningful texts.* In its simplest form, this principle completes the cycle of reading–word study–reading. We wish students' developing word knowledge to assist them in accessing texts more efficiently and engagingly, and their word knowledge is in turn exercised as they apply this knowledge in reading. Specific activities, however, can help them apply more deliberately and reflectively their knowledge as they peruse texts. For example, after comparing and contrasting CVC and CVC*e* words in word sorts, students may buddy-up and look back through a selection they have already read, searching for other words that they believe may fit these patterns. They will record these words in their word notebooks and later compare their findings with the rest of their word study group.

It is a common practice among teachers who are new to word sorting and wish to initiate this type of activity in their class to rely almost exclusively on the sorting itself to develop word knowledge. Without modeling, guidance, and variety, however, sorting alone will not lead to students' richer processing of and insights about words. Teachers must determine the degree to which they determine the categories into which students will sort words with the students' own determination of categories. Activities should include *writing* of the words. As we've seen, completed sorts can be recorded in word notebooks, but students should also engage in *writing sorts.* Writing sorts involve students pairing up and then taking turns calling out to each other words sorted earlier in the week. The words are written in appropriate columns; for example, students exploring three different common spellings for long *a* will set up three columns headed by a key word that represents each pattern. The key words may be *game, day,* and *rain*; one student calls out the word *paint* and the other student decides in which column to write it, then *fade* is called out, and so forth. Writing sorts reinforce patterns as well as memory for the spelling of specific words.

Some practices that have been around for a while are supported by research. For example, the pretest/study routine is quite effective when followed by self-correction. Importantly, however, *all* of the words should then be included in the word sorts and activities throughout the week—not just those that were missed on the pretest—because ultimately the spelling patterns are the focus rather than specific words per se, and by utilizing all of the words the likelihood of abstracting the pattern(s) is greater. Games are also quite effective as well as motivating, provided they reinforce the patterns that have been under study (Bear et al., 2004).

High-frequency words that do not follow regular patterns in terms of sound–spelling correspondence may be added to a core list or group of words each week. A number of activities support their learning and they should not be avoided; neither, however, should they constitute the primary or sole focus of spelling instruction. This is often the case, unfortunately, and reduces spelling to a strictly memorization task focused on individual words rather than on principles of alphabetics, pattern, and meaning.

How Spelling Instruction Relates to Other Content Areas

In terms of learning about word structure, spelling/word study that honors the principles outlined above will integrate effectively with the texts students are reading. Because of the importance of word knowledge and of spelling in the development of that knowledge, spelling instruction in the intermediate and middle grades should continue to be addressed directly. Most logically, this instruction can occur in the language arts. This instruction may also accommodate and relate to other areas of the curriculum (e.g., science and mathematics). For example, in a weekly list in which most of the words for which students will be held accountable in terms of their correct spelling are developmentally appropriate, a few additional words from a thematic unit may be added. Second graders who are studying dinosaurs may have a handful of "dinosaur words" they wish to learn to spell (e.g., *tyrannosaurus* and *Jurassic*), but these words should not replace the study of spelling words that are developmentally appropriate. When new content-related words *are* the sole source for the new spelling words, then students do not have sufficient underlying word knowledge to support memory for the correct spelling of these new vocabulary words. Moreover, these new spelling words rarely share spelling patterns, so each word must be learned as a discrete entity without spelling/structural relationships to any other words—not unlike an adult memorizing 20 new phone numbers (with different area codes) every week and being expected to recall each without error several days or weeks later. When classroom teachers examine science or math content for words that represent important concepts and therefore potential vocabulary words, they may *carefully* and *judiciously* include a few such words for spelling as well, thus reinforcing the meaning of the words. Again, however, it is important that such words be few in number in relation to the spelling words that are developmentally appropriate and which the students can already read.

Spelling Instruction for Struggling Readers and Writers

I have suggested that these instructional recommendations are appropriate not only for normally developing students but for most of those for whom literacy learning does not come easily. For such students, there is a significant research base at the beginning levels of literacy development that supports this approach to word study and spelling as part of a comprehensive and congruent intervention program (see Invernizzi, 2001, for an excellent review). Similarly, Moats (2000) emphasizes the importance of spelling/decoding instruction that is active, constructive, and promotes pattern recognition rather than rule memorization. Only after sustained and appropriate instruction for most struggling readers and writers do we have enough information to determine whether a difficulty has a biological basis (Vellutino et al., 1996) in which real-time processing and/or language-related issues are precluding normal progression. For the latter type of student, there has been success with an active and constructive approach as well (Zutell, 1998). Our fundamental instructional adjustments are in the pace of the instruction and the number of contrastive features we present along the way. For example, we would be sensitive to the pace at which we would introduce word categorization activities with several categories, relying primarily on two and at most three categories until the students clearly understood the format, understood the nature of the activity, and had achieved some degree of fluency in their sorting. This latter criterion is apparent when students do not linger for a period of time over every decision about which category in which to place or write a particular word.

There are those few students whose difficulty has a biological basis and for whom a more direct, systematic, and linear instructional approach is most effective (e.g., Torgesen, Wagner, & Rashotte, 1994). Rather than engaging the students in comparing and contrasting words with different spelling patterns to determine why the patterns are spelled as they are, direct and systematic approaches are "bottom-up" in that each element—for example, a particular letter–sound correspondence—is taught directly. After a few individual sounds and corresponding letters are taught, students are shown how to blend these letters/sounds together to form simple words.

GETTING THE WORDS OUT

In the last quarter of the 20th century research in developmental spelling helped to construct a stronger foundation for a scope and sequence in spelling or word study instruction, specifically *when* to teach *which* aspects and features of the spelling system (Templeton, 2003). The challenge is to disseminate this foundation effectively to novice and experienced teachers alike. How might the words get out to educators at all levels?

I often compare the present situation with respect to word study/spelling instruction to that of writing instruction a couple of decades ago. It took a long time to disseminate and develop teachers' knowledge about teaching writing, and this development of necessity included teachers' exploration of the writing process themselves, trying it out at first tentatively and then more determinedly, eventually becoming more comfortable in sharing their own process with their students in the course of modeling how prewriting, drafting, revision, and editing work and feel. So it is today with word study and spelling. Because they have internalized a phonocentric perspective of the spelling system (Templeton & Morris, 1999, 2000), most educators are not used to looking at words in exploratory ways, expecting consistency. They tend to believe the system is illogical, inconsistent, indeed incomprehensible. Teacher preparation and professional development can help to break through that "sound barrier," revealing the principles of pattern and meaning and how they bring a degree of consistency and coherence to the system that works on the levels of both sound and meaning. As they gain more understanding of the system and confidence in their own knowledge, educators can in turn help to convey the excitement and wonder about words to their students.

Over the last several years the number of books addressing word study has grown significantly. The majority of sales of these texts have been for professional development of in-service teachers. In some cases, this professional development has been voluntary; in other cases, it has been mandated from the state and/or district level. Though the ownership of such development is important (grassroots vs. top-down), we must in any case work to separate the wheat from the chaff. This emphasis on words may eventually promote the more reasoned and well-constructed approach toward helping all educators understand the elements of language and their role in helping students at different levels explore these elements. This understanding includes not only the elements—the phonemes, graphemes, morphemes, syntax, semantics, and pragmatics of it all—but ultimately an appreciation of the array of languages and cultures that express our common humanity. It will take a number of years. One can hope that at some point down that road we can look back and conclude it was a sea change in learning and instruction and a fair-winded one at that.

REFERENCES

Allal, L. (1997). Learning to spell in the classroom. In C. A. Perfetti & L. Reiben (Eds.), *Learning to spell: Research, theory, and practice across languages* (pp. 129–150). Mahwah, NJ: Erlbaum.

Baker, B. (1999). The dangerous and the good?: Developmentalism, progress, and public schooling. *American Educational Research Journal, 36*(4), 797–834.

Bear, D. R., Invernizzi, M., Templeton, S., & Johnston, F. (2004). *Words their way: Word study for phonics, vocabulary, and spelling instruction* (3rd ed.). Upper Saddle River, NJ: Merrill/Prentice-Hall.

Bear, D., Templeton, S., Helman, L., & Baren, T. (2003). Orthographic development and learning to read in different languages. In G. Garcia (Ed.), *English learners: Reaching the highest level of English literacy* (pp. 71–95). Newark, DE: International Reading Association.

Deese, J. (1992). Foreword. In S. Templeton & D. R. Bear (Eds.), *Development of orthographic knowledge and the foundations of literacy: A memorial festschrift for Edmund Henderson* (pp. ix–xi). Hillsdale, NJ: Erlbaum.

Downing, J. (1986). Cognitive clarity: A unifying and cross-cultural theory for language awareness phenomena in reading. In D. B. Yaden Jr. & S. Templeton (Eds.), *Metalinguistic awareness and beginning literacy: Conceptualizing what it means to read and write* (pp. 13–29). Portsmouth, NH: Heinemann.

Ehri, L. C. (1997). Learning to read and learning to spell are one and the same—almost. In C. A. Perfetti, L. Rieben, & M. Fayol (Eds.), *Learning to spell: Research, theory, and practice across languages* (pp. 237–269). Mawah, NJ: Erlbaum.

Gentry, J. R. (2000). A retrospective on invented spelling and a look forward. *The Reading Teacher, 54,* 318–332.

Graham, S. (2000). Should the natural learning approach replace spelling instruction? *Journal of Educational Psychology, 92,* 235–247.

Henderson, E. (1990). *Teaching spelling* (2nd ed.). Boston: Houghton Mifflin.

Henderson, E., & Templeton, S. (1986). A developmental perspective of formal spelling instruction through alphabet, pattern, and meaning. *Elementary School Journal, 86,* 305–316.

Henry, M. K. (1993). Morphological structure: Latin and Greek roots and affixes as upper grade code strategies. *Reading and Writing, 5,* 227–241.

Hughes, M., & Searle, D. (1997). *The violent e and other tricky sounds: Learning to spell from kindergarten through grade 6.* York, ME: Stenhouse.

Invernizzi, M. (2001). The complex world of one-on-one tutoring. In S. B. Neuman & D. K. Dickinson (Eds.), *Handbook of early literacy research* (pp. 459–470). New York: Guilford Press.

Moats, L. C. (2000). *Speech to print: Language essentials for teachers*. Baltimore: Brookes.

Perfetti, C. A. (1993). The representation problem in reading acquisition. In P. B. Gough, L. C. Ehri, & R. Treiman (Eds.), *Reading acquisition* (pp. 145–174). Hillsdale, NJ: Erlbaum.

Perfetti, C. A. (1997). The psycholinguistics of spelling and reading. In C. A. Perfetti, L. Rieben, & M. Fayol (Eds.), *Learning to spell: Research, theory, and practice across languages* (pp. 21–38). Mahwah, NJ: Erlbaum.

Rayner, K., & Polatsek, A. (1989). *The psychology of reading*. Hillsdale, NJ: Erlbaum.

Sabey, B. L. (1997). *Metacognitive responses of syllable juncture spellers while performing three literacy tasks*. Unpublished doctoral dissertation, University of Nevada, Reno.

Snowling, M. (1994). Towards a model of spelling acquisition: The development of some component skills. In G. D. A. Brown & N. C. Ellis (Eds.), *Handbook of spelling: Theory, process, and intervention* (pp. 111–128). Chichester, UK: Wiley.

Templeton, S. (1989). Tacit and explicit knowledge of derivational morphology: Foundations for a unified approach to spelling and vocabulary development in the intermediate grades and beyond. *Reading Psychology, 10*, 233–253.

Templeton, S. (1991). Teaching and learning the English spelling system: Reconceptualizing method and purpose. *Elementary School Journal, 92*, 183–199.

Templeton, S. (2003a). Spelling. In J. Flood, D. Lapp, J. R. Squire, & J. M. Jensen (Eds.), *Handbook of research on teaching the English language arts* (2nd ed., pp. 738–751). Mahwah, NJ: Erlbaum.

Templeton, S. (2003b). Spelling instruction. In J. Guthrie (Senior Ed.), *Encyclopedia of education* (2nd ed., pp. 2302–2305). New York: Macmillan.

Templeton, S. (2004). The vocabulary–spelling connection: Orthographic development and morphological knowledge at the intermediate grades and beyond. In J. F. Baumann & E. J. Kame'enui (Eds.), *Vocabulary instruction: Research to practice* (pp. 118–138). New York: Guilford Press.

Templeton, S., & Bear, D. R. (1992a). Summary and synthesis: "Teaching the lexicon to read and spell." In S. Templeton & D. R. Bear (Eds.), *Development of orthographic knowledge and the foundations of literacy: A memorial festschrift for Edmund Henderson* (pp. 333–352). Hillsdale, NJ: Erlbaum.

Templeton, S., & Bear, D. R. (Eds.). (1992b). *Development of orthographic knowledge and the foundations of literacy: A memorial festschrift for Edmund H. Henderson*. Hillsdale, NJ: Erlbaum.

Templeton, S., & Morris, D. (1999). Questions teachers ask about spelling. *Reading Research Quarterly, 34*, 102–112.

Templeton, S., & Morris, D. (2000). Spelling. In M. Kamil, P. Mosenthal, P. D. Pearson, & R. Barr (Eds.), *Handbook of reading research* (Vol. 3, pp. 525–543). Mahwah, NJ: Erlbaum.

Templeton, S., & Spivey, E. M. (1980). The concept of "word" in young children as a function of level of cognitive development. *Research in the Teaching of English, 14*, 265–278.

Templeton, S., & Thomas, P. W. (1984). Performance and reflection: Young children's concept of "word." *Journal of Educational Research, 27,* 139–146.

Torgesen, J. K., Wagner, R. K., & Rashotte, C. A. (1994). Longitudinal studies of phonological processing and reading. *Journal of Learning Disabilities, 27,* 276–286.

Treiman, R. (1998). Why spelling?: The benefits of incorporating spelling into beginning reading instruction. In J. L. Metsala & L. C. Ehri (Eds.), *Word recognition in beginning literacy* (pp. 289–313). Mahwah, NJ: Erlbaum.

Vellutino, F. R., Scanlon, D. M., Sipay, E. R., Small, S. G., Pratt, A., Chen, R., & Denckla, M. B. (1996). Cognitive profiles of difficult-to-remediate and readily remediated poor readers: Intervention as a vehicle for distinguishing between cognitive and experiential deficits as basic causes of specific reading disability. *Journal of Educational Psychology, 88,* 601–638.

Venezky, R. L. (1999). *The American way of spelling: The structure and origins of American English orthography.* New York: Guilford Press.

Worthy, M. J., & Invernizzi, M. (1990). Spelling errors of normal and disabled students on achievement levels one through four: Instructional implications. *Annals of Dyslexia, 40,* 138–151.

Zutell, J. (1998). Word sorting: A developmental spelling approach to word study for delayed readers. *Reading and Writing Quarterly: Overcoming Learning Difficulties, 14,* 219–238.

11

✕

Integration of Language Components in Spelling

Instruction That Maximizes Students' Learning

KENN APEL
JULIE J. MASTERSON
PAM HART

Spelling is a complex, linguistically based literacy skill. An individual's ability to spell is dependent upon his or her underlying knowledge of phonology, orthography, morphology, and mental graphemic representations (MGRs) (Apel & Masterson, 2001; Masterson & Crede, 1999). These linguistic factors play influential roles in the development of an individual's spelling skills (Bourassa & Treiman, 2001). In addition to these four factors, the method of instruction also plays a critical role in facilitating the development of spelling abilities (Bear, Invernizzi, Templeton, & Johnson, 2000; Berninger, 1999; Masterson & Crede, 1999; Scott, 2000). While research has supported the importance of individual skills in phonology, orthography, morphology, and MGRs for developing literacy skills, the majority of instructional methods utilized today do not address these factors in an integrated manner (Bailet, 2004; Masterson & Crede, 1999; Scott, 2000). Additionally, little has been written on the role(s) different school-based professionals, such as general and special education teachers and speech–language pathologists, should take in spelling instruction and intervention for students with spelling disabilities.

The questions of whose responsibility it is to help students who are struggling with spelling and how instruction should be structured are likely due to a long history of an inadequate or incorrect definition of spelling (Moats, 2000). Additionally, a lack of understanding of spelling and its linguistic underpinnings has led to confusion and uninformed instructional practices far removed from any theoretical and research bases (Moats, 2000; Scott, 2000). In this chapter, we make the case for an integrated view of spelling and spelling instruction. First, we offer an integrated view of spelling acquisition, which involves a consideration of the multiple linguistic factors that influence spelling development. Within this review, we report on research regarding current spelling instruction techniques, including methods that may facilitate or hinder attention to the multiple language properties of spelling. Following this, we describe a project that translated research into practice in the area of spelling instruction. Finally, we conclude with a discussion of several challenges facing school-based professionals in regard to spelling. These include the integration of spelling components into an instructional approach, integration of spelling across subject matters, and integration of various professionals' expertise when serving students who struggle with spelling.

FACTORS INFLUENCING
SPELLING DEVELOPMENT

Phonological Awareness

Phonological awareness is the ability to think about, reflect on, and manipulate the sound structures of a language. As reviewed by Masterson and Apel (2000), phonological awareness involves a progression of the following skills, presented here in their typical order of development: sound play, rhyming, alliteration, initial and final sound identification, and blending and segmenting sounds into syllables and phonemes. *Phonemic awareness*, an aspect of phonological awareness that focuses on manipulation at the phoneme level (e.g., segmentation), is considered to be a good predictor of early childhood spelling abilities (Nation & Hulme, 1997). It is challenging for beginning spellers to strengthen their phonological awareness skills in the absence of explicit instruction (Ehri, 2000); consequently, speech–language pathologists and teachers must provide systematic instruction and experience in phonological awareness as one component of spelling instruction in order for all children to develop optimal spelling skills (for more detailed information on phonological awareness, see Troia, Chapter 4, and Gillam & Goram, Chapter 3, this volume).

Orthographic Knowledge

Orthographic knowledge involves the skills necessary to translate spoken language into its written form. This includes an understanding of the orthographic rules present in the English language, such as knowledge of appropriate letter sequences (e.g., a *qp* combination is not present in the English language) and understanding of appropriate word positions of letter sequences (e.g., *ck* does not occur in the word initial position in the English language) (Apel, Masterson, & Niessen, 2004; Treiman & Bourassa, 2000). Orthographic knowledge also includes the understanding of orthographic rules, such as the doublet principle (i.e., consonant letters are never doubled after long vowels), long and short vowel patterns (e.g., in monosyllabic words, short vowels are routinely marked by one vowel letter whereas long vowels are marked by two vowel letters), and silent *e*-conditioned consonants (i.e., when the letters *c* or *g* are followed by the letter *e*, the consonant sounds change from the hard [stop] sound to a soft [fricative or affricate] sound) (Masterson, Apel, & Wasowicz, 2002; Scott, 2000; Treiman & Bourassa, 2000).

Morphological Knowledge

Morphological knowledge involves the awareness of the semantic aspects of a root word and its inflections and derivations (Carlisle, 1995; Fowler & Lieberman, 1995; Wasowicz, Apel, & Masterson, 2003). The use of morphological knowledge in spelling is important, as many words in the English language cannot be spelled using only phonological awareness skills or orthographic rules. In the past, morphological awareness has been considered a later developing spelling skill, used by more sophisticated spellers (Bear et al., 2000; Henderson, 1990). However, recent reports suggest that children demonstrate some inflectional and derivational morphological knowledge early in development (e.g., Lyster, 2002; Treiman & Bourassa, 2000). The relationships between morphological knowledge and spelling may be bidirectional. That is, use of morphological knowledge, specifically knowledge of root words and their meanings, not only facilitates spelling skills, but conscious attention to these factors during the act of spelling may strengthen vocabulary skills as well.

Mental Graphemic Representations

Mental graphemic representations (MGRs; also referred to as "visual orthographic images") are mental images of syllables, morphemes, or words that are created and stored in memory through multiple experiences with a printed word or word form (Apel & Masterson, 2001; Ehri & Wilce, 1982; Glenn & Hurley, 1993). These images can speed the process of reading and spelling because they aid in recognizing or accessing images of words successfully stored. "Fuzzy" MGRs can interfere with an individual's spelling ability. Masterson and Crede (1999) reported on previous studies that suggested that reading alone may not provide adequate opportunities for creation of mental images, as children may focus only at beginnings and endings of challenging words and use context as a decoding strategy. In addition, it was suggested that poor handwriting also could contribute to "fuzzy" representations of words. Therefore, explicit instruction regarding the use and importance of MGRs as a spelling strategy may be beneficial to spelling development.

Spelling Development: An Integrated View

Past descriptions of spelling development emphasized *stages* (Bear & Templeton, 1998; Bear et al., 2000; Henderson, 1990; Templeton & Morris, 2000). Spellers in the earlier stages were thought to use phonological and orthographic information, while spellers in the later stages of development added morphological awareness to their repertoire of skills. For example, according to the stage theory of spelling, in the *prephonetic stage* children begin to spell by scribbling, paying little attention to specific letter shapes and the relationship between sounds and letters. Next, in the *semiphonetic stage*, children become aware of the names of letters and how letters are written, and use this knowledge to make their first attempts at spelling words. Thus, in the semiphonetic stage, children often use one letter to represent a whole word, with the one letter chosen based on how the name sounds rather than the sound of the letter. The *phonetic stage* follows, with children relying more on their knowledge of letter–sound correspondence in their attempts to spell simple words with multiple letter combinations. In the next stage, the *within-word stage*, children begin to develop an appreciation for the orthographic rules or patterns of English orthography, such as marking long vowels with two vowel letters. In the final two stages, the *syllable juncture stage* and the *derivational constancy stage*, children use inflectional and derivational morphological knowledge and rules for modifications made at syllable boundaries to spell multisyllabic words.

While stage theories of spelling continue to be applied to methods of spelling assessment and instruction (e.g., Templeton & Morris, 2000), recent research suggests that children rely on various linguistic knowledge sources concerning the multiple linguistic factors *throughout* the process of learning to spell (e.g., Berninger & Amtmann, 2003; Lyster, 2000; Reece & Treiman, 2001; Treiman & Bourassa, 2000). As Treiman and Bourassa (2000) contend, stage theories do not address the fact that children use multiple strategies and different kinds of knowledge (phonological, orthographic, morphological) as they acquire their spelling knowledge. Across several studies, Treiman and her colleagues (Reece & Treiman, 2001; Treiman & Cassar, 1996; Treiman, Cassar, & Zukowski, 1994) have shown how children apply orthographic and morphological knowledge to their spellings during stages of spelling development that would suggest this was not possible. For example, Reece and Treiman (2001) found that first-grade children, assumed to be within the semiphonetic or phonetic stages, did not demonstrate the consistency of spelling proposed by stage theory. Instead, their spellings suggested that the children were utilizing their orthographic knowledge *in addition to* their phonological knowledge. That is, the children utilized phonological knowledge to spell some words, but orthographic knowledge to spell other words.

The extent to which each type of linguistic knowledge influences spelling varies throughout the course of development. For example, beginning spellers rely more heavily on phonological information, whereas experienced spellers use morphological information more frequently. Additionally, descriptions of children's spelling development reveal that a skill that appeared to be learned at one point in development may seem to be problematic again when either the complexity of the word or the complexity of the writing task increases. For example, a student in second grade may consistently represent each sound in a single-syllable word with a letter. However, when the student attempts multisyllabic words, all sounds may not be represented by a letter.

Children's ability to differentially access their knowledge for a number of linguistic factors across development is consistent with Sulzby's (1996) *repertoire theory of language development*. This theory, based on the relationship between oral language and written language development, suggests that children have several linguistic knowledge bases at their disposal, and the amount and frequency with which they use those knowledge bases depends on their exposure to and experience with those linguistic factors as well as the demands of the task at hand. Thus, spelling development may best be represented by a growth in the number and actual use of children's linguistic repertoires (Sulzby, 1996).

Summary

Professionals providing spelling instruction should not rely solely on stage models of spelling development (Masterson & Apel, 2000; Masterson et al., 2002; Treiman & Bourassa, 2000). Rather, an appreciation and understanding of the multiple linguistic factors underlying spelling development and knowledge of the student's skills at a given point in development should guide educators and language specialists in targeting the most appropriate factors for students (Apel & Masterson, 2001; Kelman & Apel, in press; Masterson & Apel, 2000).

While phonological, orthographic, and morphological knowledge, along with adequate MGRs, have been shown to contribute to the development of spelling abilities, classroom instruction has historically approached spelling development without addressing these factors in concert. Typically, classroom spelling instruction has been provided following either direct or indirect models. The method employed within these models varies as well.

CLASSROOM INSTRUCTIONAL PRACTICES

Classroom instructional practices are often guided by tradition rather than by current research (Bailet, 2004; Moats, 2000). These practices may take the form of explicit instruction or more authentic, real-time instruction. At the same time, professionals may or may not focus students' attention on one or more linguistic factors underlying the words studied.

Spelling Instruction Methods

The most commonly practiced model of spelling instruction is the direct method of *rote memorization of weekly target words*, beginning around second or third grade and continuing throughout elementary school (Bailet, 2004; Johnston, 2001; Scott, 2000). This form of instruction is applied through in-class activities (e.g., writing a word three times, then using it in a sentence), or relying on the student to learn these spellings through practice at home. Often, words are chosen based on published lists of the most frequently read or written words by children of varying ages and grade levels (e.g., Graham, Harris, & Loynachan, 1993). The salient feature of this approach is the emphasis on rote memorization of the list of words, as opposed to encouraging students' attention to orthographic, lexical, or morphological properties of the words to establish an appreciation for regularities in spelling. In fact, words may be chosen on a thematic basis (e.g., words that are within the classroom's unit on pirates) without any consideration of the linguistic properties of the words.

Rote memorization has been criticized for lacking individualization and relevance, and for reinforcing the idea of spelling as arbitrary in nature (Scott, 2000). This direct approach to spelling provides little guidance in helping students see the spelling patterns or rules that guide much of spelling (Heald-Taylor, 1998). Indeed, children report that these lists do little to aid their spelling development (Hughes & Searle, 1997).

Another direct method of instruction focuses on *word analysis via word sorts*. Typically, word sorts require students to sort words that are contrasted by a specific orthographic rule, such as the sorting of words that contain long or short vowels. This practice provides students with opportunities to identify specific patterns, or spelling rules, to help formulate generalizations from what has been identified, and to transfer that knowledge when spelling other words that follow similar rules or patterns (Bear et al., 2000; Scott, 2000). The use of word sorts varies in the amount of guidance the teacher provides. In some interpretations of this method (e.g., Darch, Kim, Johnson, & James, 2000), teachers actively direct students' attention to the rule represented through the sort. In other interpretations of this method, teachers provide leading questions to guide students to self-discovery of the target rule or pattern (e.g., Bear et al., 2000).

Researchers have found that word sorts are a viable means for increasing students' knowledge of specific orthographic patterns or rules (Fresch, Wheaton, & Zutell, 1998; Hall, Cunningham, & Cunningham, 1995; Joseph, 2000; Weber & Henderson, 1989; Zutell, 1998). For example, Hall et al. (1995) reported that third graders increased their spelling skills when provided instruction via word sorts compared to more traditional spelling instruction methods, such as writing words repeatedly or using visual strategies to learn word spellings. Joseph (2000) also found that word sorts resulted in significantly higher spelling accuracy compared to traditional spelling instruction practices such as discussions of phonograms (i.e., words spelled similarly, such as *tent* and *rent*) and choral readings of target words. Although additional studies are required to confirm these initial findings, it appears that word sort activities hold more promise for improving spelling abilities than approaches that encourage rote memorization.

A third method used for teaching spelling, *indirect instruction*, integrates spelling into the reading and writing curriculum. Words that become the focus of the spelling instruction may be selected by the teacher or by the student. For example, in some variations of this method, the teacher circulates around the room while students participate in authentic writing activities. The teacher then capitalizes on "teachable moments" by identifying correctly and incorrectly spelled words in a student's written material, discussing the spellings with the student, and then providing explicit instruction regarding frequently erroneous spelling patterns (Hayward, 1998; Scott, 2000). Other versions of this method encourage students to self-select the words they wish to learn to spell (Johnson, 1998; Wright, 2000). Often with these versions of indirect instruction, students are encouraged to keep their own spelling notebooks where they record the words they self-select and learn to spell.

The Focus of Spelling Instruction

Because a number of different linguistic factors contribute to spelling development, it would seem intuitive that spelling instruction involves attention to all of these factors. However, as the discussion of spelling methods suggests, the focus of spelling instruction may vary in the amount of attention provided to each of the underlying factors contributing to spelling development. For example, with some direct method approaches (e.g., rote memorization), the teacher is likely to focus on correct spelling, and to pay little attention to the underlying bases of spelling knowledge. While word analysis and sorting tasks promote orthographic knowledge, and perhaps morphological awareness (see Bear et al., 2000), this method of instruction does not focus students' attention on other sources of linguistic knowledge used for spelling, such as phonemic awareness and the development of MGRs. Finally, while some children initially may learn about and begin to use the multiple linguistic factors supporting spelling development through their experiences with reading and writing (i.e., indirect spelling instruction), there is limited research to support the benefits of a natural learning approach extending beyond the first and second grades (Graham, 2000). Additionally, those students who are challenged in spelling development will not be able to learn what is not explicitly taught, including strategies for using the multiple linguistic factors to spell correctly (Kelman & Apel, in press; Wasowicz, Apel, Masterson, & Whitney, in press; Scott, 2000).

Over the last decade, however, several proponents of spelling instruction programs that target multiple linguistic factors have come forward (e.g., Apel & Masterson, 2001; Brooks, Vaughan, & Berninger, 1999; Butyniec-Thomas & Woloshyn, 1997; Kelman & Apel, in press; Wasowicz et al., in press). As a whole, these researchers have argued for spelling instruction or remediation programs that target phonological awareness, orthographic knowledge, morphological knowledge, and MGRs in concert. For example, Butyniec-Thomas and Woloshyn (1997) compared the whole-language approach, the explicit-strategy approach (direct multiple-linguistic-factor instruction), and a combination of the two approaches in their study involving 37 third-grade students. The whole-language approach, similar to the indirect instruction discussed earlier, addressed spelling through immersion in literature (reading and writing), while the explicit-strategy approach consisted of teaching multiple linguistic factors as strategies for spelling unfamiliar words. The strategies taught consisted of syllable segmentation (a phonemic awareness skill), forming mental images of words (supporting use of MGRs), and constructing words (addressing both orthographic and morphological knowledge). The researchers found that the students who received explicit-strategy instruction combined with natural learning opportunities demonstrated the most progress in their spelling abilities, and an explicit-strategy approach alone was more beneficial than a whole-language approach alone.

Additionally, Apel and Masterson (2001) reported on the case study of an adolescent with spelling and reading impairments. Intervention focused on multiple linguistic factors to facilitate development of this student's spelling abilities. The student attended a short intensive-treatment program, receiving 23 hours of direct intervention provided in a group setting. The student demonstrated improvement in spelling performance between pre- and posttest measures, and results revealed a relatively large effect size ($d = 0.84$). *Effect size* is a descriptive statistic used to estimate the magnitude or strength of the relationship between two sets of variables (Kromrey & Foster-Johnson, 1996). In this case, the relationship between the treatment provided and the outcomes (spelling performance) was strong.

School-based professionals should use theory and current research to guide their instructional practices (Apel, 1999). In the case of spelling instruction, professionals should guide students in their development and use of multiple linguistic strategies to spell words. Recent research suggests that this approach will lead to advancing children's spelling abilities. What faces school-based professionals at this point, then, is how to translate the research on spelling instruction into everyday practices (Templeton, 2003).

TRANSLATING RESEARCH INTO PRACTICE

The current understanding of spelling development is that multiple linguistic factors influence how spelling skills are acquired. Also, as reviewed, the preliminary findings of instructional spelling programs are positive. Therefore, school-based professionals should consider implementing these findings and knowledge into their curricular practices. However, implementation of research into practice is not always an easy task (Fey & Johnson, 1998). Classroom practices may not always mirror research practices (Ingram, 1998). In this section, we provide an overview of one project that took current spelling research and theory and translated those findings and ideas into practice in an elementary classroom.

A Multiple-Linguistic-Factor Approach to Classroom Spelling Instruction

To illustrate the use of the multiple-factor approach to spelling instruction, we next describe a small study (Apel & Masterson, 2002) in which these principles were used in a classroom. We solicited the participation of children in two elementary-school classes situated in a semirural town in the Pacific Northwest. Class 1 was a third-grade class, Class 2 was a third-fourth-grade split. Both classes had similar numbers of participating students, with similar numbers of students from culturally or linguistically diverse backgrounds or students receiving special services.

Before initiating the project, we documented that the students in the two classrooms had comparable spelling skills. Each student completed a spelling test consisting of 40 words. The words represented a range of spelling complexity, such that some words were simple consonant–vowel–consonant words (e.g., *bed*), while other words were multisyllabic words containing prefixes or suffixes (e.g., *prisoner*). The students in both classes performed similarly on this pretest. That is, there was no statistical difference, based on a paired t-test, between the number of correctly spelled words produced by students in each class.

Between October and December of the school year, Class 1 received the traditional school spelling curriculum. This instruction consisted of a spelling pretest (words from a weekly spelling list) on Monday, brief amounts of in-class practice (multiple writings of the target words both in isolation and in sentences), encouragement to practice at home, and a final spelling test on Friday. While current literature suggests this is not the optimal means for spelling instruction or remediation (e.g., Bear et al., 2000), this approach was consistent with approaches that dominate U.S. classroom spelling instruction (Johnston, 2001).

Class 2 received a spelling instruction program aligned with current spelling theory and empirical research. The instruction was provided by a speech–language pathology graduate student who worked in collaboration with the classroom teacher. This particular project spanned a 9-week period, consisting of 17 days of instruction with 50 minutes per session. Each spelling instruction session in Class 2 followed the same general format:

1. Except for the initial session, the session began with a review of the previous lesson and the introduction of a new spelling strategy (i.e., linguistic factor).
2. Then the teacher modeled use of the new strategy on an overhead or blackboard.
3. Next the entire class practiced the new strategy.
4. Then the students did pair or group work that enhanced discussion and their problem-solving processes.
5. Finally, the teacher led a whole-class discussion relating awareness of the newly learned strategy to the use of various textual materials, such as classroom textbooks.

Throughout the remaining portions of the week, the classroom teacher conducted activities to promote the ongoing use of the target strategy within and outside of the classroom. Thus, in this way, spelling received a focal emphasis within the traditional "spelling time" or language arts period while it also received attention during other subjects and class activities.

As noted earlier, the instruction Class 2 received spanned a 9-week period, which was divided into three "units": phonological awareness

(6 sessions), orthographic principles (6 sessions), and morphological awareness (5 sessions). Like Class 1, the words targeted in the lessons were selected from a collection of words from which all students were required to
be exposed during the academic year, according to the district guidelines.
A brief description of these units follows.

Phonemic Awareness Unit

Phonemic segmentation activities were used to draw attention to and
facilitate students' knowledge of sounds in a word and the corresponding
graphemes used to represent those sounds. Previous research suggests that,
among various phonemic awareness tasks, phonemic segmentation abilities best predict students' spelling skills (e.g., Hoien, Lundberg, Stanovich,
& Bjaalid, 1995; Muter, Hulme, Snowling, & Taylor, 1997; Nation & Hulme,
1997). "Sound strings" (i.e., seven different colored beads threaded onto a
string approximately 4–5 inches long) were provided to each student and
were used to facilitate phoneme segmentation. The students were instructed to segment the word by moving one bead per sound on their sound
string, and then to write the word on their dry erase board or on the class
overhead or blackboard. Additionally, students were informed that they
must represent every sound with at least one letter and also encouraged
to consider single sounds that were represented by two letters (i.e., digraphs, such as *sh* and *th*). Students spontaneously discovered that the letter
x represented two sounds (/ks/) and determined that *x* was an exception
to the "represent every sound with at least one letter" rule.

Initially the instructor introduced two-, three-, and four-phoneme
words and nonsense words that did not contain liquids, nasals, or clusters,
given that research has shown these to be exceptionally difficult to segment
in words (Treiman & Bourassa, 2000). These were followed by words containing liquids, nasals, and clusters. Gradually, the instructor introduced
longer and more syllable-complex words containing up to six phonemes.

Outside of this specific instruction, the teacher engaged students in
activities that encouraged them to think about sounds in words. For example, the teacher (1) stopped while in the course of reading aloud to the
class to focus on the segmentation of words (drawing emphasis to challenging words and having students attempt oral or written spellings);
(2) asked students to segment their own names, as well as those of friends
and family members, before lining up to go out of class; (3) encouraged
students to segment the name of the upcoming subject of study during transitions; and (4) encouraged students to segment and spell words that they
used in conversation or while asking questions in class. Students also were
given homework assignments, such as finding words in magazines or books
that contained a specific number of phonemes.

Orthographic Knowledge Unit

Sorting activities (e.g., Apel & Masterson, 2001; Bear et al., 2000; Masterson & Crede, 1999) were used to engage students in a process of word analysis, specifically allowing students to discover orthographic patterns (e.g., short and long vowels, vowel teams, r-influenced vowels) that occur frequently in many words. Sorting activities as tools for facilitating orthographic rule learning are empirically supported in the literature (see Zutell, 1998, for a review). While sorting, students were encouraged to attend to what they were seeing and hearing. A hypothesis is that the exposure to, and students' identification of, typically occurring patterns in words generalizes to the use of rule-based decision making while engaged in the spelling process (Apel & Masterson, 2001). Additionally, word sorts provide a means for integrating spelling and reading (Fresch et al., 1998).

Initially, students used sorting tasks to identify long and short vowels, using all vowel types. Subsequently, sorts focused on r-influenced vowels (as in _for_ and _car_), vowel teams (e.g., _ee, ea, oa_), /k/ patterns (when /k/ is represented by the letters _k, c,_ or _ck_), complex clusters (e.g., _spl, scr,_ and _squ_), and various complex digraphs containing "silent letters" (e.g., _kn, gn,_ and _wr_). These particular patterns or rules were based generally on their occurrence in spelling development (e.g., Bear et al., 2000). Students were required not only to sort but also to generate words that followed the patterns or rules of study. Throughout this unit, the level of difficulty of sorts and targeted patterns was gradually increased at intervals deemed appropriate by the instructor (e.g., the number of words contained in each sort was increased or the level of difficulty of the patterns was adjusted). As suggested by Bear et al. (2000) and Fresch et al. (1998), "oddballs" were used as a contrastive mechanism (e.g., although the word _give_ shares the same orthographic feature of the vowel–consonant–silent _e_ pattern with the words _thrive_ and _hive_, the phonological feature of a long vowel is not shared, and therefore _give_ was considered to be an "oddball").

Teacher activities and student assignments outside of the unit included having students generate oral and written spellings of words that followed learned patterns and rules. The teacher was encouraged to highlight words that followed learned patterns throughout various classroom activities and subject studies. Also, students performed "word searches" to find and write words that followed the current patterns or rules of study.

Morphological Awareness Unit

Morphological awareness activities required students to identify and understand the relationships between base words and their inflected and derived forms. Specific attention was paid to the phonological, orthographic, and morphological differences that occurred in various words that were related to one another. A "family" analogy was used to highlight the relationships between words that were described as "relatives" (Cunningham, 1998; Wasowicz et al., 2003). Using this analogy, students learned that some family members (inflected and derived words) looked and sounded the same as the parent (base word), some looked the same but sounded differently, some looked differently but sounded the same, and some looked and sounded differently but still were related. Then, when given a word orally, students were required to identify and spell the base word, as well as to spell as many "family members" as they could. Examples of base words targeted were *act, serve, play, see, read, real, use, complete, produce,* and *discuss.*

When possible, base words were contrasted with words that were phonologically close in form, though not true "relatives" as identified by underlying meaning. For example, when working with the word *discuss,* the instructor suggested the word *disgust* as a possible family member. These types of discussions led to increased understanding of the meaning shared among base words and their inflected and derived forms.

Teacher activities and student assignments outside of the sessions followed the above line of work (i.e., to identify base words and to find and spell as many family members as possible). At the end of this unit and the orthographic knowledge unit, the students were presented with words and were requested to use the two to three strategies (e.g., using their phonemic segmentation skills) that they had learned as they spelled the words. The students then shared all of the possibilities with the entire class. In the process, students discovered that, for many words, an awareness of and the application of the multiple linguistic factors were necessary to correctly spell words.

The progress of the children in each classroom indicated that the multiple-linguistic-factor approach does indeed improve spelling skills to a greater extent than typical classroom methods. After 9 weeks of instruction, students in Class 2 significantly improved their word accuracy spelling skills, whereas students in Class 1 did not. Specifically, an effect-size measure (Kromrey & Foster-Johnson, 1996) was calculated to determine the extent to which treatment had a clinically significant effect on the participants' spelling abilities, as measured by the number of correctly produced words and bigrams on the pre- and posttest samples. A *bigram* represents two letters in correct sequence within a word (e.g., in the word *boat,* the following bigrams occur: *bo, oa,* and *at*) (White & Haring, 1980). For Class 2, effect size for word accuracy was $d = 0.65$, suggesting a moderate gain in spelling accuracy. For Class 1, effect size for word accuracy was $d = -0.07$, indicating no improvement in spelling performance between pre- and posttest administrations. These results revealed that the students who received spelling instruction that targeted multiple linguistic factors demonstrated statistically and clinically significant growth in their spelling abilities, while the class that received the standard school curriculum did not demonstrate measurable gains.

Like many pilot projects, the results bring more questions than they do answers. While an integrated approach to spelling instruction appears promising, there is much more information to be learned. In the project reviewed, the instructor had a great deal of background knowledge in the multiple linguistic factors that underlie spelling, thus enabling instruction to be informed by research and theory. Because many preprofessional programs tend to ignore specific coursework in spelling development and instruction (Moats, 2000), it may be that school-based professionals are ill prepared to provide such instruction. Likewise, the notion of incorporating spelling instruction across the curriculum or school day, via either indirect (e.g., teachable moments) or direct methods (e.g., active attention to spelling outside of the spelling lesson or language arts time) needs to be considered. Additionally, it remains unclear whether a multiple-linguistic-factors approach might facilitate the spelling development of students with specific spelling disabilities. While the one case study reviewed (Apel & Masterson, 2001) provided some initial confirmation of the usefulness of a multiple-linguistic-factors approach, further data are required, especially with larger groups of students with special needs. Finally, the question of who should provide remedial instruction for these students needs to be considered. The roles and responsibilities of school-based professionals for spelling instruction and remediation may not be clear at this point in time. Thus, there are several challenges facing school-based professionals as they move toward providing best practices in spelling instruction.

INTEGRATED SPELLING INSTRUCTION APPROACHES: ADDRESSING THE CHALLENGES

It is hoped that as professionals' understanding of spelling development deepens and new instructional programs are assessed, students will eventually receive optimal spelling instruction that meets their needs and encourages further development of their spelling skills. With this hope, however, come several instructional and research challenges. Among these are the challenge of providing a spelling approach that integrates all underlying components of spelling development, the challenge to infuse attention to spelling development across the school day, and the challenge of meeting the needs of students with specific spelling disabilities.

Challenge 1: Integrated Spelling Instruction Approaches

According to the current understanding of spelling acquisition and recent empirical findings regarding successful spelling instruction, there is a need to emphasize the integration of the multiple linguistic factors that contribute to spelling development within spelling instruction. This may not be an easy task on a number of different levels. First, many professionals still do not recognize the linguistic nature of spelling. The predominance of the direct method/rote memorization approach to spelling instruction exemplifies this tendency.

Second, most studies that have recognized the linguistic nature of spelling have focused almost exclusively on the phonological aspects of spelling (Ball & Blachman, 1991; Post, Carreker, & Holland, 2001; Schneider, Roth, & Ennemoser, 2000). Not surprisingly, these studies have found that phonemic awareness activities, such as phonemic segmentation, lead to improvements in spelling. However, because of the limited scope of these studies, the translation to practice has had a decidedly heavy emphasis on phonemic awareness skills. While phonemic awareness plays an important part in spelling development, the challenge is to see what it can and cannot do for spelling development. Spelling simple single-syllable words can be successful when one uses both phonemic awareness and letter–sound correspondence. However, the benefits of phonemic awareness are considerably less when one spells more complicated multisyllabic words, especially when those words include one or more morphological inflections (e.g., prefixes, suffixes) or are derivations of base words or roots. Thus, spelling instruction, with a focus solely on phonemic awareness, will lead to positive yet limited increases in spelling development. Based on recent reports of morphological awareness training (e.g., Berninger et al., 2003; Lyster, 2002), multiple-factor approaches that include attention to morphological awareness hold promise for improving students' spelling skills and should be empirically validated.

Third, even more recent approaches to instruction that emphasize stage theory do not necessarily encourage an integrated approach to spelling (e.g., Bear et al., 2000; Ganske, 2000). In such programs, students are taught first to learn about letter sounds, and then how to use this knowledge with their developing phonemic awareness skills to spell words. After reaching a certain competency, students then are provided word sorts to help them develop knowledge about specific orthographic patterns and rules. Finally, after obtaining a certain ability level, students are encouraged to tap into their morphological knowledge to spell inflected and derived words. Traditional, and even many nontraditional, spelling instruction approaches do not emphasize the integration of the multiple linguistic factors underlying spelling. While such approaches should be applauded for informing professionals about the multiple sources of linguistic knowledge spellers use to spell and encouraging them to address more than one of these factors throughout students' education, they do so in a linear versus an interactional manner. Thus, an integrated approach involving simultaneous and developmentally appropriate attention to the linguistic sources of knowledge is not provided.

The challenge, then, is to help professionals understand that spelling is a linguistic skill and that it taps into more than one area of language. Children should be encouraged to use a repertoire of knowledge bases to spell. This may not be an easy task. Professionals do not always agree on what language is (Apel, 1999), much less on whether spelling is a language skill (Moats, 2000). Professionals also must become knowledgeable about the phonological, orthographic, morphological, and visual underpinnings of English spelling, and be able to use that knowledge in an integrated manner as they instruct students. This will take considerable revisions of current preprofessional programs and revamping of common language arts curricula. It is hoped that when professionals *do* understand the linguistic nature of spelling, they will be able to address the second challenge, that of integrating spelling across the school day.

Challenge 2: Integrating Spelling across the Curriculum

Given that optimal spelling instruction will likely require focusing students' attention on multiple linguistic factors simultaneously, a significant portion of time in the language arts curriculum will need to be devoted to the study of these factors. The good news, however, is that such systematic word study aids not only spelling but also reading performance. Spelling must be viewed as a language skill that continues to be developed, and, as such, should be addressed throughout all grades. In other words, spelling will not be optimally mastered if instruction begins in the third grade and ends in the sixth or seventh grade.

Although we advocate an increased focus on spelling within the language arts curriculum, we also emphasize that spelling is more than a subject that is *limited* to language arts. Like reading, spelling permeates the curricula of the classroom. To limit attention to it during one segment of a day would not only ignore the research that calls for the explicit, repeated, and continuous attention needed to improve this skill, it also would belittle its importance as a skill that interacts with and affects other areas of literacy.

Spelling is used in almost every content area of the school curricula. Research reports provide direct evidence of the importance of focusing on spelling in the multiple subjects addressed throughout the school day (e.g., Hughes & Searle, 1997; Rymer & Williams, 2000). Spelling instruction infused across subject matter likely leads to increases in students' focused and active attention to the properties of English orthography, although this requires additional study. Additionally, it likely will lead to students' deeper understanding of content area vocabulary. For example, when teachers take advantage of morphological similarities among content vocabulary (e.g., the words *computer, compute, computation*), the student benefits not only by developing knowledge about the morphosemantic similarities of these words, but also by developing a more thorough understanding of the base that forms these words, thus leading to understanding of future vocabulary and expressions that are related (e.g., "*calculated* moves").

An integration of spelling across the curricula areas also acknowledges the impact spelling has on other literacy domains. Previous research has confirmed the powerful relationship between spelling and reading, and between spelling and written composition (Berninger, 2000; Cassar & Treiman 2004; Singer & Bashir, 2004). Increases in spelling ability often lead to increases in reading decoding (Berninger, Cartwright, Yates, Swanson, & Abbott, 1994). Undoubtedly, this is due to the linguistic factors shared by these two literacy skills, including phonological, morphological, and orthographic knowledge, as well as stored MGRs. Spelling also impacts the writing process (Graham, Berninger, Abbott, Abbott, & Whitaker, 1997; Singer & Bashir, 2004). For example, spelling may at times limit the length or quality of the written product. Students may focus on spelling to the exclusion of or to a greater extent than other components of the writing process. In other cases, students may avoid writing words they are unsure how to spell, thus affecting the content of their written compositions (Apel & Swank, 1999). Cross-curricular attention to the demands spelling places on written composition and the interactions between reading and spelling should strengthen both students' skills and the ability of the teacher to meet the specific needs of those students.

Integrating spelling across the curriculum of the classroom will likely benefit students in several ways. Additionally, it should raise the awareness of the teacher regarding the impact of spelling on student performance, thus leading to a better match between professionals' instructional practices and students' individual needs. A final challenge, though, is how best to meet the needs of students with specific spelling disabilities, those students for whom additional or more intensive instruction is required.

Challenge 3: Integrating Professionals' Expertise to Meet the Needs of Students with Spelling Disabilities

Because spelling is a linguistic and literacy skill, it seems that collaboration among professionals who typically provide services to children with special needs in the areas of language and literacy should be involved. By definition, then, this would involve at least the classroom teacher, the special education teacher, and the speech–language pathologist. Currently, however, it is unlikely that many schools use such professional teams to meet the needs of students who struggle with spelling. This may be due to an uncertainty about the role of the speech–language pathologist in serving students with written language needs as well as hurdles accompanying such a collaborative approach (Apel, 2002).

Historically, many, if not most, speech–language pathologists did not consider reading, much less writing and spelling, to be part of their role in helping students with language learning disabilities. However, the American Speech–Language–Hearing Association (2001), the national organization for speech–language pathologists, audiologists, and speech and hearing scientists, recently published a position statement, along with a set of guidelines and a technical report, that clearly delineated the roles and responsibilities of speech–language pathologists regarding serving children and adolescents with reading and writing disabilities, including spelling disabilities. This document states that, given the linguistic nature of spelling, reading, and written composition, speech–language pathologists are uniquely qualified to consult, participate in preventative procedures, and provide direct assessment and intervention services to children and adolescents struggling in these areas. Thus, given the language basis of spelling and their education and experience with language development and disabilities, speech–language pathologists should be one of several school-based professionals who serve students with spelling disabilities.

To say that speech–language pathologists, along with general and special education teachers, should be involved in spelling instruction for students with spelling disabilities is one thing; putting this idea into practice is another. Although there may be several hurdles to this team approach toward spelling remediation, two specific obstacles are clear (Apel, 2002). First, the criteria that speech–language pathologists' use to determine student eligibility may inhibit or discourage them from becoming involved in remediating students' spelling skills. Second, the mechanism of collaboration among professionals is not an easy one.

Most, if not all, federal and state definitions of language include spoken and written language, specifically phonology, morphology, and so on.

Likewise, federal and most state definitions of learning disabilities include all aspects of language: speaking, listening, reading, and writing. Thus, speech–language pathologists, whose expertise includes language, seem like a natural fit to serve *any* student with problems in *any* of these areas. However, there seems to be an unwritten rule regarding these definitions: *speech–language pathologists do not work with students' written language (reading, writing, and spelling) disabilities.* Instead, it seems to be the norm that speech–language pathologists are to focus only on spoken language disabilities. This unwritten limitation undoubtedly stems from a lack of awareness about the linguistic properties of spelling and other literacy skills, poor or no preprofessional preparation in these literacy areas, and tradition (i.e., speech–language pathologists have historically worked with students who had speech or other spoken language difficulties). However, historical practices do not need to dictate what is to occur in the present or the future. All school-based professionals will need to understand the background and knowledge base that speech–language pathologists bring to the endeavor of helping students with spelling disabilities improve their spelling skills.

To acknowledge the contributions that speech–language pathologists, as well as general and special education teachers, bring to spelling instruction for struggling students is one part of this particular challenge. The other part is the actual team collaboration that must occur. All professionals who will potentially serve students with spelling disabilities must understand the varied roles they may take in this process (American Speech–Language–Hearing Association, 2001). In regard to spelling instruction, team members may be involved in the planning and/or implementation of a prescriptive program for increasing students' spelling skills. They must all be aware of state and local guidelines and benchmarks to help students meet these requirements. They also must be aware of the classroom curricula, so as to help students access and succeed in the general education curriculum. To do this, they will need to understand the developmental aspects of spelling and how they relate to the demands of the classroom, and then teach students those developmental underpinnings or help modify the curriculum to meet the developmental level of the students. The team also must share a common instructional language so that clear communication occurs among team members as well as with the students they jointly serve (Moats, 2000). The challenge, then, is to focus attention on team approaches to spelling instruction, empirically and in everyday practices.

In conclusion, although spelling has been part of the school curriculum for hundreds of years, it has been the neglected child of education. In recent years, researchers and educators have come to understand its complex linguistic nature and are beginning to recognize the importance of an integrated understanding and instructional approach toward spelling. The more professionals have a shared definition, viewpoint, and understanding of spelling development and instruction, the more likely it will be that students will benefit from those professionals. In addition, as more school-based professionals further develop their understanding of spelling development and theory- and research-guided instruction, they will begin to understand the important contributions they can bring to forming students into literate citizens of the classroom and the community.

REFERENCES

Apel, K. (1999). Checks and balances: Keeping the science in our profession. *Language, Speech, and Hearing Services in Schools, 30*, 98–107.

Apel, K. (2002). Serving students with spoken and written language challenges: It's in the cards. *The ASHA Leader, 7*(1), 6–7.

Apel, K., & Masterson, J. (2001). Theory-guided spelling assessment and intervention: A case study. *Language, Speech, and Hearing Services in Schools, 32*, 182–194.

Apel, K., & Masterson, J. J. (2002, April). *Incorporation of linguistic properties and components for spelling*. Paper presented at the Rutgers Conference on Language and Literacy, New Brunswick, NJ.

Apel, K., Masterson, J. J., & Niessen, N. L. (2004). Spelling assessment frameworks. In C. A. Stone, E. R. Silliman, B. J. Ehren, & K. Apel (Eds.), *Handbook of language and literacy: Development and disorders* (pp. 644–660). New York: Guilford Press.

Apel, K., & Swank, L. K. (1999). Second chances: Improving decoding skills in the older student. *Language, Speech, and Hearing Services in Schools, 30*, 231–242.

American Speech–Language–Hearing Association. (2001). *Roles and responsibilities of speech–language pathologists with respect to reading and writing in children and adolescents: Position statement, guidelines, and technical report*. Rockville, MD: Author.

Bailet, L. L. (2004). Spelling instructional and intervention frameworks. In C. A. Stone, E. R. Silliman, B. J. Ehren, & K. Apel (Eds.), *Handbook of language and literacy: Development and disorders* (pp. 661–678). New York: Guilford Press.

Ball, E. W., & Blachman, B. A. (1991). Does phoneme awareness training in kindergarten make a difference in early word recognition and developmental spelling? *Reading Research Quarterly, 26*, 49–66.

Bear, D. R., Invernizzi, M., Templeton, S., & Johnson, F. (2000). *Words their way* (2nd ed.). Upper Saddle River, NJ: Merrill.

Bear, D. R., & Templeton, S. (1998). Explorations in developmental spelling: Foundations for learning and teaching phonics, spelling, and vocabulary. *The Reading Teacher, 52*(3), 222–242.

Berninger, V. W. (1999). Coordinating transcription and text generation in working memory during composing: Automatic and constructive processes. *Learning Disability Quarterly, 22*, 99–112.

Berninger, V. W. (2000). Development of language by hand and its connection with language by ear, mouth, and eye. *Topics in Language Disorders, 20*(3), 65–84.

Berninger, V. W., & Amtmann, D. (2003). Preventing written expression disabilities through early and continuing assessment and intervention for handwriting and/or spelling problems: Research into practice. In H. L. Swanson, K. R. Harris, & S. Graham (Eds.), *Handbook of learning disabilities* (pp. 345–363). New York: Guilford Press.

Berninger, V. W., Cartwright, A., Yates, C., Swanson, H. L., & Abbott, R. (1994). Developmental skills related to writing and reading acquisition in the intermediate grades: Shared and unique variance. *Reading and Writing: An Interdisciplinary Journal, 6,* 161–196.

Berninger, V. W., Nagy, W. E., Carlisle, J., Thomson, J., Hoffer, D., Abbott, S., & Johnson, C. (2003). Added value of morphology treatment for dyslexics in grades 4–6: Behavioral and brain evidence. In B. Foorman (Ed.), *Proceedings of the National Dyslexia Research Foundation Extraordinary Brain Conference on Instructional Interventions* (pp. 382–417). Timonium, MD: York Press.

Bourassa, D. C., & Treiman, R. (2001). Spelling development and disability: The importance of linguistic factors. *Language, Speech, and Hearing Services in Schools, 32,* 172–181.

Brooks, A., Vaughan, K., & Berninger, V. (1999). Tutorial interventions for writing disabilities: Comparison of transcription and text generation processes. *Learning Disability Quarterly, 22,* 183–190.

Butyniec-Thomas, J., & Woloshyn, V. E. (1997). The effects of explicit strategy and whole-language instruction on students' spelling ability. *Journal of Experimental Education, 65,* 293–302.

Carlisle, J. F. (1995). Morphological awareness and early reading achievement. In L. B. Feldman (Ed.), *Morphological aspects of language processing* (pp. 189–209). Mahwah, NJ: Erlbaum.

Cassar, M., & Treiman, R. (2004). Developmental variations in spelling: Comparing typical and poor spellers. In C. A. Stone, E. R. Silliman, B. J. Ehren, & K. Apel (Eds.), *Handbook of language and literacy: Development and disorders* (pp. 627–643). New York: Guilford Press.

Cunningham, P. M. (1998). The multisyllabic word dilemma: Helping students build meaning, spell, and read "big" words. *Reading and Writing Quarterly: Overcoming Learning Difficulties, 14,* 189–218.

Darch, C., Kim, S., Johnson, S., & James, H. (2000). The strategic spelling skills of students with learning disabilities: The results of two studies. *Journal of Instructional Psychology, 27*(1), 15–26.

Ehri, L. C. (2000). Learning to read and learning to spell: Two sides of a coin. *Topics in Language Disorders, 20*(3), 1–18.

Ehri, L. C., & Wilce, L. (1982). Recognition of spellings printed in lower and mixed case: Evidence for orthographic images. *Journal of Reading Behavior, 14,* 219–230.

Fey, M. E., & Johnson, B. W. (1998). Research to practice (and back again) in speech–language intervention. *Topics in Language Disorders, 18*(2), 23–34.

Fowler, A. E., & Lieberman, I. Y. (1995). The role of phonology and orthography in morphological awareness. In L. B. Feldman (Ed.), *Morphological aspects of language processing* (pp. 189–209). Mahwah, NJ: Erlbaum.

Fresch, M. J., Wheaton, A., & Zutell, J. B. (1998). Thinking aloud during spelling word sorts. *National Reading Conference Yearbook, 47*, 285–294.

Ganske, K. (2000). *Word journeys.* New York: Guilford Press

Glenn, P., & Hurley, S. (1993). Preventing spelling disabilities. *Child Language Teaching and Therapy, 9*, 1–12.

Graham, S. (2000). Should the natural learning approach replace spelling instruction? *Journal of Educational Psychology, 92*, 235–247.

Graham, S., Berninger, V., Abbott, R., Abbott, S., & Whitaker, D. (1997). The role of mechanics in composing of elementary students with learning disabilities: A new methodological approach. *Journal of Educational Psychology, 89*, 170–182.

Graham, S., Harris, K. R., & Loynachan, C. (1993). The basic vocabulary list. *Journal of Educational Research, 86*, 363–369.

Hall, D. P., Cunningham, P. M., & Cunningham, J. W. (1995). Multilevel spelling instruction in third grade classrooms. In K. A. Hinchman, D. L. Leu, & C. Kinzer (Eds.), *Perspectives on literacy research and practice* (pp. 384–389). Chicago: National Reading Conference.

Hayward, C. C. (1998). Monitoring spelling development. *The Reading Teacher, 51*(5), 444–447.

Heald-Taylor, G. (1998). Three paradigms of spelling instruction in grades 3 to 6. *The Reading Teacher, 51*, 404–413.

Henderson, E. (1990). *Teaching spelling.* Boston: Houghton Mifflin.

Hoien, T., Lundberg, I., Stanovich, K. E. & Bjaalid, I. (1995). Components of phonological awareness. *Reading and Writing, 7*, 171–188.

Hughes, M., & Searle, D. (1997). *The violent E and other tricky sounds: Learning to spell from kindergarten through grade 6.* York, ME: Stenhouse.

Ingram, D. (1998). Research–practice relationships in speech–language pathology. *Topics in Language Disorders, 18*(2), 1–9.

Johnson, A. P. (1998). Word class: Using thinking skills to enhance spelling instruction. *Reading Horizons, 38*, 257–265.

Johnston, F. (2001). Exploring classroom teachers' spelling practices and beliefs. *Reading Research and Instruction, 40*, 143–156.

Joseph, L. M. (2000). Developing first graders' phonemic awareness, word identification and spelling: A comparison of two contemporary phonic instructional approaches. *Reading Research and Instruction, 39*, 160–169.

Kelman, E., & Apel, K. (in press). The effects of a multiple linguistic, prescriptive approach to spelling instruction: A case study. *Communication Disorders Quarterly.*

Kromrey, J. D., & Foster-Johnson, L. (1996). Determining the efficacy of intervention: The use of effect sizes for data analysis in single-subject research. *Journal of Experimental Education, 65*, 73–93.

Lyster, S. H. (2002). The effects of morphological versus phonological awareness training in kindergarten on reading development. *Reading and Writing: An Interdisciplinary Journal, 15*, 261–294.

Masterson, J. J., & Apel, K. (2000). Spelling assessment: Charting a path to optimal intervention. *Topics in Language Disorders, 20*(3), 50–65.

Masterson, J. J., Apel, K., & Wasowicz, J. (2002) *SPELL: Spelling performance evaluation for language and literacy.* Evanston, IL: Learning By Design.

Masterson, J. J., & Crede, L. A. (1999). Learning to spell: Implications for assessment and intervention. *Language, Speech, and Hearing Services in Schools, 30,* 243–254.

Moats, L. C. (2000). What is the role of the speech–language pathologist in assessing and facilitating spelling skills? *Topics in Language Disorders, 20*(3), 85–87.

Muter, V., Hulme, C., Snowling, M., & Taylor, S. (1997). Segmentation, not rhyming, predicts early progress in learning to read. *Journal of Experimental Child Psychology, 65,* 370–396.

Nation, K., & Hulme, C. (1997). Phonemic segmentation, not onset-rime segmentation, predicts early reading and spelling skills. *Reading Research Quarterly, 32,* 154–167.

Post, Y. V., Carreker, S., & Holland, G. (2001). The spelling of final letter patterns: A comparison of instruction at the level of the phoneme and rime. *Annals of Dyslexia, 51,* 121–146.

Reece, C., & Treiman, R. (2001). Children's spelling of syllabic /r/ and letter–name vowels: Broadening the study of spelling development. *Applied Psycholinguistics, 22,* 139–165.

Rymer, R., & Williams, C. (2000). "Wasn't that a spelling word?": Spelling instruction and young children's writing. *Language Arts, 77*(3), 241–249.

Schneider, W., Roth, E., & Ennemoser, M. (2000). Training phonological skills and letter knowledge in children at risk for dyslexia: A comparison of three kindergarten intervention programs. *Journal of Educational Psychology, 92,* 284–295.

Scott, C. M. (2000). Principles and methods of spelling instruction: Applications for poor spellers. *Topics in Language Disorders, 20*(3), 66–82.

Singer, B. D. & Bashir, A. S. (2004). Developmental variations in writing composition skills. In C. A. Stone, E. R. Silliman, B. J. Ehren, & K. Apel (Eds.), *Handbook of language and literacy: Development and disorders* (pp. 559–582). New York: Guilford Press.

Sulzby, E. (1996). Roles of oral and written language as children approach literacy. In C. Pontecorvo, M. Orsolini, B. Burge, & L. B. Resnick (Eds.), *Children's early text construction* (pp. 25–46). Mahwah, NJ: Erlbaum.

Templeton, S. (2003). Spelling: Best ideas–best practices. *Voices from the Middle, 10*(4), 48–49.

Templeton, S., & Morris, D. (2000). Spelling. In M. Kamil, P. Mosenthal, P. D. Pearson, & R. Barr (Eds.), *Handbook of reading research* (Vol. 3, pp. 525–543). Mahwah, NJ: Erlbaum.

Treiman, R., & Bourassa, D. C. (2000). The development of spelling skills. *Topics in Language Disorders, 20*(3), 19–36.

Treiman, R., & Cassar, M. (1996). Effects of morphology on children's spelling of final consonant clusters. *Journal of Experimental Psychology, 63,* 141–170.

Treiman, R., Cassar, M., & Zukowski, A. (1994). What types of linguistic information do children use in spelling?: The case of flaps. *Child Development, 65,* 1310–1329.

Turbill, J. (2000). Developing a spelling conscience. *Language Arts, 77,* 209–217.

Wasowicz, J., Apel, K., & Masterson, J. J. (2003). Spelling assessment: Applying research in school-based practice. *Perspectives on School-Based Issues Newsletter, 4*(1), 3–7.

Wasowicz, J., Apel, K., Masterson, J. J., & Whitney, A. (in press). *SPELL-links to reading and writing.* Evanston, IL: Learning By Design.

Weber, W. R., & Henderson, E. H. (1989). A computer-based program of word study: Effects on reading and spelling. *Reading Psychology, 10,* 157–162.

White, O. R., & Haring, N. G. (1980). *Exceptional teaching* (2nd ed.). Columbus, OH: Merrill.

Wright, K. A. (2000). Weekly spelling meetings: Improving spelling instruction through classroom-based inquiry. *Language Arts, 77*(3), 218–223.

Zutell, J. (1998). Word sorting: A developmental spelling approach to word study for delayed readers. *Reading and Writing Quarterly: Overcoming Learning Difficulties, 14,* 219–238.

PART IV

❧

Integrating Education and Clinical Practices

12

❧

Putting Humpty Dumpty Together Again

What's Right with Betsy

ELAINE R. SILLIMAN
LOUISE C. WILKINSON
ROBIN L. DANZAK

"I do better expressing myself in writing than orally because, if I write, I think . . . and I can stop without trying to shoot it out really quick. . . . It's hard to think and talk at the same time to let it all be expressive, like do it smoothly. Like writing, you can go back and change like this paragraph I want first, second, third. Then talking you won't understand me 'cause I'm like confusing you 'cause I was talking about this. Then I switched to this that should have been first and then. So, in writing." (Betsy, age 17 years)

Betsy is a telling case of the struggles and victories of a youngster who has grappled with a language learning disability for most of her 17 years.[1] Her story is a fitting way to conclude this volume because she represents how a child with motivation and resilience can confront the educational and interpersonal obstacles she has experienced. Her story, which predates the passage of the No Child Left Behind Act of 2001 (hereafter NCLB) and the 1997 Individuals with Disabilities Education Act (hereafter IDEA; see Silliman & Wilkinson, Chapter 1, this volume), is a metaphor for the ongoing debates in theory and practice about the meanings of a *learning* disability versus a *language* disability. Her chronicle also illustrates the value of cross-disciplinary cooperation in the service of a child's language and literacy needs and crystallizes the research directions that evidence-based practices might take in melding together different research frames.

In a manner of speaking, Betsy's story reflects the Humpty Dumpty tale. Although it is not generally known, Humpty Dumpty was an atypically large egg prone to taking risks. In his eagerness to see the king and his court as they returned to the palace, Humpty sat on a high stonewall. Despite warnings from the king's daughter to take care so that he would not fall, the excited Humpty forgot caution and crashed to the ground, shattering into so many pieces that he could never be put "together again." Humpty Dumpty's tale captures how Betsy, a child with a fractured system, long struggled to keep her self-esteem from shattering. If the individual needs of students with language learning problems are to be met in a comprehensive way, Betsy's story of self-discovery is a motivating one because it makes a persuasive case for joining together the preventive educational services that have been fragmented for many years.

To tell her story and its implications, we connect Betsy's patterns of development and her educational history to three issues that surround all children with language learning disabilities. These issues are the ambiguous definition of a language learning disability, its causes, and its long-term outcomes. First, we examine Betsy's changing profile from grade 1 in 1986 to grade 6 in 1991. Next, we allow Betsy herself to speak about her journey through school, offering insights about her strengths and needs in language and literacy. Finally, we offer some future directions for achieving collaborative and integrated services for students like Betsy.

BETSY'S STORY

Not Ready to Leave the Nest: The Preschool Years

Betsy, a healthy neonate, was the second of two children born to a middle-class family. Her motor skills followed a pattern of normal development; however, her language was delayed and her speech was unintelligible. Betsy's mother reported that throughout early childhood Betsy became easily frustrated by her inability to express herself adequately. This frustration was often manifested as violent temper tantrums. At age 3 years and 2 months, at her mother's request, Betsy was referred by her pediatrician to a speech–language pathologist who identified a severe articulation disorder. Betsy then attended private therapy sessions for her speech and vocabulary development until the age of 5 years, when she entered kindergarten. At that point, Betsy began to receive services from the school-based speech–language pathologists for her "articulation," which had since improved in intelligibility. The continuing concentration on Betsy's speech production beginning at age 3 years and 2 months, while not inappropriate, was not sufficient. As Betsy progressed through the preschool years and early elementary grades, this narrow focus became symbolic of many lost opportunities for preventing more serious problems with language and literacy learning.

Language Impairment and a Learning Disability: Specific and General Views, Causes, and Outcomes

Betsy's developmental profile through the preschool years is consistent with the "late talker" pattern (Rescorla, 2000; Thal, Reilly, Seibert, Jeffries, & Fenson, 2004), or a preschool-age child who appears normal in all other ways except for an unexpected delay in speech. At the same time, her profile captures the clash between two perspectives about the diagnostic definition of a language disability or impairment, the *specific view* and the *general view*, as well as portraying two controversies about the causes and long-term consequences of a language learning disability.

The Controversy about "Specific" in Specific Language Impairment

The prevailing view frames language impairment as a disruption in the system of verbal communication specific to the linguistic system. More explicitly, despite normal development in the nonverbal domain (Bishop & Clarkson, 2003), *specific language impairment* (SLI) is defined as "'unexpected and unexplained variations' in language acquisition" (Rice, 2003, p. 63). Figure 12.1 displays two debates about the meaning of SLI.

The first controversy is "big modularity" (Schaeffer, 2004, p. 135). In the modularity perspective, syntax, or grammar, is viewed as a specialized innate system, or *module*, separate from other cognitive processes (de Villiers, 2003) (see Figure 12.1). The reason offered for this specialization is that a system is dedicated to the processing of grammar (Elman et al., 1996). Because the brain is organized in a unique way for language, SLI is then considered as a distinctive disorder because it is the verb system through which tense is marked that is selectively disrupted (de Villiers, 2003; Rice, 2003). This selective disruption of tensing is speculated to have broad ramifications for basic development of grammatical morphology well beyond the preschool years. *Grammatical morphemes* are linguistic devices for indicating subject–verb agreement when agreement is obligatory in Standard American English. Examples of these required tense inflections include –s and –ed as in "Paul walks home," when referring to a present, ongoing action, and "Paul and Michael walked home," when referring to a

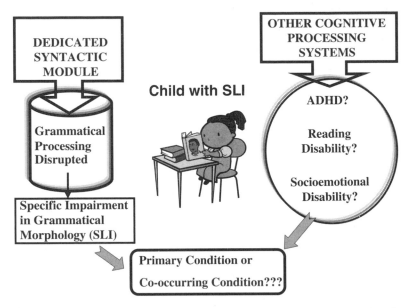

FIGURE 12.1. The modularity and co-occurrence controversies associated with the specific view of specific language impairment (SLI).

past action. Disruptions in the timing of the acquisition of these grammatical tense markers may represent a general delay, or a selective "delay-within-delay" (Rice, 2003, p. 71), in linguistic development.

A detailed discussion of modularity is beyond the scope of this chapter. Nevertheless, on first appearances and consistent with the SLI perspective, it seemed that all that was "wrong" with Betsy during her preschool years was her delayed language production in combination with her severe expressive phonological difficulties. Not all agree with the SLI view. For example, Elman et al. (1996) suggest that the more interesting question is *not* the innateness of a grammar module, but the extent to which brain structure for language and speech becomes progressively more specialized over time by virtue of children's continuous interactions with the talk that serves as the input for further brain development. In addition, an important clinical question that goes beyond the innateness controversy concerns the reliable prediction of transient delays in language development that may resolve versus language difficulties that will persist. By age 3 years and 2 months, Betsy so concerned her mother that she wanted an evaluation by a speech–language pathologist for Betsy's speech problems, not her problems with language development. Recent research (Bishop, Price, Dale, & Plomin, 2003) indicates that a parent who seeks professional services for significant speech difficulties as a primary concern by the time a child is age 4 years may be a predictor of the boundary between transient language delays and chronic problems in language development that have a genetic component.

The Co-Occurrence Controversy

A second controversy about SLI is one that also overlaps with the big modularly account. As shown in Figure 12.1, this is the co-occurrence issue in which two or more impairments appear together with an overlap of symptoms (Kaplan, Dewey, Crawford, & Wilson, 2001). The question of interest is whether the language impairment is the primary condition, which implies causality, or whether it coincidentally occurs at the same time with another impairment that then influences the "look" of the SLI (Botting & Conti-Ramsden, 2004; de Villiers, 2003). One example of co-occurrence would be SLI and attention-deficit/hyperactivity disorder (ADHD), or the inability to readily self-regulate one's learning (Westby, 2004). A second illustration is the overlap between a language impairment and a child's ongoing struggles with decoding and reading comprehension (Catts, Fey, Zhang, & Tomblin, 1999; Catts, Fey, Tomblin, & Zhang, 2002). A third example is the coexistence of SLI and socioemotional difficulties, such as the violent temper tantrums that Betsy's mother described her as exhibiting when others did not readily understand her. Donahue and Pearl (2003) note the complexity of the problem of unraveling whether persisting language learning difficulties are "causes, outcomes, correlates, or simply coincidental with . . . social interactional difficulties, at any one point in time" (p. 92) (for further discussion of social interactional issues, see Donahue & Foster, Chapter 7, this volume).

A radically different perspective on the co-occurrence issue reworks the old notion of minimal brain dysfunction into a new concept based on neurobiological research. What appear to be associations between two developmental conditions, such as a reading disability and ADHD, may actually reflect varying expressions of atypical brain development (Gilger & Kaplan, 2001; Gilger & Wise, 2004; Kaplan et al., 2001). In effect, based on the nature and quality of gene–environment interactions, atypical brain development may be evidenced in multiple ways across children in a variety of behavioral areas, including the social, emotional, attentional, linguistic, and academic domains. One important point is that co-occurrence of disabilities seems to be the rule, not the exception, because pure cases of a disability seldom occur (Gilger & Kaplan, 2001; van Geert, 2004). Often the overlapping diagnostic labels that a child receives, such as "SLI and ADHD" or "dyslexia and ADHD," are arbitrary because they originate from the professionals who see the child (Bishop, 2004). A second critical point is that the term "atypical brain development" does not describe a disorder but instead references an integrative concept about etiology that then is expressed as a "scatter of strengths and weaknesses" (Kaplan et al., 2001, p. 563) depending on how a child's genetic makeup interacts with his or her unique experiences and the compensatory strategies that he or she develops (Bishop, 2004). In other words, there are no sharp boundaries between seemingly different impairments, such as a language impairment and a reading disability. When children like Betsy are viewed through a multidimensional continuum of strengths and weaknesses, rather than as "a category of disability," the unevenness of their language skills (Leonard, 1998) may become more understandable as individual profiles that reflect varying gene–experiential interactions. Different instructional and intervention implications should also emerge from a more multidimensional view.

The "Specific" as Part of Broader General Systems Interactions

In stark contrast with those who promote the SLI perspective, Bates (2004) views the same pattern of disruption in oral language development as evidence of a more *general* involvement of information-processing systems that are broadly distributed in the brain and restrict how linguistic representations can be employed for an infinite variety of purposes. As shown in Figure 12.2, variations in cognitive information-processing systems—for example, the speed of processing or encoding events in memory—may reflect alternate types of brain organization that are not related directly to language, but that nevertheless can affect the timing of brain events necessary for "on-schedule" language development (Bates, Vicari, & Trauner, 1999). Disturbances in the timing of interactions among these general information-process systems are represented as gaps in Figure 12.2. For example, Bates (1997) acknowledges that grammatical morphology can be disrupted in some children; however, disturbances in grammatical morphology may selectively occur not because the verb tense system is specifically impaired, but because this linguistic aspect is "a weak link in the processing chain, one that is highly likely to fall apart when things go awry" (p. 467).

To expand further on Figure 12.2, Bates and Roe (2001) offer a vivid account of the "Humpty Dumpty Principle," or what happens when things go awry and cannot readily be put together again. As a backdrop for this view of fractured development, a brief journey through the process of emerging, and well-timed, word learning is required. When a child initially attempts to break into the linguistic code, he or she relies on extracting and storing critical perceptual details in the acoustic stream, such as " 'the little sounds' and 'little words' " (Elman et al., 1996, p. 309). According to Bates et al. (1999), this major activity engages the left temporal cortex and is cru-

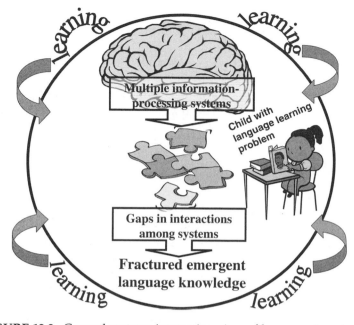

FIGURE 12.2. General systems interaction view of language impairment.

cial for the child's eventual production of new word meaning—for example, when the child is attempting to "fast map" the initial meaning of *hammer* as a new concept. While these perceptual bits may contribute to the child's initial connections between sound and meaning, these bits cannot stand alone for strong linkages to develop. They must be integrated over multiple sources of information in order to eventually derive the patterns that indicate the conventional meaning, an "emergent" process that draws extensively on right-hemisphere resources (Elman et al., 1996). The multiple sources requiring integration involve (1) visual information about the shape and size of a hammer; (2) tactile information about how a hammer feels, as well as knowledge of its functions and movements; and (3) prior experiences with a hammer, including emotions connected with hitting one's thumb accidentally with a hammer. In Bates's (2004) analysis, producing a new word requires greater perceptual analysis than does recognizing a word whose meaning is typically supported by the surrounding social and physical context; therefore, the bias of the left temporal cortex toward perceptual detail is not specific to language or even to hearing, but is a reflection of brain systems with enormous computing power that are "sculpted" (p. 249) by learning, including language learning.

As we mentioned earlier, the "gaps" indicated on Figure 12.2 are the results of disruptions to the timing of interactions among (nonlinguistic) brain infrastructures, their neural substrates, and experiences that propel brain changes. These disturbances then affect how adequately cortical regions specialize for specific cognitive functions based on their engagement in particular activities, like language learning (Bates & Roe, 2001). In this general systems interaction perspective, caution is warranted in assuming that "a particular neural correlate of language impairment reflects the behavioral state of the system. That is, the brain may still be in a relatively immature state because the relevant experience-driven events have not yet taken place" (Bates, Thal, Finlay, & Clancy, 2003, p. 37). In Bates's (2004) opinion, "we may never observe a true case of specific language impairment. If language is impaired in some fashion, then we should always be able to detect at least some subset of nonlinguistic skills that are also impaired" (p. 252), such as symbolic play, spatial imagery in older children, nonverbal attention, working memory, and planning (Bates, 1997; Berninger & Richards, 2002; Bishop, 2004). Another nonlinguistic domain that might show some degree of impairment is inferencing, which relies on the integration of multiple sources of information for both oral and reading comprehension and may be independent of working memory to some extent (Cain & Oakhill, 1998; Cain, Oakhill, Barnes, & Bryant, 2001; Cain, Oakhill, & Bryant, 2004).

An assumption is that Betsy entered the world with brain systems that were fractured. As some suggest (Edwards & Lahey, 1998; Maillart, Schelstraete, & Hupet, 2004), it may be that, as a preschooler trying to break into the linguistic code, she had difficulty formulating solid phonological representations from the perceptual bits in the acoustic stream, which then affected her vocabulary development, and ultimately expressed itself in her early unintelligible speech. Alternately, Betsy experienced protracted problems with the efficient integration of multiple sources of information, which impacted on her development of an interconnected repertoire of conceptual and linguistic knowledge and subsequently hindered her emergent inferencing skills. The two possibilities are not mutually exclusive, however, making it a prime challenge for Betsy, like Humpty Dumpty, to put the splintered pieces back together again through her learning experiences.

Finally, a practical point about the two conflicting perspectives on language impairment is worth mention. Berninger (2003) notes that, regardless of the perspective on the nature of a language impairment, the often unrecognized learning difficulties that children with this condition experience during the school-age years has resulted in their becoming "the most underidentified and underserved group at present" (p. 27).

What Is "Specific" in Specific Learning Disabilities?

Resolving these conflicting frames is also essential for understanding whether a *language disability* and a *reading disability* are two co-occurring and independent conditions, as assumed by the phonological core deficit account (Keogh, 2002; Lyon, Shaywitz, & Shaywitz, 2003; Stanovich, 2000; Torgesen, 2004), or whether they are intertwined beyond the well-documented domain of phonological processing (Dickinson & McCabe, 2001; Dickinson, McCabe, Anastasopoulos, Peisner-Feinberg, & Poe, 2003). The phonological core deficit theory continues to dominate as the primary "language-based" explanation for a reading disability (see also Troia, Chapter 4, this volume), which is typically equated with dyslexia.

A new working definition of dyslexia now refers to this condition as a *specific* learning disability that is the product of three unexpected, but distinctive and interrelated, breakdowns in learning to read (Lyon et al., 2003):

- *Word recognition* as defined by the accurate and fluent identification of real words
- *Spelling*, which entails the translation and encoding of phonemic information into an integrated code of phonological, orthographic, and morphological knowledge (Cassar & Treiman, 2004)
- *Decoding* as defined by the rate of the oral reading of nonwords wherein meaning is relatively absent and only the phonological structure is available for accurate pronunciation

This cluster of difficulties is said to differentiate the phonological core deficit underlying a specific reading impairment from other kinds of learning disabilities that may co-occur with a reading impairment such as SLI, but whose characteristics differ in theory from those of a particular problem with reading and writing (including spelling and handwriting). Moreover, dyslexia, as a neurogenetic impairment viewed on a behavioral level, is considered a condition that is nonresponsive over a reasonable period of time to scientifically based instruction implemented "by well-prepared teachers" (Lyon et al., 2003, p. 9; see also Silliman & Wilkinson, Chapter 1, this volume, for the highly qualified teacher controversy arising from the NCLB legislation). Because of this nonresponsiveness, significant problems with vocabulary learning and reading comprehension become predictable.

Given this cluster of difficulties, two interrelated questions arise about the extent to which a reading disability occurs in "pure" form.

1. *How common is a pure type of dyslexia (specific reading disability)?* An often cited, research-based estimate is that, in grades 2 and 3 (Shaywitz,

Shaywitz, Fletcher, & Escobar, 1990), dyslexia "affects one child in five . . . [in other words] . . . when administered a test of intelligence and a reading test individually . . . 20% of children were reading below their age, grade, or level of ability" (Shaywitz, 2003, p. 30). However, there is longitudinal evidence indicating that, to the contrary, a pure form of dyslexia is relatively uncommon. Using some measures comparable to those used by Shaywitz et al. (1990) combined with oral language measures, Catts et al. (1999) found that only 14% of grade 2 poor readers had experienced difficulties with phonological processing alone in kindergarten, suggesting that the phonological core deficit as a primary explanation for a reading disability may have limited scope. In comparison, 37% of poor readers in grade 2 demonstrated both phonological-processing and oral language difficulties in kindergarten, while 22% had oral language problems only, and 27% did not show either problem in kindergarten.

2. *To what extent do the key diagnostic features of dyslexia and SLI overlap?* The second question derives from research-supported assessment in the differential diagnosis of dyslexia and concerns whether key features of this differential diagnosis are specific only to dyslexia. According to Berninger and O'Donnell (in press), one diagnostic marker of dyslexia is that a child's phonological representations are not well specified, which then affects the efficiency of the child's phonemic awareness as well as affecting the ultimate efficiency of decoding. A second diagnostic marker is characterized by inefficiencies in verbal working memory, which we will return to shortly.

However, Berninger and O'Donnell (in press) propose that children with dyslexia differ from children with a language learning disability along a continuum of severity. The claim is that, in addition to problems with phonological representations, children with a language learning disability also have distinctive problems with morphological and syntactic awareness in the oral domain, unlike those with dyslexia.

In terms of morphological awareness, one pattern pertains to problems with the morphological representation of derived meanings, such as how two words are related or unrelated in meaning through suffixes. For example, "Does *quickly* come from *quick*?" "Does *mother* come from *moth*?" (Nagy, Berninger, Abbott, Vaughn, & Vermeulen, 2003, p. 733). This task requires phonological segmentation of the word and the ability to analyze whether the segmented portion is related in meaning to the target word (Carlisle & Fleming, 2003). Similarly, as children with a language learning disability enter the upper elementary grades, they may encounter significant difficulty in the generation of morphologically complex words that require the simultaneous integration of phonological, syntactic, and semantic (morphological) relationships—for example, "*Major*. He won the vote by a _____" (Carlisle, 2000, p. 187).

The second pattern that Berninger and O'Donnell (in press) cite for distinguishing dyslexia from a language learning disability involves problems with more explicit syntactic processing, such as the verbatim repetition of sentences that increase in length and complexity—for example, "*Was the van preceded by the ambulance? The boy stopped to buy some milk, even though he was late for class*" (Semel, Wiig, & Secord, 1995). While this kind of task does call for the activation of syntactic knowledge, it also requires the activation of verbal working memory strategies for accurate recall, thus calling into question whether this task involves only syntactic processing. For example, in children at least age 11 years old with oral language status in the normal range of variability, sentence repetition appeared to identify more accurately those with relatively resolved SLI histories than did nonword repetition tasks (Conti-Ramsden, Botting, & Faragher, 2001). Reduced performance on sentence repetition also characterized younger children with poor reading comprehension who had unrecognized oral language problems (Nation, Clarke, Marshall, & Durand, 2004). These outcomes suggest that protracted inefficiencies with verbal working memory also contribute to performance on syntactic processing tasks.

As we mentioned previously, the second hallmark of dyslexia also pertains to problems with verbal working memory, which then limit children's ability to translate letters into sound readily and to maintain appropriate attention to key aspects of language processing. Both of these features clearly overlap with the SLI perspective: children's difficulty in encoding or storing new oral word meanings is related to problems in verbal (and/or phonological) working memory. The outcome is the formation of fuzzy phonological and morphosyntactic representations that then affect the scope and depth of their vocabulary learning (e.g., Conti-Ramsden, 2003; Dollaghan & Campbell, 1998; Edwards & Lahey, 1998; Leonard, 1998; Rice, Cleave, & Oetting, 2000) and their sentence comprehension (Montgomery, 2002a, 2002b).

Recently, studies of SLI have been extended to reading comprehension. What must be kept in mind in evaluating results are variables that can affect the validity of findings, such as the demographic characteristics of the samples and the cutoffs set to differentiate normal from atypical performance. In one study, more than half of the children, ages 7 to 9 years, with specific reading disability were found to have an SLI (McArthur, Hogben, Edwards, Heath, & Mengler, 2000). Similarly, about 50% of the children with an SLI were also found to have a reading impairment. In a second study, children with poor reading comprehension (mean age = 8½ years), without any residual phonological processing problems as measured by phonemic segmentation tasks, were found to have "relative weaknesses across a range of [oral] language skills that are important to reading comprehension, from understanding the meaning of individual words to understanding figurative expressions" (Nation et al., 2004, p. 208). One suggestion is that inferencing might be a common breakdown that bridges both language comprehension and reading comprehension (Cain et al., 2004). However, there is a caution for the design of studies investigating the relationship between types of oral language skills and reading comprehension. Unless problems with oral reading fluency are ruled out with measures of rate and accuracy—for example, the child who orally reads slowly but accurately—difficulties may be falsely attributed to reading comprehension, such as inferencing failures, when the root problem is the overall fluency of word recognition (Duke, Pressley, & Hilden, 2004). Neither the McArthur et al. (2000) nor the Nation et al. (2004) studies clearly eliminated rate and accuracy factors as possible confounding variables (see Whitaker, Gambrell, & Morrow, Chapter 5, this volume, for exemplary instructional practices in teaching children to read).

On the one hand, this overlap between characteristic indicators of dyslexia and SLI may be coincidental. On the other hand, the notable similarity between the diagnostic portraits of dyslexia and SLI—or a language learning disability—may possibly represent related expressions of atypical brain development (Gilger & Kaplan, 2001; Gilger & Wise, 2004; Kaplan et al., 2001) or a more general involvement of certain cortical functions that remain less specialized for particular language activities (Bates, 2004). Given their different diagnostic and intervention outcomes, these three possibilities remain to be explored. Applied to Betsy, the important questions to consider relate to what can be predicted for her as she enters formal schooling and how her profile of strengths and weaknesses may change over time.

What Can We Predict for Betsy as She Steps from the Nest?

Consensus does not yet exist that almost all children with reading problems likely have a "fundamental impairment in language, beginning in the early preschool years" (McCardle, Scarborough, & Catts, 2001, p. 235). What can be agreed on, however, is that the profiles of a language impairment and a reading disability, including their severity, will vary within children and may take different forms depending on the nature of interactions between genetic and experiential factors (Snowling, Gallagher, & Frith, 2003). Some children may chronically struggle with new vocabulary learning and decoding fluency, while others may be continually challenged by the semantic, syntactic, and inferential demands of text comprehension due to the underdevelopment of these synergistic processes in the oral domain (Carlisle & Rice, 2002; McGregor, 2004; Scott, 2004; see also Gillam & Gorman, Chapter 3, this volume).

Based on a variety of prospective longitudinal studies in the United States and Great Britain, including twin studies, it is now well established that a preschool-age child whose delayed language or severe phonological impairment[2] does not resolve by kindergarten entry, like Betsy, is at least five to six times more likely to be at risk for a language learning disability and subsequent academic problems than peers without any visible evidence of a language delay (Bird, Bishop, & Freeman, 1995; Bishop et al., 2003; Botting, Faragher, Simkin, Knox, & Conti-Ramsden, 2001; Catts et al., 1999; Catts et al., 2002; Felsenfeld, Broen, & McGue, 1994; Johnson et al., 1999; Rescorla, 2000, 2002; Stothard, Snowling, Bishop, Chipchase, & Kaplan, 1998; Thal et al., 2004). Regardless of how the disability is expressed, the combination of a quality curriculum and its early introduction (Berninger & O'Donnell, in press) plays a pivotal role in moderating the effects of a language-based disability on educational outcomes in reading, writing, and spelling (see Silliman & Wilkinson, Chapter 1, this volume; Silliman, Wilkinson, & Brea-Spahn, 2004).

Trying to Be a Good Egg, but Anxious about Doing So: The Elementary Years

Betsy entered kindergarten in 1984 when the whole language approach was the dominant method for teaching children to read in her school district. As we noted earlier, she continued to receive speech services in kindergarten for articulation. By the end of grade 1, when Betsy was 7 years, 3 months old, her grade 1 teacher referred her for a school psychological evaluation. According to the school psychologist's report, the reason for the referral was the teacher's concerns that, although Betsy had made "good progress" and was ready for grade 2, she had difficulties in learning "a series of items, such as the alphabet, understanding new skills and concepts, expressing her ideas, and phrasing questions." In addition, the teacher said that Betsy "sometimes forgets almost immediately what she has seen or heard, and has difficulty following oral directions." In terms of her coping skills, the teacher found that Betsy appeared anxious at times and tended to have perfectionist tendencies. There was no mention of what Betsy did "right."

Given the current stress on the prevention of reading failure, one can only wonder how Betsy may have responded at that time to a comprehensive program of preventive intervention in her first-grade classroom. In the best of all possible worlds, this program would have been crafted to her oral language and basic reading needs and delivered collaboratively by an

educational team knowledgeable about "oral and written language structure, developmental sequences in oral and written language learning, and
the ways in which speech and print can be problematic for children" (Moats,
2004, p. 274). Instead, Betsy was placed in the position of waiting to fail.

A Profile of Uneven Abilities

From the end of grade 1, when Betsy was first referred for special education services, to grade 6, her first year in middle school, she displayed increasing mismatches between her considerable intellectual abilities and her
proficiency as a reader, writer, and speller. Most likely, this widening gap
was an outcome of at least two variables. One concerned the increasing
metacognitive and metalinguistic demands that schooling requires for full
participation in the academic discourse of the classroom and textbooks. The
other variable involved the regular and special education instruction in
which Betsy participated. Both functioned on Betsy's behalf as separate
entities with goals that did not necessarily relate to Betsy's changing needs.

- *Intellectual ability*. At the end of grade 1, based on the school psychologist's evaluation of her intellectual potential, Betsy attained a performance score of 124, a verbal score of 119, and a full-scale score of 124,
indicating that she was functioning at the 94th percentile intellectually
relative to chronological age. This suggested that she had developed sufficient conceptual knowledge, including vocabulary skills, to achieve such
high scores. Obviously, Betsy was bright.
- *Academic achievement in reading, vocabulary, spelling, and grammar*. At
the time of her original referral at the end of grade 1, based on a basic skills
measure that the school psychologist administered, Betsy's word recognition and spelling skills were equivalent to the beginning of grade 2. Table
12.1 shows Betsy's subsequent academic achievement from grades 2 to 6
on the nationally normed comprehensive assessment program that her
school district administered to all students beginning in grade 2.[3] Four
trends can be discerned from the scores: (1) Although her scores declined
significantly over time, Betsy still managed to score consistently within
normal ranges of variability on the vocabulary and grammar portions of
the comprehensive assessment (vocabulary was assessed as part of the
reading comprehension measure); (2) grade 3 was a hallmark for her in
reading comprehension, spelling, and grammar; (3) by grade 5, her spelling skills were no longer advancing; and (4) by grade 6, she had reached
the cutoff between the normal range of variability in reading comprehension for grade-level and below-grade-level skill.
- *Oral language ability*. Unfortunately, the only available results from
oral language assessments consisted of a single reevaluation conducted in

TABLE 12.1. Betsy's Achievement in Reading Comprehension (Including Vocabulary) and Language Arts (Spelling and Grammar) on the Comprehensive Assessment Program from Grade 2 (CA 8; 2) to Grade 6 (CA 12; 2) Administered by Her School District (Scores Are Reported in Percentiles)

Grade	Reading comprehension	Vocabulary	Spelling	Grammar
2[a]	58	61	20	75
3[b]	68	34	53	90
4	51	75	51	50
5	39	52	5	44
6	25	40	7[c]	48

[a]Decoding (word attack skills) was not assessed beyond grade 2. Betsy scored in the 68th percentile.

[b]Beginning with grade 3, percentiles reported were national percentiles (local percentiles were unreported).

[c]Assessment of derivational morphology (affixes) did not begin until grade 6. Betsy's percent correct in this area was 33%, below the national average percent correct of 42%. Her percentage of correct vowel spellings was 71% (only vowels were assessed at grade 6), which was equivalent to the national percent correct average of 72%.

grade 6 when Betsy was 12 years, 3 months old, and in her first year of middle school. By this time in her school career, Betsy was still in a general education classroom and had been receiving pullout resource services for 5½ years for language impairment and a specific learning disability. Two general language measures and two additional measures of vocabulary comprehension and vocabulary production were administered.

On one of the language measures, Betsy performed within the lower limits of –1 standard deviation on the receptive (comprehension) subtests (standard score = 89). Her major area of weakness was inferring relationships within semantic categories—for example, "Which words go together: *eagle, wing, hand*." On the expressive (production) subtests, she scored below –1 standard deviation (standard score = 70), experiencing the most difficulties with formulating "compound and complex sentences incorporating age-appropriate vocabulary" and in recalling sentences increasing in length and complexity. As we noted earlier, children with superficially resolved SLI histories who manage by age 11 years to score within normal ranges on certain standardized language measures may continue to perform below expectations on sentence repetition tasks (Conti-Ramsden et al., 2001). On the second language measure, a similar pattern was found for resolving sentence ambiguity and formulating sentences that fit particular situations. Betsy had less difficulty with making pragmatic, or social, inferences, which drew more on her world knowledge of conventional social behaviors and required less demanding metalinguistic processing of relational and morphosyntactic patterns. These configurations are consistent with characteristics of SLI, as well as the Berninger and O'Donnell (in press) profile of a language learning disability. Finally, on both of the general vocabulary measures, Betsy scored within the normal range of variability; however, neither of these measures required that she understood or produced multiple meanings.

Sitting on the Wall, Waiting to Fall

The conclusion by the diagnostic speech–language pathologist was that, despite "making steady progress in language processing and production, Betsy continues to present the profile of a student experiencing significant deficits in the development of receptive and expressive language skills." The recommendation was to continue Betsy in the language intervention resource program. In other words, Betsy's eligibility for special education services beginning in grade 2 was based on the considerable gap between her high intellectual level and her average to below-average performance on standardized language measures.

Moreover, in grade 1 her desire to achieve (the "perfectionism" that her teacher described) combined with her fear of failure provoked a metamorphosis. By grade 6, the diagnostic speech–language pathologist now described Betsy as "becoming easily frustrated and giving up at times." It seemed that trying to be a good egg was no longer worth the effort. As she approached adolescence, Betsy, like Humpty Dumpty, appeared poised to take a big fall off the educational achievement ladder. Now that we have an overview of how professionals saw Betsy, the next section focuses on what we can learn from Betsy's own perspectives on her strengths and struggles as a communicator and a learner.

BETSY'S PERSONAL JOURNEY

As Betsy's story continued from grade 6, she managed to "squeak by" academically until grade 10, where the academic demands, especially in social studies and science, proved to be more than she could handle. For example, she "hated" reading in middle and high school because her reading was slow, a fluency factor that must have significantly influenced her reading comprehension as shown in her decreasing performance over time on the annual comprehensive assessment measure (see Table 12.1). According to Betsy's description of reading, "It's just so slow, so slow. Like I read it once and it's just words and I have to read it again to get the pictures, 'cause I'm so worried that I get it mixed up." In grade 10 Betsy became withdrawn and often spoke of dropping out of school because she felt that she did not belong there. School officials, hoping to keep Betsy in school, asked her if she was willing to attend an alternative public high school designed for potential dropouts who were struggling with the academic and social demands of a traditional high school, and she agreed with this plan. At the same time that Betsy was experiencing internal turmoil about her lack of membership in the high school community, her mother characterized Betsy as a social individual who made and sustained friendships. She also saw Betsy as a creative and imaginative person who expressed herself through sculpture and writing. It was through her active pursuit of writing, particularly when experiencing emotional conflict about her feelings and identity, that Betsy produced an extensive body of work.

Most relevant for our purposes here, over an 8-year period, Betsy had produced stories, letters, and poems that met three criteria: (1) all were self-generated and unrelated to any school purpose or school assignment—these expressive writings were created at home where Betsy often spent hours alone in her bedroom, writing in a notebook or on a scrap of paper; (2) all were written for Betsy's own communicative purposes—she described this purpose as analogous to writing letters to herself: "Everything I write is a journal. Like more my poems are a journal 'cause I remember that same day I wrote that. I remember the feeling. And like when I read it, the feelings come back"; and (3) only Betsy edited or corrected what she wrote. As changes evolved in her life circumstances and combined with the development of her personal identity, so differences became apparent in the moods and feelings expressed in her creative/imaginative writing.

In addition to her letters, stories, and poems, at age 17 years Betsy also participated in two interviews that told her story. We draw on the interviews and expressive writings to tell this story from Betsy's perspective.

Expressive Writing in the Elementary Years: Creating Involvement

Betsy's first memory of being encouraged to write occurred when she was in grade 2. Her speech–language pathologist at that time encouraged Betsy to write: "She wanted me to write all the time. And I wrote like really scary stories, horror stories, and I liked that."

While in grade 2, Betsy began tutoring outside of school to help her with her reading. She recalled that she and her tutor frequently went to the library to read books. Apparently sensing Betsy's resistance to reading, the tutor encouraged her to write stories about the books they shared. By grade 4, Betsy's enjoyment of narrative writing was such that she wanted to be an author. She also remembered that her grade-4 teachers also encouraged her writing. In grade 5, she became a member of Young Authors and was selected to write a story. She wrote about a little girl who was adopted by a rich family and an older boy, who also wanted to be adopted, but was never chosen. Betsy said that she got the idea for the story after watching a television program about adoption, stating that "I learned that, you know, older kids don't get adopted." Tables 12.2 and 12.3 display two of the "scary" stories that Betsy wrote at ages 9 and 11 years, "The Grandma Story" and "The Wolf Story," respectively.

During Betsy's elementary-school years, fear and loss are major themes of her fictional stories, which appear to function as a communicative medium for working through social problem solving. "The Grandmother Story" is told in the first person. It deals with the fear of losing loved ones, as well as the fear generated when the grandmother tells about her brother who died, who "did bad stuff to people," and returns to "haunt you and scare you very much." "The Wolf Story" also has the storyteller as a main character, whose friend, Amelia, turns into a wolf, and kidnaps the storyteller's mother. The strategy for returning Amelia to her normal state involves tickling her feet. In both of these stories, Betsy conveys emotional involvement with the characters that she has created, which indicates a developing theory of mind, through the syntactic devices she selects.

In "The Grandma Story," Betsy uses a relatively long sequence of quoted dialogue or utterances that are projected onto story characters (T-units 14–20 and 22–23). The quoted dialogue types that she employed were the free direct form where the dialogue sequence lacks a framing clause to mark either the projected talk or change in speaker roles—for example, "Yes I do! Well he is back! What?" and the direct form (Nordqvist, 1998). With this second type, the dialogue sequence is syntactically marked by a framing clause that contains a mental state verb—for example, "She *said* you now my brother died at 40 years old" (see also "The Wolf Story," T-units 14–15). While the free direct form is less developmentally complex, it still commonly appears in the narrative writing of 9-year-old children, which suggests that many children, like Betsy, are still influenced by "thinking-for-speaking," or writing like talking, rather than thinking (planning)-for-writing at that age (Strömqvist, Nordqvist, & Weneglin, 2004). Prosodic and gestural cues are absent in writing; therefore, as a way to "perform" her narrative, Betsy relied on two nonlinguistic counterparts in "The Grandmother Story," rather than on the linguistic mode, to convey the attitudinal viewpoints of her characters. These nonlinguistic devices were underlining and exclamation points, both of which served the function of emphasis. In neither story does Betsy explicitly mark quoted dialogue with quotation marks, which may indicate that her engagement in story creation took precedence over punctuation refinements.

While her writings (and oral interviews) were rich with psychological verbs that denoted awareness of characters' internal mental states (e.g., "know," "want," "love," "decide") and psychological adjectives that de-

TABLE 12.2. Fictional Narrative, "The Grandma Story," Written by Betsy at Age 9 Years (Grade 3)[a]

T-unit[b]	Number of words	Number of clauses	The Grandma Story[c]
1	8	2	It started *when I was 9 years old.*
2	5	1	I loved my **grat** [great] grandmother.
3	5	1	We were like best friends!
4	8	1	She lived with my grandmother & my grand-father.
5	7	1	I **visted** [visited] everyday & watched her sew.
6	6	1	But one day I went there.
7	7	2	I thought Φ it was a **nornmol** [normal] day
8	4	1	but it wasn't.
9	7	1	Momo & PoPoP that's my grandparents
10	4	1	They were not there
11	4	1	but grandmother was there.
12	4	1	She seemed very **serrys** [serious].
13	6	1	So I **lest** [listen] in very good.
14	11	2	She said you **now** [know] my brother died at 40 years old.
15	7	1	And he did bad stuff to people!
16	3	1	Yes I do!
17	4	1	Well he is back! What!
18	5	1	Shh! Shh! You may not **belive** [believe] this
19	3	1	I can't!
20	13	2	But *when* he **now's** [knows] **A bot** [about] you he will haunt you and scare you very much!
21	5	1	And then the door slammed!
22	6	1	Oh! mom let's go home!
23	4	1	OK! **By**! [Bye] Take care!

[a]Original word spacings, capitalizations, underlining, and spellings have been retained.

[b]The T-unit is a clause, the basic unit of spoken language (Hunt, 1965). At a minimum, a T-unit consists of one main clause (a subject and a predicate) that can stand alone plus all dependent (subordinated) clauses or nonclausal structures (noun phrases, verb phrases, adverbials, etc.) attached to or embedded within it. A clause attached to another clause by a coordinating conjunction (*and, or, but, so*) would be considered two different T-units (see T-units 6, 8, 13, 15, 20, and 21), unless the second clause has a subject deletion that can be semantically linked back to the previously mentioned subject. For example, T-unit 20, ". . . he will haunt you *and* scare you very much!," is one T-unit because the deletion of "he" can be recovered from the original pronoun in subject position.

[c]Contractions were counted as two words; vocalizations such as "Shh" were not counted as words; italicization indicates a subordinating or dependent clause; a single underline indicates Betsy's own underlining; words with spelling violations are in bold type; Φ indicates an implied sentential complementation marker ("that").

- Average T-unit length (Hunt, 1965): Total # of words in sample (138)/Total # main + subordinate clauses (27) = 5.1.
- Subordination index (ratio of clauses to main clauses [Hunt, 1965, p. 33]): Total # of main + subordinate clauses (27)/Total # of T-units (23) = 1.20.

TABLE 12.3. Fictional Narrative, "The Wolf Story," Written by Betsy at Age 11 Years (Grade 5)

T-unit	Number of words	Number of clauses	The Wolf Story
1	12	2	*When* the night was dark I was **waching** [watching] tv in my room
2	5	1	I **herd** [heard] a **holing** [howling] noise.
3	3	1	I looked **out sid** [outside]
4	3	1	It was Amelia
5	6	1	She was turning **in** [into] a wolf
6	9	1	I ran to the front door and **locket** [locked] it
7	6	1	I ran back to my room
8	3	1	She was gone.
9	6	1	I **whent** [went] to my mom's room
10	4	1	she was gone too.
11	3	1	I was crying
			ring ring
12	4	1	I answered the door
13	3	1	it was Heather
14	3	1	she said help!
15	7	2	Why a wolf is **traing** [trying] *robb* [rob] me.
16	7	2	I saw Amelia *turning* **in to** [into] the wolf
17	4	1	she took my mom
18	6	2	we have to *teakle* [tickle] her feet
19	5	1	And she will turn back.

- Average T-unit length (Hunt, 1965): Total # of words in sample (103)/Total # main + subordinate clauses (19) = 5.42.
- Subordination index (ratio of clauses to main clauses [Hunt, 1965, p. 33]): Total # of main + subordinate clauses (23)/Total # of T-units (19) = 1.21.

scribed characters' emotional states (such as "lonely," "scared," "happy," "surprised," "sorry"), she did not always follow through in her stories to express the important distinction between her own voice and those of the characters that she created in these texts. For example, she did not always consistently differentiate between first and third person in her writing. Other linguistic aspects gleaned from her earliest writings pertain to multidimensional issues with grammatical morphology, grammatical complexity, and her patterns of spelling errors.

Grammatical Morphology and Complexity

As we discussed earlier, a hallmark of SLI is the protracted oral development of the grammatical tense system in clauses where subject–verb agreement is obligatory. Neither "The Grandmother Story" nor "The Wolf Story" (see Tables 12.2 and 12.3) indicated that Betsy, in her spontaneous narrative writing at age 9 years was having difficulty with the grammatical tense system—for example, in marking the past tense for both regular and irregular verbs. This pattern implied that, at a minimum, by age 9 years, Betsy had consolidated the phonological, morphological, and orthographic aspects of past tense representations into a flexible unit. The time at which this development occurred, of course, is unknown; but the selective delay pattern referred to by Rice (2003) does not seem to apply to Betsy at this age. Instead, Betsy's control of the basic grammatical tense system in her personal narrative writing is consistent with the findings by Green et al. (2003). Children in grade 3 have command of past tense and complex verb inflections (e.g., participles, copula, and auxiliaries) in their narrative text generation, although equivalent mastery of plural inflections may take somewhat longer.

At the same time, the grammatical complexity of both stories might be questioned, if not for a 9-year-old of Betsy's socioeconomic background (Story 1), certainly for an 11-year-old (Story 2). A common measure of advances in a child's grammatical complexity is average T-unit length, which represents a child's ability to pack in more information within either oral or written clauses (Scott & Windsor, 2000). It is defined as the average number of words per T-unit in a given sample (Hunt, 1965). A second general measure of advances in grammatical complexity is the clause density ratio, defined as "the extent to which utterances/sentences [T-units] contain subordinate [dependent] clauses" (Scott & Stokes, 1995, p. 310). The expectation is that, in both the spoken and the written domains, a child's clause density ratio will increase over time, providing evidence of the ability to advance information complexity through the use of subordination devices (see "The Grandmother Story" and "The Wolf Story" in Tables 12.2 and 12.3 for how each measure is determined).

The average length of Betsy's T-units for the two stories, written approximately 2 years apart, is essentially identical, 5.1 and 5.4, respectively. Similarly, the clause density ratios are identical at 1.20, which means that Betsy used subordinated clauses 20% of the time in both stories. The exact meaning of this ratio is unclear since there are few developmental standards for written narratives available for comparison. Moreover, it is also unclear if these figures reflect a leveling off, or plateau, in her ability to generate sentences containing more information density, as found when children incorporate more subordination into their narrative writing. For example, Betsy did not use multiple subordinators, such as "I didn't go *to answer* the door *because* I was afraid *that* Amelia might be there, " a development in middle childhood and preadolescence that has distinguished children with a language learning disability from their typically developing peers (Gillam & Johnston, 1992). Certainly, the increasing obstacles that Betsy faced with reading comprehension may have impacted on the expansion of her grammatical awareness. In turn, less available grammatical awareness may affect the continuing growth and assimilation of linguistic complexity with academic discourse proficiency (Silliman et al., 2004). Both influence whether a child is able to process text at deeper levels of comprehension and employ more literate grammatical complexity in writing (Scott, 2004). In general, there has been minimal research on the specific role of syntactic processing and sentence-level grammatical knowledge in either reading comprehension or writing (Scott, 2004; Treiman, Clifton, Meyer, & Wurm, 2003).

Spelling Patterns

Some authors (e.g., Scott, 2004) make the case that spelling is a primary reason why too many children write poorly, a problem that may be interrelated with children's overall skills in generating written sentences (Graham, Harris, & Chorzempa, 2002; see also Englert & Dunsmore, Chapter 8, and Singer & Bashir, Chapter 9, this volume), their rate of writing fluency (Berninger et al., 2002), and how spelling is taught. All or some of these factors may have been operating in Betsy's case, although Betsy could not be considered a "poor" speller based on her own compositions.

It is beyond our scope to analyze the misspellings in the two stories that Betsy wrote at ages 9 and 11 years (see Tables 12.2 and 12.3); however, her misspellings were systematic and not even unusual at this age since most related to vowel variations, particularly at syllable boundaries, and the conventional ways that these vowels were represented in the orthography (Berninger et al., 2002; Kessler & Treiman, 2003). In sum, it appeared that Betsy was still grappling with how consonants following the vowel affected consonantal spelling in two-syllable and multisyllabic words, for example, *nornmol*, *serrys*. Templeton (see Chapter 10, this volume) refers to this phase as discovering within-syllable patterns. In other cases, Betsy seemed to be dealing with when prepositions were (and were not) compound words, for example, *in to*, the orthographic marking of *–ed* ("The Wolf Story," T-unit 6), and vowel reduction ("visted," "The Grandmother Story," T-unit 5). Vowel reduction occurs when a vowel receives less stress and is less phonetically salient. Mastering the phonetic contexts of vowel alterations in spelling tends to precede the mastery of reduced vowel stress (Templeton, 2004).

Summary

Two related conclusions can be drawn from Betsy's elementary years. First, she demonstrated budding competence with narrative writing and spelling outside of the school setting. Had school professionals recognized what she was doing right, this insight about her strengths might have been harnessed to create an intervention plan that would have explicitly assisted her with reading comprehension and her more literate use of syntax and derivational morphology. Second, although various classroom teachers and her speech–language pathologist individually encouraged Betsy's narrative writing interests, this encouragement was insufficient as a comprehensive strategy for facilitating her language and literacy needs in an integrated way. We now move onto Betsy's middle-school years. An important question, based on this review of her uneven patterns of strengths as a writer and speller and weaknesses as a reader, is whether linguistic and academic discourse issues grew to be ever bigger obstacles for her sense of competence as a learner.

Expressive Writing in the Middle-School Years: Growing Self-Awareness

Betsy fondly recalled the help she received in elementary school from her teachers and speech–language pathologists. But her memories of middle school were less fond because, in her opinion, the educational staff, including her special education teachers, did not "know how to handle kids" and did not seem to be as qualified as her elementary teachers. Moreover, it was during her middle-school years that Betsy became increasingly aware of the problems she had with easily expressing herself orally and the anxiety it created, which drew her even more into writing as her means of personal communication. As she explained:

> "'Cause I can ramble, ramble writing. I love rambling. I can't ramble speaking because my words just like, like get all mixed up. Like I meant this word and that one paragraph, but it came down here. And like when I write, I'm just like . . . I'm speaking what my mind's really speaking. Not how it talks, like I get . . . like my tongue gets caught. So my tongue gets stuck on things. But my hand doesn't. I believe your hand connects to your mind, you know, like you don't have to worry about if a word comes out."

A Focus Inward with Poetic Writing

Betsy described middle school as a miserable time, noting that she "lived in hell for a period of time"; however, she recognized that "every kid is miserable in middle school." It was during this time that Betsy began to write poems, stating "I liked dark poems and really sad poems in that stage of my life and stuff." Two poems reflecting her dark period, "The Beholder of Love" written at age 12 years and "The Canvas White" written at age 13 years, are shown in Figures 12.3 and 12.4. Although both are short, they reflect a new look at Betsy's more literate command of linguistic complexity.

Advances in Linguistic Complexity

Betsy's poems portray her application of compensatory strategies that appeared to allow flexibility in the expression of linguistic complexity. The poems have minimal subordination; however, they incorporate nonclausal devices for elaborating meaning in a more literate way, specifically, by altering sentence voice and expanding verb and noun phrases. For example, "The Beholder of Love" poem, written in Betsy's first year of middle school, has two occurrences of the passive voice following the copula (see Figure 12.3). "The Canvas White" poem, which she wrote at age 13 years (see Figure 12.4), is even more complex as it is characterized by the inclusion and coordination of three literate linguistic devices. These are: (1) an end-focus principle whereby new information is emphasized through reversals of noun and adjective positions ("The canvas *white*"; "the pencil *sharpened*"), combined with (2) a derivational form ("the pencil *sharpened*"), and (3) noun postmodification ("the pencil sharpened *at the tip*"; "turning the canvas *into*

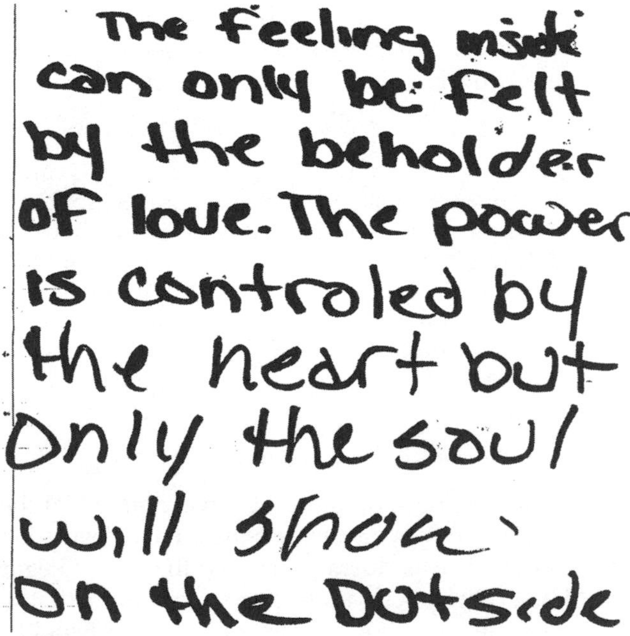
The feeling inside
can only be felt
by the beholder
of love. The power
is controled by
the heart but
only the soul
will show
on the outside

FIGURE 12.3. Betsy, age 12 years, in grade 6: "The Beholder of Love" poem.

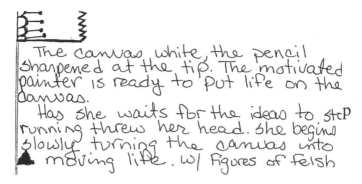

The canvas white, the pencil
sharpened at the tip. The motivated
painter is ready to put life on the
canvas.
   Has she waits for the ideas to step
running threw her head. She begins
slowly turning the canvas into
   moving life. w/ figures of felsh

FIGURE 12.4. Betsy, age 13 years, in grade 7: "The Canvas White" poem.

moving life w/figures of felsh [flesh]"). Thus, at a time when the diagnostic speech–language pathologist was casting Betsy's language-processing problems as difficulty in formulating complex sentences, Betsy was creating poetry by manipulating her linguistic knowledge of semantic–syntactic relationships to create metaphorical images of her feelings.

One speculation is that, as a result of her language learning disability, Betsy had a limited, but still powerful, set of complex semantic and morpho-syntactic resources that she applied in creative ways to achieving a more literate mode for her self-expression within the narrative genre. In these natural literacy contexts, Betsy was making the most efficient use of the relatively unlimited time available to plan what she wanted to say, and, most importantly, how to express and revise it using her limited repertoire of linguistic resources. During her interview, Betsy seemed to suggest that this was the case. She described her goal in written self-expression, elaborating on the advantages of the planning time offered through writing, as well as the advantages of computer programs as a support:

> "To get it out is my first goal, just to get it out, and understand may be. No one else does. But then put it in. Like there should be an 'and' there or there should be something to finish. That's not a full sentence, but at least I got it out. And I can finish it and I don't really mind. Computers do the spelling for me."

A small caution is indicated here about how adequately spell-checking programs produce "good spellers" from inadequate ones by eradicating misspellings. Graham et al. (2002) report that spell checkers are only partially successful in eliminating the misspellings of students with learning disabilities. We now shift to the final years of Betsy's educational journey, her high-school years.

The High-School Years: Searching for the Road Back

By her second year in high school, Betsy reported that she no longer wrote her "ramblings" because she had become depressed again and did not even want to touch paper: "I just didn't want to do anything." As we mentioned at the outset of this section, by grade 10, Betsy had just about fallen off the educational ladder and was prepared to become a school dropout. However, her enrollment in an alternate public high school for grades 11 and 12 slowly changed her worldview.

Being Challenged

The curriculum at the alternate high school was presented as a self-paced plan, and, rather than lectures, consisted of "worksheets" containing the information that had to be learned. Betsy said that she preferred the worksheets to oral lectures because she read the printed material at her own pace; therefore, she felt less "stupid" because she did not have to publicly ask the teacher "What did you just say?" Another positive aspect of the alternate high school was the personal attention that teachers gave students, which made Betsy feel safe in being able "to ask them anything 'cause the teacher's right next to me." Additionally, Betsy was no longer receiving special education services, a fact that did not disturb her because she felt increasingly comfortable in her new setting. Moreover, she felt comfortable because "everyone in the school has—um—I think a disorder."

However, a major curriculum barrier for her was the composing of expository text. Her prior educational experiences had not sufficiently provided her with the explicit writing, linguistic, and self-regulation strategies by which she could generate well-formed informational and persuasive text structures (see Singer & Bashir, Chapter 9, this volume). For example, at the end of grade 8 when Betsy took the state writing assessment, the task was "writing to convince." Betsy received a score of 2.5 (on a scale of 1 to 5), which indicated that her response only slightly addressed the topic, did not clearly express her thoughts, and contained some misspellings and incorrect uses of punctuation.

For the first time in a long while, Betsy encountered a teacher, her English teacher, who held high expectations for her and made her "do more than what she was giving to the other kids. She expected too much from me." Initially, this made Betsy angry. However, this same teacher introduced activities on persuasive texts that motivated Betsy's interest and drew on her situational knowledge, while also offering opportunities for her to acquire new content knowledge and expand her cultural literacy (see also Pressley & Hilden, Chapter 6, this volume, for more on this topic).

These activities included producing 30-second commercials on the "Wonder Bra," comparing an older and newer version of the novel *Little Women*, and preparing oral debates on controversial topics pertinent to teenagers. In retrospect, Betsy evaluated these challenging activities as positive because she developed some procedural strategies for constructing persuasive texts in a more competent manner. Although still ambivalent about preparing persuasive texts, Betsy started to "love persuasives" because she came to believe "I can do that . . . and I could even do them more after she sent me back to the computer like 500 times." Betsy also discovered other strategies to support her reading comprehension of more complex literary and expository content. For example, she used books on tape, following the text as she listened to the tape; however, these taped books were not always readily available.

Feeling more comfortable with herself, Betsy began her poetry writing again. Even her terminology changed in describing the kind of writing that she now enjoyed. Instead of "ramblings," poetry was an activity more like "a journal 'cause I remember that same day I wrote that. I remember the feelings and when I read it, the feelings come back . . . and when you read it, it like soaks in your skin."

Coming to the End of the Road and a New Beginning

As high-school graduation approached, Betsy was selected by her classmates to give the graduation speech. As might be expected, Betsy was terrified to do so, but with her mother's encouragement she took on the task, preparing her written remarks, rehearsing them endlessly, and then taking center stage as the honored speaker. This accomplishment was the pinnacle of her life; the individual who could not smoothly plan out how to talk, whose tongue seemed to get stuck whenever she attempted to verbally express herself, now stood in front of her peers and their families and pointed them to their futures with her words. At 17 years old, Betsy had earned her high-school diploma. However, the alternate high school, which helped her to reach a new level of competence, "to be a strong person," in Betsy's own words, closed immediately following the graduation. The school board's reason for the closure was to save money.

Epilogue

The following fall, Betsy enrolled in a community college, while living at home. However, she soon encountered major difficulties in her ability to keep pace with class lectures, take notes, comprehend the expository texts she had to read, and produce expository essays. This time, Betsy did drop out. Eventually, she made the decision to pursue a career as a graphic arts designer and moved away from home for the first time to realize this goal. There is no further information about what happened to Betsy as she began traveling down this new path.

FINAL THOUGHTS: MELDING PRACTICES AND MAKING THEM WORK

As evidenced through her writings and oral history, Betsy spent much of her school years struggling to piece together a fractured sense of self as professionals in her schools simultaneously sought to "repair" the presumed broken pieces of her linguistic and discourse systems. Betsy's ultimate success in finding value in her strengths and abilities far outshone these well-intentioned, but often disjointed, attempts at "fixing" her. In this way, Betsy's story is again reminiscent of Humpty Dumpty's tale. Perhaps if all the king's horses and all the king's men would have communicated with one another, united their skills, and worked collaboratively toward a common goal, they could have solved the Humpty Dumpty puzzle.

The issues raised in this volume make clear that proficiency with the multiple dimensions of literacy require many interacting components. Based on the dynamic systems view of language impairment outlined earlier (Bates et al., 2003; Bates, 2004; Gilger & Wise, 2004), disruptions in the timing of ongoing interactions between the genetic and the neural underpinnings of brain function and the nature and quality of experiences influence the appearance of a language learning disability at different points in a child's development. For this reason, it is imperative that educators, speech–language pathologists, and other professionals, as well as parents, work together as early as possible to target instruction, intervention, and the development of related socioemotional factors at levels that address the student's general, as well as specific, difficulties in language and literacy learning.

In addition to sustaining the best practices presented in the various chapters of this book, there is another priority. Much emphasis has been placed on scientifically supported instructional practices in reading, but unequal attention has been paid to assessment practices that have a solid research foundation—for example, in profile diagnosis (Berninger, Dunn, & Alper, in press). The profile analysis approach is geared to identifying individual strengths and weaknesses in language and literacy learning, or uneven abilities, which should then lead to a plan for appropriate curriculum modifications prior to any referral to special education. Of course, as Wallach and Ehren discuss (see Chapter 2, this volume), professionals face multiple challenges in developing and implementing collaboratively created programs designed to maximize students' language and literacy learning through curriculum modifications and the careful and continuous monitoring of students' subsequent response to instruction (Silliman et al., 2004). Large caseloads and piles of paperwork come to mind, as well as other obstacles such as time and scheduling constraints, administrative issues, and so on. However, in spite of these challenges, professionals who take the time to recognize and explore areas of overlapping service as well as the unique contributions that each can offer will achieve an important first step: the creation of a space in which open dialogue among colleagues is supported and valued.

As evidenced by current research and Betsy's poignant story, students with language learning impairments daily confront complex linguistic and social challenges (Brinton & Fujiki, 2004; Donahue & Pearl, 2003). As Wallach and Ehren (see Chapter 2, this volume) suggest, these students may have particular difficulty adapting to the language and culture of the school community. One way to mediate this issue is to create a safe, nurturing, and predictable schoolwide environment. This involves collaboration of the entire staff to develop common school procedures, expectations, and classroom environments that maximize student learning. The development of common structures and strategies implemented throughout the school will benefit particularly from the contributions of speech–language pathologists and other professionals working with students who face daily trials in language and learning. In addition, coming to a mutual understanding about the definition of literacy and how to help students reach related objectives will aid in the delivery of services that support and complement one another.

Moreover, collaboration is not despecialization, as some would argue. The ultimate goal is not to cross or erase the lines that define multiple educational services, but rather to step outside of a dominant paradigm that keeps each specialist boxed inside these lines. Rather than an overlap or distortion of roles and responsibilities, the integration of services can be considered as a blending of colors: each one contributes unique visual properties as it mixes with others to create a richer, more distinctive, hue. Betsy, whose fragile language-processing skills were splintered like the pieces of Humpty Dumpty's shell, exemplifies the student who would benefit most from an integrated form of literacy instruction and a collaborative approach to language intervention. Imagine how Betsy's experiences in elementary, middle, and high school would have changed had she continually received services from a team of highly qualified professionals (to use the terminology of the NCLB Act) whose goals for her were aligned not only with one another's but also with grade-level curricula and expectations. This collaborative team might have included Betsy's classroom teacher, her learning disability teacher, her speech–language pathologist, a school psychologist or guidance counselor, the administration, and her parents. Had these people invested the time necessary to investigate the potential of each other's contributions and entered into one another's workspaces, they could have offered Betsy a dynamic, integrated, and collaboratively developed model of services.

But there are also others whose perspectives should be valued. From Betsy's perspective, an essential aim should be to assist children who are struggling with literacy to believe that they "can do." In her framework, "Make the kid read a lot. Then have discussions after the book to make sure you're really understood. That helps your writing a lot. . . . You should try to do activities outside of school too [to] try to get them encouraged to read." From the viewpoint of a parent (Krishnan, 2004), individuals who are highly qualified to serve students with special needs would share certain values and beliefs. Among these are the understanding that:

- All behavior is communication.
- Schools model the values of their communities, reflecting how communities feel their most vulnerable students should be treated.
- The assistance of a team for differentiating the curriculum for all students in a classroom is the rule, not the exception.
- The love of learning as a lifelong process must be infused daily into all aspects of classroom life. (pp. 1–2)

In conclusion, literacy learning as a collection of processing strategies and skills that continuously interweave with experiences can be thought of as an orchestra playing a symphony. Though they can function independently, each instrument and each part of the score contributes to the complex and dynamic sound of the whole concert. Harmony occurs when multiple instruments simultaneously produce individual yet related melodies. If one instrument is out of tune, the sound of the whole orchestra will be adversely affected. In the case of reading, writing, and spelling, students with language learning disabilities may experience "out-of-tune" elements that cause dissonance when they attempt to integrate the tools of literacy. Educators and clinicians alike should understand that every instrument forms a necessary part of the whole of literacy skills development. It is our collective responsibility to work together to seek out and actively investigate effective ways to tune each instrument in a student's literacy tool kit. It can be said that Betsy, like Humpty Dumpty, was an atypical egg who was in constant danger of falling off the wall and being shattered. The question to ask ourselves is not how to put the pieces back together for individual students but how to support what is right about them. Betsy's voice provides a signpost for us to follow: "If you read one of my stories, or you read one of my poems, you'd know how my mind works . . . 'cause I write exactly how it's in my head."

ACKNOWLEDGMENT

We are highly indebted to Brenda Mortensen-Reed and Kamlah Scheer, who brought Betsy to life by their transcriptions and analyses of her narratives, letters, poems, and oral interviews. In addition, we are grateful to C. Addison Stone for his detailed and thoughtful review of the initial version of this chapter.

NOTES

1. Betsy choose to be an active participant in the telling of her story as a way of helping others who must struggle daily with the multiple and complex challenges presented by a language learning disability. Both Betsy and her mother consented to have her story published.

2. Preschool-age children who have persisting unintelligible speech, like Betsy, combined with equally serious delays in lexical development, also similar to Betsy, are at significant risk for persistent language and literacy learning problems (Bird et al., 1995; Felsenfeld et al., 1994; Johnson et al., 1999; Leonard, 1998). However, mild-to-moderate difficulties with the precise motor execution of speech segments (articulation), if the only presenting symptom, is neither indicative of language learning difficulties nor predictive of problems in learning to read and spell (Bishop & Clarkson, 2003; Catts, Hu, Larrivee, & Swank, 1994; Hodson, 1994).

3. Although not shown in Table 12.1, in grade 6, Betsy's ranks in math computation and math problem solving fell below the 14th percentile, while her performance on math concepts ranked at the 23rd percentile.

REFERENCES

Bates, E. A. (1997). Origins of language disorders: A comparative approach. *Developmental Neuropsychology, 13,* 447–476.

Bates, E. A. (2004). Explaining and interpreting deficits in language development across clinical groups: Where do we go from here? *Brain and Language, 88,* 248–253.

Bates, E. A., & Roe, K. (2001). Language development in children with unilateral brain injury. In C. A. Nelson & M. Luciana (Eds.), *Handbook of developmental cognitive neuroscience* (pp. 281–307). Cambridge, MA: MIT Press.

Bates, E. A., Thal, D., Finlay, B., & Clancy, B. (2003). Early language development and its neural correlates. In I. Rapin & S. Segalowitz (Eds.), *Handbook of neuropsychology* (Vol. 8, Part 2, pp. 2–62). Amsterdam: Elsevier.

Bates, E. A., Vicari, S. & Trauner, D. (1999). Neural mediation of language development: Perspectives from lesion studies of infants and children. In H. Tager-Flusberg (Ed.), *Neurodevelopmental disorders* (pp. 533–581). Cambridge, MA: MIT Press.

Berninger, V. W. (2003). Understanding the "lexia" in dyslexia: A multidisciplinary team approach to learning disabilities. *Annals of Dyslexia, 51,* 23–48.

Berninger, V. W., Dunn, A., & Alper, T. (in press). Integrated multi-level assessment for branching, instructional, and profile diagnosis. In A. Prifitera, D. Saklofske, L. Weiss, & E. Rolfhus (Eds.), *WISC-IV: Clinical use and interpretation*. San Diego, CA: Academic Press.

Berninger, V. W., & O'Donnell, L. (in press). Research-supported differential diagnosis of specific learning disabilities. In A. Prifitera, D. Saklofske, L. Weiss, & E. Rolfhus (Eds.), *WISC-IV: Clinical use and interpretation*. San Diego, CA: Academic Press.

Berninger, V. W., & Richards, T. L. (2002). *Brain literacy for educators and psychologists*. Boston: Academic Press.

Berninger, V. W., Vaughn, K., Abbott, R. D., Begay, K., Coleman, K. B., Curtin, G., Hawkins, J. M., & Graham, S. (2002). Teaching spelling and composition alone and together: Implications for the simple view of spelling. *Journal of Educational Psychology, 94*, 291–304.

Bird, J., Bishop, D. V. M., & Freeman, N. H. (1995). Phonological awareness and literacy development in children with expressive phonological impairments. *Journal of Speech and Hearing Research, 38*, 446–462.

Bishop, D. V. M. (2004). Specific language impairment: Diagnostic dilemmas. In L. Verhoeven & H. van Balkom (Eds.), *Classification of developmental language disorders: Theoretical issues and clinical implications* (pp. 309–326). Mahwah, NJ: Erlbaum.

Bishop, D. V. M., & Clarkson, B. (2003). Written language as a window into residual language deficits: A study of children with persistent and residual speech and language impairments. *Cortex, 39*, 215–237.

Bishop, D. V. M., Price, T. S., Dale, P. S., & Plomin, R. (2003). Outcomes of early language delay, Part 2: Etiology of transient and persistent difficulties. *Journal of Speech, Language, and Hearing Research, 46*, 561–575.

Botting, N., & Conti-Ramsden, G. (2004). Characteristics of children with specific language impairment. In L. Verhoeven & H. van Balkom (Eds.), *Classification of developmental language disorders: Theoretical issues and clinical implications* (pp. 23–38). Mahwah, NJ: Erlbaum.

Botting, N., Faragher, B., Simkin, Z., Knox, E., & Conti-Ramsden, G. (2001). Predicting pathways of specific language impairment: What differentiates good and poor outcomes. *Journal of Child Psychiatry and Psychology, 42*, 1013–1020.

Brinton, B., & Fujiki, M. (2004). Social and affective factors in children with language impairment: Implications for literacy learning. In C. A. Stone, E. R. Silliman, B. J. Ehren, & K. Apel (Eds.), *Handbook of language and literacy: Development and disorders* (pp. 130–153) New York: Guilford Press.

Cain, K., & Oakhill, J. (1998). Comprehension skill and inference-making ability: Issues and causality. In C. Hulme & R. M. Joshi (Eds.), *Reading and spelling: Development and disorders* (pp. 329–342). London: Erlbaum.

Cain, K., Oakhill, J. V., Barnes, M. A., & Bryant, P. E. (2001). Comprehension skill, inference-making ability, and their relation to knowledge. *Memory and Cognition, 29*, 850–859.

Cain, K., Oakhill, J. V., & Bryant, P. E. (2004). Children's reading comprehension ability: Concurrent prediction by working memory, verbal ability, and component skills. *Journal of Educational Psychology, 96*, 31–42.

Carlisle, J. F. (2000). Awareness of the structure and meaning of morphologically complex words: Impact on reading. *Reading and Writing, 12,* 169–190.

Carlisle, J. F., & Fleming, J. (2003). Lexical processing of morphologically complex words in the elementary years. *Scientific Studies of Reading, 7,* 239–253.

Carlisle, J. F., & Rice, M. S. (2002). *Improving reading comprehension: Research-based principles and practices.* Baltimore: York Press.

Cassar, M., & Treiman, R. (2004). Developmental variations in spelling: Comparing typical and poor spellers. In C. A. Stone, E. R. Silliman, B. J. Ehren, & K. Apel (Eds.), *Handbook of language and literacy: Development and disorders* (pp. 627–643). New York: Guilford Press.

Catts, H. W., Fey, M. E., Tomblin, J. B., & Zhang, X. (2002). A longitudinal investigation of reading outcomes in children with language impairments. *Journal of Speech, Language, and Hearing Research, 45,* 1142–1157.

Catts, H. W., Fey, M. E., Zhang, X., & Tomblin, J. B. (1999). Language basis of reading and reading disabilities: Evidence from a longitudinal investigation. *Scientific Studies of Reading, 3,* 331–361.

Catts, H. W., Hu, C. F., Larrivee, L., & Swank, L. (1994). Early identification of reading disabilities in children with speech–language impairments. In R. V. Watkins & M. B. Rice (Eds.), *Specific language impairments in children* (pp. 145–160). Baltimore: Brookes.

Conti-Ramsden, G. (2003). Processing and linguistic markers in young children with specific language impairment (SLI). *Journal of Speech, Language, and Hearing Research, 46,* 1029–1037.

Conti-Ramsden, G., Botting, N., & Faragher, B. (2001). Psycholinguistic markers for specific language impairment (SLI). *Journal of Child Psychology and Psychiatry, 42,* 741–748.

Dale, P. S., Price, T. S., Bishop, D. V. M., & Plomin, R. (2003). Outcomes of early language delay, Part 1: Predicting persistent and transient language difficulties at 3 and 4 years. *Journal of Speech, Language, and Hearing Research, 46,* 544–560.

de Villiers, J. G. (2003). Defining SLI: A linguistic perspective. In Y. Levy & J. Schaffer (Eds.), *Language competence across populations: Toward a definition of specific language impairment* (pp. 425–447). Mahwah, NJ: Erlbaum.

Dickinson, D. K., & McCabe, A. (2001). Bringing it all together: The multiple origins, skills, and environmental supports of early literacy. *Learning Disabilities Research and Practice, 16,* 186–202.

Dickinson, D. K., McCabe, A., Anastasopoulos, L., Peisner-Feinberg, E. S., & Poe, M. D. (2003). The comprehensive language approach to early literacy: The interrelationships among vocabulary, phonological sensitivity, and print knowledge among preschool-aged children. *Journal of Educational Psychology, 95,* 465–481.

Dollaghan, C., & Campbell, T. F. (1998). Nonword repetition and child language impairment.*Journal of Speech, Language, and Hearing Research, 41,* 1136–1146.

Donahue, M. L., & Pearl, P. (2003). Studying social development and learning disabilities is not for the faint-hearted: Comments on the risk/resilience framework. *Learning Disabilities Research and Practice, 18,* 90–93.

Duke, N. K., Pressley, M., & Hilden, K. (2004). Difficulties with reading comprehension. In C. A. Stone, E. R. Silliman, B. J. Ehren, & K. Apel (Eds.), *Handbook of language and literacy: Development and disorders* (pp. 501–520). New York: Guilford Press.

Edwards, J., & Lahey, M. (1998). Nonword repetitions in children with specific language impairment: Exploration of some explanations for their inaccuracies. *Applied Psycholinguistics, 19,* 279–309.

Elman, J. L., Bates, E. A., Johnson, M. H., Karmiloff-Smith, A., Parisi, D., & Plunkett, K. (1996). *Rethinking innateness: A connectionist perspective on development.* Cambridge, MA: MIT Press.

Felsenfeld, S., Broen, P. A., & McGue, M. (1994). A 28-year follow-up of adults with a history of moderate phonological disorder: Educational and occupational results. *Journal of Speech and Hearing Research, 37,* 1341–1353.

Gilger, J. W., & Kaplan, B. J. (2001). Atypical brain development: A conceptual framework for understanding developmental learning disabilities. *Developmental Neuropsychology, 20,* 465–481.

Gilger, J. W., & Wise, S. E. (2004). Genetic correlates of language and literacy impairments. In C. A. Stone, E. R. Silliman, B. J. Ehren, & K. Apel (Eds.), *Handbook of language and literacy: Development and disorders* (pp. 25–48). New York: Guilford Press.

Gillam, R., & Johnston, J. (1992). Spoken and written language relationships in language/learning impaired and normally achieving school-age children. *Journal of Speech and Hearing Research, 35,* 1303–1315.

Graham, S., Harris, K. R., & Chorzempa, B. F. (2002). Contribution of spelling instruction to the spelling, writing, and reading of poor spellers. *Journal of Educational Psychology, 94,* 669–686.

Green, L., McCutchen, D., Schwiebert, C., Quinlan, T., Eva-Wood, A., & Juelis, J. (2003). Morphological development in children's writing. *Journal of Educational Psychology, 95,* 752–761.

Hodson, B. W. (1994). Helping individuals become intelligible, literate, and articulate: The role of phonology. *Topics in Language Disorders, 14*(2), 1–16.

Hunt, K. W. (1965). *Grammatical structures written at three grade levels* (Research Report No. 3). Champaign, IL: National Council of Teachers of English.

Johnson, C. J., Beitchman, J. H., Young, A., Escobar, M., Atkinson, L., Wilson, B., et al. (1999). Fourteen-year follow-up of children with and without speech/language impairments: Speech/language stability and outcomes. *Journal of Speech, Language, and Hearing Research, 42,* 744–760.

Kaplan, B. J., Dewey, D. M., Crawford, S. G., & Wilson, B. N. (2001). The term *comorbidity* is of questionable value in reference to developmental disorders: Data and theory. *Journal of Learning Disabilities, 34,* 555–565.

Keogh, B. K. (2002). Research on reading and reading problems: Findings, limitations, and future directions. In K. G. Butler & E. R. Silliman (Eds.), *Speaking, reading, and writing in children with language learning disabilities: New paradigms in research and practice* (pp. 27–44). Mahwah, NJ: Erlbaum.

Kessler, B., & Treiman, R. (2003). Is English spelling chaotic?: Misconceptions concerning its irregularity. *Reading Psychology, 24,* 267–289.

Krishnan, S. (2004, March 25). *Highly qualified teachers: A parent's dream.* Retrieved March 25, 2004, from *www.ourchildrenleftbehind.com/pages/1/index.htm.*

Leonard, L. B. (1998). *Children with specific language impairment*. Cambridge, MA: MIT Press.

Lyon, G. R., Shaywitz, S. E., & Shaywitz, B. A. (2003). A definition of dyslexia. *Annals of Dyslexia, 53*, 1–14.

Maillart, C., Schelstraete, M., & Hupet, M. (2004). Phonological representations in children with SLI: A study of French. *Journal of Speech, Language, and Hearing Research, 47*, 187–198.

McArthur, G. M., Hogben, J. H., Edwards, V. T., Heath, S. M., & Mengler, E. D. (2000). On the "specifics" of specific reading disability and specific language impairment. *Journal of Child Psychology and Psychiatry, 41*, 869–874.

McCardle, P., Scarborough, H. S., & Catts, H. W. (2001). Predicting, explaining, and preventing children's reading difficulties. *Learning Disabilities Research and Practice, 16*, 230–239.

McGregor, K. (2004). Developmental dependencies between lexical semantics and reading. In C. A. Stone, E. R. Silliman, B. J. Ehren, & K. Apel (Eds.), *Handbook of language and literacy: Development and disorders* (pp. 302–317). New York: Guilford Press.

Moats, L. C. (2004). Science, language, and imagination in the professional development of reading teachers. In P. McCardle & V. Chhabra (Eds.), *The voice of evidence in reading research* (pp. 269–287). Baltimore: Brookes.

Montgomery, J. W. (2002a). Information processing and language comprehension in children with specific language impairment. *Topics in Language Disorders, 22*(3), 62–84.

Montgomery, J. W. (2002b). Understanding the language difficulties of children with specific language impairments: Does verbal working memory matter? *American Journal of Speech–Language Pathology, 11*, 77–91.

Nagy, W., Berninger, V., Abbott, R., Vaughn, K., & Vermeulen, K. (2003). Relationship of morphology and other language skills to literacy skills in at-risk second-grade readers and at-risk fourth-grade writers. *Journal of Educational Psychology, 95*(4), 730–742.

Nation, K., Clarke, P., Marshall, C. M., & Durand, M. (2004). Hidden language impairments in children: Parallels between poor reading comprehension and specific language impairment? *Journal of Speech–Language–Hearing Research, 47*, 199–211.

Nordqvist, A. (1998). Projecting speech to protagonists in oral and written narratives: A developmental study. *Psychology of Language and Communication, 2*(2), 37–46.

Rescorla, L. (2000). Do late-talking toddlers turn out to have reading difficulties a decade later? *Annals of Dyslexia, 50*, 87–102.

Rescorla, L. (2002). Language and reading outcomes to age 9 in late talking toddlers. *Journal of Speech, Language, and Hearing Research, 45*, 360–371.

Rice, M. L. (2003). A unified model of specific and general language delay: Grammatical tense as a clinical marker of unexpected variation. In Y. Levy & J. Schaeffer (Eds.), *Language competence across populations: Toward a definition of specific language impairment* (pp. 209–231). Mahwah, NJ: Erlbaum.

Rice, M. L., Cleave, P., & Oetting, J. (2000). The use of syntactic cues in lexical acquisition by children with specific language impairment. *Journal of Speech, Language, and Hearing Research, 43,* 582–594.

Schaeffer, J. (2004). Pragmatics and SLI. In Y. Levy & J. Schaffer (Eds.), *Language competence across populations: Toward a definition of specific language impairment* (pp. 135–150). Mahwah, NJ: Erlbaum.

Scott, C. M. (2004). Syntactic contributions to literacy learning. In C. A. Stone, E. R. Silliman, B. J. Ehren, & K. Apel (Eds.), *Handbook of language and literacy: Development and disorders* (pp. 340–362). New York: Guilford Press.

Scott, C. M., & Stokes, S. L. (1995). Measures of syntax in school-age children and adolescents. *Language, Speech, and Hearing Services in Schools, 26,* 309–317.

Scott, C. M., & Windsor, J. (2000). General language performance measures in spoken and written narrative and expository discourse of school-age children with language learning disabilities. *Journal of Speech, Language, and Hearing Research, 43,* 324–339.

Semel, E., Wiig, E., & Secord, W. (1995). *Clinical evaluation of language fundaments* (3rd. ed.). San Antonio, TX: Psychological Corporation.

Shaywitz, S. E. 2003). *Overcoming dyslexia: A new and complete science-based program for reading problems at any level.* New York: Knopf.

Shaywitz, S. E., Shaywitz, B. A., Fletcher, J. M., & Esobar, M. D. (1990). Prevalence of reading disability in boys and girls. *Journal of the American Medical Association, 264,* 998–1002.

Silliman, E. R., Wilkinson, L. C., & Brea-Spahn, M. R. (2004). Policy and practice imperatives for language and literacy learning: Who will be left behind? In C. A. Stone, E. R. Silliman, B. J. Ehren, & K. Apel (Eds.), *Handbook of language and literacy: Development and disorders* (pp. 97–129). New York: Guilford Press.

Snowling, M. J., Gallagher, A., & Frith, U. (2003). Family risk of dyslexia is continuous: Individual differences in the precursors of reading skill. *Child Development, 74,* 358–373.

Stanovich, K. E. (2000). *Progress in understanding reading: Scientific foundations and new frontiers.* New York: Guilford Press.

Stothard, S. E., Snowling, M. J., Bishop, D. V. M. , Chipchase, B. B., & Kaplan, C. A. (1998). Language impaired preschoolers: A follow-up into adolescence. *Journal of Speech, Language, and Hearing Research, 41,* 407–418.

Strömqvist, S., Nordqvist, A., & Weneglin, A. (2004). Writing the frog story: Developmental and cross-modal perspectives. In S. Strömqvist & L. Verhoeven (Eds.), Relating events in narrative: Typological and contextual perspectives (pp. 359–394). Mahwah, NJ: Erlbaum.

Templeton, S. (2004). The vocabulary–spelling connection: Orthographic development and morphological knowledge at the intermediate grades and beyond. In J. F. Baumann & E. J. Kame'enui (Eds.), *Vocabulary instruction: Research to practice* (pp. 118–138). New York: Guilford Press.

Thal, D. J., Reilly, J., Seibert, L., Jeffries, R., & Fenson, J. (2004). Language development in children at risk for language impairment: Cross-population comparisons. *Brain and Language, 88,* 167–179.

Torgesen, J. K. (2004). Lessons learned from research on interventions for students who have difficulty learning to read. In P. McCardle & V. Chhabra (Eds.), *The voice of evidence in reading research* (pp. 355–382). Baltimore: Brookes.

Treiman, R., Clifton, C. Jr., Meyer, A. S., & Wurm, L. H. (2003). Language comprehension and production. In A. F. Healy & R. W. Proctor (Eds.), *Experimental psychology* (Vol. 4, pp. 527–547). New York: Wiley.

van Geert, P. (2004). A dynamic systems approach to diagnostic measurement of SLI. In L. Verhoeven & H. van Balkom (Eds.), *Classification of developmental language disorders: Theoretical issues and clinical implications* (pp. 327–348). Mahwah, NJ: Erlbaum.

Westby, C. (2004). A language perspective on executive functioning, metacognition, and self-regulation in reading. In C. A. Stone, E. R. Silliman, B. J. Ehren, & K. Apel (Eds.), *Handbook of language and literacy: Development and disorders* (pp. 398–427). New York: Guilford Press.

Index